# Joy of Crafts

# Joy of Crafts

BLUE MOUNTAIN CRAFTS COUNCIL

**Holt, Rinehart and Winston**

New York

Published simultaneously in Canada by Holt, Rinehart and Winston
of Canada, Limited.

Library of Congress Cataloging in Publication Data

Blue Mountain Crafts Council
    Joy of Crafts.

    1. Handicraft.   I.   Title.
TT157.B65        745.5        74-24777
ISBN 0-03-014481-7

Printed in the United States of America

Produced for the Blue Mountain Crafts Council,
300 East 40th Street, New York, N.Y. 10016
by Plenary Publications International, Inc.

# Contents

# Preface

The Blue Mountain Crafts Council is dedicated to preserving our priceless heritage of craft skills. It has participated in the planning of JOY OF CRAFTS to help make these skills accessible to people who enjoy making beautiful and useful objects with their hands. The Council members are for the most part working artisans representing a wide range of talents and teaching experience. Their contributions to this collection reflect the rich variety of hand skills practiced in this country today.

The one hundred twenty projects in this volume have been selected to appeal both to the beginner desiring instruction in various basic craft skills and to the more experienced craftsperson. Many of the elementary projects can be completed quickly using low-cost, commonly-available tools and materials, so that beginners can easily create useful and decorative objects while mastering basic skills. Experienced craftspeople will find other projects with more complex techniques and designs to challenge their skills.

The directions for each project are presented in a concise, step-by-step format, starting with a large color photograph of the finished object and followed by clearly stated instructions and diagrams with a list of the tools and materials needed. The projects utilize a great variety of techniques and materials, and the designs range from the bold spontaneity of contemporary forms to the traditional patterns of our Colonial heritage. Wherever possible the projects have been designed so that the reader may choose alternate materials and motifs that fit his or her own creative tastes and practical needs.

Surrounded as we are by push-button entertainment and ready-made accessories, we hope this collection of craft projects opens new doors for the increasing number of people who are relying more and more on their own resources for enjoyment and satisfaction.

On behalf of the Council, we would like to thank the many talented people who contributed to this book and shared with us their joy of crafts.

The Editors

# 1 / Beginner's potpourri

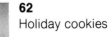

# 2 / Family projects

# 3 / Dolls, toys, and playthings

# 4 / **Celebrations and decorations**

# 5 / Wearables and baubles

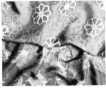

**204**
Batik scarfs

**207**
Bracelet and pendant

**211**
Silkscreen T-shirt

**218**
Silver necklace

**223**
Knitted shawl

**226**
Tie-dyed shirt

**233**
Embroidered clutch purse

**233**
Leather bag

**243**
Macramé vest
Macramé necklace

**249**
Wrap-around skirt

**249**
Kite caftan

# 6 / Stitchery and accessories

# 7 / **Flora and fauna**

**296**
Pressed-flower picture

**305**
Knotted plant hanger

**305**
Acrylic cube planter

**311**
Terrarium

**311**
Miniature gardens

**315**
Indoor light garden

**319**
Simulated bonsai

**322**
Fresh and dried herbs

**331**
Patio blocks

**335**
Tire planter

**335**
Hemp hammock

**339**
Birdhouse and feeder

# 8 / Moneymakers

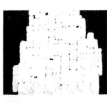

# 9 / Nifty gifts

**382**
Enameled jewel box

**382**
Enameled cuff links

**387**
Tooled leather belts

**392**
Leaded-glass belt buckle

**396**
Carved walking canes

**399**
Needlepoint acrobats

**403**
Turtle pillow

**406**
Appliquéd shoulder bag

**410**
Etched aluminum tray

**413**
Crocheted eyeglass case

**416**
Knitted hat with mittens

**420**
Baby bunting

**423**
Ceramic lamp

**431**
Handmade buttons

# 10 / Folk crafts

**434**
Silhouette with
shears

**436**
Rushed chair seat

**439**
Dried-apple heads

**444**
Pine-needle basket

**448**
Braided rug

**451**
Hooked rug

**455**
Patchwork quilt

**459**
Tinsel glass
painting

**463**
Cornhusk doll

**467**
Embroidered place
mats

**470**
Découpage wall
plaque

**475**
Stenciled furniture

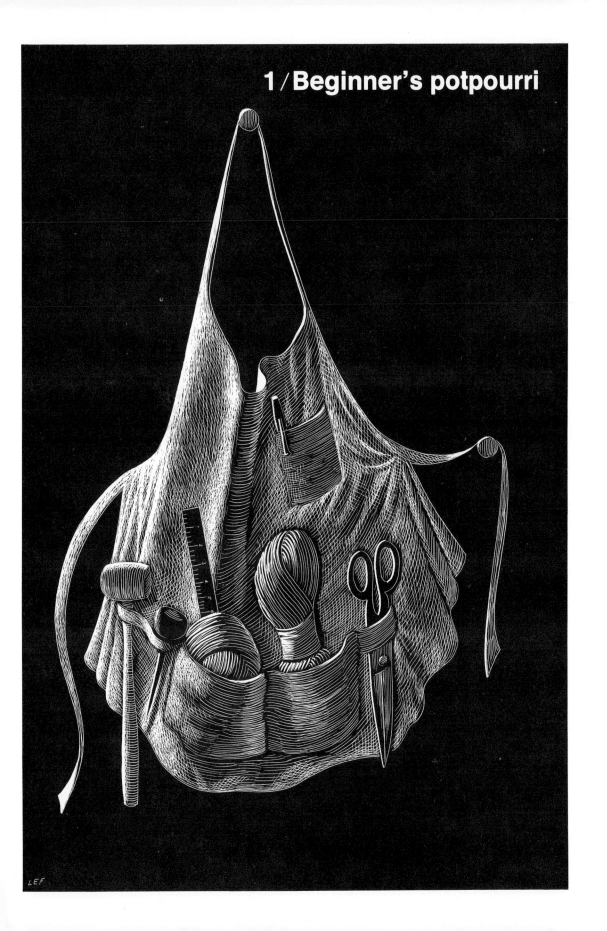

LEF

# Button and cord necklace

Jewelry made from variety store sewing notions has become a current fashion. Using buttons, sequins, silk cord or curtain rings, you can create colorful, smart-looking necklaces, bags, bracelets, belts and earrings for literally pennies. You can also use leftover trims and buttons from old clothes, so the supplies for this unique and easy craft may cost you nothing! You need only know how to thread a needle and make a simple braid to produce, within an hour, a necklace like the one described below. The beads used for this design are inexpensive and available at craft stores.

Be sure to use flat buttons with at least two holes, so that a needle can pass through in two directions. Sort the notions you are using by item and color and place them in small trays, muffin cups or dishes to serve as an organizing aid to help your work go smoothly and quickly.

Materials: 4 yards of satin-covered cord; 1 yard elastic sewing thread; ½- or ⅝-inch flat, two-hole buttons in three colors—48 of a main color (A), 32 of a second color (B), and 16 of a third color (C). You also need 12 round, ⅜-inch beads; one ⅝-inch bead of the same color; one café curtain ring; a sewing needle; and a pair of small, sharp scissors.

### Braiding cord

Cut and set aside a 6-inch length of cord. Cut remainder of cord in four equal lengths. Fold two lengths in half and, starting from the folded end, braid for about 5 inches. Knot and leave ends free for ties. Repeat for the other two lengths. Set aside the two braided cord lengths. These will be attached to the strands of beads to complete the necklace.

### Stringing buttons and beads

Thread needle with elastic and join buttons and ⅜-inch beads in the following sequence: (work down through one buttonhole and up through the opposite hole) eight buttons of color A; one button of color C; one bead; one button of color C; eight buttons of color B; one button of color C; one bead; one button of color C; eight buttons of color A; one button of color C. Repeat, eliminating last button of color C, and fasten thread securely to complete first strand of necklace. Make a second strand exactly like the first.

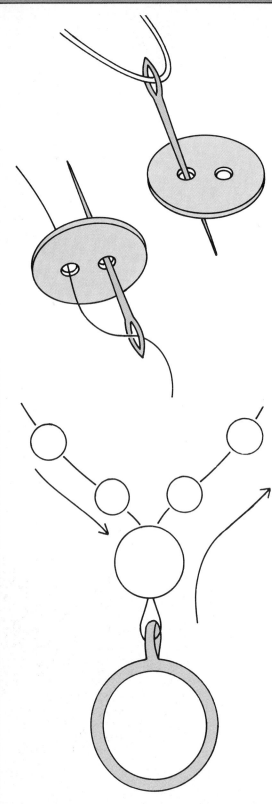

### Making the pendant

For the pendant portion of the necklace, take the 6-inch length of cord and thread through two ⅜-inch beads, the ⅝-inch bead, and the curtain ring, then back up through the ⅝-inch bead and through two more ⅜-inch beads (see lower left).

### Finishing the necklace

Use a square knot to attach each side of pendant to one end of each strand of buttons, reinforcing with a few loops of regular sewing thread. Sew braids to opposite ends of button strands. This step completes your necklace and your introduction to the craft of button

jewelry. Now that you are familiar with the simple method and materials involved, you will want to experiment with different sizes, group-ings, and color combinations to create your own original designs.

# Dried flower bouquet

For centuries, flower-lovers have known how to air-dry certain everlasting flowers and herbs by hanging them upside down in a dark, dry place. The results were not colorful but they did provide a memory of summer through the long winter months. In recent years, however, through the introduction of a fine granular substance called silica-gel, it has become possible for amateurs to give all sorts of flowers eternal youth. Silica-gel has remarkable water-absorption abilities, and when it is sprinkled carefully on freshly picked flowers and left to work for a week, it blots up all the flowers' natural moisture before the colors have had a chance to fade. There are two types of chemicals necessary for this project: #28-200 mesh crystals and #6-16 mesh crystals; they are sold at florist shops or chemical supply houses. The #6-16 mesh crystals (a blue compound) turn pink when they are saturated with the flowers' moisture. It is important to use fresh flowers, as every hour between the time the flower is picked and the time you begin to dry it takes its toll in beauty. Ideally, the flowers should be picked at the hottest hour of a sunny day, when the moisture levels are at their lowest. If the flowers are obtained from a florist, more time will have elapsed between the field and the drying process, so be very selective.

Materials: five parts #28-200 mesh crystals; one part #6-16 mesh crystals; a shallow airtight container large enough to hold about 8 to 10 flowers; florist wire and green tape; clear acrylic fixative; and a selection of fresh flowers.

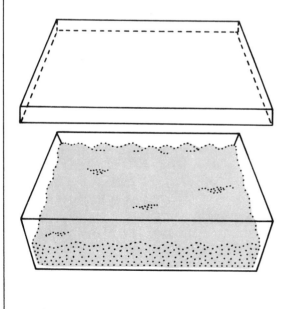

### Preparing crystals
Mix five parts of #28-200 mesh crystals with one part #6-16 blue crystals. (If you are only able to buy the #28-200 crystals, the process will still work. The blue crystals merely serve as a convenient indicator of moisture levels.) Put a 2-inch deep layer of the crystals in the bottom of a shallow, airtight container.

### Placing flowers in crystals
Gather fresh flowers. Daisies, cosmos or simple field flowers which are flattish on top are easy for beginning experiments in flower drying. Large, heavy-headed fleshy flowers like roses need more attention. Cut the stems 2 inches below the blossoms. Place the flower, stem down, in the container, allowing enough space between flower heads so that they do not touch. The bottom layer of petals

## Dried flower bouquet

should rest on the silica-gel. Sprinkle the chemical gently in and around the petals, filling in the various layers of petals from the bottom up so that they are supported and not crushed. Keep filling the container until the tops of the flowers are barely covered. Cover the container and seal the lid with tape.

**Pour off silica-gel**
After one week, open the container and slowly pour off the top silica-gel. The flowers are now dry and brittle, and must be handled carefully to prevent damage. Lift each flower out of the container. Blow off the remaining dust and crystals.

**Making wire stems**
To make the flowers suitable for use in a bouquet, place them on artificial stems. Tape each short, dried natural stem to a length of florists' wire, wrapping the splice in green tape and continuing for the length of the wire to camouflage it. (If the original stem is very brittle, poke the wire into the underside of the flower itself. This must be done gently.)

## Dried flower bouquet

### Spraying flowers

To make dried flowers more durable and resistant to household humidity, spray each one separately, underside and top, with a clear acrylic fixative, holding the can about 18 inches away. Let the fixative dry and spray again. (Fixative can be purchased in stationers' and art supply stores.)

### Arranging bouquet

In arranging the finished flowers, vary the stem lengths. Add a few naturally dried fillers, such as Lunaria, babies' breath, yarrow, straw flowers, artemesia, and wild grasses. You will find some of these standing in the fields in the late fall, dried by the sun and autumn winds. If you are using a low bowl for the arrangement, place a piece of foamed plastic snugly in the bottom to anchor each stem. Florists can also provide these items.

### Reactivating silica-gel

Although the initial cost of silica-gel is relatively expensive, it can be reused over and over by removing the moisture from the crystals after the compound has been used to dry flowers. Spread the silica-gel in a shallow pan and place in a warm (250 degrees Fahrenheit) oven for about a half hour, or until the pink crystals return to their blue color. Cool and store the compound in an airtight container.

Three pounds of silica-gel is the minimum amount needed to cover about a dozen blossoms at one time, however, if you invest in five pounds of silica-gel, it is possible to dry more flowers at one time. It is advisable to keep a chart of the drying time required for various flowers. Record the date the flowers are placed in the drying agent and then check the results after the fourth or fifth day. The silica-gel mixture should be stored for reuse.

# Brass rubbing

Rubbing, one of the world's oldest art forms, is a simple technique of making a reproduction of an incised or sculptured surface. It is accomplished by securing a sheet of paper over an interesting surface and using a pencil or crayon to mark or rub the paper so the raised portions of the surface are colored and the recessed portions remain unmarked on the paper. The result is a reverse impression or negative of the surface design over which you rubbed. Carefully produced rubbings are suitable for wall hangings, collages, and patterns for needlepoint.

The art of rubbing was perfected in China about 300 B.C., and prior to the invention of the printing press, the technique was used as a means of communication. Royal decrees were cut in stone and erected at a central marketplace. Travelers passing through paused to make a rubbing of the stone, and then passed the rubbing on to others in the remote areas outside the city.

In selecting a surface to rub, choose a relief that is not too deep, with the raised surface flat and smooth. Examples include coins and medallions, wood carvings, etched glass, hammered metal trays, old doorknobs, antique cast-iron pieces, textile stamps and even ornate gravestones.

Materials: white, black or light-colored paper; masking tape (drafting weight); fixative spray; and crayons or shoemakers' heels. These supplies are available at art supply stores, except the heels, which you can purchase at a shoe repair store.

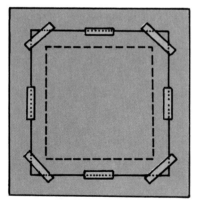

## Mounting the paper
Select a surface that you find interesting and prepare it for rubbing by cleaning it with a soft cloth or an old toothbrush. Cut the paper to fit over the surface, leaving a margin of one or two inches around the area in which the rubbing will appear. Secure the paper to the surface with drafting-weight masking tape, which peels away easily and will not damage the paper when the tape is removed. Make sure the paper stretches tightly over the surface.

## Making the rubbing
Using the shoemakers' heel or the broad edge of a crayon, press strokes across the paper, from left to right, starting at the top and work-

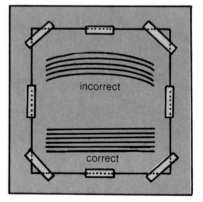

incorrect

correct

ing down. Use uniform pressure and make even strokes, so the lines are crisp and sharp. Don't go over an area more than once, because it will cause the lines of the rubbing to blur. In larger rubbings there is a tendency for stroke lines to curve downward at the sides. This will happen if your arm isn't strong enough to reach across the width of the rubbing. In such a case, move your body as you move your hand back and forth across the surface instead of standing in one position while doing the rubbing. To keep the rubbing from smudging, spray fixative over it while it is taped to the surface and let it dry.

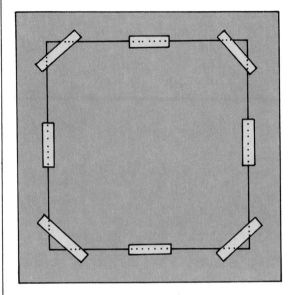

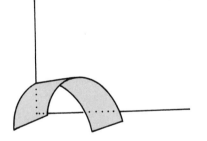

### Removing the paper

Remove the paper from the rubbing surface by peeling the tape off very carefully so the paper will not be damaged. Peel the tape off the paper slowly toward the surface to which the paper is taped, using a rolling, rather than pulling motion. After safely removing and storing paper, remove tape from rubbing surface. The rubbing is ready to frame or to store. To store, roll the paper with the rubbing surface on the inside, then insert into cardboard mailing tubes, or tubes used to roll up fabric or wrapping paper. They are available in varying lengths, so select a clean tube that will fully protect your rubbing.

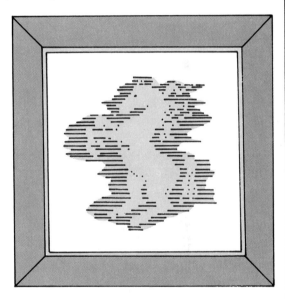

### Coordinating rubbings

You can mix and match rubbed designs, rubbing only parts of a cornerstone or gravestone ornamentation, and then coordinating the parts. Select a part of one gravestone or cornerstone because it has an interesting design, and take the inscription from another cornerstone or gravestone. Popular subjects for rubbings include ornate scrollwork, faces of angels and cherubim, and parts of complex scenes carved in panels of stone. Use the rubbings to make collages, or just frame them as you would a picture. It is also possible to arrange a series of rubbings and paste them directly on a wall.

# Crocheted hat

If you have never crocheted, you can start now with any one of the hats illustrated. The child's hat will work up the fastest because it is smaller; however, all three are basically the same, worked in the single crochet stitch. Crocheted fashion accessories coordinate especially well with casual clothes and often add a special flair to high-style ensembles; the beret, for example. The most popular crocheted hat is the pull-on type with either a cuff or a simple roll-up brim. It is practical for cold weather and at the same time style oriented.

Materials: size H crochet hook, for child's hat; size J hook, for adult's hat; one skein (four ounces) of four-ply yarn in any color and two ounces of a contrasting-color yarn (enough yarn for either child-or adult-size hat); a pair of scissors; safety pins; and an embroidery needle.

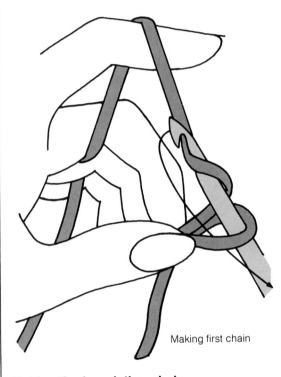

Making first chain

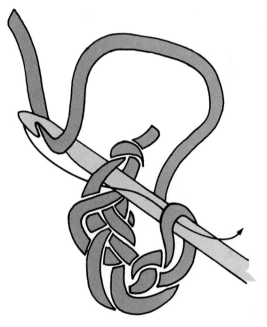

Joining chain

## Making the foundation chain

Make a slip knot on the crochet hook, which is held in the right hand. Thread the yarn over the left ring finger, under the middle finger and over the index finger. Hold the short end between your thumb and middle finger.

Then, to crochet a chain stitch, pass the hook under and over the yarn and draw it through the loop on the crochet hook. Make four chain stitches. As you crochet, gradually let the yarn slide through your fingers so the stitches do not become too tight. Each chain stitch should be approximately ¼ inch in length.

## Making a ring

Join the four chain stitches by making a slip stitch in the first chain. (Insert the hook in the first chain stitch. Bring the yarn over the hook and with a single motion, draw the yarn back through the chain stitch, and at the same time through the loop already on the hook.)

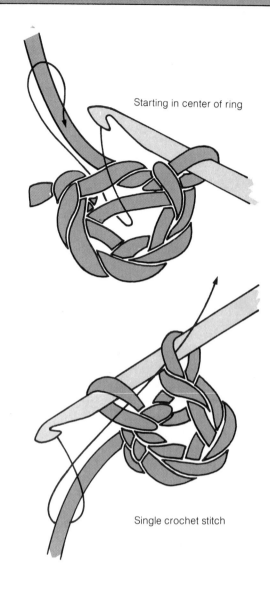

Starting in center of ring

Single crochet stitch

### Beginning first round of child-size hat

Hold the ring with the thumb and middle finger of the left hand. Make six single crochet stitches on the ring as follows: insert hook through center of ring, wrap the yarn around the hook and draw it through the ring; wrap the yarn over hook again and draw the yarn through both loops on the hook. Be careful not to cover stitches already made (use a safety pin to mark beginning of each round).

### Crocheting the next rounds

For the second round, work two single crochet stitches in each of the six single crochet stitches in the first round (total of 12 stitches).

Round 3: work two single crochets in the first stitch; one single crochet in the second stitch; repeat around (total 18 stitches).

Round 4: work two single crochets in the first stitch; one single crochet in each of next two stitches; repeat around (total 24 stitches).

Round 5: two single crochets in first stitch, one single crochet in each of next three stitches; repeat around (total of 30 stitches).

Round 6: two single crochets in first stitch; one single crochet in each of next four stitches; repeat around (total 36 stitches).

Round 7: two single crochets in first stitch; one single crochet in each of next five stitches; repeat around (total 42 stitches).

Round 8: two single crochets in the first stitch; one single crochet in each of the next six stitches; repeat around (total 48 stitches).

Round 9: two single crochets in the first stitch; one single crochet in each of the next 11 stitches; increase one stitch every twelfth stitch; repeat around (total 52 stitches).

Round 10: two single crochets in the first stitch; one single crochet in each of the next 12 stitches; repeat around (total 56 stitches).

Round 11: two single crochets in first stitch; one single crochet in each of the next 13 stitches; repeat around (total 60 stitches).

Round 12: work two single crochets in first stitch; one single crochet in each of next 14 stitches; repeat around (total 64 stitches).

Round 13: work one single crochet in each stitch around. Continue working on rounds of 64 stitches (being sure to mark beginning of each round) until the piece measures 5 inches from the crown to edge.

Next round: work single crochet in each stitch around; join to first stitch with a slip-stitch. Break off yarn (color A) and attach trim yarn (color B), chain one.

To change color of yarn, complete the last row of yarn, then leave an excess of approximately two inches of yarn. Securely knot the yarn, and using your crochet hook, continue

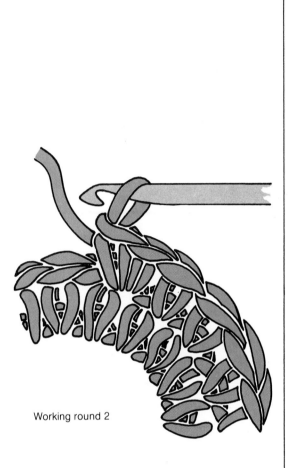

Working round 2

to crochet, working the end back into the last row. Always break off color after slipstitch, join new color, and chain 1 with new color.

### Crocheting trim border

With color B, single crochet around, joining end of round with a slipstitch. (Each following round will be joined with a slipstitch.) Chain 1.

Next round: work one single crochet in BACK LOOP of each stitch all around. Join color A.

Round 3: chain 1, crochet in back of each stitch around.

Work the next four rounds, continuing to crochet in back of stitch, using yarn colors in this order: B, A, B, A.

### Making pompon

Wrap yarn around a two-inch piece of cardboard as follows: place a 4-inch length of yarn color A at the top edge of cardboard in a horizontal position. Then, using yarn colors A and B together, wrap the two strands around the cardboard 50 times. Break off the yarns. Tie the horizontal yarn length at top around the wool tightly. Cut through all strands of yarn at the bottom edge of cardboard, trim and fluff. Make another in the same manner, then attach both pompons together and attach securely to top of hat.

### Crocheting adult-size hat

Using size J hook, follow instructions for child's hat for the first 12 rounds.

Round 13: work single crochet in each stitch around. Then repeat round 13 until piece measures 6½ inches or desired length from crown to edge. Continue to mark the beginning of each round with a safety pin. Make a slipstitch in the first stitch at the end of the last round.

### Border or brim

To make a brim, follow the instructions for the child's hat. For an interesting border in place of a brim, follow the instructions below.

Border round 1: chain 2, work one double crochet (See CRAFTNOTES for instructions on double crochet stitch.) In next stitch; continue around making 1 double crochet in each stitch and join at end with a slip stitch.

Round 2: chain 1, make 5 double crochets in the next stitch; 1 single crochet in the second stitch; then repeat this pattern around and end by joining with a slipstitch in the chain stitch. Break off yarn as described previously.

The art of crocheting takes a great deal of patience and practice. Once you are adept, you will soon find yourself spending leisure hours designing fashion accessories as well as numerous articles for your home.

### Crocheting brim

Using yarn A, work the following round crocheting in both loops of each stitch as follows: two single crochet in the first stitch, one single crochet in next three stitches; continue around increasing every fourth stitch, ending with a slipstitch, chain 1.

Round 2: work one single crochet in each stitch all around.

Round 3: begin by working one single crochet in each of next two stitches, then work the following pattern around: two single crochets in next stitch, one single crochet in next three stitches. Break off yarn and attach yarn color B.

Round 4: chain 1, then work one single crochet in each stitch around, ending with a slipstitch. Break off yarn, leaving a tail to weave yarn end into edge, and pull through stitch tightly.

# Bean-bag toss

Bean-bags are easy to make and fun for children to toss back and forth. They are easier for them to catch and hold on to than balls, and they serve as favorite cuddly toys, too. You can make a simple game by cutting holes in a board, holes that are a bit larger than the bean-bags. Then support the board with a stand. The youngsters aim their bean-bags at the board, scoring each time a bean-bag finds its way into a hole. The cat, frog, and owl bean-bags shown here are only a sampling of the many animals that can be designed.

Materials: scraps of felt or duck fabric, approximately 6 inches by 18 inches; ordinary thread; embroidery thread or yarn; and a package of dried beans (any kind will do).

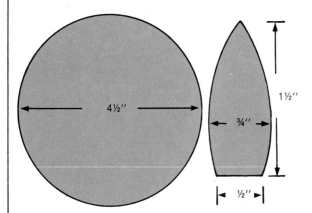

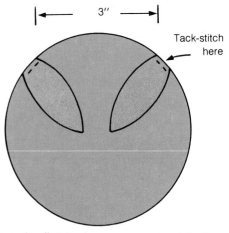

**Cutting and sewing the bean-bag**
Make two paper patterns as shown above. (You can use a bowl or similar object to trace the outline of the circle.) Using the patterns

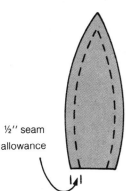

½'' seam allowance

as a guide, cut two cloth circles for the cat's head, and four petal-shaped pieces for the ears. With the fabric inside out, stitch together two sets of ears, using a ½-inch seam allowance and leaving the bottoms open. Trim away excess and turn ears right side out.

Place the finished ears approximately 3 inches apart on the outer side of one of the circles, with the flat edges of the ears touching the outer edge of the circle. Then tack-stitch in position as shown.

On the second circle, embroider the cat's face with colored thread or yarn and/or use buttons for eyes and nose.

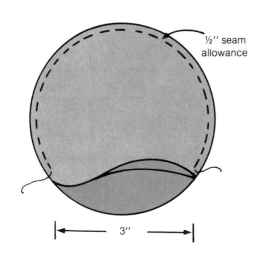

½'' seam allowance

3''

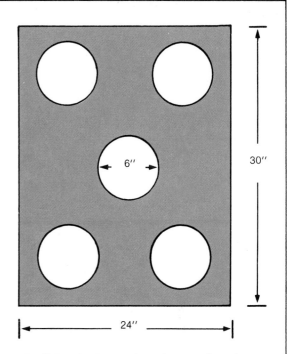

6''

30''

24''

Or from a contrasting color fabric, cut out and appliqué the features to face as shown in illustration. (For appliqué technique, see Appliquéd pillows and wall hanging.)

Place the second circle face down on the embroidered face and stitch together along the outside edge, allowing a ½-inch seam. Leave an opening of approximately 3 inches at the bottom. Trim off excess material around the sewn edge and turn material right side out.

Stuff the dry beans into the opening, then turn under the remaining exposed edges of the two circles and bind together with an overcast stitch to complete the bean-bag.

### Sawing and decorating the board

To make a bean-bag game board you can use just about any piece of wood; a piece of plywood 24 by 30 inches is a good size. Use a saber saw or compass saw to cut four or five holes approximately 6 inches in diameter. Or cut holes of different sizes, with a higher score for throwing the bean-bag through the smaller holes. Sand the inside edges of the holes so that the bean-bag doesn't catch on rough splinters. You can paint colorful circles around the holes if you wish, and cut out paper numbers and paste them on, to indicate the score for hitting each hole.

Or use your imagination to make whatever kind of game your child will enjoy. For example, exercise your artistic talents by painting mice running for each hole, and see if the bean-bag cat can beat them to their lairs. Finish off board with a coat of shellac or varnish.

You can make a simple angular stand to support the board, or just lean it against a wall to serve as a target for the bean-bag tossers.

# Coiled pot

In making pottery, the coiled method of shaping clay forms provides an excellent opportunity for the novice to learn the basic skills in working with clay and the clay binder called slip; in using simple modeling tools; and in applying stains and glazes. For this project, the pliable and flexible stoneware clay is rolled into long coils. The coils are assembled on a flat surface within a rectangular clay coil frame, and then this shape is formed into a cylinder by joining the two short sides. The bottom of the cylinder is formed by using a rolling pin to flatten a piece of clay into a circle. The staining and glazing process for this project is also elementary. It is recommended that the pottery piece prepared for this project be fired by a professional. Pottery or porcelain workshops fire pieces for moderate fees. The supplies needed are inexpensive and easily obtained from clay suppliers or art supply stores. Use any water-based stone clay, but do not use plasticene or kiln clay. Make a binding agent, slip, by mixing clay and water together into a paste consistency.

Materials: a rolling pin; a pointed stick or butter knife; a ceramic needle tool, which can be made by embedding the eye end of a darning needle in a cork; powdered ferric oxide; a plastic bag or sheet; a paintbrush; sponge; and about 10 pounds of clay. To prepare the work area, lay several layers of newspaper on a large, flat, nonmetallic surface (preferably unfinished wood, because it is porous enough to absorb the water that seeps through the newspaper from the clay).

### Making coil frame

Roll sausage-shaped clay rolls with palms of hands, rolling on a flat surface until they become elongated. The first four coils should be about ⅜ inch in diameter. Approximate length of coils depends on size of object.

For project illustrated use two coils 12 inches long and two 24 inches long. Join at corners to form a geometric shape (for the design illustrated here, a rectangular outline or frame is used). If clay sticks to the newspaper, it will peel easily. Coils should be moist enough for flexibility.

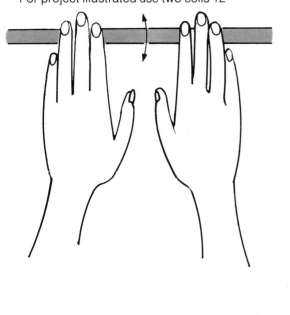

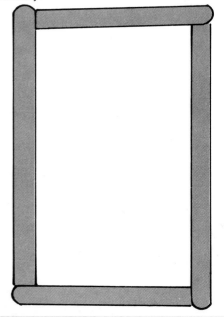

## Coiled pot

### Assembling coils

Lay coils of different lengths inside the coil frame to form the design. Whenever you join clay to itself, score both surfaces with X-marks using the needle tool; use modeling tools and fingers to apply a thin layer of slip between coils to bond them together. Do not use too much, or coils will become loose. There should be grooves, but no gaps, between coils.

Smooth clay between coils to join tightly.

This side of the piece will become the inside of the pot, so it does not matter if the design texture is lost. Place newspaper on a clean area of the working surface. With a rolling pin, roll a ball of clay into a flat circle ¼ inch thick. The base of the pot will be cut out of this circle.

### Joining pot to base

Gently rest the rectangle on your arm, newspaper side up, and carefully peel off the paper.

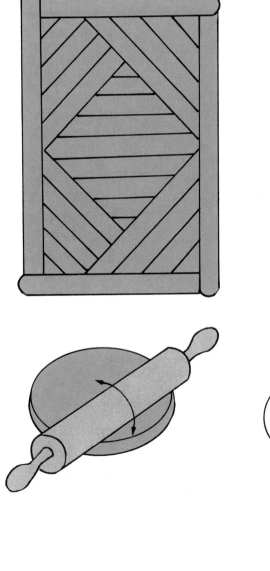

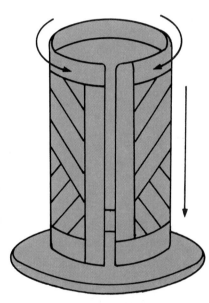

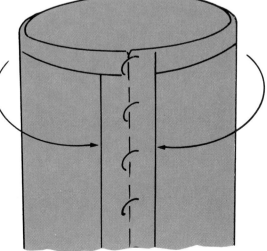

## Coiled pot

Lift and bend the rectangle, so the two short ends are brought together to form a cylinder. Leave a narrow opening to join cylinder seam.

Place cylinder on top of circular base and buttress to base where the two shapes meet. Reinforcement is done by working an additional coil of clay onto the inside, between the cylinder and the base. The base circumference should be slightly larger than the diameter of the cylinder. Apply a thin layer of slip to inside and outside edge of cylinder seam, pressing both edges together after smoothing with fingers, and work seam closed.

Lay another coil of clay inside along the cylinder seam and smooth it onto the inside surface with your finger. Cut away excess clay from base with knife, and smooth edges. If the cylinder is not quite rigid enough to stand by itself, loosely stuff cylinder with crumpled newspaper. Remove newspaper after drying stage.

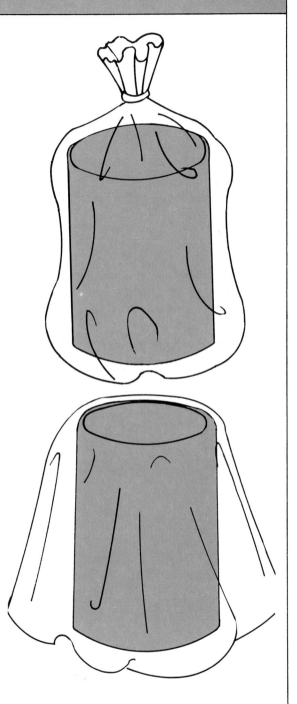

### Drying the pot

Since clay tends to pull apart, let the pot dry very slowly. The drying process, which takes about a week, consists of three stages. First, cover the pot completely with a plastic bag or sheet to make it airtight.

After 24 hours, let some air circulate between the plastic and the pot. When clay becomes stiff, but not totally dry, remove plastic. The pot has now reached the leather-hard stage. Let it dry, completely uncovered, for four more days. When the piece is at the bone-dry stage (no moisture present), it is ready for firing.

Test bone-dryness from the temperature of

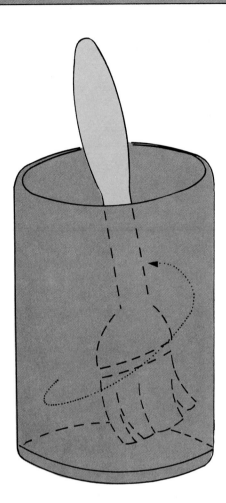

the pot; if cold, it must dry longer; if it is about room temperature, it is safe to fire. Never fire a piece that is not bone-dry, or it will explode inside the kiln. Firing time and temperature depend on the type of clay used. This information should be obtained from the supplier at the time of purchase. Firing generally takes at least eight hours, plus cooling time, before a piece can be removed from the kiln.

### Staining and glazing
The first firing will bring the pot to a "bisque" temperature, indicated by a light pink color. (At this temperature it is still porous enough to absorb stain or clear glaze. It has not reached a vitrified, or "hard" stage.) Stain piece at this stage.

Stain is made by combining powdered ferric oxide with water to make a red, watery liquid. Apply oxide with brush, first on the inside to prevent water seepage when the pot is completed, and then onto the outer surface. Sponge and scrub the outside of the pot until the oxide comes off the raised surface of the coils but remains in the grooves. This will emphasize the texture of the design. Allow to dry one hour before firing again.

To glaze the piece with clear or colored glaze, it must be stained and fired first. (If clear glaze is used, the stain will show through.) Apply the glaze in the same sequence as for staining: inside to seal piece for water tightness and then outside.

Use brush to apply glaze, following directions given on the glaze container. Never stain or glaze the bottom of the base; it will fuse to the inside of the kiln. When the glaze has dried for the time period recommended by the supplier, test for dryness with a wet finger. If it sticks slightly to the pot, the piece is ready for firing.

Fire to "glaze" temperature recommended by supplier (temperature varies with the type of clay and glaze). The finished pot can be used as a planter, pencil holder or decorative piece, depending on its size.

# Ceramic painting

Much of the beauty in earthenware, stoneware and porcelain is its decorative finish: the design or the high-gloss glaze or both. Ceramic ware may be glazed or unglazed. A glaze is a glass coating that is applied and then fired to make the clay surface non-porous and to enhance the appearance of the piece. Designs can be painted on the unglazed surface of a ceramic piece before it is glazed. For some pieces, the glaze is applied first, then fired before the design is painted on its surface. Sometimes a decorative piece of pottery is not glazed after it is painted, which gives it a soft, matte finish. For the inexperienced potter, it is recommended that the glazing and firing be done by a ceramics studio.

Purchase unfinished ceramic pieces at a hobby or crafts shop or from a professional ceramist, then decorate and have glazed. Or take a plainly finished, ordinary dish, bowl or mug and embellish the piece with a painted design. Examples of three techniques of ceramic painting are shown. The shallow bowl is left unglazed; the heart-shaped box is painted over the glaze; the pitcher is painted and then glazed.

Materials: dry pigment; water colors or poster paints; clear ceramic cement; a small dish; a palette knife or wooden stick; an artist's brush; furniture wax; paraffin wax (optional); oil-based enamel; a piece of glass or palette; linseed oil; and a soft lead pencil. All are available at art supply or hobby stores.

### Decorating with dry pigments
Prepare the unglazed ceramic surface by covering with clear ceramic cement and allow it to dry. In a small dish, blend pigments with additional cement, using a palette knife or wooden stick, until you obtain the desired

color. Then apply to the ceramic surface with an artist's brush, holding it as you would hold a pencil. Complete the larger background areas first, then the decorative lines. In the example shown, ridged and grooved areas are painted in colors that complement and contrast with the blue background.

When all the colors have dried completely, use a soft cloth to apply a coat of furniture wax to the outside of the piece. The inside may be coated with hot paraffin wax to prevent leaking, if it is used to hold water and fresh flowers.

### Decorating with water colors
Another technique for decorating a piece that is to be left unglazed is to use watercolors or poster paints. Proceed as above. To finish the piece, do not use paraffin wax, as it may blur the colors. Instead, finish the piece by spraying the inside and outside surfaces with clear acrylic or lacquer.

### Decorating a previously glazed piece

To paint over a glazed ceramic piece, as on the heart-shaped box, use oil-based artist's pigments. Squeeze small amounts of the desired colors around the edge of a clean palette

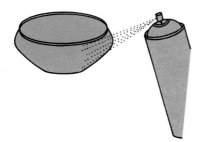

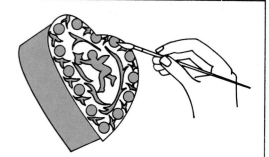

or piece of glass; and experiment in obtaining the exact tones you want by mixing two or three colors together, blending with a palette knife. For example, the cupids on the heart-shaped box are painted with a mixture of

white and small amounts of burnt sienna and cadmium yellow. The leaves are painted with green and with white and burnt sienna. Use linseed oil, a few drops at a time, to thin to a medium-thin consistency, just thick enough to avoid running.

When the color and consistency are satisfactory, apply a small amount to the bottom of the glazed piece, where it will not show. If the color is right, apply paint to the ceramic surface to be decorated, using an artist's brush. Work sure strokes; don't lift the brush until each stroke is completed. On the heart-shaped box, paint is applied to the raised design and border of the top.

### Decorating a piece to be glazed

Use either oil or water paints. The pitcher shown is decorated with water paints; these present no problems when the piece is glazed and fired in a high-temperature kiln. If oil paints are used, add as little linseed oil as possible; it may blister during the firing process.

Trace or draw a design on the unglazed ceramic surface with a soft lead or crayon pencil before painting. Do not use a sharp pencil; it may score the unglazed surface. Pencil marks will disappear during the firing process.

To give the appearance of depth, apply at least two coats of paint to the design. The first coat should be pale in tone; allow it to dry

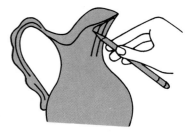

completely before applying a second, slightly darker coat. Subsequent coats, about three, each slightly darker than the one before, will heighten the effect. Allow the paint to dry about one week before glazing and firing.

43

# Fringed wall hanging

To make this simple, open-weave design, a few thick wefts of green, yellow and brown are woven through thin, neutral-colored warp cords that hang loosely, allowing sun and air to filter through. The 5-inch fringe along the bottom edge adds a graceful finish to this hanging, which measures 9 inches by 21½ inches when complete.

Materials: a spool of cotton or linen warp yarn or a ball of crochet cotton in a neutral shade; ¼ ounce each of knitting worsted in green and brown; ¼ ounce of bulky rug or quickpoint yarn; one 10-inch dowel for hanging; a stretcher frame or canvas stretchers to fit finished dimensions; a large, blunt-tipped needle; nails and a hammer; and a large comb with widely spaced teeth.

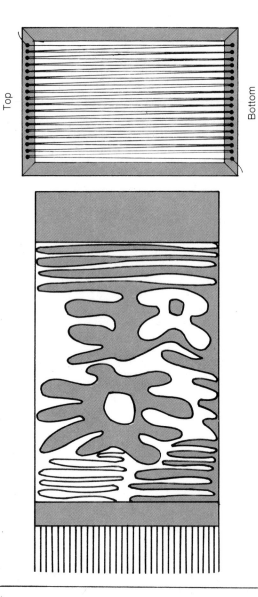

### Preparing frame and weaving

Assemble frame so the shorter lengths become top and bottom of frame. Insert nails ¼ inch apart at top and bottom edges of frame. Attach end of warp yarn to bottom left nail and wind as shown. Beginning 5 inches up from the bottom, weave over and under across the entire warp with green for 1½ inches. Use comb as a beater to push rows together. Using the over-and-under weave throughout, work yellow and brown floral design free style until about 3 inches from the top. (No comb is needed for this section of the weaving.) Finish remaining 3 inches with closely spaced over-and-under green weft rows, pushed together with comb.

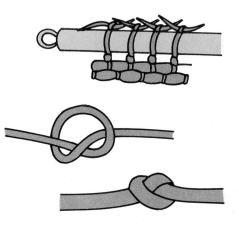

### Finishing

To finish, cut warp at top and bottom and knot top ends of warp around the dowel. Tie overhand knots with the warp ends just below bottom edge of weaving, to form fringes.

# Play apron

No matter how easy it is to toss soiled clothing into a washing machine, it behooves us to take advantage of any protective covering that allows children complete freedom with crayons, paints or modeling clay. An attractive apron makes playtime more fun for the youngsters and easy on their jeans, T-shirts and pinafores. Children can paint with abandon and never ruin clothing when it is protected by a colorful cobbler's apron. It is easy to make, with vinyl material that wipes clean with a damp cloth.

Materials: an 18-inch square of fabric-backed vinyl in a bright color; matching thread; bowl or other round object; scissors; scraps of vinyl in a contrasting color for decoration; 56 inches of narrow twill tape; twine or ribbon; and rubber cement.

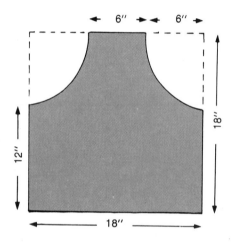
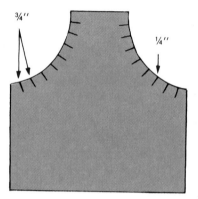

### Cutting apron
Cut the fabric-backed vinyl according to the measurements indicated on pattern shown, using a bowl or similar object as a guide for making the circular cut for the armholes.

### Notching
Make ½-inch cuts at ¾-inch intervals along the two arm cutouts.

### Hemming
Turn the material wrong side up and fold over the notched edge, wrong side to wrong side. Machine stitch, using a zigzag attachment, if you have one. Otherwise, use a straight stitch.

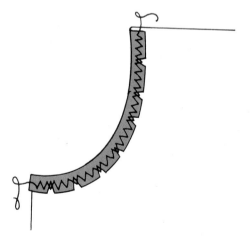

# Play apron

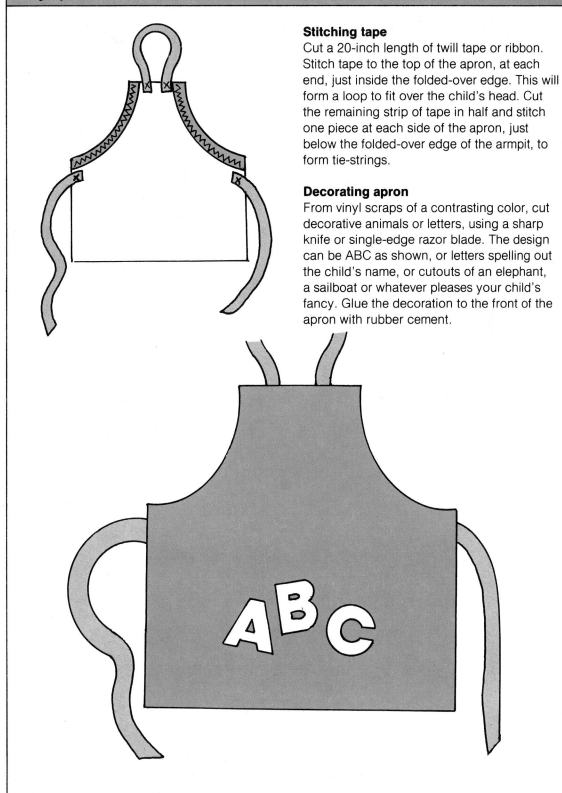

## Stitching tape

Cut a 20-inch length of twill tape or ribbon. Stitch tape to the top of the apron, at each end, just inside the folded-over edge. This will form a loop to fit over the child's head. Cut the remaining strip of tape in half and stitch one piece at each side of the apron, just below the folded-over edge of the armpit, to form tie-strings.

## Decorating apron

From vinyl scraps of a contrasting color, cut decorative animals or letters, using a sharp knife or single-edge razor blade. The design can be ABC as shown, or letters spelling out the child's name, or cutouts of an elephant, a sailboat or whatever pleases your child's fancy. Glue the decoration to the front of the apron with rubber cement.

# Foil trinket box

This handsome box looks like an antique of finely crafted metal, but actually it is of far more humble origin. It is made from an empty wooden cigar box, obtainable from a tobacconist. The antique finish is easy to achieve with aluminum foil and black paint; and to create the embossed effect, the foil is worked over a raised design, made of cardboard cutouts and string glued to the box.

Materials: an empty cigar box; aluminum foil; 30-ounce can of black flat latex paint; 1-inch paintbrush; cardboard; heavy string; white glue; a can of clear acrylic spray; a piece of green felt, large enough to line the inside bottom of the box; scissors; and some rags.

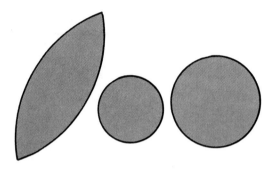

### Cutting patterns
If the cigar box has a hook or catch, remove it and set it aside before covering the box. There is no need to remove the hinges; apply foil right over them.

From cardboard, cut the leaves (ovals) and petals (circles) for the top flower design as illustrated. Cut three leaves, six large petals and five small petals. Trace around coins to outline the petals; a quarter for the large ones and a dime for the small.

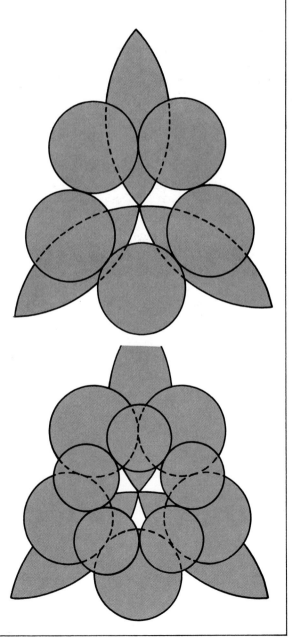

### Mounting design on box

In the center of the box top, glue down the three leaves in a triangular pattern. Next, glue five of the large petals on top of the leaves in a circular pattern, so that each petal touches the adjacent one. Glue the five small petals over the large ones in a similar manner, ending with the remaining large petal in the center.

### Gluing string to design

Draw guidelines in a freehand fashion for embossed designs on all sides of the box and around the flower on the top. Adapt design to size of cigar box. Glue string along these lines. Cut off excess string and allow to dry.

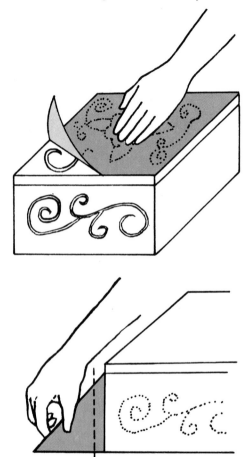

Pinch and Trim

### Working foil over design

Cut pieces of aluminum foil to fit the box top and around the sides, allowing an excess of about ⅜ inch along edges. Crinkle the foil pieces, then smooth out slightly but not completely. Spread glue thinly on the cover of the box, then place foil on top cover. Starting in the middle and working outward, press the foil in and around the flower design, the string and the hinges. Pinch the foil at corners, trim off excess and press over the remaining foil. Trim off excess foil all around.

# Foil trinket box

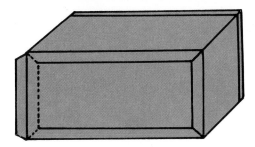

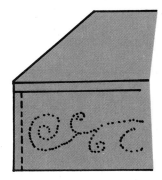

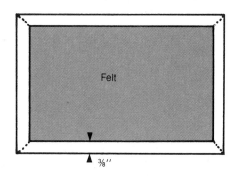

## Mounting foil on sides

In similar manner, glue foil in place around the four sides of the box, starting at a back corner. Press foil around the string and over the hinges. Fold the foil under ⅜ inch at the bottom on all four sides. Trim off excess foil at the top edges.

## Antiquing box

Apply flat black paint to the foil, wiping it off before it dries to give an aged appearance. Allow to dry, then spray the box with acrylic finish. Again, allow to dry.

Applying Paint

|  |
|---|
| Felt |
| ⅜" |

To complete the box, cut a piece of felt to fit inside at the bottom of the box. Trim felt piece about ⅜ inch all around and glue in place. Fasten the catch in place if the box has one.

# Geometric collage

Collage is a technique that was originated by Kurt Schwitters, an early twentieth century artist. Many European artists of this period incorporated into their paintings a real object, such as a fragment of paper or snip of lace. The significance of the technique lies not in its eccentricity but in its relevance to reality. Contemporary collage is an outgrowth of abstract and nonobjective art, consisting primarily of cutouts mounted in layers in a specific or free-form design. The illustrated geometric design collage is really quite simple for a first-time project. It measures about 11½ inches by 14 inches. If you prefer a more traditional theme than the modern geometric design shown, use the same technique to create a collage of flowers or any other prints cut from gift wrap, magazines, wallpaper or greeting cards.

Materials: a piece or two of shirt cardboard; several pieces of tissue paper of various colors (colors used in the work shown include pale blue, dark blue, red, yellow and green); white glue; a can of clear spray enamel; a picture frame and a piece of white mounting board to fit the frame; a sharp knife to cut the board; and a ½-inch soft-hair artist's brush.

### Cutting paper circles

To make patterns for the cutouts, trace two circles on a sheet of cardboard, one approximately 2½ inches in diameter and the other 2 inches. Use any round object as a guide for tracing, such as a juice can, spool or bottle. Cut out the patterns. Stack several layers of tissue paper, varying the colors. Using the patterns as guides, cut out circles. Repeat until there are approximately 30 circles of each size. Do not be concerned if the circles are not perfectly round; slight imperfections will be camouflaged by the design.

### Mounting large circles

In a mixing dish, thin the white glue with two parts water to one part glue. Use the artist's brush to spread an even coating over the face of the mounting board. Place the larger circles of tissue paper around the outer edge of the board, alternating spacing and colors to achieve a pleasing pattern. Overlap the circles to create a variety of tinted shadings. The diluted glue makes it easy to shift the circles until the best effect is achieved.

### Mounting small circles

With all outer circles in place, apply another coat of the diluted glue on the board and place the smaller circles, partially overlapping

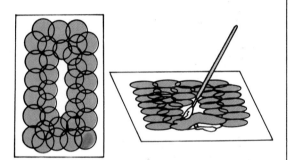

the larger ones, working around the rectangle and toward the center of the mounting board. Again, arrange the circles for the most pleasing effect. With all circles in place, cover the entire surface with another coat of diluted glue. Let dry.

### Finishing collage

Spray the collage with a coating of clear enamel. Spray across from one edge to the other, holding the spray can at an even distance from the board and working from top to bottom of the collage. Allow to dry thoroughly, then mount the collage in the frame. Use picture wire and screw eyes in back of the frame to hang on a picture hook.

# Eggshell mosaic butterfly

Creating mosaic designs with eggshell pieces is similar to the traditional mosaic work of various colored stone or marble pieces; however, in the eggshell medium, designs are more delicate and their application considerably more versatile. Eggshell pieces apply easily on glass, metal cans, wood surfaces or cardboard cut-outs; and the range of colors is almost limitless. Shell pieces can be colored with crayons or oil pastels; painted with oils, tempera, acrylic or enamel; spray painted; or brushed with food coloring or fabric dye. The choice of coloring materials depends on the object, its surface and the desired visual effects. The number of eggshells required for each project depends on the size of the surface to be covered; and with practice in the craft, it becomes easier to estimate accurately the quantity needed. Save the shells until a sufficient quantity is collected, or obtain them from restaurants. For a first project, try the illustrated small mosaic butterfly.

Materials: approximately five whole or ten half eggshells, cleaned and dried; white glue or modeling paste used for rounded objects; acrylic paints; clear acrylic; a small container of water; paper towels; a piece of sturdy cardboard about 9 by 12 inches; a nail file; and a large flat working surface, covered with newspapers.

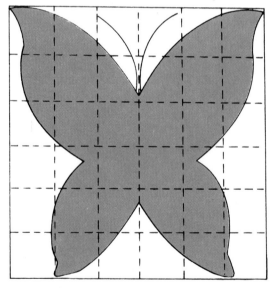

**Drawing pattern and preparing eggshells**
Draw and cut a paper butterfly pattern measuring about 6 by 6 inches overall. Lay the pattern flat on the cardboard and trace around the outline. Cut out cardboard butterfly.

Clean eggshells in a solution of cold water and a few drops of detergent. Dry on a paper towel. Then break dry eggshells into small pieces about the size of your fingertip. The exact size is not as important as your ability to manipulate the pieces in the mounting process.

**Mounting the shell bits**
Place one piece of eggshell between your thumb and index finger with the interior part of the shell facing you. Squirt a bit of glue onto the interior side of the shell and spread with your finger as evenly as possible. The glue should be about $\frac{1}{16}$ inch thick; if less than that, the shells will not adhere to the cardboard. Excess glue can always be scooped up with fingers and placed on another piece of shell. Press shell onto center of butterfly.

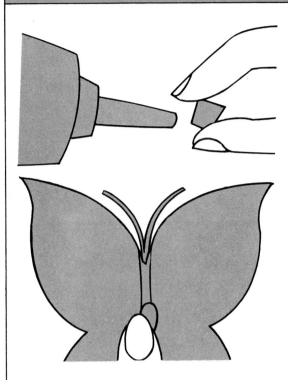

ens underneath the shells. While working, wash your hands periodically to remove glue from fingers.

### Applying shells to edges

To apply shells to edges, select shell pieces that conform most closely to the outline of the butterfly. Apply glue 1/16 inch thick to shell interior and place on edge of pattern, pressing

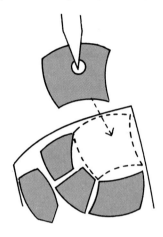

Apply glue in the same manner to the second piece of shell and place on the cardboard next to first shell. The shells should touch each other but not overlap. Continue gluing shell pieces to cardboard pattern, working from center to edge. If any shells pop up, simply press them down again until they lie flat. This sometimes occurs before the glue hard-

firmly and making sure piece touches other shells without overlapping. Mount shells to pointed areas or corners with a toothpick. Cover toothpick end with glue and apply to cardboard at this particular part of the design, making sure glue is 1/16 inch thick. Dip point of toothpick in glue, touch to shell and place gently on corner or point of butterfly. Allow glue to dry for time recommended on container. Remember that all pieces of eggshell should lie flat when dry.

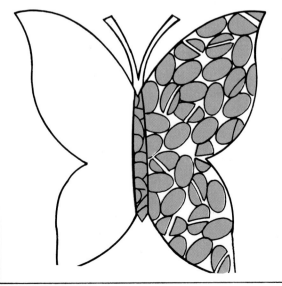

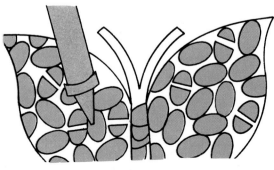

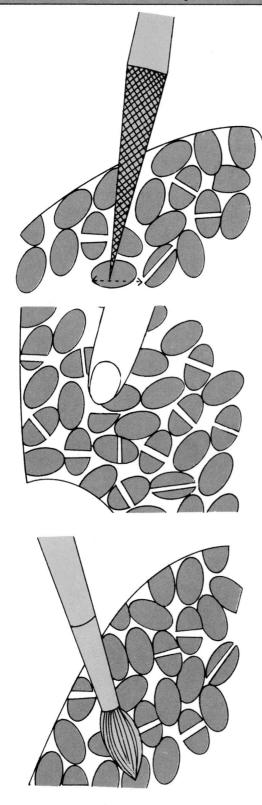

### Coloring the butterfly

To color the mosaic design with paints, select a variety of bright colors and paint eggshells, using one color at a time. Apply second color in the same manner. When color effect is satisfactory, spray with clear acrylic to give it a glossy finish. If a matte finish is desired, do not apply acrylic. Hang the butterfly directly on the wall with adhesive hanging attachments found in art supply stores, or glue it to a backing and place in a picture frame or between two pieces of glass or clear plastic.

This also adapts easily to mobiles. Simply cut out several smaller butterflies and apply eggshell pieces on both sides of the cardboard, and suspend from the ceiling. Once you master the technique of working with eggshells on a flat surface, create more complex three-dimensional mosaics.

# Teneriffe embroidery

Teneriffe embroidery is most frequently used as a decorative border on tablecloths, window curtains, children's dresses and aprons. The pattern is worked in a rectangular area and the stitching runs up and down and across the fabric in rows to form the design. To simplify the placement of stitches for a first project, use a checked fabric such as the green and white gingham illustrated. Here a dark-green embroidery thread was used.

Materials: six-strand embroidery floss or No. 5 cotton thread, quantity depends on the size of the area to be covered; gingham fabric with ¼-inch checks; embroidery needle; pins; and scissors.

### Working horizontal stitches

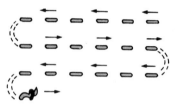

Determine how wide and how deep the Teneriffe border will be. The depth should include an odd number of checked rows. For this project, nine rows were used. Block off the rectangular area to be embroidered and mark the corners with pins. Thread the needle and begin the horizontal stitches which will be worked on the even numbered rows (2 through 8). Start at the end of the second row. Run a series of horizontal stitches centered over each shaded square and under each white square. Complete the row, skip to the fourth row and repeat the procedure. Repeat similarly in sixth and eighth rows.

### Working vertical stitches

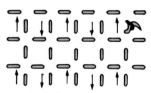

For the vertical stitches, work on the odd numbered rows (1 through 9), starting on the shaded square, one square in from the end of the first row. Run a series of vertical stitches centered over each shaded square and under each white square in the first vertical row,

working from top to bottom. Skip next vertical row and repeat from bottom to top. Continue to end of pattern.

### Stitching the circles

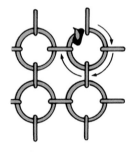

Starting in one corner of the work, bring the needle up through the right side of the first vertical stitch. Working clockwise, slide the needle and thread under the horizontal stitch, then under the next vertical stitch (directly below the first vertical stitch), and under the opposite horizontal stitch. Then bring the needle and thread down through the left side of the vertical stitch, completing a circle. Repeat, starting at the next vertical stitch, and continue across first row of vertical stitches until all circles are completed. Repeat for each row, always starting at the vertical stitch. Circles enclose white squares.

### Completing the design

In the dark square of each octagonal area surrounded by the circles, stitch a cross consisting of a horizontal stitch topped by a vertical stitch. Start at one corner of the work and stitch up and down across the pattern until the Teneriffe is completed.

# Patchwork pillow

In our great-grandparents' time, all types of fabrics were both expensive and hard to find. People learned to be ingenious in using and reusing the materials at hand. Patchwork was a creative way to recycle an old dress, a bit of shirting and the scraps from a new sewing project. By stitching them together in bold geometric patterns, unique effects were produced at virtually no expense. The same advantages can be enjoyed today, though you may prefer to use some new materials to obtain the proper mixture of colors for the setting you have in mind. When you have mastered the simple patchwork techniques on a pillow, you can go on to make comforters and wall hangings.

Materials: a piece of upholstery material large enough to cover the back of the pillow, and small pieces of five or six different lightweight fabrics to make your patches. We recommend cottons in bright small-scale designs, such as calicoes. In addition, you will need a foundation to which you will sew the patches. This will be covered by the patches when the project is finished. Use any lightweight piece of fabric large enough to cover the front of the pillow. Also needed: a ready-made pillow or materials to make one as described in the instructions below.

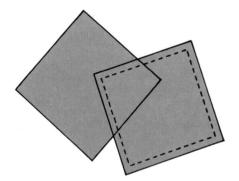

Machine stitch the two squares together on three sides, 1 inch in from the edges. Turn the assembled piece inside out so that the seam allowances do not show. Fill this to plumpness with cut-up pieces of foam rubber, old nylon stockings, or the like. Hand sew the fourth side. You now have a square pillow to cover.

### Making the pillow
Before you start your patchwork, you must know the dimensions of your pillow. Ready-made muslin-covered pillows can be purchased for finishing at home. However, if you would prefer to make your own, it is an easy task. Begin by cutting out two squares of material the size of the desired pillow with 1 inch extra on each side for the seams.

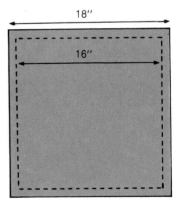

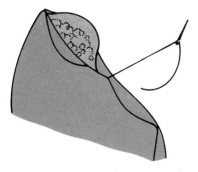

### Cutting cloth for the pillowcase
Measure the size of your pillow. Mark off on your foundation fabric a square equal to the size of the pillow plus 1 inch on each side for the seam allowance. (A 16-inch pillow will take an 18-inch-by-18-inch square of fabric.)

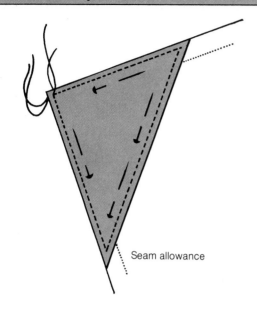

Seam allowance

Cut a second piece of patchwork of a different color and in a different shape. Fold the edges as before and position the patch so that one edge is touching the first patch and another edge is along the margin of the foundation fabric. Cut a third patch, shaping it to fit within the spaces created by the previous patches. Continue to cover the foundation fabric in this manner, positioning your patches in a variety of shapes.

## Patching the pillow

Lay the foundation fabric on a flat surface. From one of your lightweight cottons, cut out a triangular shape. Fold the three edges under. Place the patch at the top left corner and pin. Using a brightly colored thread, machine stitch close to edges around triangle.

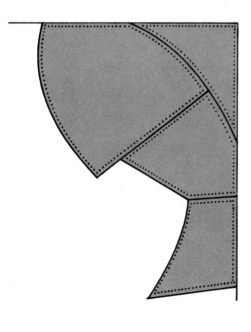

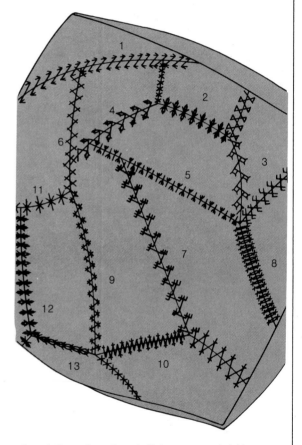

Descriptions of numbered stitches appear at right

## Decorating the patchwork

Turn the pillow cover to right side. Go over all the machine-stitched patches with a decorative embroidered stitch in the same bright-colored thread you used in the machine, or with a matching embroidery thread if you prefer an even bolder effect. Hand stitch, so that the stitches cover all seams between patches from the edge of one patch to the edge of the adjoining patch. More than a dozen stitches are described below.

For the decorative stitches described below, see numbered diagram at left.

1. A decorative border combining straight and fly-stitching.

2. The cross-stitch, consisting of two rows of whipped-stitches, one worked backward to cross over the middle of another. It is worked two crosses at a time.

3. Faggoting ordinarily joins two pieces of material. Here, since it is decorative only, it is not necessary to hem both pieces and baste them a desired distance apart on a firm piece of paper. Merely stitch up from the underside of one patch, then stitch down on the adjacent patch. Bring the needle back under the thread stitched between both patches and stitch up from underside through the first patch. Continue for the entire seam.

4. This decorative border stitching resembles the feathered chain.

5. One of several variations on faggoting (See number 3 for stitch description).

6. Herringbone stitch is sewn similarly to cross-stitch, but the cross goes through the ends, rather than the middle of each stitch.

7. Like feather-stitching, the feathered chain stitch is a double row of stitches interlocking through the loop of each chain.

8. Hemstitching consists of vertical stitching between two edges, wrapped with a back stitch, every few threads, at top and bottom.

9. Tack herringbone at each cross point with a back stitch to create tacked herringbone stitch.

10. A row of long and short stitches simply consists of two adjacent, alternating lengths of straight stitch.

11. The star-stitch is just that: two stitches form a T shape, topped by a cross-stitch to equal an eight-point star.

12. A bundle stitch is three straight stitches backed at midpoint.

13. The wheat-ear stitch joins two straight stitches, slanted at the bottom toward each other, with a chain stitch.

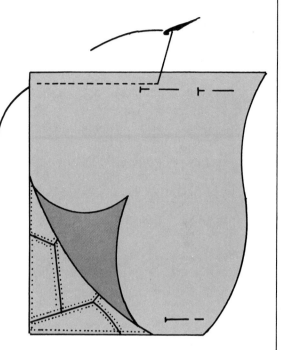

### Finishing the pillow

When the foundation square is completely covered with patches and decorative stitching, place your square of upholstery fabric for the pillow right sides together with the patchwork. Pin together along three sides and stitch with a ½-inch seam allowance.

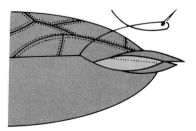

Insert the pillow into the finished pillow-case. Fold in the edges of the fourth side and hand stitch to close the pillowcase.

# Holiday cookies

In almost every country where Christmas is celebrated, traditional cookies are always included in the festive array of sweets and delicacies prepared for the holidays. Like the gingerbread cookies (see Gingerbread sculpture), the Danish vanilla cookies shown are suitable to hang on the Christmas tree or, as illustrated, on a decorative stand. You may choose to arrange the cookies on a large silver tray with other holiday favorites for family and friends to enjoy. These crisp cookies do not crumble and take well to frosting and decorating. The dough is cut into shapes, baked and frosted.

Materials: for the cookies you need: 1 cup butter or margarine; 1 cup granulated sugar; 1 beaten egg; 2 tablespoons vanilla flavoring; 3 cups flour (whole-wheat flour is nice for variation and better nutritional value); ½ teaspoon baking powder; and ⅛ teaspoon salt. To make the decorative frosting you need: 1 cup confectioners' sugar; 1 tablespoon water; and any desired food colorings. This recipe will make 4 to 6 dozen cookies.

### Preparing cookie dough
Cream the butter or margarine in a large bowl. Add granulated sugar gradually, beating well until fluffy; then add beaten egg and vanilla flavoring and beat until well blended. Sift dry ingredients and add gradually, blending in well to make a stiff dough. Wrap the dough in waxed paper and chill in the refrigerator for about three hours, or until it is very firm.

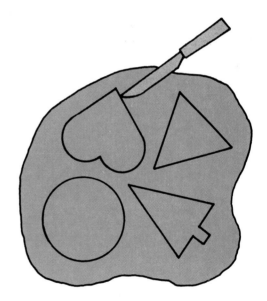

### Shaping and baking cookies
On a lightly floured board, roll dough out into a large circular sheet about ⅛ inch thick if cookies are to be eaten or ¼ inch thick if cookies are to be hung as decorations. Cut out shapes with cookie cutters. Or copy shapes shown: a circle, a tree, a heart and a triangle. Trace shapes onto heavy waxed paper, cut out, and place on dough to use as patterns. Trace outlines on dough with a dull knife, and then cut out with a sharp knife. If cookies are to be hung, cut holes at center tops with a plastic straw. Cut out centers of some of the dough pieces with a thimble.

Place cookies on an ungreased baking sheet and bake 10 or 11 minutes at 350 degrees Fahrenheit. If necessary, adjust time and temperature to suit the characteristics of your oven. When cookies are delicately browned, remove from oven and allow to cool on wire racks.

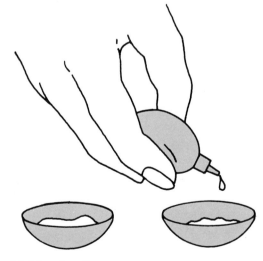

### Making frosting
In a small bowl, mix the confectioners' sugar and water. Spoon the frosting into several smaller dishes, one for each color desired.

Add one or two drops of food coloring to each dish of frosting and blend.

### Decorating cookies
Spoon frosting into a pastry bag, then force icing through tip of bag to decorate cookies

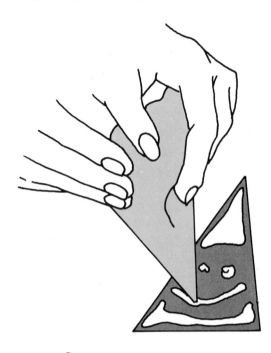

with such details as dots and stripes, fir-tree branches, concentric hearts, ruffles or rosettes. Decorate the circular cookies with the centers cut out to resemble holly or evergreen wreaths. Let cookies stand until frosting is firm. Store in tins or jars for Christmas Day or string short lengths of gilded cord through top holes and hang on your Christmas tree.

LEF

# Pysanky eggs

Elaborately dyed eggshells are a traditional Easter specialty throughout the Christian world, but nowhere is the decorating skill practiced with more care than in the Slavic countries. Elaborate geometric and floral designs, often symbolic, are applied by techniques involving melted wax and vegetable dyes. The Ukrainians call the craft pysanky; the Lithuanians, margutis.

The craft requires white hen's eggs, either hard cooked or the whole eggshell, from which the raw egg has been blown out. Liquid candle wax is then applied to each eggshell, describing lines and spaces in the design which are to remain white when the eggshell is dyed. (The dye colors will not penetrate the waxed portions.) The egg is then dipped in a dye bath. By waxing, dyeing, and then waxing and dyeing again, several times in sequence, each time using a darker dye color, a multicolor effect is achieved. Here's how to achieve results like those known in the Old World.

Materials: darning needle; drip candle; medium-sized speed-ball straight pen, or a stylus with a hollow point; vinegar; pencil and paper; rubber band; vegetable dyes; slotted spoon; fixative spray; variety of containers for dyeing; paper towels; and white eggs.

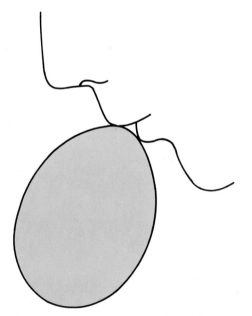

## Preparing eggshells
Remove eggs from refrigerator and allow them to reach room temperature. This prevents cracked shells whether eggs are to be hard cooked or blown. To blow eggs from shells, use a darning needle or large pin to pierce each egg at both ends, turning the needle as you press gently to help it penetrate the shell. Make the hole at the round end slightly larger than that at the pointed end of the egg.

Hold the egg over a bowl, round end down, and blow into the smaller, upper hole. Should the yolk resist being blown out, pierce the yolk sac by gently poking a needle up through the bottom hole and stir the yolk about. Blow again. Repeat procedure with as many eggs as the number of shells you plan to decorate. (Use raw eggs for omelets or some other culinary purpose.)

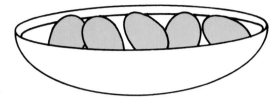

To rinse out the eggshells, place the large round end in a bowl of cool water and draw water into the shell by sucking in from the top. Then blow out the water so the interior of the shell is thoroughly cleansed. Any egg particles left inside might produce an unpleasant odor. Place the shells in a bowl of vinegar, to prime the eggshell surface for the dyes to adhere better. Set the shells aside to drain and dry.

### Filling stylus
Place a drip-type candle in a holder. Light the candle and wait for melted wax to gather in a pool around the wick. Dip the pen tip into the candle flame to heat it and then dip it into the melted wax, or if a hollow stylus is used, dip the open end in the melted wax to load it.

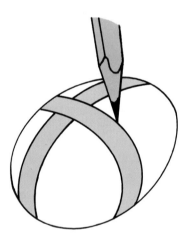

### Creating designs
Plot the designs on paper, one for each egg. For your first experiments in pysanky, avoid elaborate motifs like the one shown. Try stripes, dots within circles, dashes and other such combinations, plotting the design so larger areas are covered and few, if any, intricate patterns are used. Restrict dye colors to two or three. When the designs are completed, sketch them on the eggs with very light lines so they will not show through the dyes. Lines running the length or breadth of the egg can be traced lightly with the use of a rubber band snapped in place as a guide for tracing lines running completely around the middle of the shell or lengthwise around the eggshell.

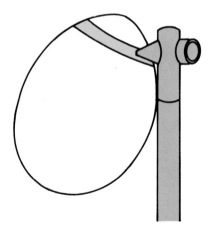

### Waxing design
Draw a line of wax wherever the neutral white color of the eggshell is to show through. Repeat the dipping and filling of the pen tip or stylus each time the line of wax begins to thin or skip spaces.

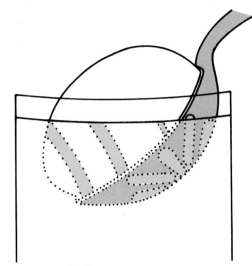

Prepare for the second dye bath, color B, if two or more colors are desired. If the area protected by wax is to be white in the final design, leave the wax as it is and, using the pen or stylus as before, fill in additional dyed areas with more wax motifs. These will remain color A after the egg has been immersed in dye bath B. Repeat the steps for the second dye bath exactly as the first, and allow to dry. Repeat the waxing and dyeing procedure for each additional color desired.

### Dyeing eggshell

While the wax on the egg is cooling, prepare the dye solutions, starting with the lightest in the series of colors you plan to be used. This is color A. Mix according to the directions on the vegetable dye package. Add two tablespoons of vinegar to each pint of dye solution to aid in distributing the color evenly over the entire eggshell surface. Before immersing the egg, check to be sure that the dye bath is cool; a warm bath will soften the wax. Immerse the egg in the dye; and when the color has reached the intensity desired, remove the egg with a slotted spoon and place it on a paper towel to dry. (Do not rub as this will smear the wax.)

### Removing wax

To make the decorated egg glow with soft highlights, remove the wax by placing the egg in a slotted spoon and hold over a gas flame, far enough away from the flame to prevent scorching the surface. (Do not hold it above the candle flame; the candle smoke is likely to darken the egg.) Gently wipe the egg with a paper towel to remove the melting wax, leaving just enough of a film to shine.

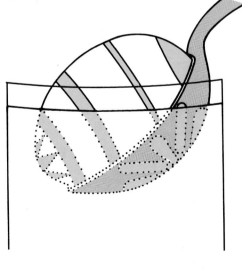

The colors on the decorated eggshells will not fade, provided they are not kept in direct sunlight.

# Puppet theater

The puppet theater is a very important element in working with any type of puppet. Even if it is a makeshift arrangement of a cardboard carton set on a table, a set is essential for the puppeteer to work behind. It focuses the audience's attention on the puppets and at the same time conceals the person manipulating the puppets. There are many types of theaters, ranging from the cardboard carton to the more durably constructed stage and theater. This three-panel puppet assembly is one type used by professionals that is practical and simple to construct. Attractive, portable and usable indoors and out, it utilizes a three-panel folding screen with an opening for the puppet stage in the center panel. Lightweight fabric curtains are hung from rods and wires to complete the theater. The model illustrated is 6 feet high, and each panel is 2 feet wide. The back curtains extend 2 feet from each side for the center panel when the puppets are in action. The side panels extend outward so the center back curtain extends across an area 5 feet wide, to give the puppeteer sufficient working room.

Materials: three pieces of plywood, each 6 feet by 2 feet by 2 inches thick; six double-acting hinges with screws to fit; 6½ yards of 30-inch felt or burlap to cover the front panels; a lamp with a tubular-shaped light bulb, a shade, and fixtures to affix overhead to the inside of the theater (see illustration); 2 flood lamps for placing crosslighting in front of the theater; 5 feet of heavy-gauge household wire; an extension-type curtain rod with caps on each end that can extend up to 9 feet; one thin rod or dowel ½ inch in diameter and 23 inches long to serve as a weight for the front curtain; 13 screw eyes; about one dozen screw-in cup hooks; 9 yards of string or cord; a hammer and tacks or staple gun; an electric power drill with ½-inch bit, and sanding and screw-driving attachments (or substitute sandpaper and a manual screwdriver); a keyhole saw and a crosscut saw; seven 2-yard lengths of matte finish, lightweight, drapable fabric, 1 yard wide, such as jersey, for the back curtain and side extensions; three 1¼-yard lengths of similar material for the middle curtain (each 1 yard wide); and for the front curtain, two 1-yard-square lengths of matte finish fabric such as corduroy, velveteen, cotton, or matte jersey; a sewing machine or needle and thread. It is important to select matte finish fabrics in solid colors so that they will enhance the total effect of the theater, rather than detract attention from the puppets. Apply simple trim or sequins in a matching color to the back curtain extensions only for accent, if desired.

### Cutting stage opening in panel
Mark a 20-inch-square area on one of the plywood panels, 2 inches in from each 6-foot edge, at a height comfortable for the puppeteer. Mark and drill a hole through each corner of the square, being careful not to drill outside the outline of the square. With the keyhole saw, cut along the lines marked, between the holes you drilled. This opening is the puppet stage. Sand all edges of the opening smooth. On the square you cut out of the panel, mark a 20-inch-long straight line 3 inches in from one edge and parallel to that edge. Cut along the line marked with a crosscut saw. Sand the edges smooth on this 20-by-3-by-2-inch piece of wood. This strip forms the apron of the puppet stage. Mark and cut a notch in the apron strip 2 inches wide and 1 inch deep into the 2-inch thickness of the wood, along the entire length of the strip. Sand inside of notch smooth.

### Drilling holes in two side panels
Mark a ½-inch-diameter circle on each of the

other two panels, 2 inches in from one 6-foot edge, and 2 inches in from the adjacent 2-foot edge. Drill a ½-inch hole through the thickness of the wood. Mark and drill another ½-inch hole 1 foot across from the first hole and 2 inches in from the same 2-foot edge. Sand inside of circles smooth with sandpaper or an electric sanding attachment.

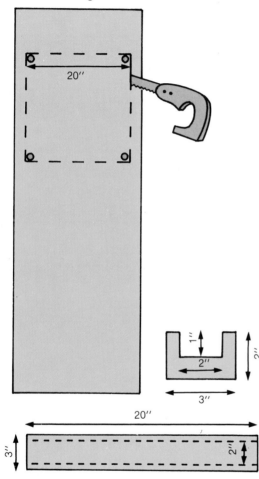

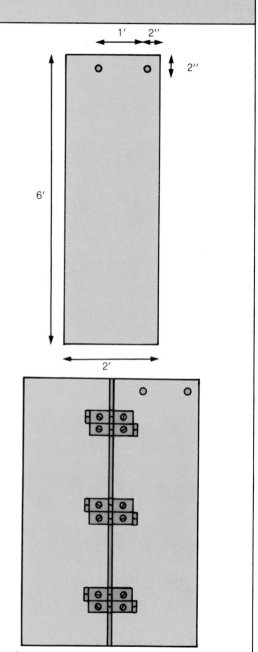

### Attaching hinges to panels

Mark positions for three hinges along the 6-foot edges of each side panel, 10 inches opposite each inner ½-inch hole: one at center, one 12 inches from top and one 12 inches from bottom of panel. Mark hinge positions on both sides of center panel at center, and 1 foot from top and bottom. Place hinges in position one at a time, and drive screws through hinge openings with a screwdriver or screwdriving attachment.

### Covering panels with fabric

Cut three lengths of felt or burlap, each 6½ feet long by 2½ feet wide, to cover one side of each panel. Tack over all edges, along thickness of panel, turning raw edges under 1 inch. Cut away and tack cloth around hinges and drilled holes, turning and tacking raw edges under. Cut away fabric covering stage opening, leaving sufficient allowance to fit over the thickness of stage opening, plus 1 inch. Turn each under, clipping at corners

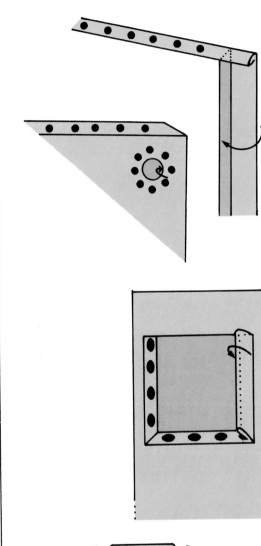

where necessary, and tack to thickness of stage opening. Set screen upright, with covered panels facing out to the audience, so that side panels open to a width of 5 feet at back. Place notched apron over bottom edge of stage opening.

## Assembling curtain rigging

On the uncovered side of the center panel, space and fasten screw eyes for curtain rigging evenly around the stage opening, evenly spaced, and in line, on each of the four sides as follows: two along each side, one at the center along top, one at the center below apron along bottom edge, and one at each of

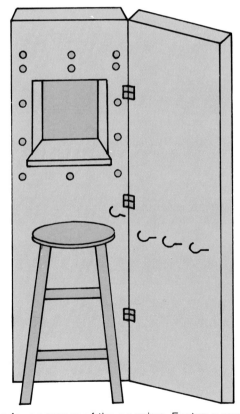

the four corners of the opening. Fasten a row of four more screw eyes, three directly above those along the top of the stage opening, plus one at the far right corner of the center panel. Screw a cup hook along lower side of center panel, near edge, directly below the last corner screw eye, to hold curtain rigging taut when curtain is raised. Place the stool to be used by the puppeteer inside the theater and mark positions for cup hooks on each side panel at a comfortable height in relation to stool height. These hooks will hold puppets so that the puppeteer can change the cast of characters quickly. If the puppets are too heavy, use larger hooks.

### Stitching stage curtain

To make the front curtain, seam two 1-yard lengths of fabric lengthwise, right sides to-

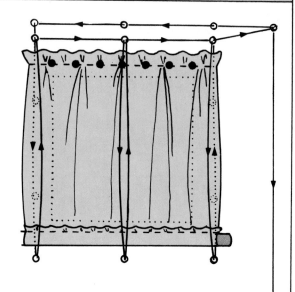

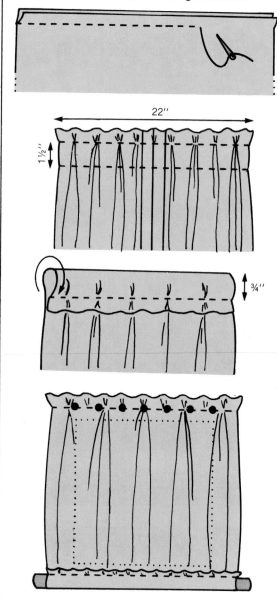

gether, allowing ½-inch seam allowance. Press seam open. Turn under all raw edges ¼ inch and baste to wrong side. Turn under ¼ inch again, covering raw edges, and backstitch securely by hand or machine. Baste, gather to a width of 22 inches, and backstitch curtain fabric ¾ inch from each hemmed edge, perpendicular to piecing seam. Run a second row of gatherstitching and backstitching 1½ inches in from one gathered row. Pin this row of stitching to the first gathered row, wrong sides of fabric together. Backstitch over previous stitching lines, to form a bottom hem, through which the 23-inch rod or dowel will slip easily.

### Rigging stage curtain

Tack opposite edge of fabric over top of stage opening on the inside. With curtain in place, thread string or cord through screw eyes, beginning at top far right corner eye. Knot string or cord around this screw eye, then pass across through top row of screw eyes, working toward the left, then thread downward through all eyes on the left side of stage opening; bring string back up as the string lies over the wrong side of the curtain and draw string through the top screw eye directly above the bottom eye just threaded, through next eye on the second-from-top row and down over the wrong side of curtain through center bottom eye; back up again through top center eye in the same horizontal row of eyes and across through next eye; down through all remaining right-side eyes; up around wrong side of curtain and directly back through top eye on same side; then across to far-right corner eye and downward through it to cup hook. To raise curtain, pull string downward and wrap securely around cup hook below to keep it

dicular to piecing seams, and another ¾ inch below that. Measure distance between the inner holes on opposite side panels and gather width of fabric to fit. Backstitch over each row of gathers. Turn and pin one row of gathers to the other, wrong sides together, and backstitch to form a tubular hem. Turn opposite edge of fabric 2 inches under to wrong side. Pin and hemstitch. Pass heavy gauge household wire through inner drilled hole on one side and wrap it over and around top of panel, then around itself several times to secure. Pass heavy gauge household wire through the thin tubular hem and across to opposite hole on other side panel. Wrap wire around and through the hole and around itself several times.

Now the middle curtain is in place. It serves as a scrim curtain, which means that cross-lighted from in front of the theater, it enables

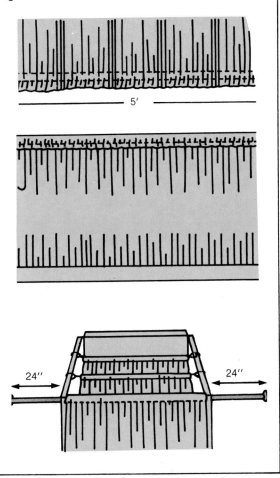

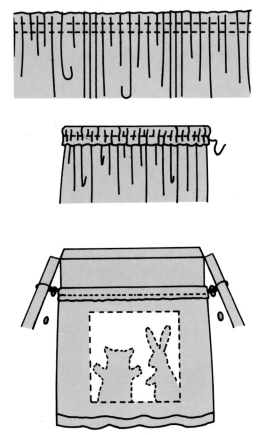

raised. To lower curtain, unwrap string from cup hook and release tension gradually until curtain falls.

### Making scrim or center curtain
Hem raw edges and piece together the three 1¼-yard lengths of lightweight material for the center curtain in the same manner as for the front curtain, pressing open the two piecing seams. Run two rows of gather stitching, one ¾ inch below one hemmed edge, perpen-

the puppeteer to manipulate the puppets and see the audience without being visible to them. Therefore, it is important that the fabric for this curtain be lightweight and have a matte finish.

### Stitching and hanging back curtain

To make back curtain and extensions, turn under all raw edges of each 2-yard length of fabric ¼ inch to wrong side and stitch, then turn under ¼ inch again and stitch. Piece five of the lengths together with backstitched lengthwise seams, pinning wrong sides together and allowing ½-inch seam allowances. Gatherstitch one side of the pieced length ¾ inch in from one hemmed edge, with piecing seams perpendicular to gatherstitching, adjusting gathers to a 5-foot width. Backstitch over gathers. Run a second row of gathers 1½ inches in from the first and backstitch. Pin the two rows wrong sides together and backstitch over previous rows of stitching. Turn opposite edge of fabric under 6 inches to wrong side and hemstitch. Unscrew caps from curtain rod and pass one end of the rod through the outer

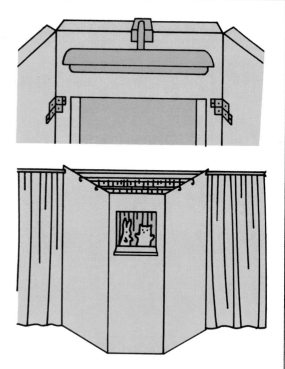

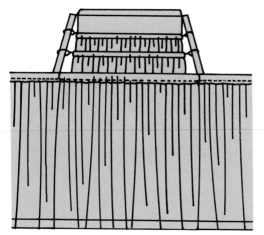

hole on one side panel, extending it 2 feet outside the panel. Pass other end of rod through tubular upper hem and through the outer hole on the other side panel, extending it 2 feet.

### Stitching and hanging side curtains

Turn under all raw edges of remaining two pieces of fabric ¼ inch to wrong side and stitch. Turn under ¼ inch again and stitch.

Gatherstitch along width of each piece ¾ inch from one hemmed edge to a width of 2 feet and backstitch over gathers. Gather and backstitch another row 1½ inches in from the first row. Pin the two gathered rows wrong sides together and backstitch over previous stitching. Turn opposite end of each piece 6 inches in to wrong side and hemstitch. Pass one side extension of curtain rod through the thin tubular top hem and cap each end of the curtain rod.

### Testing the puppet theater

Clamp overhead light inside the theater over the stage and position front lights to right and left of stage, so that the light beams cross and focus on the front curtain. Bring stool and puppets inside the theater, along with a tape player or phonograph to provide background music, and set yourself up while the audience assembles. Then raise the curtain and let the show begin. After the puppet cast has taken its curtain calls, you can disassemble the theater by removing rod and wire, back and middle curtains, folding panels into a ''Z'' shape, and storing the theater in a convenient closet until time for the next performance.

# Hand puppet

Children are enchanted with puppets and they are really a breeze to create. Hand puppets, such as the clown shown, can be made out of felt or fabric and an original pattern. Once the clown pattern is sketched and cut out, you can re-use the two essential parts, the body and the head, to make your children's favorite cartoon characters, animals, or fictional figures.

   Materials: four sheets of 1-inch-square graph paper, 9 inches by 12 inches (or rule out 1-inch squares on plain paper); common pins; two pieces of orange felt, 9 inches by 12 inches; two pieces of white felt, 4 inches by 4 inches; one piece of pink felt for the collar, 3 inches by 6 inches; additional small scraps of felt; 16 inches of orange knitting worsted or rug yarn; four pink pompons; household and manicure scissors; needle; thread; white glue; and a toothpick.

Scale: ⅜″ represents 1″

Actual size

### Cutting out the pieces

To make the clown's body, collar, ears, and head, trace them and transfer the patterns onto graph paper to enlarge the dimensions to actual size. The facial features and hat are shown actual size; trace them directly from the illustration. Carefully draw each of the four major puppet parts on the grids, using the measurements indicated. Iron the felt, cut out the patterns, and pin them to the respective pieces of colored felt. Cut two orange body shapes; two white head shapes; one pink collar; two each of the ears, eyes, and eyebrows, using varied scraps; and one each of the mouth, nose and hat. Use sharp household scissors and, for curved cuts, manicure scissors.

Press each part into place and allow a few minutes' drying time before gluing the next part. If any excess glue gets on the felt, wipe it immediately with a tissue. Glue the collar to the body; the face to the collar; and facial features and hat (without the band) to the face. Turn the clown over and glue the ears in place. As mentioned before, these should overlap the collar slightly; secure this spot with glue. Cut the orange yarn into eight lengths, 2 inches each. Loop the strands and glue them to the inside of the top of the back headpiece. Proceed to glue the back of the head in place. Then glue the four pompons to the front of the clown; one centered on the collar, and the others 1 to 2 inches apart.

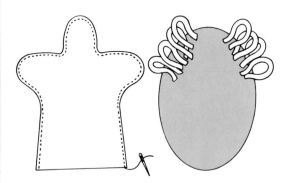

### Making the flower

The tiny flower is the difficult part in making the clown. If you want to avoid this, buy a small flower with a wire stem and glue it on the hatband. To make your own felt flower, follow the illustration, which shows the flower actual size. Cut out a circle with a scalloped edge about ½ inch wide. Use a hole punch to cut smaller circles, and glue these to the scalloped circle to form flower petals. Glue the flower to the hat, then secure the band, partially covering the flower.

### Assembling the clown

Place the felt parts together to make sure the pieces are in proportion and to determine whether any additional trimming is needed. Note that the bottom edge of the face overlaps the collar; and the ears are placed slightly behind the face with the ear lobes touching the collar. To assemble the clown, sew the two body parts together (one on top of the other), leaving a ¼-inch seam. Leave the bottom seam open so that your hand can operate the finished clown.

The rest of the features are glued together. For small areas, spread the glue over the entire back with a toothpick; for the large parts, a bead of glue spread flat near the edges will do.

### Working the puppet

To manipulate the puppet, simply place your hand into the body with thumb and little finger in the clown's hands, and index and middle fingers in the head. Design other circus puppets so your children can present their own puppet show. Use the basic body and head measurements and vary the features and decorations.

Pinus sylvestris

PINEAPPLE FRITTE

Combine one egg, one cup mi
tablespoons sugar, two and
spoons baking powder, one
pineapple, two tablespoo
(melted), two and one-half

# Picture frames

There are so many ways to use mat and molding materials to create unusual picture frames. Picture framing serves both a utilitarian and artistic purpose. The primary consideration is the proper balance of frame to picture; the frame should complement but never dominate the picture. Variations of molding and mats used to frame pictures can be helpful in creating the proper showcase for the painting, print or etching.

Materials: a miter box and hacksaw to cut the wood molding at clean, sharp angles; two C-clamps to hold the wood and the miter box firmly; an eggbeater drill; a 6-ounce hammer; white glue; a box of brads (small nails); a box of glazier's points (optional); a mat cutter set which includes a T-square and knife; a length of wood molding 96 inches (or longer if needed); a sheet of mat board; and a sheet of wrapping paper (optional). Check both a hardware store and an art supply store for these items.

There are many variations in framing. This project illustrates the basic techniques with a few options. You can make the frame the same size as the picture or mount the picture on a mat and make the frame to accommodate the perimeter of the mat. You can also frame two or three small pictures by using a mat to separate the pictures (see below, left).

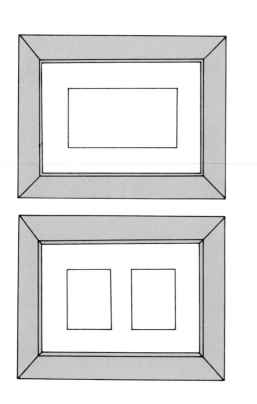

## Selecting and cutting mat

If a mat is used, check the selection at your local art supply store and choose one that will complement the picture and frame. Ask to see the seconds, rejects or odd-sized mats first, then the regular stock. When you have selected the mat, cut it to the size needed. First mark off the outside area on the mat, and then

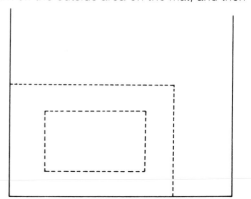

mark the area in the center of the mat to be cut out. Be sure the entire picture is visible when it is mounted on the mat. Make all marks on the reverse side of the mat. Do not place the picture exactly in the center of the mat; leave a larger border at the bottom than at sides and top. The sides and top should be the same width. The outside dimensions of the mat should be about ¼ inch wider than the inside perimeter of the frame.

To cut the mat, place it face down on a newspaper-covered worktable. Place the mat cutter on top of the mat, with the T-square against the edge of the table. Put the bottom

# Picture frames

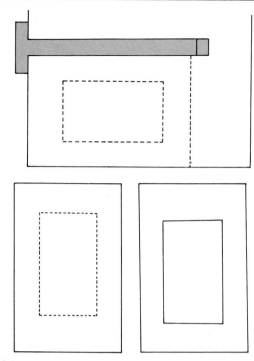

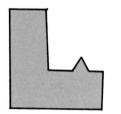
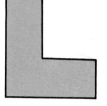

walls. The molding comes in 8-foot lengths. Before you start working, cut it down to lengths easy to handle, but plan the cuts so there are no useless scraps left over. Mark on the lengths the exact dimensions of each side of the frame and cut pieces, using a miter box and hacksaw.

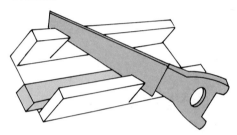

of the mat against the "T" and lean against the T-square with your body holding it firmly. Line up the mat cutter with the lines drawn on the mat, insert the knife into the perpendicular slot of the cutter, insert the knife into the mat and through it into the newspapers below and draw the knife toward you, making the cut in one firm motion. Reposition the mat cutter and repeat this procedure, cutting on the second line. To cut out the center of the mat, where the picture is visible, repeat the procedure, but this time insert the knife into the angled slot in the mat cutter, to obtain a beveled edge. Cut on all four lines drawn. Place the mat over the picture to check the fit. Then mount picture to back of mat.

## Making the frame
Now make the frame. Use scrap wood or buy molding, the kind used around doors and

## Cutting the molding
The miter box has three sets of grooves to guide the hacksaw: grooves angled to the right; and left; and one perpendicular. For picture framing, use the angled grooves. Each of the four sides of the frame will require two angled edges, one to the right and the other to the left. Place the molding in the miter box; place the clamps so they embrace the molding, the miter box and the worktable; slip the hacksaw into the groove and make the cut. Repeat the process until all four sides of the frame are cut.

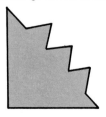
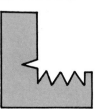

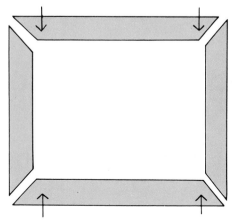

### Assembling the frame

Lay the molding pieces on the floor, match all four sides and assemble, to check the fit. Insert one of the brads into the eggbeater drill and using it as a bit, drill holes in the side pieces through each of the four joints of the frame, so brads can be inserted in a horizontal position rather than perpendicular to the ground. This will lessen the strain of gravity on the frame when it is hung. After drilling the holes, smear some white glue on the inside joints of the frame, place them together, insert a brad into each drilled hole and, using the 6-ounce hammer, tap the brads all the way into the holes. Wipe away the excess glue and allow to dry.

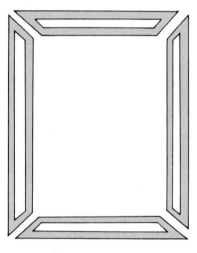

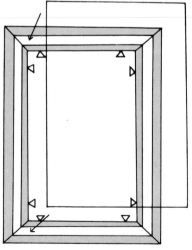

### Mounting the rabbet

To hold the picture in the frame, you need a groove called a rabbet. There are two ways to make it. The first is to use a table saw to cut the groove *before* assembling the frame. This is difficult and takes great care. The alternative is much easier. Using the miter box and hacksaw, cut strips of ⅛- or ¼-inch plywood, ¼ inch narrower than the width of the molding,

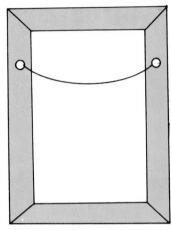

and with glue fasten them to the back of the frame about ¼ inch from the inside edge.

Place the picture, or the mat on which picture is mounted, inside the rabbet and fasten it in place along the four sides with brads or glazier's points. If you decide to protect the picture with glass, have the glass cut to size.

### Finishing frame

Finish the back of the frame with a dust cover, if desired. To make a dust cover, soak a sheet of wrapping paper in water and lay flat on the working surface. Blot up excess moisture and cut to fit the frame. Glue or staple paper to the back along edges of frame. When the paper dries, it will stretch tight, sealing the back of the picture frame.

To hang, screw two eye-hooks, one into each side of frame, about one third of the way from the top. Stretch picture wire loosely from one hook to the other. Drive a picture hook into the wall (the hooks come in a variety of sizes rated by the weight of picture they can support) and hang your picture, adjusting the wire if necessary.

Practical space savers as well as decorative room accents, custom-designed shelving systems utilize wall space to best advantage and serve as a coordinating force for the decor of the room. Storage and display space is created in a balanced and attractive design for books, plants, art, audio and bar equipment or any combination of these items. Most hardware and home furnishing stores feature a wide variety of components from which a shelving system can be designed and assembled.

Materials: shelves; slotted rails, also called shelf standards; brackets; screws; a screwdriver; and lead anchors. Another type is the floor-to-ceiling poles that are held in place by tension springs. You may also create a shelving system with bricks or cinder blocks and planks.

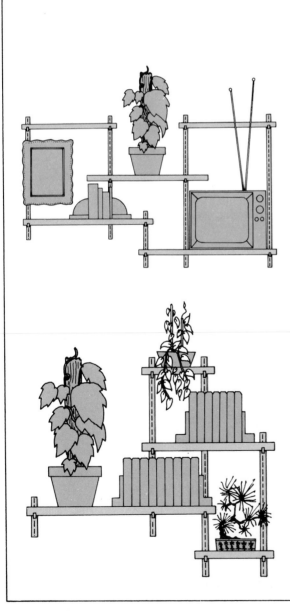

### Planning the system

First determine the use of the shelving system; is it to be for display, entertainment, work space, or a combination of these? Also, what kinds of objects are to be placed on the shelves: books, plants, audio equipment, television or bric-a-brac. Measure the area in which the system is to be installed (measuring from top to bottom and from side to side). Visit several hardware stores to see what choice of components there is available, before designing the wall system. Vary the shelves in length and in height. One very good way to break up a shelving system is to leave a roughly symmetrical gap between shelves near the center of the system. This gap can be used to hang a painting, or to display a piece of sculpture, or for a large plant or a small indoor tree. The shelving system should be in harmony with the rest of the room and the wall. This is especially important when the shelves are mounted on only one side of the wall space.

### Determining dimensions

The objects to be placed on the shelves will determine the distance between the slotted rails (the heavier the objects, the closer the rails which support the brackets). If books are to be placed on the shelves, the rails should be no more than 32 inches apart; for heavier objects, such as a television, the rails should be even closer. Shelves are available in a variety of lengths and depths, and as many rails as needed can be used, so the options are practically limitless.

5 inches on other. On the longer extension, place a number of objects, such as a small plant, a candle or a figurine, which will visually balance the television.

### Visualizing completed system

Consider the above guidelines in planning the shelving system. Draw it on paper, then chalk the plan full scale on the wall where the shelving system is to be mounted. This will help you visualize the completed system. Once the plan is finished, list the components needed.

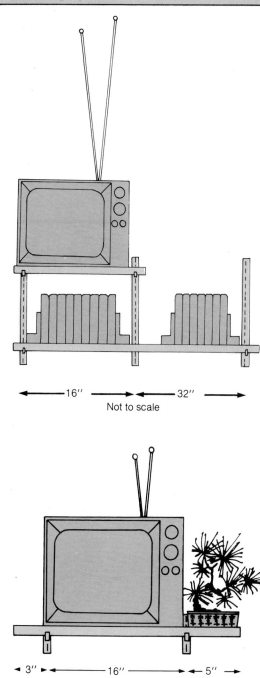

16″ ⟶ ⟵ 32″

Not to scale

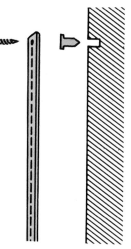

In designing the system, plan to place the shelves so that they extend from 2 to 6 inches beyond their supporting brackets. To support a television set, for example, mount rails about 16 inches apart. For variety, use a 24-inch-long shelf and place it so that it extends 3 inches beyond the bracket on one side and

3″ ⟵ 16″ ⟶ 5″

### Preparing for installation

Installation of the system varies with the type of wall. For wood walls, simply drill holes and drive screws through the rails and into the wall. For concrete or brick walls, drill holes and insert lead or plastic anchors into holes before driving the screws. The plugs expand as the screw is driven in, insuring a tight fit. For plasterboard walls, plan the system so that each slotted rail is mounted over one of the studs inside the wall. To find the studs (which are 2-inch-by-4-inch beams inside the wall), tap the wall until you hit a solid spot, or drill holes in the wall along the baseboard near the floor until a stud is hit. After finding one stud, locate the adjacent one and measure the distance between them to establish the distance between studs in all the walls. Another method for mounting the rails on plasterboard is to use flange fasteners or expansion bolts (available at all hardware stores).

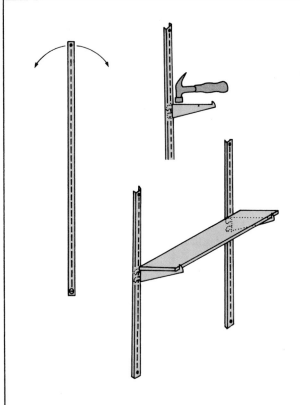

and push up while moving the bottom of the pole to the corresponding spot on the floor. Use a carpenter's level to check the vertical. After the poles are in place, attach the brackets and mount the shelves. This system can also serve as a room divider. A more flexible system is easy to create with bricks or cinder blocks and finished or unfinished planks. Make a stack of three or four bricks, or stand a cinder block on end to create space between shelves. This system is inexpensive and easily put together or taken apart.

### Installing rails

To install the rails, simply place them over the chalk marks made on the wall. Drill the top hole first and drive that screw in. Let the rail swing freely to find the vertical and then drill the hole for the bottom screw. Always mount the other rails in relation to the first rail you mounted. With the rails fastened, attach the brackets by slipping the tabs into the slots in the rails. Tap the back of the bracket with a hammer to make sure the tabs are firmly in place. Place the shelves on the brackets.

### Installing poles

For a system of floor-to-ceiling poles held in place by springs, measure the distance between the floor and ceiling, and purchase poles to fit the space. The poles are available in several lengths. To install poles, mark the spots on the floor and ceiling where the poles are to be set. The springs which provide the tension to hold the poles are located at the top of the poles; therefore, place the top of the pole against the spot marked on the ceiling

# Memory box

During the Victorian Period, memory boxes reached a peak of popularity, with almost any object a potential keepsake. To preserve and display tiny objects, they were mounted in a shallow box or frame, sealed by glass, and the boxes were usually hung on the wall. Basically, the display of personal significance included such items as a bow, a dance card, a dried flower, a shoe buckle, or a brilliant butterfly.

Memorabilia boxes are still in vogue, particularly as gifts designed to display the specific interests of the recipient. More popular, however, are the abstract designs and use of common objects that vary in color and texture. It is challenging to create designs similar to the one illustrated which was assembled with a variety of dried beans, seeds, shells and single objects.

Materials: a picture frame and shallow box to fit behind the frame. Start with the frame and make a box to fit behind it, or start with the box and cut the frame to size. It all depends on which part is available ready-made. For a frame 12 to 15 inches by 15 to 20 inches, construct the box to fit the inside dimensions of the frame and between 1 and 2 inches deep, depending upon the materials you plan to put in it. The shallower the box, the easier it is to work with it. Also required for making the box are: a sheet of heavy cardboard or plywood; a mat knife; white glue; clear glue; wood stain; masking tape; strips of balsa wood about ¼ to ½ inch thick and as wide as the box is deep, to make the compartment dividers inside; a sheet of glass or piece of acrylic to fit the frame; and picture hangers and wire. The choice of items to be stored in the memory box is optional, but be sure to select light-weight, small objects.

### Starting with a frame

If you can't find a ready-made box to fit a frame that you have, cut a sheet of heavy card-

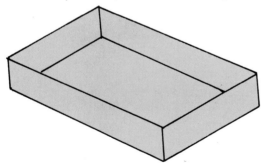

board or plywood the same size as the inner dimensions of the frame.

Using the mat knife, cut four pieces of the 1-inch-wide, ¼-inch-thick balsa. Determine the lengths of each piece by laying each on edge one by one inside the edges of the cardboard, trimming each in turn so that it butts against the one preceding it. With white glue, bond the four pieces on edge to the cardboard and to

each other at their right-angle corners and allow to dry. You should now have a 1-inch-deep box.

### Starting with a box

If you are starting with a suitable 1-inch-deep ready-made box and need a frame to match it,

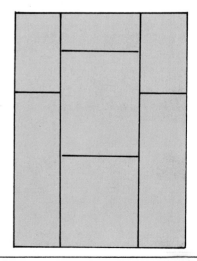

you have three choices: you can use an old picture frame that is larger than the box and cut it down to fit; have a frame shop make one to your specifications; or buy separate pieces of frame molding and make a frame to fit. (See instructions for Picture frames.)

### Making partitions

To make the partitions for the box, make a rough sketch of your partition plan on paper. Keep in mind the kind of materials you are going to mount in the box and try to arrange the items so the overall effect is pleasing in a sense of design. Cut the partition pieces as needed out of 1-inch-wide (or as wide as your box is high) balsa. Cut them carefully and individually and check that they fit together at the joints cleanly and snugly. Glue the partition pieces to the cardboard and to each other. Allow to dry.

### Staining box

Stain all the balsa parts to match the color of the frame. If any parts of the backing are going to show in the completed memory box (such as the space behind the bottle in the example shown), either stain that part or put a small piece of decorative paper in the space and glue it down. Once the box is assembled, it has to be filled.

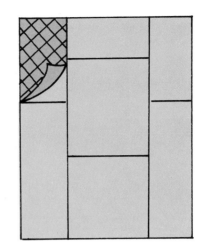

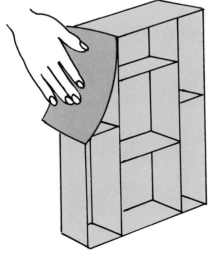

### Arranging objects

To fill the memory box, gather up a colorful assortment of things you can find right on the pantry shelf: kidney beans, navy beans, split peas, seeds of any and every type, as well as any other dry, hard items such as buttons, pebbles and the like. Compose an arrange-

ment by piling your selections in various sequences on a sheet of paper until you are satisfied that colors, textures and sizes work well together. Your eye is the only judge. You may want to accent one very bright color or coordinate your color choices with the area where you intend to hang the memory box.

### Mounting objects

Spread a generous coating of transparent glue on the backing and following your plan, sprinkle in a first layer of each of the materials in its respective box. Allow the glue to dry. Repeat the gluing process for two or three more layers until each of the boxes is filled and its contents fixed in place. (This is to prevent the seeds from slipping to the bottom of the box when it is hung.)

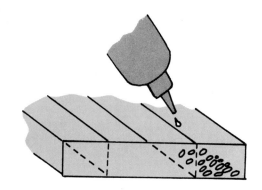

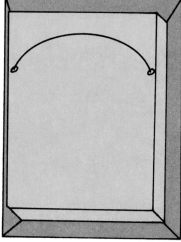

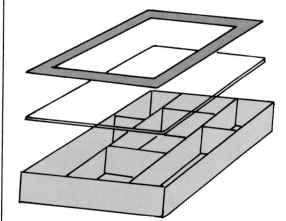

In those compartments where you wish to mount a single object, such as the bottle or bird on the rock shown in the illustration, simply glue the object to the compartment divider rather than the backing. Use a bright-colored background, either heavy paper or fabric glued to the back of the compartment. There are any number of ways to vary the individual compartment with either color or texture. Mount a single layer of glass chips or tiny shells to the background or mount a photograph of a waterfall or sunset to punctuate a single object in a compartment.

## Sealing box

Have a sheet of glass or piece of acrylic cut to fit the frame. Remove finger marks with glass cleaner, or rubbing alcohol for the acrylic sheet.

Be careful to touch only the edges of the glass and lay it squarely atop the compartmented box. Lay the picture frame squarely atop the glass and box, taking care that frame, glass, and box are nested together. Check to see that the glued memory items are thoroughly set; then carefully pick up the assembled memory box and turn it face down on the table. Run a wide strip of masking tape around the frame so that it laps over to the cardboard backing and seals the whole assembly together.

Screw two tiny picture hangers on either side of the back of the box, and stretch a lightweight picture wire between them for hanging.

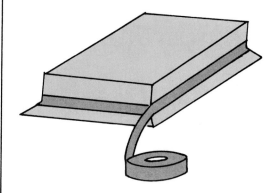

# Coiled vase

This bark-textured vase is an interesting variation of coiled pottery. Made of white, low-fire clay and thickly glazed, the vase is constructed in one of two methods. Either assemble a rectangular coiled shape and form a cylinder which is joined to a ½-inch-thick circular base; or layer coils atop each other, smoothing and pressing as the cylinder forms. Instructions for both methods are described below. Before starting, check CRAFTNOTES and the Coiled pot project.

   Materials: about 10 pounds of white, low-fire clay; triangular-shaped modeling tool or butter knife; metal kidney-shaped smoothing tool, or the back of an old spoon; shaving tool with a triangular wire at one end and an oval wire at the other; an old paintbrush; several layers of newspaper to cover work area; plastic food wrap or a plastic bag; water; powdered ferric oxide, to make stain; wooden spoon; rolling pin; and commercial low-fire glaze in golden brown, or another color. The clay, ferric oxide, glaze, and tools are available from clay suppliers; the other items can be found at home. Use a large, nonmetal working surface, preferably unfinished wood, because it is porous and will absorb water seepage from clay. Prepare a binder called slip (or slurry) made of clay mixed with water to a paste consistency.

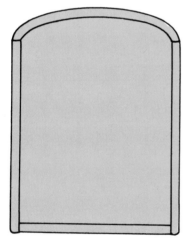

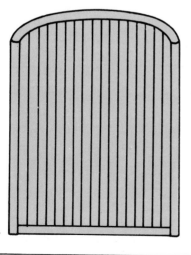

### Forming the clay rectangle

To piece the vase together from an almost-rectangular coiled shape and a circle, start by rolling four coils ½ inch thick. Two coils should be 12 inches in length, one 20 inches, and the fourth coil 22 inches long. Lay these four coils on newspaper and join to form a frame with the two 12-inch sides opposite each other, 20 inches apart. Lay the 22-inch coil so that it forms a convex curve between the two 12-inch sides, with the widest part of the curve at approximately midpoint. Lay the 20-inch coil at bottom between the two side coils. Within the frame, lay ½-inch-thick coils parallel to the 12-inch sides until all the space within the frame is filled. Smooth slip between the grooves formed by the coils with fingers and modeling tool to bind and fill any gaps between the coils. Smooth as evenly as possible. This surface will be the inside of the vase.

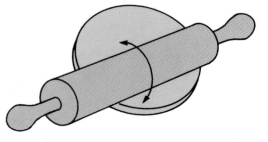

# Coiled vase

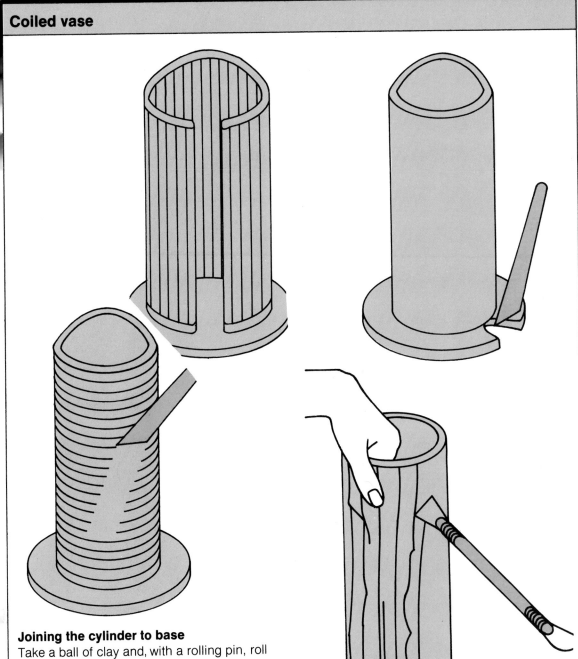

## Joining the cylinder to base

Take a ball of clay and, with a rolling pin, roll out a ½-inch-thick circle about 5 or 6 inches in diameter. Place the four-sided shape upright atop the circle, with the 12-inch sides vertical and the curved side on top to form a cylinder. The circle should be a little larger than the circumference of the cylinder. Before joining the sides of the cylinder, apply slip to inside where cylinder and circle meet. When you have joined the edges of the cylinder with slip, smooth the outer surface all around with modeling tool and metal kidney until grooves between the coils are practically erased.

Cut away excess clay from bottom of vase. With triangular end of shaving tool, scrape gently upward from bottom to top all around outside of vase, overlapping strokes slightly and supporting vase on inside with palm of hand. Be careful not to scrape too heavily, or vase will be too thin and break when fired.

# Coiled vase

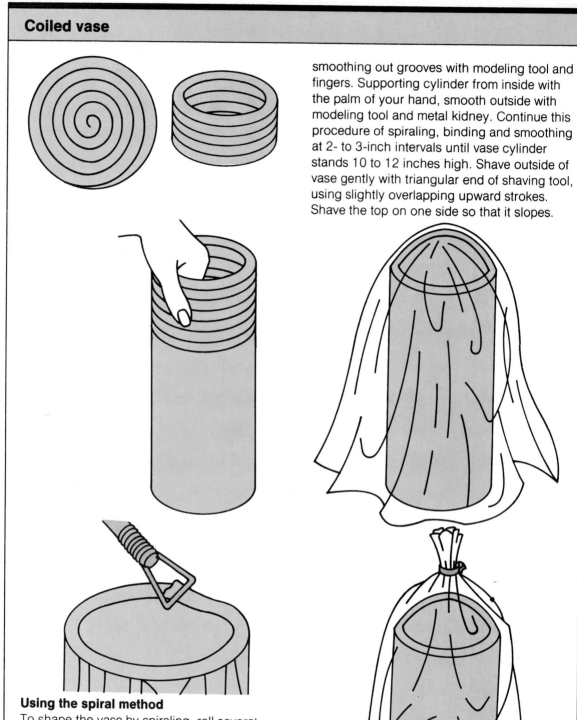

smoothing out grooves with modeling tool and fingers. Supporting cylinder from inside with the palm of your hand, smooth outside with modeling tool and metal kidney. Continue this procedure of spiraling, binding and smoothing at 2- to 3-inch intervals until vase cylinder stands 10 to 12 inches high. Shave outside of vase gently with triangular end of shaving tool, using slightly overlapping upward strokes. Shave the top on one side so that it slopes.

## Using the spiral method

To shape the vase by spiraling, roll several long, ½-inch-thick coils of different lengths. Form a closed 8½-inch-circumference circle from one coil to make a base, smoothing out grooves with slip and modeling tool. Layer other coils atop the base circumference with a spiraling motion, until you have a cylinder 2 inches high. Apply slip to inside, filling and

## Coiled vase

### Drying the vase

To dry vase before first firing, cover it tightly with plastic for 24 hours. Loosen plastic on the second day to allow some air to seep through. When clay is hard, but still a bit moist (leather-hard), remove plastic and allow to dry until no trace of moisture remains. When the vase has reached this bone-dry stage, take it to a pottery studio to be fired at the proper temperature. Have it fired to bisque temperature, indicated by a light pinkish color.

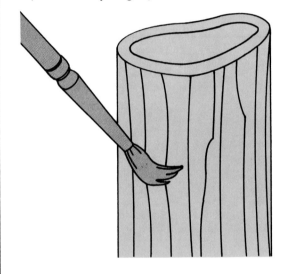

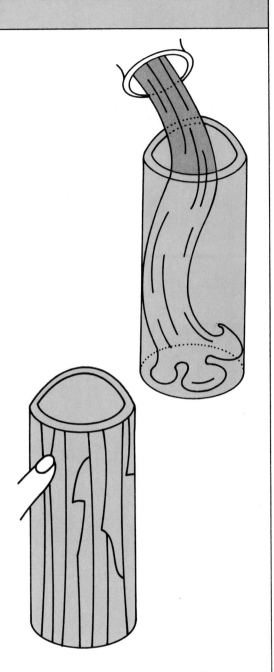

### Staining

Mix a stain of red, watery liquid with powdered ferric oxide and water. Brush first on inside, then outside of vase. Although staining the base is not usually recommended, stain it if you wish to give the vase greater watertightness; but be sure to tell the studio firing your piece to rest it on special stilts to prevent the vase from sticking to the bottom of the kiln. When stain sticks only slightly to your wet finger, it can be fired.

### Glazing

After stained piece has been fired, spread a glaze all over the inside and outside of the vase. Be sure to use a glaze compatible with the firing temperature of the clay. Do not glaze the bottom of the base. If glaze accidentally splashes on, wash or scrape it off. Glaze will dry thickly, enhancing the barklike texture.

Test the glaze for dryness with a wet finger; if it sticks just slightly to the surface, the piece is ready to be fired once again. The completed vase will hold freshly cut flowers or a bouquet of dried pods and field flowers.

# Batik mobiles

A mobile featuring circles and ovals of batik is a conversation piece that adds a personal accent to almost any room in your home.

   Materials: You need different shapes in various sizes. For larger circles, embroidery hoops approximately 12 inches in diameter and 4½ inches in diameter are suitable. Smaller circles should be made of wooden curtain hooks or circles with attached hooks approximately 2½ inches in diameter. Old bed sheets can be used for the fabric. Additional materials: household dyes; batik wax; a tjanting tool; pen; scissors; nylon threads; white glue; and small cup hooks or screw eyes, to hang the completed mobiles.

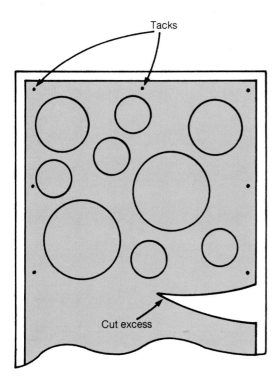

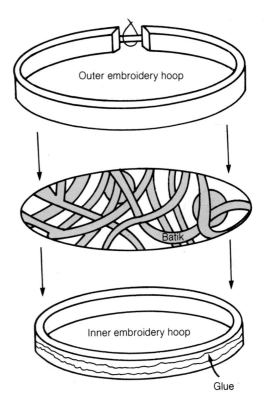

### Dyeing the cloth and making shapes

Thumbtack a large piece of an old sheet tautly to a wooden surface. Arrange the desired number of shaped circles on it so that they are at least 3¼ inches apart. Using a pen, outline the shapes. Then follow the instructions for Batik party invitations. For other suggestions about applying the wax, see Batik scarfs.

   When you have completed waxing and dyeing the sheet, allow it to dry and remove the wax by ironing. Cut out the individual circles (allowing about ½-inch margin all around) and stretch them on the embroidery hoops, or glue them to the wooden circles. Attach screw eyes to the hoops and tie various lengths of nylon thread through them.

# Batik mobiles

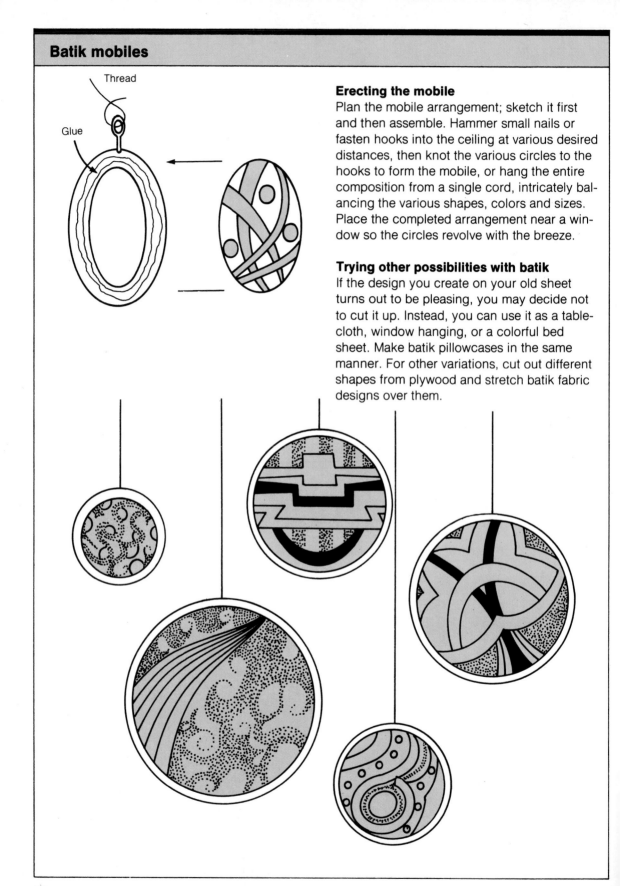

Thread

Glue

## Erecting the mobile
Plan the mobile arrangement; sketch it first and then assemble. Hammer small nails or fasten hooks into the ceiling at various desired distances, then knot the various circles to the hooks to form the mobile, or hang the entire composition from a single cord, intricately balancing the various shapes, colors and sizes. Place the completed arrangement near a window so the circles revolve with the breeze.

## Trying other possibilities with batik
If the design you create on your old sheet turns out to be pleasing, you may decide not to cut it up. Instead, you can use it as a tablecloth, window hanging, or a colorful bed sheet. Make batik pillowcases in the same manner. For other variations, cut out different shapes from plywood and stretch batik fabric designs over them.

# Cruciform kite

Kite flying is a very happy family experience, especially when the kite is constructed from scratch with each member making his or her contribution. Simple as it may seem to make a kite, it must conform to certain principles if it is to soar properly. This three-dimensional type is aerodynamically more sophisticated than most conventional and basic flat-sectioned kites sold in toy stores. It can be built with a few common materials; and between solo flights, it makes a handsome piece of wall sculpture. Don't be dismayed if the directions seem complicated. Simply follow them carefully step by step and you will have a truly unique kite in flight when the project is finished. Once aloft, the kite will attain good height and withstand high winds.

Materials: nine 36-inch lengths of stripwood, cane, or balsa for the struts (three of them measuring ½ inch wide by ¼ inch thick, and six measuring ¾ inch wide by ¼ inch thick); 3 skeins of embroidery thread; needle; 3 yards of lightweight, two-way-stretch jersey fabric; five-minute two-component epoxy glue or white glue; ruler; T-square; protractor; mat knife; scissors; ¼-inch paintbrush; and non-water-soluble paint (use a color that contrasts with the jersey fabric).

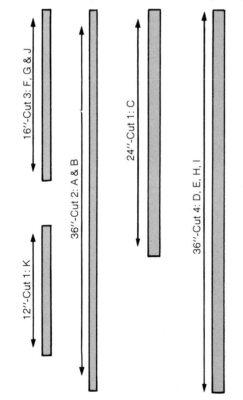

16″-Cut 3: F, G & J

36″-Cut 2: A & B

24″-Cut 1: C

36″-Cut 4: D, E, H, I

12″-Cut 1: K

¼-inch strut cut one piece 16 inches long and one 12 inches long. Cut from one of the ½-inch-by-¼-inch struts a 24-inch length. For convenience, each of the eleven struts will be referred to in our instructions by a letter name, with the following measurements. Struts A and B each measure 36 inches by ½ inch by ¼ inch. Strut C measures 24 inches by ½ inch by ¼ inch. Struts D, E, H and I each measure 36 inches by ¾ inch by ¼ inch. Struts F, G and J each measure 16 inches by ¾ inch by ¼ inch. Strut K measures 12 inches by ¾ inch by ¼ inch.

### Assembling backbone
Measure and mark the midpoint of strut B, and measure and mark 2 inches from one end of A. Then place strut B, the crossbar, over strut A, the backbone, to form a cross with B perpendicular to A at 2 inches from one end of A, and 33½ inches from the other end. With a T-square, check the angles formed by the two struts to be sure they are exactly 90 degrees. Glue into position with five-minute epoxy (a mixture of equal parts epoxy and hardener). Let dry for at least an hour.

### Extending backbone
Next, at the short end of strut A, where it crosses B, place strut C, the 24-inch strut,

### Preparing struts
Before you begin construction, paint all struts with non-water-soluble paint. Allow to dry for up to 12 hours. With a mat knife, cut from the length of one of the ¾-inch-by-¼-inch struts two 16-inch lengths. From another ¾-inch-by-

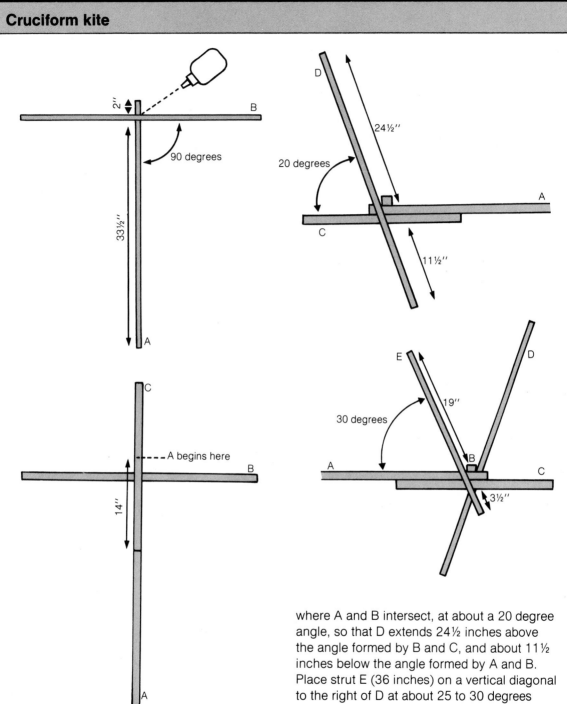

over strut A, so that C overlaps A for 14 inches. (See diagram for positioning.) Glue C in position and let epoxy set for one hour.

## Mounting struts D and E

Place D (a 36-inch strut) to the left on a slight vertical diagonal over A and C at the point where A and B intersect, at about a 20 degree angle, so that D extends 24½ inches above the angle formed by B and C, and about 11½ inches below the angle formed by A and B. Place strut E (36 inches) on a vertical diagonal to the right of D at about 25 to 30 degrees under and to the right of the intersection of struts A and B and under A and C, so that E extends 19 inches above A and about 3½ inches below C. Glue E into position until it sets; then soak some string with epoxy and wrap it firmly around all sides of the strut intersection area. (Use a protractor to determine the angles for positioning these struts.)

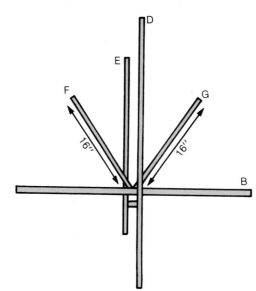

### Mounting struts H and I

Place side struts H and I (36-inch struts) so that one end of H rests on one end of B and one end of I rests on the other end of B. The opposite ends of H and I are placed, and beveled, to meet in a perfect "V" along strut A. Glue H and I into position and wait one hour for glue to dry. Coat a length of thread with glue and wrap it around the area where A, H and I intersect. If necessary, clamp until glue hardens.

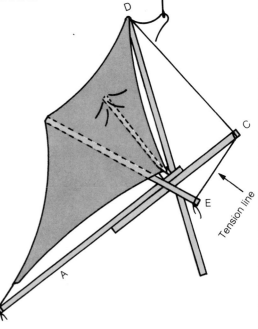

### Mounting struts F and G

Position struts F and G (16 inches long) between struts D and E, with one end of each along strut B. With a mat knife, bevel the points where F and G meet so that they form a perfect "V" along B. To bevel correctly, place each strut alongside B in the position where it is to be glued, then mark the desired degree of bevel. Glue F and G into position and allow to dry.

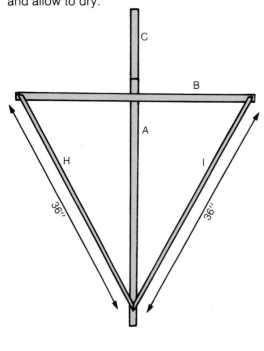

### Draping fabric on frame

Drape the jersey over the kite framework, positioning it and stretching it taut over all free ends of the struts until you are satisfied with your arrangement. (A vertical center seam may be necessary to achieve complete tautness.) Cut away excess jersey extending beyond strut ends. Fasten the material at outer ends of the struts by tacking embroidery thread to fabric, then wrapping the thread several times around the end of the strut and securing with a small knot. To ease stress on areas of greatest tension, secure thread between strut end and an opposing point. (From the end of E to C to D.)

# Cruciform kite

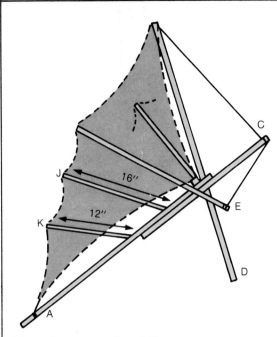

## Mounting struts J and K

The last two struts, J and K, are placed along strut A. Place strut K at 20 inches from the outer end of A at a 45 degree angle, and place strut J at 27 inches from the outer end of A, at a 65 degree angle. Mark and bevel the ends of J and K where they meet at A, then glue in position and allow to set.

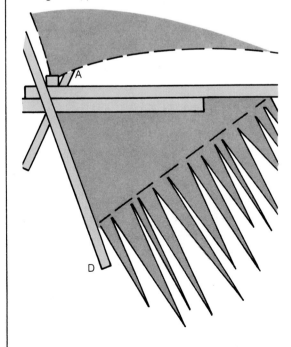

## Mounting fabric on bottom

Drape and cut a piece of jersey to fit the angle between the longer side of A near the point where it overlaps C, and the shorter side of D. Cut pointed fringes along the outer edge of the material, spacing them closely by eye as you cut. Staple or tack fringe and glue into place.

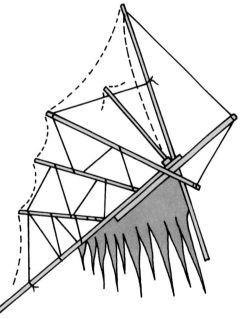

## Bracing with string

Wrap thread between and around all vertical struts along the backbone of the kite in an attractive, random pattern. This will serve as both decoration and bracing. If desired, turn under and hem raw edges of jersey between struts. Also, if you want a taut fit, sew zigzag stitches through the edge of the material and around pieces H and I. If you live in a windy area, cut a long, thin strip of jersey (the windier the locale, the longer the strip), and cut fringe along the long edges as instructed in the previous steps. Use a thumbtack and glue to fasten the fringed jersey to the bottom of the backbone, strut A. This will secure the tail properly. To fly, use stout cord for the bridle and flying line. Tie the bridle at two points along the backbone, strut A, in the form of a slack loop, then slipknot the flying line to the bridle.

# Stuffed seating unit

Oversized pillows, easy to make and comfortable enough to please a pasha, have become serious rivals of expensive seating pieces. The type of pillow shown is set directly on the floor; or a group of six pillows, arranged on a platform, substitutes beautifully for a sofa. Special skills are not required to create this project.

Materials: allow three 22-by-22-inch squares of 3-inch-thick foam rubber sheeting for each pillow core; 3 yards of polyester batting (usually 27 inches wide); 2 yards of muslin; and 2 yards of a medium to heavyweight upholstery fabric, such as corduroy, brushed denim, velvet, fake fur, or a cotton suede fabric, preferably with a stain-resistant finish; a yardstick; a fine-point felt marker; shears; two sharp knives with long blades, one smooth edged and the other serrated; straight pins; and a large spool of heavy-duty thread to match the upholstery fabric.

### Cutting foam squares

Cut out three 22-inch squares of foam rubber, using the smooth-edged knife. Press down on

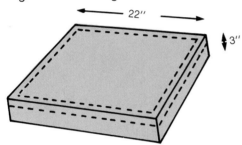

the foam with a slow, steady stroke as you cut. Set one of the cushions aside and place the other two flat on a firm work surface. Using the felt marker pen draw a line around the top of one cushion, 1 inch in from the edge; and a line around the sides, 1 inch down from the top.

With the serrated blade knife, cut away the foam between the lines just drawn, cutting

with a sawing motion, so that the finished cushions will be beveled along their top edges. The cut edge may be somewhat rough, but this does not matter since it will be covered eventually by the layers of muslin and upholstery fabric. Repeat for second cushion.

### Assembling cushion core

Assemble the three foam sections as a sandwich, with the untrimmed section in the middle

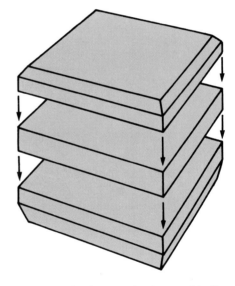

and the beveled edges at the top and bottom. Apply rubber cement to the inner faces of the foam sections, stacking them so that all three parts align neatly and adhere firmly. The cushion core is now complete.

### Covering core with batt

Cut out a 27-by-82-inch strip of polyester or cotton batt. (Batt is generally sold in 27-inch widths, but as the material does not hold its dimensions with great reliability, you may have to stretch it to the proper width in some places and trim in others.) Wrap the batt around the cushion unit, so that the ends overlap completely on the top, in effect covering the top surface with a double layer of batting. Stitch the batt along the exposed seam to hold it in place. Cut two panels of polyester batt measuring 10 by 27 inches each. Fill in the uncovered sides of the cushion with these side pieces, tucking the ends in between the attached batting and the foam core. If necessary, tack the side pieces to the rest of the cushion with a few stitches to hold it in place.

## Cutting and seaming muslin cover

Cut out two pieces of muslin measuring 32 by 32 inches. Machine stitch three of the four seams, allowing on each side and at the corners a 1½-inch seam allowance, tapering gradually to a ½-inch seam allowance at the midpoint of each side. (This will round off the corners of the finished cushion with a professional touch.)

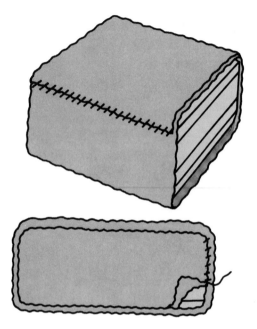

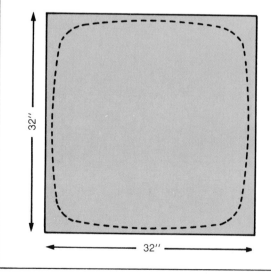

## Finishing

Invert the muslin case and slip it over the foam cushion core. Turn under the raw edges of open end and whip-stitch them together to finish the fourth side. Repeat these same steps with the upholstery fabric, making sure that the raw edge side of the upholstery cover is not on the same side as the raw edge of the muslin cover before it was whip-stitched closed. Or if desired, finish off the upholstery cover with a zipper closing, following the package instructions for stitching zipper to open end. If larger or smaller sized cushions are desired, adjust measurements proportionally for all materials needed. To make a seating platform for the pillows, see the project instructions that follow.

# Platform seating unit

Here is an easy-to-make simple platform seating arrangement that accommodates six overstuffed cushions or a single unit cushion. It is assembled with cinder blocks and a sheet of plywood. These units are less expensive than conventional furniture and distinctively simple.

Materials: six cinder blocks; a plain door (or the equivalent 1-inch-thick plywood slab); a mattress or solid foam slab about 4 inches thick; and upholstery fabric to cover the foam. (If desired, make six good-sized foam cushions, as previously explained in Stuffed seating unit.)

Arrange the cinder blocks on the floor, place the door on the cinder blocks, cover foam with fabric, as described for Stuffed seating unit, and place the foam on the door. If desired, use six stuffed cushions: three to sit on and three to place against the wall to provide cushioning for the back.

To use this simple unit as the basis for a more complex system, arrange two units in a corner of a room perpendicular to each other. Strategically placed, the platform seating unit can serve as a room divider; or in a large room, arrange three units in a box shape with one side open. This seating arrangement is especially well suited for entertaining guests. These units are rearranged easily, so you might use one setup for daily use, and another for parties or family gatherings.

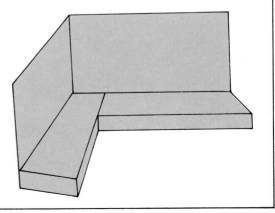

# Needlepoint patchwork pillow

If you're interested in getting into needlepoint but have reservations, this project is for you. It requires only a small square of needlepoint stitchery, six inches to be exact. The one square of needlepoint is pieced to surrounding patches of upholstery fabric, creating an unusual patchwork pillow cover. The pillow cover is 17½ inches square when complete. The decorative front is made up of nine squares: one center square of needlepoint and eight fabric squares forming the patchwork design. The back of the pillow is made with a piece of upholstery fabric. To create the illusion of patches with needlepoint, simply start with a square of needlepoint canvas the size of the pillow desired and block off nine squares on the canvas to be stitched in different colors. An example of a more subtle patchwork design, worked within a circle for a round pillow, is illustrated for those who are experienced in needlepoint.

Materials: an 8-inch square of needlepoint canvas, ten squares to the inch, to make the 6-inch-square finished needlepoint (1-inch seam allowance); several colors of needlepoint yarn (regular 4-ply wool may be used as a substitute but it tends to fray); a package of tapestry needles; 1-inch-wide masking tape; waterproof marking pens (colors to match the yarn); a pair of scissors; and a 17-inch-square, ready-made pillow. Most of these items can be purchased at a yarn or needlepoint shop. Also needed are ¾ of a yard of lightweight upholstery fabric, for the patches on the front of the pillow cover and the back of the cover; pins; needle and sewing thread; and scissors.

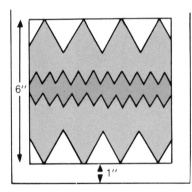

### Tracing design on canvas
To make the needlepoint square: Draw a 6-inch-square pattern on a piece of paper. Mark a 1-inch seam allowance all around. Plan a simple geometric pattern for the first project. Tape the paper pattern to a window that faces the light. Center the needlepoint canvas over the pattern (leaving a 1-inch seam allowance) and tape it into place. Draw the design on the canvas, using colored markers to match yarn colors. Mark a corner of the canvas with one of the markers, and rub with water to make sure that the marker is waterproof. If not, cover the entire design with acrylic spray once the pattern is traced on the canvas. Remove the canvas and paper pattern from the window, and bind the raw edges of canvas with masking tape to prevent raveling while sewing.

### Beginning the needlepoint
To thread the needle, make a loop near the end of a 20-inch strand of yarn, pull it taut over the eye, and slide it off the needle; then push the loop through the eye. To begin the first strand, hold about one inch against the back of the row you are working on and cover it as you work the stitches on that row. End a thread and begin a thread by weaving it through the wrong side of the stitches previously made.

### Working the Continental stitch
One of the most common needlepoint stitches is the Continental stitch, which is always worked from right to left. Start at the top right corner of the canvas (see diagram) and come up at point A below the first horizontal canvas

thread and to the left of the first vertical thread. Now put the needle in one thread to the right and above at B and come out at C, two threads to the left and one below. This lays the thread up and back at a slant. Note also that the needle goes in at a slant. With the thread at C you will be ready for the second stitch which is done exactly as the first stitch. Put the needle in at D, thread to the right and above C, and come out at E.

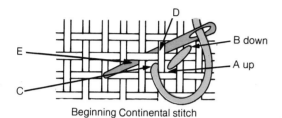

Beginning Continental stitch

Continue making stitches in this manner until you have completed one row.

Turn the piece 180 degrees and work the second row, which will then be above the first, so you will always be working from right to left. The stitches should all start in the same direction, line after line, and you will be working the lines above and below alternately.

## Working Bargello

This stitch is worked across the canvas from

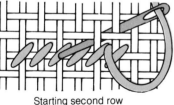

Starting second row

left to right. For the first row, bring needle up at A. Insert at B, four threads above A. Bring it up at C, two threads below and one to the right of B. Continue working from left to right, forming peaks and valleys according to your design. The succeeding rows can follow the

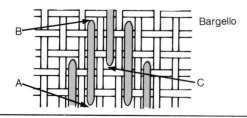

Bargello

first row exactly in different colors (or in different shades of the same color) or they can be worked upside down to form diamonds. When the needlepoint design is completed, block. (See CRAFTNOTES).

## Assembling the patchwork

Cut an 18-inch square from the upholstery fabric, for the back of the pillow cover. From the remaining fabric, cut eight 6½-inch squares for the patches, which are assembled in three rows of three patches each. Join the patches with small running stitches, allowing ¼-inch seams. Join three patches to form the top row and another three patches to form the bottom row.

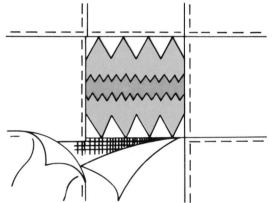

Then set aside. With right sides together, join a patch to either side of the square of needlepoint, allowing ¼-inch seams. Seam the top row of joined patches to the needlepoint row. Seam the bottom row of patches to the needlepoint row in same manner.

## Assembling the pillow

When the patchwork front of the pillow is completed, take the 18-inch square of fabric for the pillow back and lay it face down on the front of the needlepoint and patchwork. Stitch the front and back of the pillow cover along the three edges, allowing a ¼-inch seam, leaving one edge open. Reverse the pillow cover, insert the pillow, and fold under the raw edges. Then sew the edge closed with an overcast stitch.

Design your own needlepoint pattern for a pillow. The example shown in the color illustration, an original design, was worked with the Continental stitch throughout.

# Poured-acrylic trivet

Once you have experimented with liquid plastics, you will find working in this art medium a joy because of its versatility and unlimited possibilities. Liquid plastics conform to any mold and almost any object embeds successfully in them. Rigid molds, such as glass or metal, give the cast a shiny surface, while rubber or polyethylene molds (ice-cube trays or left-over containers) produce a mat finish on the cast. Interesting variations can also be achieved by tinting the resin or making it opaque. Once you become skilled in the basics of pouring and molding plastics, create variations.

Experiment with embedding weeds and other objects in small jars before trying to preserve a family heirloom. The results vary depending upon the brand and age of the polyester casting resin, the temperature of the room, the depth of the casting, and the planetary configurations. Let your imagination go with this unusual new medium.

Materials: approximately one pint of liquid casting resin, and catalyst (the catalyst will usually be included; if not, the supplier will recommend the proper amount to purchase); an eyedropper; 6-inch ovenproof glass dish; three small whiskey glasses; unwaxed paper cups (the type used for hot drinks); wood stirring sticks; carpenter's level; some rags; PVA (polyvinyl alcohol) mold release; auto or furniture paste wax; and a felt-tip pen. Our trivet is embedded with a sprig of dried and pressed Queen Anne's lace, and chips of yellow, orange and red glass. Substitute other dried flowers, or herbs, or use any colorful small objects, such as dried kidney beans, colored eggshells or paper cutouts.

### Preparing the embedments
Before making the trivet itself, place the Queen Anne's lace, flowers or herbs, stems and leaves still attached, between two layers of facial tissue inside a heavy book and leave in place until the tissues show no signs of moisture. This should take about three weeks.

Before embedding, spray the foliage with several coats of clear acrylic to be sure that no moisture remains to inhibit the cure of the resin. Allow each coat to dry before applying the next one.

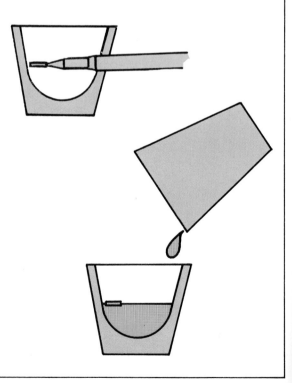

### Casting the legs
Start by casting the three legs of the trivet, using clean, dry whiskey glasses for the molds. If you have three whiskey glasses you can make them all at the same time; otherwise, make one at a time and wait for each to harden. With a felt-tip pen, mark the outside of each glass ¾ inch from the inside bottom. Thinly coat the inside of each glass with 2 or 3 light coats of paste wax, buffing between each coat. Let dry and apply 2 to 3 coats of

## Poured-acrylic trivet

PVA (polyvinyl alcohol) mold release, allowing each coat to dry according to manufacturer's directions. This will facilitate removal of the hardened resin. Prepare the casting plastic for each glass mold separately.

Pour 1 liquid ounce of resin into a paper cup and add 4 drops of catalyst, or the amount recommended by the manufacturer. Stir gently with a wood stick, trying not to make air bubbles. When thoroughly mixed, pour it into the whiskey glass up to the mark and cover the glass with plastic wrap.

Let the resin harden for at least three hours, until it is firm, then turn the glass over and tap the bottom. The trivet leg should come out. If not, gently pry with a stir stick. As soon as the air is introduced, the piece will pop out. If you use the same whiskey glass, wash it with soapy water to remove the wax and PVA. Dry it thoroughly before repeating the procedure for the other two legs.

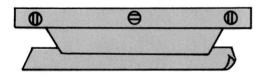

### Casting the trivet
Lay out the dried flowers, stems and leaves as they will be placed for embedment in the trivet. Check arrangement in empty glass dish mold, then set them aside. Coat the ovenproof (ovenproofing is recommended because heat is given off during the hardening process) dish with wax and mold release, as explained above. Spread newspapers on a table and place the dish on them. Use the level to make sure the dish height is even all around. This is important for a perfectly formed trivet.

Pour 3½ ounces of resin into a paper cup and add 15 drops of catalyst. Stir gently until the mixture changes color. Pour it slowly into the dish. Let it stand for 15 minutes, then test with a stirrer to see if it has a firm, jellylike consistency, and does not stick to the stirrer.

In a paper cup, mix 2½ ounces of resin and 10 drops of catalyst, then pour into the dish. Immediately slide the foliage to be embedded

into the liquid layer so that it rests on the firm layer underneath. Remember to place the embedment *face down,* for you are pouring from the top down. Let dry to a firm, gelatin consistency, before pouring next layer.

In a clean paper cup, mix the third layer of 3½ ounces of resin and 15 drops of catalyst and pour into the dish; then sprinkle in the glass chips. Let dry until almost (but not quite) hard, so that the legs will embed successfully, but not sink too deeply. Place the 3 legs on the surface of the almost-hard resin, equally spaced about ⅝ inch in from the edge. Press each leg gently into the plastic, to embed. Be sure all legs are embedded evenly. Move the dish as little as possible during the hardening stage so the plastic will set properly.

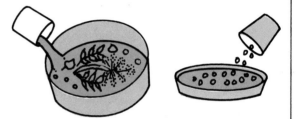

### Releasing the trivet
Wait at least five hours before removing the plastic trivet from its mold. Hold the casting dish over the table or other surface and tap the dish bottom. Remove surface scratches with a medium-grade file or sandpaper placed grit side up on a flat surface. Finish with a commercial plastic cleaner to give the trivet a crystal sheen.

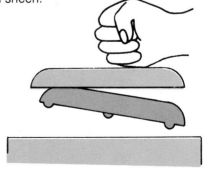

# Stenciled mitts and potholder

Fabric stenciling is an easy method to transfer colorful designs onto ready-made place mats, kitchen towels, aprons or oven mitts. The design is painted onto the fabric within the confines of a cut-out stencil. Cotton, linen and rayon are ideal fabrics for this technique, especially white or light shades. Silk, wool, felt or nylon fabrics are also suitable, but they require careful handling and are not as practical. Practice stenciling a test piece of fabric before proceeding. For your first project, use ready-made kitchen accessories such as the illustrated oven mitts and potholder. Prepare pieces to be stenciled by washing them in warm, soapy water and pressing to remove sizing.

Materials: textile paints; extender and thinner (available at art supply or hobby shops); stencil paper; a stencil cutter, razor blade or sharp knife; a stiff oil-paint brush; a blotter, soft cardboard or newspapers; mixing dishes of any material but plastic; masking tape or thumbtacks; a hard pencil; pearl cotton; and a fine needle.

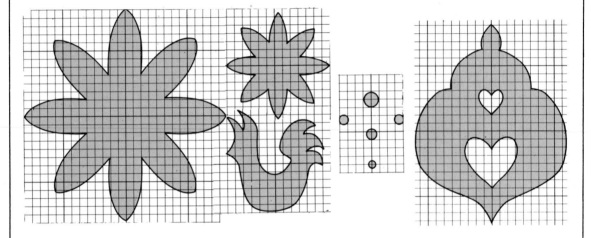

### Drawing designs and cutting stencil
Copy the simple designs shown for a first project. These motifs are not as difficult to stencil as the designs stenciled on the mitts and potholder in the color illustration. You can use the two flower patterns in different sizes for place mats or mitts; the bird and small circle motif for a mitt or towels and the heart motif for a potholder. Trace each design onto stencil paper with a hard pencil and cut out with a stencil cutter, knife or razor blade. If the design requires more than one color, a separate stencil is cut for each color of the pattern. Draw or tape a right angle to one corner of the fabric where the stencil is placed, placing each stencil for each design color to fit into the angle. Always check alignment of stencils before painting, by placing together, then holding up to the light.

### Applying paint
To prepare paint for application: Mix 3 parts color extender to 1 part textile paint in a mixing dish. Add a few drops of thinner for a smooth, thick, creamy paint consistency.

# Stenciled mitts and potholder

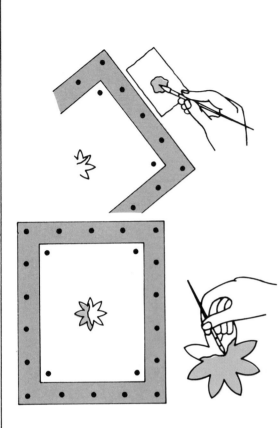

## Setting the colors

Most textile colors require heat setting for colorfastness and washability. This is done by one of two methods: using an oven or a pressing iron. Oven-cure cotton or linen for three minutes at 350 degrees Fahrenheit or five minutes at 250 degrees Fahrenheit. To cure with an iron, lay a press cloth over the design and press with a hot iron for cotton and linen, and a warm iron for rayon or other heat-sensitive fabrics. Press front, then back, in this manner. Dampen a press cloth and press well again.

## Finishing touches

Accent the bird motif with French knot eyes and tail. To make a French knot, thread needle with pearl cotton and bring needle up where knot is to be made. Wind thread 2 or 3 times around point of needle and insert needle point

Stretch item to be stenciled over cardboard or newspaper to absorb color that may pass through fabric. Secure item to work surface with tacks or tape. Work textile paint into brush, then brush off excess onto a piece of scrap cloth or paper, leaving only a small amount of color on the brush. Place stencil in position on cloth. Paint outlines first, then fill in remainder by stroking evenly toward center. Colors are heavily concentrated, so only a few coats are necessary to achieve color intensity desired. Allow work to dry for at least 24 hours.

You can also stipple colors onto fabric with an up and down motion, holding brush vertically. Each glob of color should contact the cloth fibers in order to soak into the fabric properly. Keep each coat thin. When you achieve desired shade, allow work to dry.

in fabric as close as possible to (but not directly on) the place where thread emerges, and pull through to wrong side, holding twists in place on right side. With a waterproof felt-tip pen, outline the heart motif on the potholder and add a few scrolls and circles to embellish the design.

# Floor games

Oldest among all children's pastimes, and still popular, are those games played on a chalk-marked area of an outdoor playground or on the floor of a game room. The games run the gamut from pebble toss to hopscotch and the objectives and scoring vary as widely. The playing area for floor games is quickly extemporized with paint or tape to mark the boundaries and the game equipment is as common as match sticks, bottle caps, stones, and checkers. Some of these game patterns can serve as a decorative focal point, on the floor of a child's room or family game room, while others require a very large outdoor area. Any one of the game patterns, with variations if desired, makes a cheery decoration for an exercise mat such as the mat illustrated.

Each game included in this project is accompanied by illustrated diagrams with dimensions for the game pattern. Game rules and objectives are also explained, but they may be varied as desired. To duplicate the game patterns, first check the floor space available and the dimensions of the game pattern. Then sketch the layout on paper before marking the pattern on the floor with chalk. Cover the chalk-marked boundaries with either paint or adhesive tape and use stencils to paint the numerals or letters.

Materials: wood-, cement-, or linoleum-covered floor; white or colored water-soluble paint or heavy-duty fabric-backed adhesive tape; ready-made numeral and alphabet stencils; small paintbrush; ruler; chalk; scissors; and string.

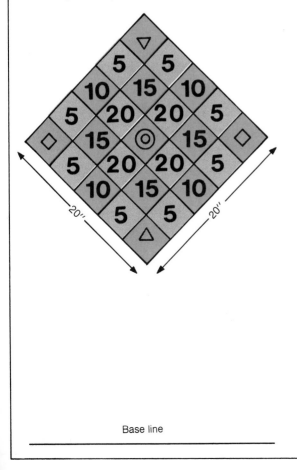

Base line

## Pebble toss

Follow the diagram to lay out the square target on the floor, with one point near the players. The game is played with two or more players. Markers are tossed on the target from a base line that is at least 6 feet away from the nearest point of the 20-inch square. Each player uses five markers per turn. At the end of each turn the score is totaled. The first player to reach 250 points (this number can be varied) wins. The bull's-eye doubles the score, triangles halve the score of that turn, and diamonds cancel the player's score up to that point. Markers on lines don't count.

## Kick hopscotch

To lay out the game pattern, use a ruler and chalk to mark the boundaries of the squares, rectangles, and triangles. Then mark the two arcs at the top (using chalk and a string as you would a compass). This version of hopscotch is played by tossing a marker (stone or bottle cap) into square I, hopping into that square on one foot, and kicking the marker out of it. The player then throws the marker into II, hops into II via I, kicks the marker out, and then hops out, again via I. The player then throws the stone into area III, jumps into squares I and II, straddling them, then hops into triangle III, kicks the marker out, and then hops back out again. These steps are repeated until the player has hopped all the way through X and back again. In moving to triangle VI, the player straddles IV and V, and square VII is a free square in which the player may land with both feet. The object of the game is to be the first to complete hopping through the entire playing area. Players take turns, with a player doing as many successful kicks of the marker as possible before going out. Tossing the marker into an improper area or landing on a line while hopping forces a player out. A player is allowed as many chances as necessary to kick the marker out of the playing area.

### Snail hopscotch

To lay out the game pattern, start by chalking a circle 12 inches in diameter. (Use chalk and string, compass fashion.) Then continue boundaries for snail course until completed, drawing lines first with chalk. (Mark points equidistant from inner circle to guide you as boundaries are drawn.) Finish with paint or tape as instructed in the introduction. Each player (any number of players) uses a different set of markers (buttons, checkers, or pebbles). The player hops from area I all the way to the circle at the center, rests there and then hops back again. Each completed circuit of the snail enables a player to "stake out" any numbered area with a personal marker.

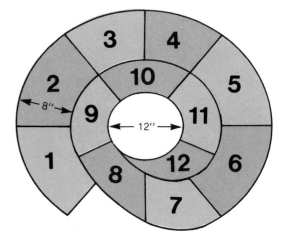

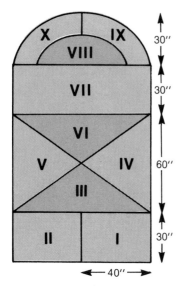

Each such area then becomes an additional "rest" spot for that player, and the opponents are not allowed to hop into it. A player who lands on a line while hopping is "out." Players are allowed to change legs in rest areas. The winner is the player who, by leaving personal markers in as many areas as possible, makes it impossible for others to complete a circuit.

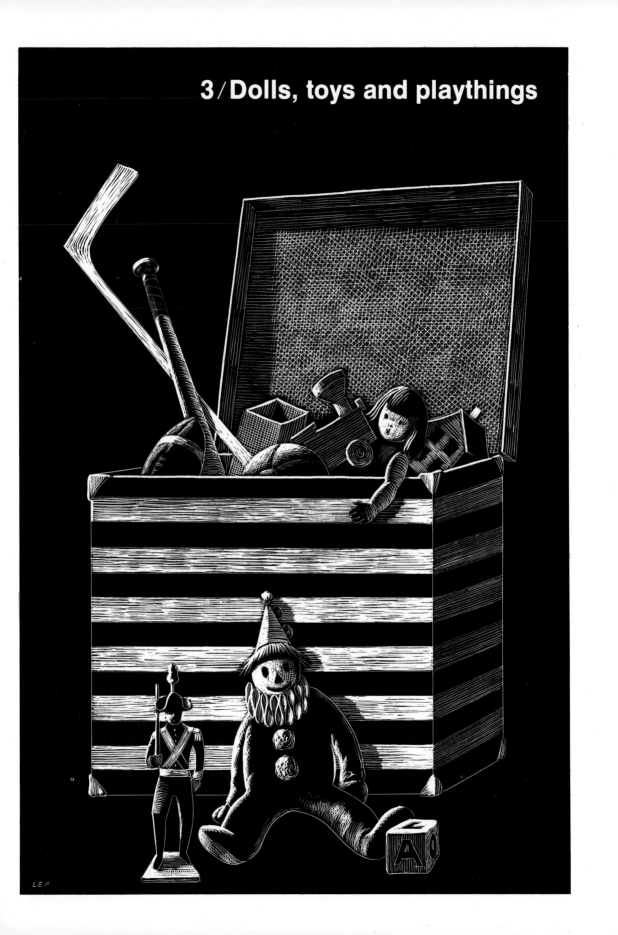

# 3/Dolls, toys and playthings

# Sock dolls

Soft and cuddly, these unsophisticated sock dolls are almost certain to win a child's affection. Surprisingly uncomplicated to make, either or both the little girl or boy doll work up rather quickly. Basically, the dolls are identical, but in their clothing and facial features, they assume their own identities. The dolls can take on almost any personality or storybook character you wish to create.

Materials: one pair of large men's socks for each doll; bright-colored fabric remnants for clothes; black felt for shoes; narrow bias binding; strong white string for outlining neck; a wooden clothespin for each doll; a small amount of yellow yarn for hair; and blue, red and pink embroidery thread for facial features. To complete the little girl, you also need rickrack tape, lace, and braid to trim her dress and panties. Cotton batting, polyester fiber material, or old nylon stockings can be used to stuff both dolls.

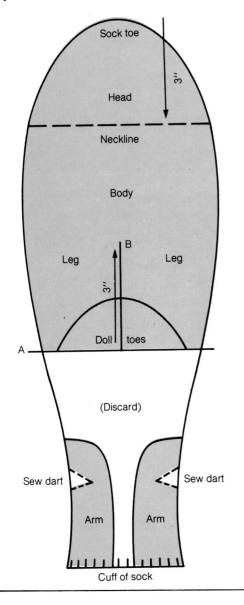

### Creating the girl doll

Place the sock flat with the heel part turned over and up and pressed flat. Cut the sock in half just below where the heel starts (line A in diagram). Then make another cut, three inches long, starting in the middle of the raw edge (line B in diagram).

Cut the arms out of the other piece of the sock and discard excess.

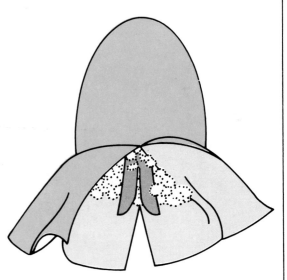

### Stuffing the body

Stuff the doll as you proceed with sewing. To keep head rigid, place a wooden clothespin inside the body, pressing its end against the end of the sock (top of head). When stuffing the feet, try to keep them as round as possible (the cut fabric forms natural points). Sew seams as you go, to keep stuffing in place. Stuff arms, sew closed, then sew to body.

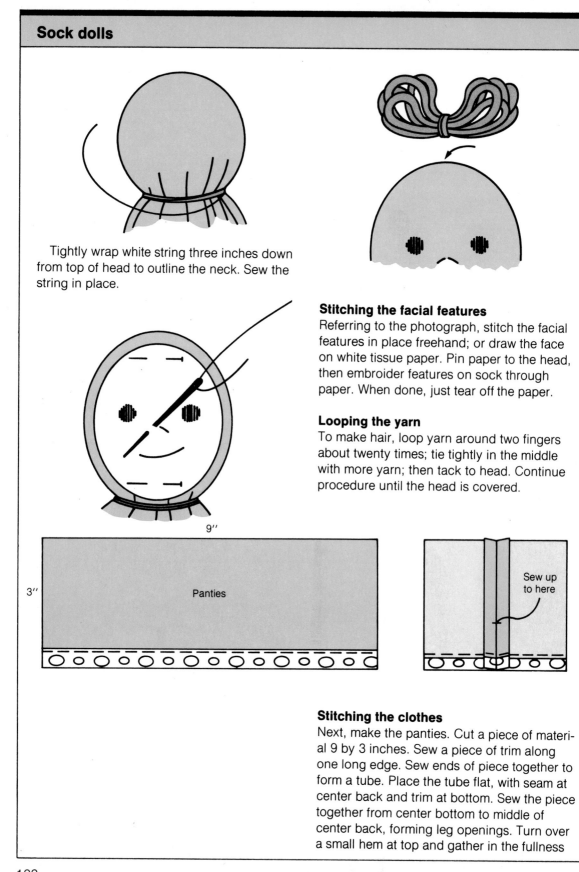

Tightly wrap white string three inches down from top of head to outline the neck. Sew the string in place.

### Stitching the facial features
Referring to the photograph, stitch the facial features in place freehand; or draw the face on white tissue paper. Pin paper to the head, then embroider features on sock through paper. When done, just tear off the paper.

### Looping the yarn
To make hair, loop yarn around two fingers about twenty times; tie tightly in the middle with more yarn; then tack to head. Continue procedure until the head is covered.

9"

3"

Panties

Sew up to here

### Stitching the clothes
Next, make the panties. Cut a piece of material 9 by 3 inches. Sew a piece of trim along one long edge. Sew ends of piece together to form a tube. Place the tube flat, with seam at center back and trim at bottom. Sew the piece together from center bottom to middle of center back, forming leg openings. Turn over a small hem at top and gather in the fullness

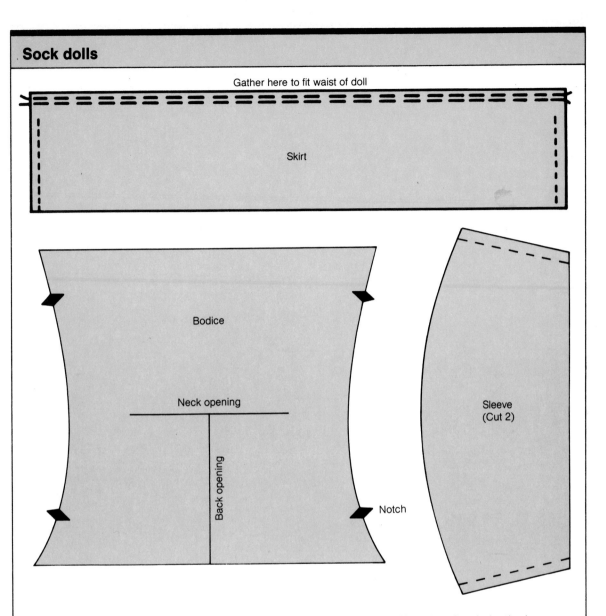

Gather here to fit waist of doll

Skirt

Bodice

Sleeve
(Cut 2)

Neck opening

Back opening

Notch

Gather

Shoulder

Sleeve

by sewing on a ⅛-inch strip of elastic, long enough to fit the doll's waist.

The dress is made up of a bodice, two sleeves, and a skirt. First, cut out all parts. (Note that the bodice has two openings cut in it for the neck and back.)

Finish the neck and back openings with bias binding. Place each sleeve flat and sew trim to each at cuff edge. Make a row of wide running stitches at shoulder edge. Then sew sleeves to bodice armhole, gathering along the running stitches to fit between the notches marked.

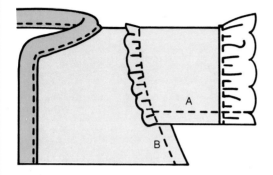

Fold the bodice over, sewing A to A, then B to B, as illustrated, to close underarm seam.

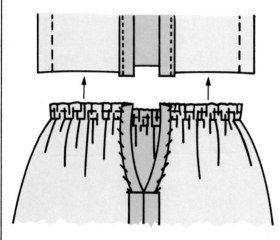

Join short sides of the skirt piece and sew together, except for ½ inch at the top. Hem this portion.

Sew skirt to bodice, gathering to fit and aligning the skirt opening with that on the bodice. (Together, they form a back opening for slipping the dress on and off the doll easily.) Then, sew snaps or buttons to the edge of the opening.

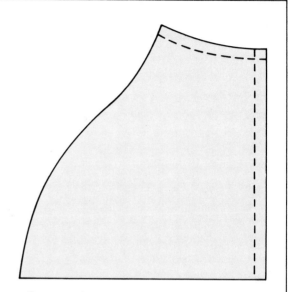

Cut two pieces of fabric for bonnet. Sew pieces together, wrong sides out, then sew back seam. Sew ribbon ties to bottom corners. Trim with lace.

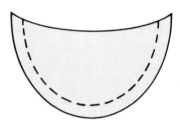

Cut four pieces of black felt for the shoes. To make each shoe, sew two pieces of felt together, wrong sides out, on the long curved edge. Turn shoe right side out, slip on foot and tack in place.

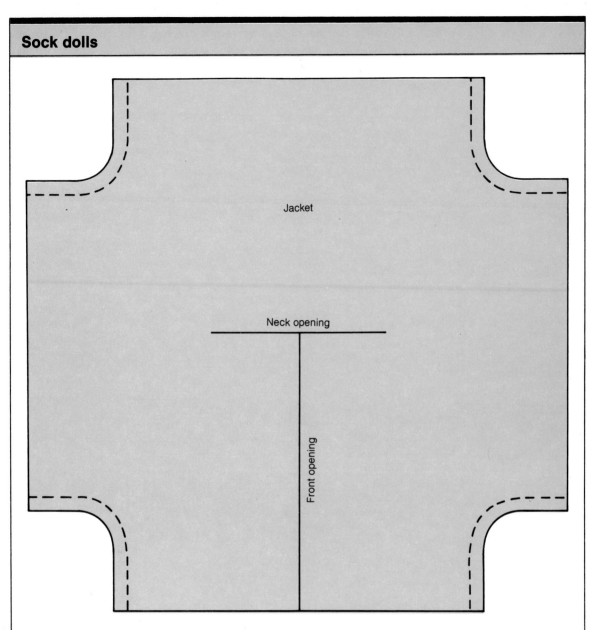

Jacket

Neck opening

Front opening

### Creating the boy doll

To make the body, follow same directions given for making the girl doll. Cut one piece of fabric for the coat, as shown, then two pieces for the pants. Turn edges to hem or trim with bias binding, and join side seams of the jacket.

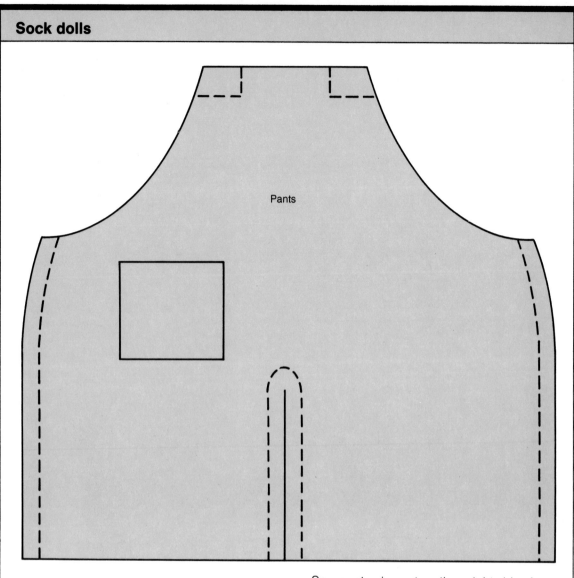

Pants

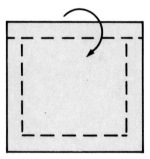

Sew pants pieces together, right sides facing. Sew along cuts to form the legs. Turn trousers right side out and sew on a small pocket, as shown. Hem legs at cuff edge.

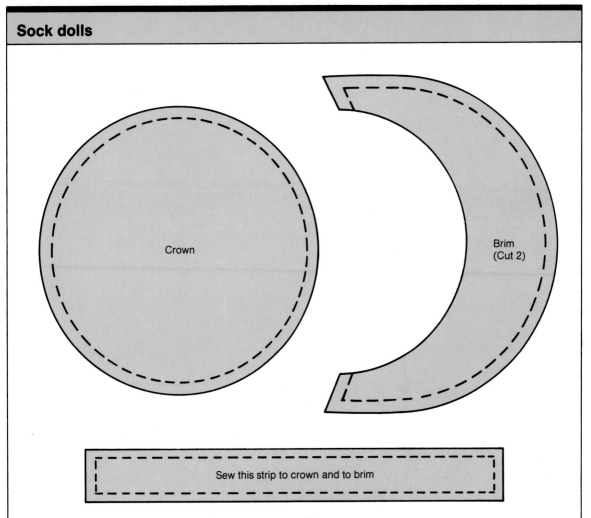

Crown

Brim
(Cut 2)

Sew this strip to crown and to brim

### Making the cap

Start by cutting one piece of circular fabric for the crown, and two pieces for the brim. Place the brim pieces together, right sides out, and sew together along curved edge. Cut a 1-inch strip of fabric of sufficient length to equal the circumference of the crown, and sew it to the crown to form the band of the cap, then sew the brim to this strip. Stuff the hat with some of the filler to keep it looking plump and perky.

# Doll clothes

Grandmothers and especially teenage granddaughters, here's a challenging project to test your ingenuity in creating a small wardrobe of doll clothes for a younger member of the family.

Handmade clothes for a favorite doll seem so much more elegant than the ready-made fashions available, but working with very small patterns can be tedious. However, these simple but fashionable doll clothes are all easy and quick to sew, with very little finishing necessary. There are no tiny buttons or snaps; everything pulls on or ties. All five fashions (skirt and top, at-home robe, bulky sweater, halter dress, and a wedding dress) are designed for grown-up dolls rather than cuddly baby dolls. Because doll sizes vary, instructions are given without specific measurements. Be sure to fit the clothes on the doll after each major step and make adjustments accordingly.

Materials: 1 pair white stretch ankle socks with lace trim (infant's size), and a small piece of elastic for the wedding dress; 2 squares of felt (orange and yellow), for the at-home robe; 1 square of dark-green felt, narrow ribbon, and a small scrap from the white stretch socks for the long skirt and camisole top; a ribbed-top sock of soft, fuzzy knit (in a child's size), and white bias tape, for the knit halter dress and bulky sweater.

### Making the wedding dress

Cut the ribbed top off one of the lace-trimmed socks (cutting into the foot of the sock, if necessary, for length). This is the skirt of the dress, with the lace trim used for the hem. Cut the top off the other sock, for the dress bodice, cutting it long enough to reach from the shoulders to below the waist of the doll. Slit both sock sections to form two flat pieces. Lay the (skirt) longer piece down, right side up; place the (bodice) shorter piece on top, right

sides and raw edges together. Baste bodice to skirt. Next, cut a narrow strip of elastic to fit snugly around doll's waist. Pin and then stitch the elastic to top of raw edges, stitching elastic to fit the width of the knit fabric.

Turn bodice up, keeping elastic turned toward the bodice to give a bloused effect. Stitch center back completely to form a tube. Tack lace edges loosely at shoulders to form open sleeves, as shown in photograph. Optional: To make a veil, cut a rectangle of sheer

129

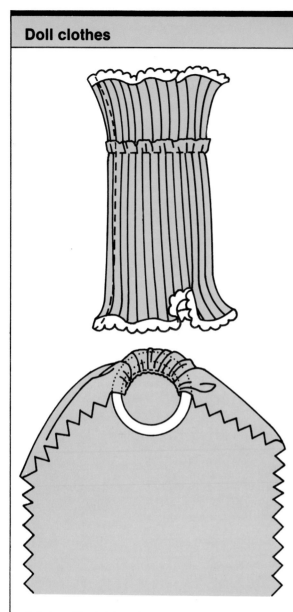

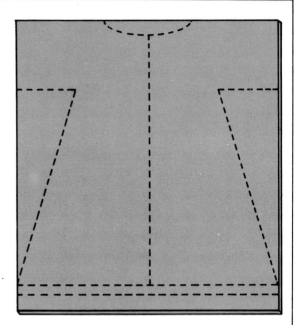

with contrasting thread. First, stitch sleeve edges, neckline curves and front edges. Seam center back, shoulders and side seams from hem to sleeve edges. Cut two narrow contrasting strips of felt for the belt. Overlap at

fabric with pinking shears, gather and stitch onto drapery ring. Pin onto doll's hair.

**The ankle-length at-home robe**
Lightly trace a T-shape for the pattern, widening it at hemlines and drawing a half circle for the neckline. Cut out pattern and check size on doll. Adjust if necessary.

Place one square of felt on top of the other and, using the pattern, cut out felt, allowing for seams. Cut both pieces from midpoint of neckline to hemline, so there are four pieces. Alternating colors, baste pieces together and fit on doll. Make any adjustments now. For a decorative finish, zigzag seams on the outside

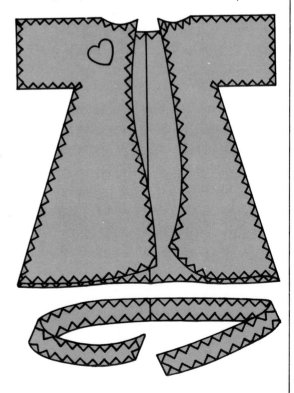

back to join and stitch all around. For a decorative touch, cut a tiny heart or small patch from the yellow felt and stitch to front orange panel. Use a decorative machine stitch or a handworked blanket stitch.

### Cutting felt skirt

For the long skirt, cut four shapes from felt like triangles, with the tops cut off. Total measurement of top (narrow) edges should equal

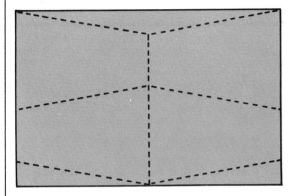

doll's waist plus a narrow seam allowance. Seam four pieces together with three seams, leaving skirt flat like an apron. Stitch ribbon over seams, turning under bottom edge to wrong side. Sew a length of ribbon to waist, leaving enough on each side for ties.

Stitch last seam, leaving an opening to fit over doll. Tie belt at side after skirt is on doll.

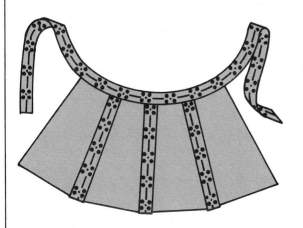

To make the camisole top for the skirt, cut a small piece from foot of sock used for wedding dress. Ribs run from top to bottom.

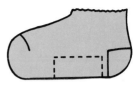

Fold under a narrow cuff at top edge and stitch. An overcast stitch will give a pretty, scalloped edge.

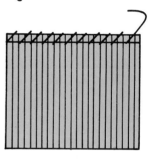

Cut two pieces of ribbon to fit over doll's shoulders. Pin the four ends of ribbon to wrong side, placed to fit over shoulders, with

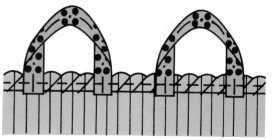

the right side of ribbon facing wrong side of bodice. Stitch in one continuous row along top edge of bodice or tack by hand. Seam center back. The finishing touch is a tie of the ribbon material in the doll's hair.

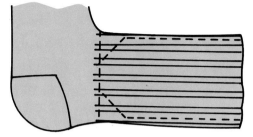

## Making halter dress

Take one of the ribbed-top, fuzzy knit socks and cut a rectangle from the front half of sock to fit doll from neck to toe. (For a tall doll, it may be necessary to cut into the unribbed part of sock.) Cut piece to fit very snugly around doll. Use finished top edge of sock as

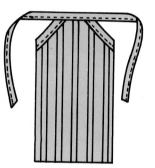

a hem. Cut corners off the raw edge to make the halter.

Bind the raw edges, where corners were cut off, with narrow bias tape. Cut another strip of bias tape long enough for ties. Center tape on top raw edge, fold over and, starting at one

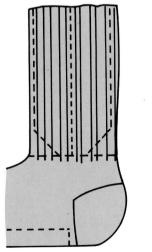

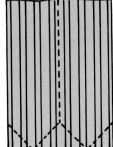

end of tape, stitch edges of tape together. At the same time, enclose top edge of dress in tape, in one continuous stitching, until the other end of tape is reached. Seam center back. Slip on doll and tie tape in back of neck.

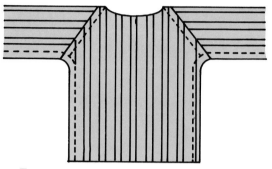

To make the bulky sweater, cut top off the other fuzzy knit sock to fit doll from neck to legs. Use finished top for hem. Cut corners to make raglan armholes. Slit center front and side edges.

From the remaining half of sock top left from halter dress, cut rectangular pieces for sleeves. Cut off corners to make raglan sleeves to fit the armhole allowance on the body of the sweater.

Seam sleeves to sweater pieces at armholes. Seam underarm and sweater side seams. Finish with decorative zigzag stitch or bind neckline and center front edges with narrow bias tape. Roll up sleeves to form cuffs. Cut tie belt from long edge of sock foot, using bottom fold as one side. Stitch other edge for neat finish or leave open.

# Scrub-brush dragon

Children enjoy imaginative handmade toys as much as they do the very expensive scale-model rockets and electric kitchens they receive on special occasions. The idea of a dragon toy is exciting, but invite a child to help create a dragon pull-toy with ordinary scrub brushes and the imagination takes flight. More than a makeshift toy assembled with brushes, it requires some woodworking skills and a good share of patience. If you are unfamiliar with dowels, drills, and the mysteries of the coping saw, don't be intimidated; try your hand at this and have fun.

Materials: three heavy-duty scrub brushes (substitute blocks of wood, if desired). The body of the dragon is a rectangular brush 8 by 3 inches and the crown and tail brushes, which should be about 5 inches long, may be whatever shape you like. You also need the following wood: one block, 6 inches long by 2 inches wide by 1⅛ inches thick; an 8-by-8-inch sheet of wood, ¾ inch thick; a 6-inch length of 1-inch-by-1-inch lumber; a 9-inch length, ½ inch by ¼ inch; 18 inches of ¼-inch-diameter dowel; and 1 inch of 1-inch-diameter dowel. Also, four metal washers about 1 inch in diameter and 1-inch-wide hinge with screws. The tools you need include: electric drill with ¼-inch bit; coping saw or jig saw; screwdriver; pencil; ruler; and wood glue (white glue). Marbles, beads, or buttons for the eyes, and varnish or stain are optional.

### Drilling holes in brush piece
Saw the 1-by-1-by-6-inch piece into two 3-inch lengths and drill a ¼-inch hole from one end to the other, through the center of each piece, lengthwise. Also, drill one hole in one corner of one end and the opposite corner of the other end of each piece. The holes should be ¼ inch deep and ¼ inch in diameter.

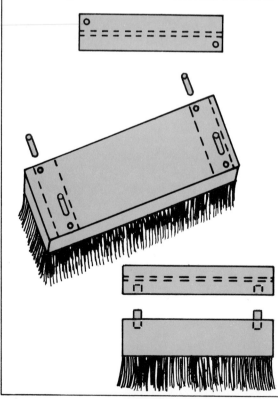

### Assembling body
Lay both 3-inch pieces across the back of the brush, one at each end, about 1½ inches from each end with the ¼-inch holes you drilled face down. Trace around the wood with a pencil and mark the area on the back of the brush corresponding to the ¼-inch holes drilled in the slats. Drill holes ¼ inch deep into the brush and ¼ inch in diameter through these marks. You should have two holes in each 3-inch length of wood and four holes in the base of the brush. Cut four ½-inch lengths of ¼-inch dowel. Brush wood glue over the areas outlined on the back of the brush, dabbing some of the glue into the four holes. Insert the cut dowels into each hole, brush some glue on the face of the pieces, dabbing some into the holes, and fit them into the dowels sticking out of the brush. Place the brush bristles down and place a weight on top while the glue dries.

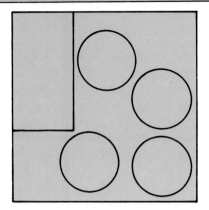

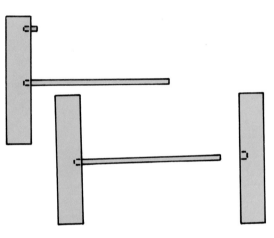

of the dragon and will control the movement of the jaws. Cut a ½-inch length from the ¼-inch dowel, brush glue into the hole and insert the dowel. Let dry.

### Making the jaws

Use the coping saw to round off one end of the 6-by-2-by-1⅛-inch block for the tip of the dragon's mouth. On the right side only, about 2 inches from the point of the jaws and ¼ inch from the top, drill a hole ¼ inch in diameter and ¼ inch deep. On each side of the rec-

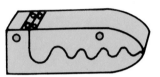

tangular end of the block, about ¼ inch from the top and ¼ inch from the back, drill a ¼-inch hole about ⅛ inch deep. These are the eyes.

Working with the same block, screw a hinge to the top of the block about 1½ inches from the flat end. Draw a line from the joint of the hinge leading straight down about 1 inch, then becoming wavy and squiggly from that point

### Cutting neck and wheels

On the sheet of 8-by-8-inch wood, mark the following pieces: a 3-by-5-inch rectangle (the dragon's neck) and four wheels, each 3 inches in diameter. Cut the pieces out with the coping saw.

At the center of each wheel, drill a hole ¼ inch deep and ¼ inch in diameter. Cut two lengths of ¼-inch dowel, each 3½ inches long. Take two of the wheels, brush glue into the holes, and insert one dowel in each. Set aside to dry. Take one of the remaining wheels and drill a ¼-inch hole, ¼ inch in diameter, about ½ inch from the outside edge of the wheel. This will be the right front wheel

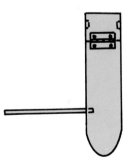

to the tip of the mouth. Make sure the line is shallow and curved; deep or pointed lines may cause the jaws to catch as they open and close. Cut along the line you drew with the coping saw.

Cut a 3¼-inch length of the ¼-inch-diameter dowel. Brush glue into the hole you drilled on the right side, about 2 inches from the end of the beak, and insert the dowel.

## Scrub-brush dragon

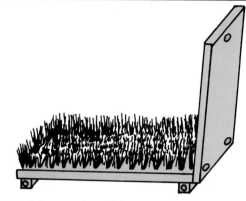

### Attaching neck and jaws

Attach the 3-by-5-inch neck block to the body brush by drilling through the neck and into the brush. Drill holes ½ inch deep and ¼ inch in diameter and fasten with glue and ¼-inch dowels. Fasten the jaws to the neck in the same way.

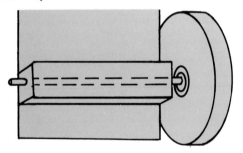

Insert a washer onto the dowels glued to two of the wheels, then pass the dowels through the holes in the wood pieces glued to the underside of the brush. Insert a washer onto each axle, dab glue into the holes of the two remaining wheels and attach them to the axles. Make sure that the wheel with the piece of dowel sticking out of it is on the right front side of the dragon, the same side as the dowel protruding from the jaw.

Drill a ¼-inch hole through the center of the 1-inch-diameter dowel. Then slice the dowel into four ¼-inch thicknesses, making wood washers. Set the right front wheel (the one with the dowel on the outside) so that the dowel is as far away as possible from the corresponding dowel sticking out of the dragon's jaw. Place the 9-inch-long slat of wood so that it touches each protruding dowel. Mark the point at which it touches and drill ¼-inch-diameter holes through the slat at those points. Place the slat over the dowels and roll the dragon forward to test the fit.

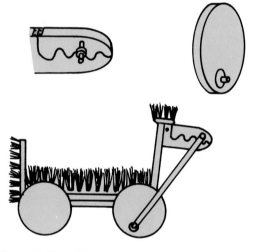

### Completing the dragon

Once you're satisfied with the fit of the slat, take it off. Dab some glue into the holes of the wooden "washer" you made and slip the washer onto the dowel sticking out of the right side of the jaw. Push the washer about 1 inch in and let it dry. Repeat this process for the dowel protruding from the front wheel, but push the dowel washer against the wheel. Replace the wooden slat and again test the snapping action of the beak by rolling the dragon back and forth. Dab glue into the holes of the other two washers and slip these onto the dowels on the jaws and wheel close to—but not quite touching—the slat, which must have a bit of free play. Attach the crown and tail using the same method you used to attach the neck and jaws. You can set marbles or beads into the eyeholes and paint, varnish or stain the monster as you wish.

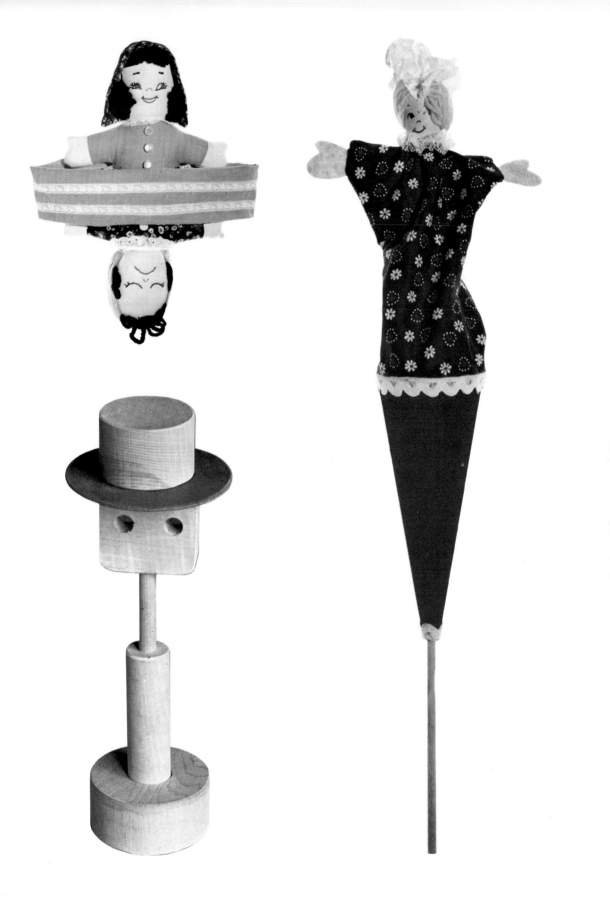

# Upside-down doll

Sometimes she is happy; sometimes she is sad. You can set the mood for this pretty little doll by simply flipping her skirt over her head to reveal either weeping eyes or a smiling face. She can be sewn together from leftover scraps of material; the largest pieces needed (for the skirt) measure just 10 by 26 inches. As shown, she wears two dresses; one solid colored, and one a print, with contrasting bonnets and aprons.

Materials: fabric scraps, for the dresses; a small piece of flesh-colored or pink fabric for the hands and faces; some wool yarn for the hair; black, blue, pink and red embroidery thread for the facial features; ordinary thread; ¼-inch-wide elastic for the waistband; small pieces of lace, ruffling, braid or ribbon for trim; buttons; and cotton batting or polyester fiberfill for stuffing.

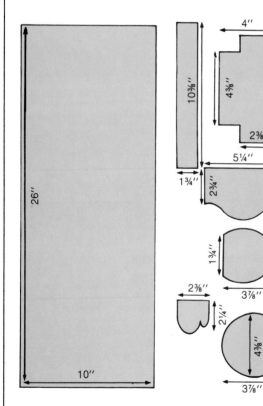

Embroider the faces, using red for mouths, pink for noses, black for eyebrows and eyelashes, and blue for the eyes of the smiling doll (the sad doll has her eyes tightly closed). Wind about fifteen loops of wool yarn around your fingers, then stitch the loops across the top of each face for hair.

Cut fabric for: faces (cut two); hands (cut eight); bonnets (cut four); brim (cut four); bodices (cut four); skirts (cut two) and aprons (cut four). One-fourth-inch seam allowances are included in all dimensions. Except for faces and hands, all pieces should be one half printed fabric and one half solid colored fabric.

With wrong sides out, sew bonnet pieces together along the curved rear edges, allowing a ¼-inch seam. With all pieces inside out, pin and baste bonnet edges to face edges, easing in fullness (leave bottom open). Stitch and turn right side out.

Sew bonnet brim pieces together along sides and outer edge with wrong sides out. If the brim is to be folded back (sad face), sew a trim piece between the outer edges. Turn right side out and stitch the unsewn edge of the brims around each face. For a full brim (happy face), cover the seam with lace.

Place apron pieces together wrong side out, with lace or other trim on the inside around the curved edges. Sew curved edges together. Turn aprons right side out. Place aprons midway along top edge of the skirt: the print apron on the solid-colored side and the solid-colored apron on the print side. The unsewn edges of the aprons should be ¾ inch below the edge of the skirt. Baste in place; stitch across the top of the skirt ⅝ inch down from the top to form a casing.

Sew hand pieces to front and back bodice pieces. With wrong sides out, sew bodice fronts and backs together, leaving openings at top for heads. Turn right side out. Sew heads to bodices. Sew the two bodies together at the front only. Stuff the bodies with cotton batting or fiberfill. Sew the back opening together.

With wrong sides out, sew both long edges of the two skirt pieces together. Turn right side out and press.

Cut a piece of ¼-inch-wide elastic to fit around the doll's waist. Insert the elastic into the casing, gathering the skirt top as you go along. Fasten securely at each end. Hand stitch the back opening of the skirt closed. Add trim pieces to the skirt. Add trim around the necks and wherever else it seems necessary. Sew buttons on front of dresses. Slip the skirt over the doll's head and arms. Now you can set her moods to match your own.

# Take-apart man

This delightful wooden man, constructed of five pieces that assemble easily and just as quickly pull apart, is an engaging toy for a preschool child and a challenge to his dexterity. The figure, which is 12 inches high when assembled, is very simple to make from disks cut out of plywood with a few commonly used hand tools. Children are fascinated with put-together toys and usually become happily engrossed while playing with them. For anyone beginning to acquire skill with woodworking tools, this project offers an opportunity to practice drilling and sawing small pieces of wood without despair and with almost certain success.

Materials: two 5-inch-long dowel sections, one 1¼ inches in diameter, the other ½ inch in diameter; a hardwood board (birch or oak) 1½ inches thick and at least 8 inches long by 6 inches wide; another hardwood board that is ¾ inch thick and 2½ inches square or larger; and a piece of ⅛-inch plywood or pressed wood sheeting, at least 6 by 6 inches. (All lengths and widths are the minimums required for cutting out the wooden rounds—larger sizes are also suitable.) Check lumber supplier or hardware store for these materials. The tools required include: a vise; clamp; small handsaw; drafting compass; bit brace with a ½-inch bit and an expansion bit used for making holes larger than 1 inch; coping saw; and coarse, medium and fine sandpaper.

### Cutting the dowel

Take the ½-inch-diameter dowel section and, if necessary, trim it to the required 5 inches, using the handsaw and the vise. Measure 1¾ inches from one end of the dowel, mark it with a pencil and, with the dowel positioned in the vise, saw as marked. The short length is used for the top of the head and the longer piece for the neck. Set both aside.

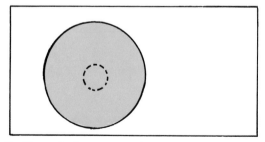

### Outline circles on wood

Lay the plywood or pressed wood sheet on a work surface, and with a compass draw a circle 4½ inches in diameter on the board. Try to locate the circle in the center of the board, as it makes for easier sawing later. The wood may split while you are sawing if the circle is too close to an edge. This piece will be used

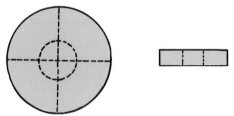

for the hat brim. Before setting it aside, mark the center of the circle (the point on which the compass rotated).

In the same manner, draw a 3½-inch circle and a 2⅜-inch circle on the 1½-inch-thick hardwood piece. The larger circle will be used for the base; the smaller will be used for the crown of the hat. Mark the center of the circles

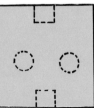

as in the previous step. Set the wood pieces aside.

### Making the head and face

Take the ¾-inch-thick hardwood piece and, if it

is not already 2½ inches square, mark it with a ruler and trim with the handsaw. This will be used for the head. Draw two circles, properly placed, for the eyes. Lay a scrap of wood on the edge of the worktable. Lay the head piece on top of it, aligning the outside edges with the table edge. (The scrap underneath is used to protect the table.) Clamp the two pieces securely to the table. Then, with the ½-inch bit and brace, drill the two eyeholes as marked. Stand the head square on edge in the vise with the two eyeholes parallel to the table. Drill a ½-inch hole in the top of the head, centered from side to side and front to back. Invert the

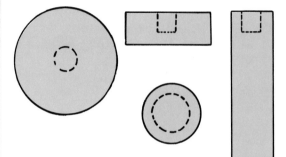

head piece and drill another hole in the bottom in the same manner. Set the head piece aside.

### Making the hat
Using the compass, find the center of the wood circle cut out for the hat brim. Position the piece on a scrap of wood and clamp as for the head. At the center point of the hat-brim circle, drill a ½-inch hole through to the other side.

In the same manner, using the ½-inch bit, drill a 1-inch-deep hole in the center of the 2⅜-inch circle for the hat crown (drawn on the thick hardwood piece).

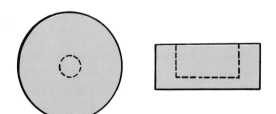

Take the 1¼-inch dowel, place it in the vise, and drill a ½-inch hole in the center of one end.

Replace the ½-inch bit in the bit brace with the expansion bit, adjusted to slightly larger than 1¼ inch, to accommodate the 1¼-inch dowel. Drill a few test holes in a scrap of wood to check how precisely the hole and the dowel match. When the correct-size hole (which fits snugly but not too tightly) is determined, you are ready to drill the base or foot. Place a piece of scrap wood on top of the wood on which you drew the 3½-inch circle. Clamp the two together to the table firmly. Use the expansion bit to drill the correct-size hole in the center, about 1¼ inch deep.

Using a coping saw, cut out the three circles drawn for the hat brim, the hat crown, and the foot or base. Saw each piece separately, using the vise or clamp to hold the piece.

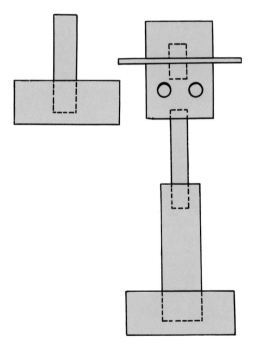

Round the edges and rough spots of all seven pieces with coarse sandpaper, then with medium sandpaper, and then with fine sandpaper, so all parts fit together smoothly.

Glue the head peg into the top of the head piece. Because of its small size, this is the only piece that is glued, to avoid losing the piece during play. The hat, brim, neck, body, and foot fit together to assemble and can easily be pulled apart and reassembled.

# Pop-up puppet

It looks a little bit like an overgrown lollipop, then pop goes the puppet, to the delight of children of all ages. It is made mostly out of scraps, but the lively puppet has a personality all its own. It may be a little girl, or a clown, or whatever you decide to make it. The fact that it is an original, rather than the way it is made, makes it endearing.

Materials: a 20-inch length of ¼-inch dowel; an empty wool or yarn cone (approximately 6¾ inches long); water-based acrylic poster paints for the cone and the face; red and black felt-tip pens; scraps of fabric, felt, lace, braid, and yarn; and a cork, spool or foam plastic ball (about 1 inch in diameter) for the head. The puppet's body is sewn together, and the rest of the assembly is done with white glue.

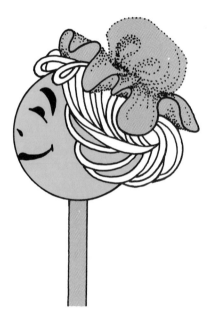

## Painting cone and head
Paint the cone with a bright poster paint. Paint the head a flesh color. When it is dry, use felt-tip pens to draw eyes, nose and mouth. Glue yarn hair to head, either straggly or in loops. Add a hat, if you wish, by gluing on a bit of lace.

With a sharp knife, hollow out a shallow hole, ¼ inch in diameter, in the bottom of the head. Place a small amount of white glue in the hole, insert the dowel, and set aside to dry thoroughly.

## Making patterns
Make paper patterns for the hands and body. To determine the width of the shirt, measure around the wide mouth of the cone. The bottom of each shirt piece should be half this measurement. Allow ½ inch for the two side seams. Use the paper patterns as guides to cut two fabric body pieces and two felt hands.

# Pop-up puppet

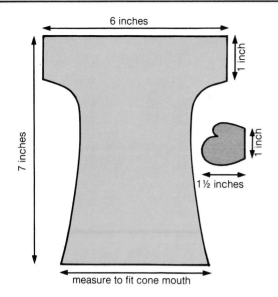

6 inches

7 inches

1 inch

1 inch

1½ inches

measure to fit cone mouth

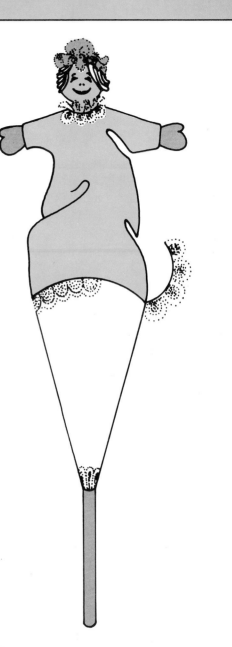

## Assembling body

Place the body pieces together, right sides to-gether, with the hands invisibly in place be-tween them. Sew together at the sides, includ-ing the arms, allowing a ¼-inch seam. Sew

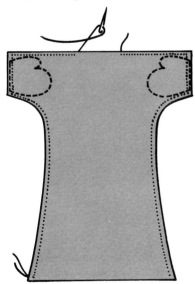

across the top, leaving a "neck" opening large enough to accommodate the widest part of the head.

## Completing puppet

Turn the body right side out. Insert the head and dowel through the bottom. Gather the neck opening snugly around the head and

glue. Tack-stitch gathered lace around the neck for a collar. Put the dowel through the cone. Glue the body-shirt around the outer edge of the mouth of the cone. Cover the edge of the shirt by gluing on a piece of deco-rative trim. Glue a small scrap of trim around the narrow end of the cone, where the dowel protrudes. Allow the glue to dry thoroughly before putting the puppet to work. Pull the dowel down and the puppet disappears; push it up and he pops into sight.

# Country miss rag doll clothes

New clothes help to spruce up a faded and tattered rag doll, the treasured doll from which a child will never part. The country-girl clothes illustrated will give almost any doll a new and crisp-looking appearance. Included are a calico dress, an apron, and a bonnet; underneath she is wearing pantaloons and a petticoat. All are easily sewn by hand. The required materials are sized for a doll approximately 20 inches tall.

Materials: 24 by 36 inches of cotton print or calico fabric for the dress; 12 by 14 inches of white cotton fabric for the apron, 24 by 36 inches of lightweight cotton fabric, such as batiste, for the pantaloons and petticoat; 18 by 32 inches of gingham for the bonnet; 12 inches of ½-inch-wide white lace trim for the apron; 12 inches of 1½-inch lace or trim for the pantaloons; 2 yards rickrack trim; sewing thread (one spool of white and one color); 1 yard of ⅛-inch-wide elastic; and 1 yard of ¼-inch-wide elastic. For larger or smaller dolls, estimate quantity of materials, trims and elastic needed after you have altered the paper pattern pieces to accommodate doll size.

### Making the pantaloons

Draw the pattern pieces to full size on graph paper following the illustration. Cut out pieces and identify each. To make the pantaloons, first fold the cotton fabric with the selvage edges together, then fold again so there are four thicknesses of fabric. Place the pattern on the fold and cut fabric, following the pattern outline. There will be two identical pieces, one

for the front and one for the back. With right sides together, join the two pieces along the angled center-front and center-back seams, sewing with a seam allowance of ¼ inch.

At the waist of the pantaloons, fold edge to the wrong side (about ⅛ inch of fabric) and press. Then fold down ½ inch and stitch around to form a casing, leaving a small opening. Cut a piece of ¼-inch elastic 1 inch less

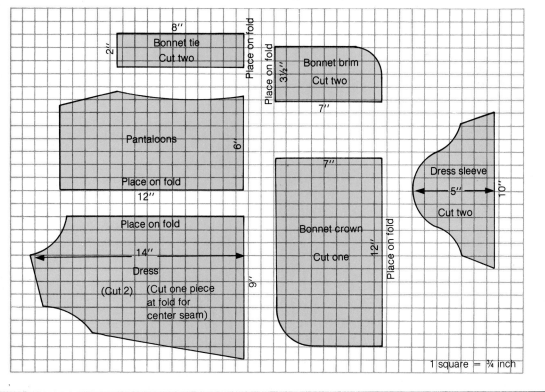

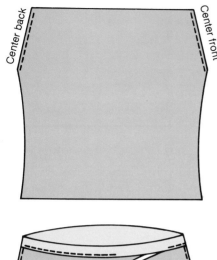

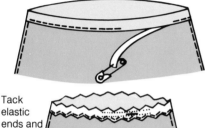

Tack elastic ends and finish stitching

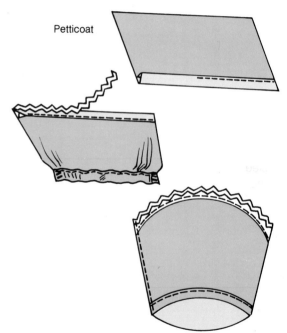

Petticoat

than the measurement of the doll's waist. Attach a small safety pin to one end of the elastic, insert it in the casing and work it around the waistband. Overlap the ends and tack securely together. Stitch the opening in the casing to close.

Still working on the wrong side, turn up a ⅜-inch hem at the bottom of each leg piece. Each pantaloon piece forms one leg. Place trim or lace along bottom hem and stitch. Approximately ½ inch above the hem, sew pieces of ⅛-inch elastic to each leg section, stretching it taut as you sew. With right sides together, stitch the crotch seam, then the leg seams, leaving a ¼-inch allowance. Turn pantaloons right side out.

**Making the petticoat**
For the petticoat, cut a piece of white fabric 8 by 24 inches. On one of the long edges, fold ⅛ inch of fabric to the wrong side and press. Then fold down ½ inch and stitch to form a casing. Cut a piece of ¼-inch elastic 1 inch less than the measurement of the doll's waist and insert in casing in the same manner as

directed for the pantaloons. Tack ends together securely. Turn up a ⅛-inch hem at the bottom edge and stitch. Sew rickrack trim or lace along hem edge. With right sides together, join the remaining sides, leaving a ¼-inch allowance. Turn petticoat right side out.

**Making the dress**
To make the doll's dress, fold the print fabric in half, selvage edges together. Fold again so there are four fabric thicknesses. Using the pattern as a guide, cut out fabric so there are two identical pieces. Then cut one of the pieces in half along the fold line. Cut two

## Country miss rag doll clothes

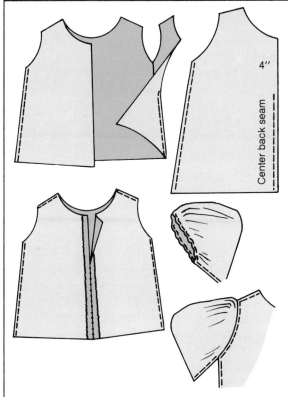

Center back seam

4"

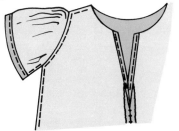

sleeves from the print fabric, again following the pattern.

Take three body pieces and, with right sides together, sew the two side seams, allowing a ¼-inch seam. Sew the center back seam (where you cut the folded edge), right sides together. Allow a ¼-inch seam. Leave a 4-inch opening at the top. With right sides together, sew the two shoulder seams, then the sleeve seams.

### Making the sleeves
Gather sleeve caps loosely and, on the wrong side, pin sleeves into armholes, matching the sleeve seam with the side seam of the dress. Adjust gathers and stitch sleeves in place. Trim seams.

### Finishing and trimming the dress
Hem the sleeves by folding ⅛ inch of fabric to the wront side and pressing, then fold under another ¼ inch, and stitch. Similarly, hem each side of the back opening. Fold ⅛ inch of fabric at the bottom of the dress to the wrong side and press, then fold under 1 inch and stitch for the hem. Turn dress right side out. Stitch rickrack trim around the bottom edge of the dress.

### Making the back tie
Cut from the remaining printed fabric a bias strip (cut on the diagonal) 1 inch wide and 20 inches long. Fold under ⅛ inch on each long edge and on each end, and press. Fold the strip in half lengthwise, wrong sides together, and press again. Put aside. Gather and stitch the neck of the dress so it measures 5 inches

after gathering. Match the center of the bias strip with the center of the gathered neckline of dress. Place the gathered fabric inside folded strip and stitch the full length of the strip, catching all gathers. Put dress on doll and tie in back.

### Making the apron
For the apron, cut a piece of white cotton 7 by 12 inches. Fold under ⅛ inch on one long edge and on both short edges and press. Then fold the three edges under again ⅛ inch and hemstitch or zigzag stitch on the right side. Trim the long edge with lace. Run a gathering stitch along the remaining long edge.

Cut a waistband of white cotton fabric, 2 by 5½ inches. Fold under ⅛ inch along each long edge and press. Fold under ⅛ inch along each short edge and press. Fold waistband in half lengthwise, with wrong sides together, and press. Gather top edge of apron to 5 inches and insert into waistband approximately ¼ inch. Top-stitch along waistband, leaving ends open.

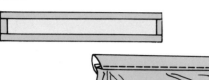

For the ties, cut two pieces of fabric 2 by 12 inches. Hem the two long edges of each tie strap by folding under ⅛ inch of fabric, pressing, then folding over another ¼ inch and stitching. At one end of each tie, fold over the fabric to form a triangle, right sides together. Stitch along the edge, then turn right side out.

Insert the raw ends of the ties ¼ inch into the open ends of the waistband. Top-stitch. If desired, stitch ready-made appliqués onto the apron.

## Making the bonnet

For the bonnet, fold gingham fabric double, with selvage edges together, so there are four fabric thicknesses. Using the patterns as guides, cut one large piece for the crown, two brim pieces, and two ties.

With right sides together, sew the two brim pieces together, stitching along the short edges and the long curved edge, allowing a

¼-inch seam. Turn right side out and press Turn the remaining raw edges in ⅛ inch and press.

Gather the straight edge of the bonnet

crown to fit into the open side of bonnet brim and stitch. Gather the bottom edge of the bonnet so it measures 7 inches. Stitch together the two tie pieces to make one long tie. Then turn under all raw edges ⅛ inch and press. Fold in half lengthwise, with wrong sides together. Match the center of the tie (where you stitched the two pieces together) with the center of the bottom edge of the bonnet. Tuck and pin the gathered edge into the tie, centered as indicated. Stitch the length of the tie; along the edges of tie, then stitch each end. Fold back brim, and place on doll's head, leaving ties loose.

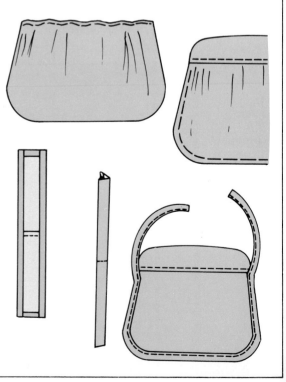

149

# Dollhouse and furniture

The dollhouse illustrated was accomplished by a six-year-old child with very little assistance. Imagine what can be achieved by an adult. Even a grandfather not oriented in crafts will enjoy this project and succeed, too.

Materials: two or three cardboard cartons or good-sized shoe boxes (or use ¼- or ⅛-inch plywood); small matchboxes for tables, beds, chests and drawers; empty thread spools to make end tables and chairs; scraps of cloth for table covering, bedspreads, carpets and wall hangings; plastic lids from food packages for tabletops; paper cups and cardboard to create other furnishings and equipment; cellophane wrapping for windows; plastic sponges to make beds, sofas, and shelf bases; and canceled postage stamps (a framed stamp makes a perfect wall hanging for a dollhouse). In addition, you need: coffee stir sticks; construction paper in different colors (available at stationery and art supply stores); scraps of adhesive-backed wall covering; scissors; glue; pipe cleaners; toothpicks; and clear plastic adhesive or masking tape.

## Making the frame
Arrange the cardboard boxes as desired to form the rooms of the dollhouse, perhaps side by side for a single-level house, or one atop the other to resemble a two-level dwell-

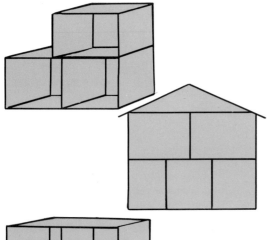

ing. Cut off the sides of the boxes which will become the back of the house, and which will remain open to make it easy to place the furniture inside and for play. To make the sloping roof, fold one large sheet of construction paper in half, or use two small sheets. Cover the outside of the house with standard white or brown paper, or use a colorful wrapping paper.

## Using wood (optional)
For a more durable and less makeshift dollhouse, build the frame out of ¼- or ⅛-inch plywood or masonite, attach 1-by-1-inch slats to the plywood with nails and glue, and fit the pieces together as shown in the diagram. Also cut and attach a piece of plywood for the front of the dollhouse.

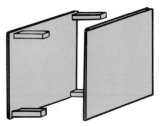

## Making room dividers
If rooms are not already formed, make further divisions by fitting a piece of cardboard or construction paper between floor and ceiling and fastening it into place with strips of masking or adhesive tape. You can also use this technique to split a large box into separate stories.

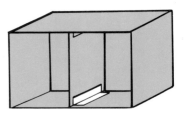

To make doors, draw a rectangle on the outside of the box and cut along three sides of the rectangle; fold back the uncut side. Use tape to reinforce the joint of the door and act as a hinge.

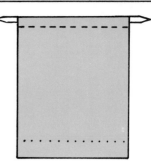

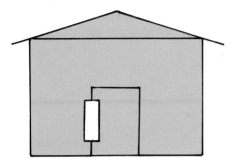

### Decorating interior

To make curtains, use tissue paper or fabric remnants. Toothpicks or pipe cleaners, fastened to the wall with tape or glue, become suitable curtain rods.

### Creating windows

There are several ways to create the windows. Mark off the window area and cut it out completely, or mark off the window area, cut

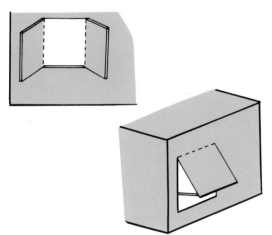

For wall hangings, cut tiny frames out of construction paper to fit around postage stamps, or smaller pieces of printed fabric, or gift wrapping paper. Scraps of cloth make colorful carpeting.

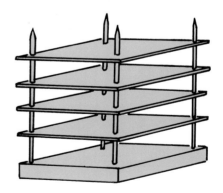

along the top and bottom lines, then mark the center of the two cut lines and cut down the middle from the top to bottom. Fold the flaps back, securing them with tape to create shutters. To make an awning, mark the window area and cut along the side lines and bottom line, then fold the cutout piece up, along the uncut line. Use toothpicks to support the flap to simulate an awning. To give the appearance of glass windows, tape or glue cellophane or transparent wrap over the cutout areas.

Make shelves by cutting a section of a plastic sponge and cutting pieces of construction paper the same size as the sponge section. Insert toothpicks, one in each corner of the sponge, then thread the sheets of paper over the toothpicks, spacing them as illustrated.

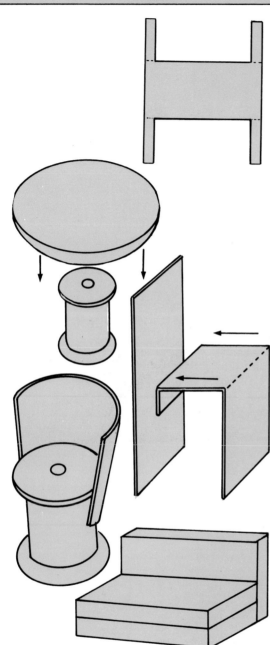

to cardboard and glue to the sides of a spool, to create a chair. Then cover top of spool with same fabric to complete. Sofas or couches are made with three pieces of sponge glued together and cut to a size that fits the room.

Beds are similarly made with sponge pieces or with large matchboxes. Scraps of cloth make excellent bedspreads, and a piece of construction paper or cardboard, cut to size,

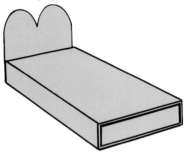

serves as a headboard. To make a bed canopy, use toothpicks or pipe cleaners glued in a vertical position to the bed corners to support a piece of cloth forming a canopy over the bed.

To make a desk, glue two small matchboxes together to form one pedestal and repeat to create the second pedestal. Cut out a piece of construction paper measuring slightly larger

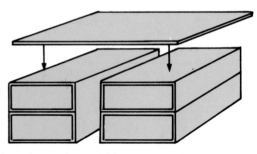

than the surfaces of the two matchbox pedestals. Glue to the tops of matchboxes as shown above. Many appliances and functional household equipment are box-shaped, so make a variety of sizes; then apply color, and sketch in some details to give them the appearance of sinks, televisions or washing machines. Remember to keep the furniture sizes in proportion to the size of the room and the dollhouse, and put only a few pieces of furniture into one room. The simpler the furnishings, the more appealing the house will look, and the more room there will be for creative play.

## Making furniture

Make tables by cutting and folding cardboard or construction paper; by placing plastic lids over empty thread spools; or by cutting circles out of cardboard and gluing them to the spools. Vary the table heights to create coffee tables, dining and lamp tables. To make chairs cut two pieces of cardboard, identical in size. Fold one in half to form the seat and front support, then glue it to the other piece. Glue fabric

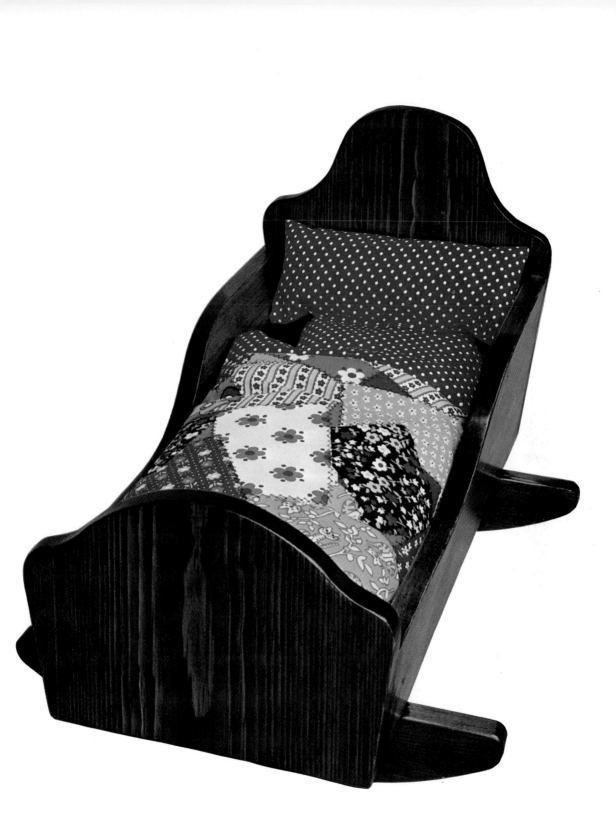

# Doll's cradle

This sturdy cradle is made to last for years, and for sentimental reasons can be passed from one generation to the next. While simple in design, the woodworking requires some skill. Even though quite inexpensive when compared to other woods, the pine used takes a fine finish that looks very elegant.

Materials: for the bottom of the cradle, one pine board 10 by 19 inches; for the sides, two pieces, each 8 by 19 inches; for the back, one piece 12 by 12 inches; for the front, one piece 7 by 12 inches; and two pieces for the rockers, each 4 by 15 inches. (All boards are ⅝-inch-thick Pine.) Other materials needed include several large sheets of cardboard about 9 by 12 inches; four 1½-by-⅜-inch-diameter screws; six 1½-inch finishing nails; hammer; saber saw; wood putty; fine-grade and medium-grade sandpaper; brace or drill press; hand plane; ruler; satin varnish; wood stain; paste wax; steel wool; paper towels or soft cloth; and white glue. Use either power or hand tools.

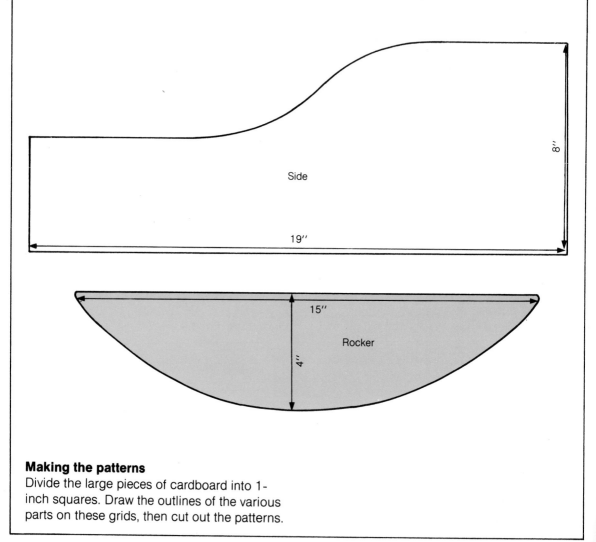

Side

8″

19″

15″

Rocker

4″

## Making the patterns
Divide the large pieces of cardboard into 1-inch squares. Draw the outlines of the various parts on these grids, then cut out the patterns.

154

# Doll's cradle

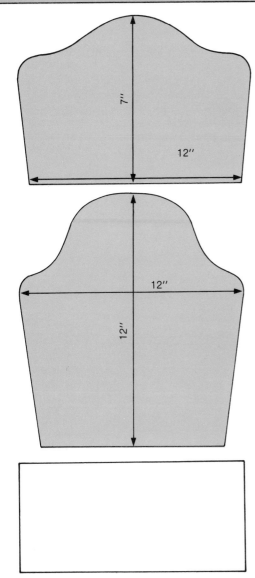

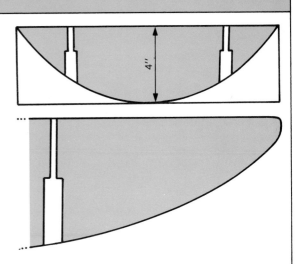

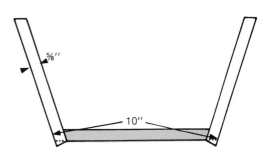

other side (the straight top edge) to meet the first holes, creating the counterbores. Use a saber saw to cut the rocker pieces to shape.

## Assembling side pieces to bottom

Sand all the pieces on all sides with medium-grade sandpaper; next, sand with fine-grade

paper. Assemble the side pieces to the bottom, using three finishing nails on each side and bead of glue where the pieces join. One way to make this easier is to clamp the bottom in a vise (with well-padded jaws). Start the nails in the side; position the side on the bottom; partially drive nails in place; apply glue; and finally drive the nails the rest of the way. Countersink nails and fill holes with wood putty or plastic wood.

## Cutting wood pieces

Using the patterns, outline on the wood all the parts except the rockers, and cut out the pieces, preferably with a saber saw. Bevel the edges of the bottom piece 8 degrees.

8 degree bevel

Outline the rocker patterns on the wood. Then, using a ⅜-inch-diameter bit in a brace (or a drill press), counterbore holes 1⅝ inches deep in the rocker pieces. Use a twist drill with an 11/64-inch bit to drill through from the

With the sides in position, clamp them for about 30 minutes. This gives the glue time to dry. Remove the clamps, then use a hand plane to trim the bottom edges of the sides so they are flush with the bottom. Then sand the planed areas thoroughly.

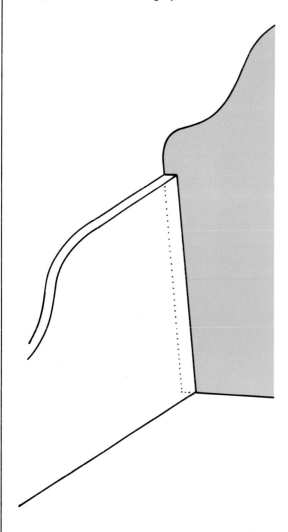

### Mounting rockers
Mark the positions of the rockers on the bottom of the cradle (3 inches from the ends). Drill small pilot holes in the bottom of the cradle, then attach rockers with No. 8 1½-inch screws through the previously drilled holes. This completes the assembly.

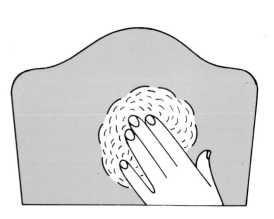

### Sanding and staining
Use medium, then fine sandpaper, to give the cradle an overall sanding. Sand all exposed edges. Use a vacuum cleaner to remove all sawdust. Apply a generous coat of stain (walnut is recommended) and allow to stand for 15 minutes. Wipe excess with a cloth. Allow to dry according to label instructions, then apply another coat of stain, let stand, wipe and allow 24 hours to dry. Apply a coat of satin varnish, and allow to dry for 24 to 48 hours. Sand very lightly with a medium-grade paper to remove minor imperfections or raised wood grain. Vacuum, then apply a generous coat of paste wax, using a wad of fine-grade steel wool. Remove excess wax immediately with a cloth or paper towels. Buff the finish with a clean cloth or towels. This time-consuming process is necessary to achieve a warm and mellow finish.

### Mounting front and back
The back and the front are attached in the same manner. Apply a bead of white glue to the end grain of the sides and bottom end; position the piece in place; then clamp and allow about 30 minutes for the glue to dry. You can also use finishing nails, but this isn't necessary. If the glue oozes out, wipe it off immediately with a cloth before it dries.

# Doll's quilt and mattress set

In the fantasy world of children, a doll-size mattress, pillow and coverlet constitute a bed. This three-piece doll's bed set does not require a cradle or carriage, just a favorite doll.

Materials: 20-inch-by-26-inch piece of patchwork fabric (or piece together colorful scraps of fabric as instructed for Patchwork pillow) for the quilt top; a piece of fabric 25 by 45 inches for the mattress, pillow and the back side of the quilt; a 20-by-25-inch piece of cotton or polyester batting, for the quilt; cotton or polyester stuffing for the mattress and pillow; and thread to match the fabrics. No special sewing skills are required, and all the pieces can be sewn by hand, although a sewing machine makes the job easier.

This three-piece set is a perfect fit for the Doll cradle project.

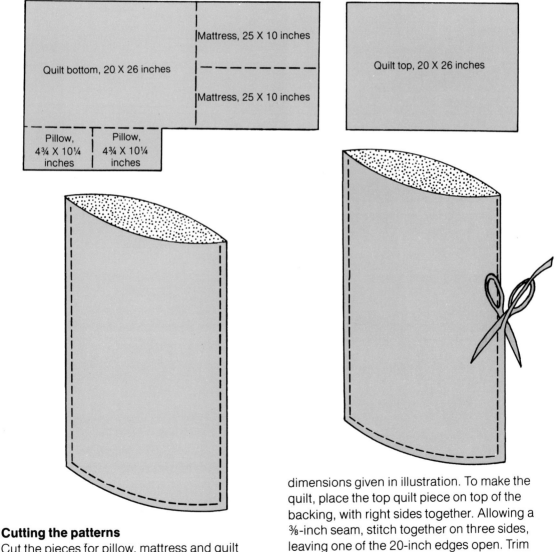

**Cutting the patterns**

Cut the pieces for pillow, mattress and quilt backing from the large piece of fabric. Follow dimensions given in illustration. To make the quilt, place the top quilt piece on top of the backing, with right sides together. Allowing a ⅜-inch seam, stitch together on three sides, leaving one of the 20-inch edges open. Trim the seams. Turn right side out and press.

## Doll's quilt and mattress set

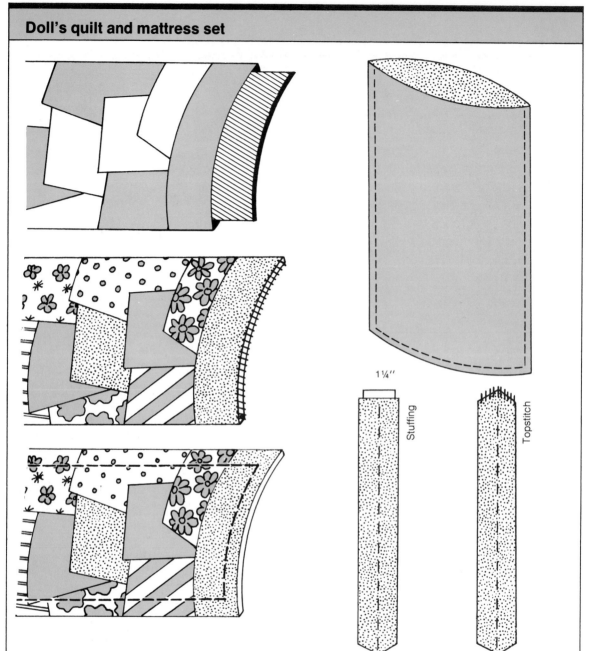

Stuffing

Topstitch

1¼″

### Finishing the quilt
Trim batting to fit the quilt cover, then place it inside the cover. Turn in the raw edges of the open side of the quilt and top-stitch across the opening. Top-stitch the quilt all around, 2 inches in from the outside edges.

### Making the mattress
To make the mattress, place the two pieces right sides together and stitch on three sides, allowing a ⅜-inch seam. Leave open one of the 10-inch edges. Trim the seams. Turn the mattress right side out and press. Stuff the mattress with the filler to a thickness of about 1¼ inches. Turn in the raw edges of the fourth side and top-stitch to complete the mattress.

### Stitching the pillow
The pillow is made similarly. Stitch on three sides, leaving one of the 4¾-inch sides open for stuffing. Turn right side out, stuff and then top-stitch.

# Bottle Santa Claus

The legendary Christmas Santa Claus known to American children is a very lovable, jolly, plump character with a flowing white beard, a twinkle in his eye and a heart of gold. Dressed in a red suit trimmed with white fur, with a black belt to cinch his ample girth and a red stocking cap cocked on his head, this traditional Santa Claus is reproduced in miniature for every type of decoration from candy wrappings to table centerpieces. In the illustrated project, the whimsical Santa Claus is made from an empty wine bottle.

Materials: 2-quart chianti bottle; a foamed plastic ball 5 inches in diameter; a piece of red felt 5 by 24 inches; a piece of white felt 12 inches square; a 12-inch-square piece of black felt; a ¾-inch red Christmas tree ball; a small package of cotton batting; a small jar of flesh-colored water paint; a can of black spray paint; white glue; a gold buckle; paper; pencil; small paintbrush; scissors; and a sharp-pointed knife.

### Painting bottle and headpiece
Wash and rinse the empty wine bottle and allow to dry completely. Spray the bottle with black paint; allow to dry. Brush a coat of flesh-colored water-base paint on the foamed plastic ball. Allow both the bottle and the ball to dry completely. Use a sharp-pointed knife to cut a hole in the ball about ⅓ inch deep, just large enough to fit over the neck of the bottle. Put a small amount of white glue into the hole in the ball and place it on the wine bottle.

### Making patterns
Working from the grid patterns, make patterns of the various pieces of felt, and cut them out. Place each pattern on the color felt indicated in the illustration. Cut out the red, black, and white felt pieces, as directed. (Note: Using paper pattern, cut two pieces for each of the following: the red hat, the white hat trim, the white lower jacket trim, and the black eyebrows.)

### Assembling felt jacket pieces
Glue the red felt jacket to the bottle with the two edges butting together in front. Glue the white collar trim in place, then glue the two pieces of white trim on the lower edge of jacket. Glue on the two front jacket trim pieces, covering the ends of the collar and lower trim pieces. Slip the gold buckle on the front black belt piece, and center on belt. Glue belt in place with buckle center front. Then glue on the back belt piece.

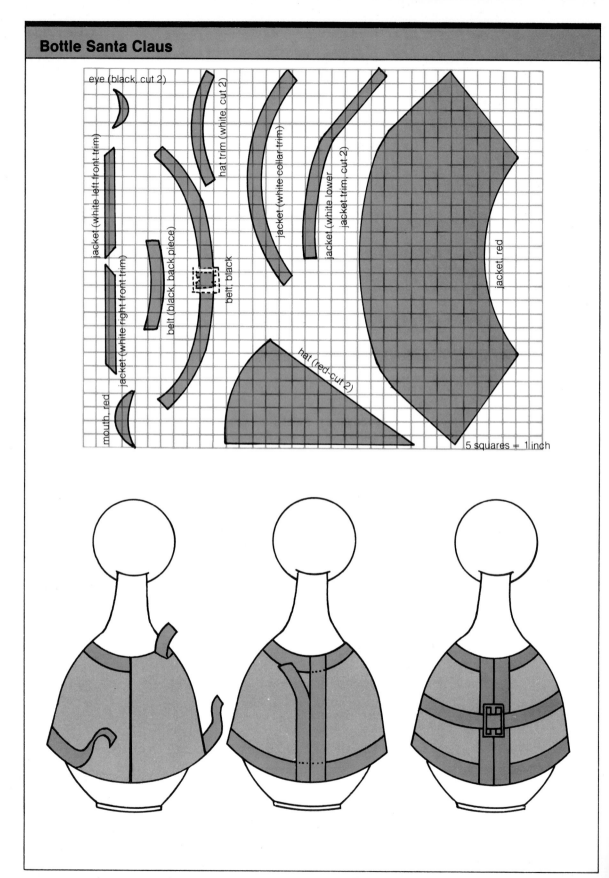

eye (black, cut 2)

jacket (white left front trim)

jacket (white right front trim)

hat trim (white, cut 2)

jacket (white collar trim)

jacket (white lower jacket trim, cut 2)

belt (black, back piece)

belt, black

jacket, red

mouth, red

hat (red-cut 2)

5 squares = 1 inch

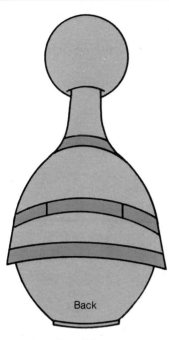

Back

### Completing head and face

Glue the two hat pieces together along the edges, leaving the bottom open to fit on the foamed plastic head. Glue the two pieces of hat trim around the lower edge of the hat, then glue the hat to the top of the foamed plastic ball. Glue felt eyes and mouth on foamed ball. Push the neck of the Christmas tree ball into the center of the face for a nose.

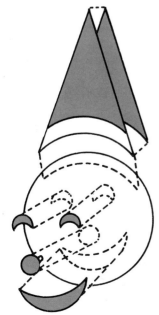

Finally, glue the cotton batting in place to make the beard, mustache, eyebrows and hair around the sides and back of the hat. Add a tassel of cotton at the tip of the hat.

# Knotted sisal wreath

This rustic Christmas wreath is very easily made from heavy rope crafted with a series of knots. Its rough texture and simple knot pattern make it a unique conversation piece. Trim the wreath with a bell and a bow of ribbon and place it over an unadorned fresh evergreen wreath.

Materials: 13 yards of heavy 2-ply sisal; 1 yard of thin cord; ¾ yard of bright ribbon; a brass bell; thin-gauge household wire; board or lid from foamed plastic cooler chest, or other flat surface for knotting; C-clamp (optional); and some T-shaped pins.

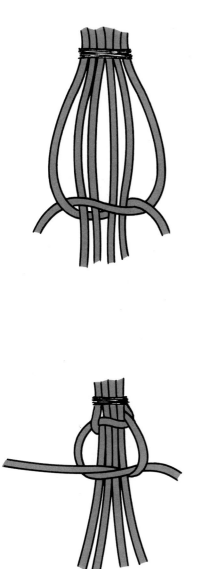

**Anchoring cords**

Cut two 4-yard lengths and four 1¼-yard lengths of sisal. Secure the 6 lengths together by wrapping with wire, 7 inches from one end. With a C-clamp, fasten the end at the point where the wire is wrapped around sisal, to the board or a desired flat working surface. This will hold the cords taut, while knotting. Using the two 4-yard lengths as knotting cords, tie square knots around the 4 shorter lengths. Make each square knot as follows: Bring left outer cord over the 4 center cords and to the right of them. Place right outer cord over left outer cord and pass it under and to left of the 4 center cords, bringing it up through the loop formed by the left outer cord and center cords. Pass the cord now on left outer side under and to the right of the center cords, then over the right-hand cord. Now bring the right-hand cord up and over the center cords, passing it through the loop formed by the left outer cord. Pull cords to tighten and complete the knot. (See diagrams at left and above.)

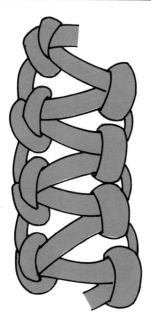

### Knotting chain

Continue working square knots in a chain, being careful to complete each knot and making sure you don't bring the same outer cord over the center cords twice in succession; otherwise your chain will twist. Secure work with T-pins at intervals between every few knots. Pin and curve the chain of knots until the knotted chain measures 26 inches.

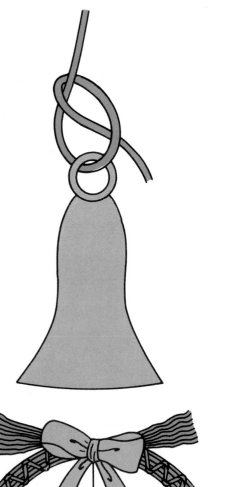

### Forming wreath

Secure end below last knot with wire. Shape knotted sisal into a circle by crossing ends and wrapping wire around the point of intersection, about 7 inches from each end. Trim ends evenly, and wrap thin cord over wire.

Thread a length of yarn, ribbon or string halfway through the top ring of a small brass bell and tie an overhand knot. Tie ends around the top of wreath at point where bell is attached and sisal ends overlap. Place the completed sisal wreath on top of a simple, fresh evergreen wreath. Then wrap the ribbon around both the sisal and evergreen wreaths, tie together at top and tie a bow. Then tack wreath to the entry door of your home to welcome Christmas visitors.

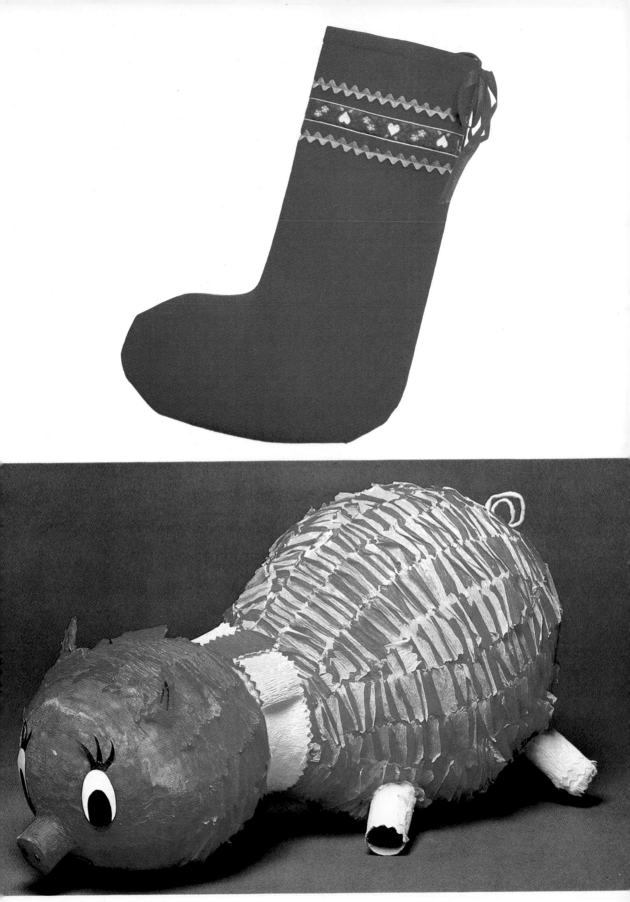

# Christmas stocking

Brightly colored Christmas stockings, bulging with small surprises and hung by the fireside or on your tree, lend a special air of expectancy to the holiday festivities. These colorful stockings, like Santa Claus, have become a part of the contemporary Christmas tradition. To make the bright-red stocking shown, you need no special skills, just enthusiasm.

Materials: a pencil and a sheet of paper at least 24 inches by 20 inches; ⅔ yard of 36-inch-wide velvet, corduroy, velour, or similar fabric; 14 inches of embroidered ribbon; 28 inches of rickrack trim; 1 yard of ribbon ½ inch wide; needle; thread; and scissors.

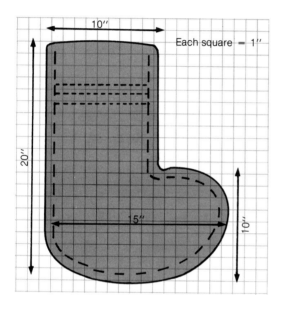

Each square = 1″

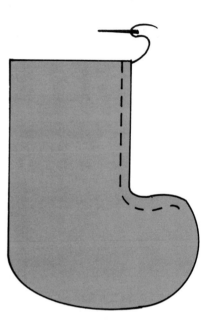

## Cutting pattern and fabric

Copy the pattern shown on the paper. Fold fabric, selvages together; pin pattern to fabric and cut two pieces for stocking, allowing ½ inch extra for seam allowance. The sock pieces should be 20 inches long from top to heel; 10 inches wide at top; 15 inches from toe to heel; and 10 inches from top of foot to sole. Mark three parallel guidelines for trim placement as follows: one 3 inches from top edge of stocking; one 3½ inches from top; and one 4 inches from top.

## Stitching the stocking

Pin the two stocking pieces, right sides together, along front, from top to toe, and stitch

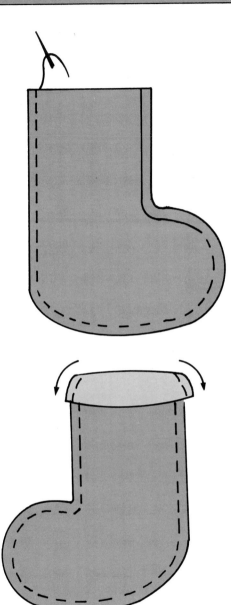

a ½-inch-wide seam. Clip curves. Trim seam to ¼ inch and press open. Pin and stitch rickrack along placement lines and press. Then, right sides together, stitch remainder of stocking together, allowing a ½-inch seam, from the top of the toe around sole and heel and up the back to top edge. Press stocking. Turn top edge ½ inch to inside of stocking, stitch and press.

**Trimming the stocking**

Fold ribbon in half, place across back seam ¼ inch from top edge, and stitch so that a 3-inch loop extends upward from line of stitching. Tie remaining ribbon into a large bow to complete the stocking.

# Piñata

In Mexico and many other Central American countries, the colorful piñata is always the center of attention at children's celebrations and traditional festivals, especially at Christmas. These papier-mâché figures of animals, birds, and clowns covering earthenware jars are hung from the ceiling, destined to be smashed open and to pour forth toys and sweets on joyful children who have broken the treasure trove with sticks.

Materials: a large balloon and a small balloon (approximately 12 inches and 6⅜ inches in diameter when inflated); flour; newspapers; tissue paper of various colors; a large bowl; cardboard tubes from inside paper towels or toilet tissue; masking tape; ⅝-inch-wide ribbon; white glue; and to fill the piñata, candies and tiny toys.

## Forming the body

Tear newspapers into strips about 1¼ inches wide. In a large bowl, make a paste of half flour and half water. Soak the newspaper strips in the paste. Inflate the balloons. Cover each balloon with a layer of newspaper strips, squeezing excess paste or water off each strip by pulling it between your fingers. Allow to dry, then apply more strips, building up four or five layers. Dry final layer overnight.

## Festooning the piñata

When the strips have dried thoroughly, burst the balloons by pricking through the strips with a pin. Cut an opening of approximately 2-inch diameter in one end of the larger papier-mâché piece which forms the body of the animal and a matching opening in the smaller piece, which will become the head, where the two are to be joined. Remove the balloons. Cover the papier-mâché with layers of colored tissue paper strips, securing them with a solution of one part white glue and one part water. Build up several layers of tissue paper so the newspaper print or bandage weave does not show through. Then cover the larger section with decorative cutouts. To cut tissue-paper decorations (hearts, flowers, diamonds, stars, triangles, circles), fold the paper several times in order to cut out several copies of each design at one time. Apply with glue to the body. Cut eyes, eyebrows and mouth out of tissue paper and glue to the head.

## Completing the piñata

With a knife, cut five 2-inch lengths of the cardboard tube, for the feet and snout, and attach to proper section with masking tape. Cover feet and snout with tissue paper the same color as the head and body. Fill body with small candies and toys. Attach head to body with cellophane tape and white glue. Cut 14-inch piece of ribbon and glue on as a tail. Curl tail by holding it tightly against one of the scissor blades, and slide the blade along the taut ribbon. Tie string around the piñata and hang from ceiling or use as a party table centerpiece.

# Batik party invitations

Wouldn't you love to send these batik note cards to your friends on special occasions? The batik process is an exciting way of making a design on fabric by a technique known as wax resist. This simply means that a wax pattern, applied to fabric, resists the color when the fabric is dyed.

Materials: a wooden block approximately 12 by 12 inches; thumbtacks; and a firm, smoothly woven fabric which will absorb the wax uniformly. Silk, linen, and wool fabrics are the easiest to use; however, they are also the most costly. To be certain of finished colors, white fabric, woven of natural fibers, is best, although colored fabrics can provide interesting surprises. You need a tjanting tool (a metal tool with a small spout) for fine-lined designs, or a calligraphic paintbrush for bolder designs. The tools are dipped into a mixture of 60 percent beeswax and 40 percent paraffin or canning wax melted at a constant temperature of 350 to 375 degrees Fahrenheit in an enamel or heat-proof glass saucepan, on top of an electric hot plate rather than over a flame (hot wax is combustible). Keep a box of baking soda or salt nearby in case of fire. Have a piece of wire handy to remove any lumps of wax on the tjanting tool or brush.

You will also need household fabric dyes; plastic or enamel containers for storage of dyes; rubber gloves (some dyes are toxic); a plastic bucket for dipping fabric; bleach to remove any sink stains; an electric iron to remove the wax; a can of dry-cleaning fluid; paper towels and newspapers; notepaper; and rubber cement.

As you experiment with this new medium, utilize found objects and interesting shapes, such as cookie cutters, which can leave an intricate impression on your fabric. Pick out fabric, glue, bond paper, and matching envelopes at any variety store.

## Preparing the cloth

All new fabrics must be washed and ironed before you begin work, to remove sizing. To make the batik greeting card, cut pieces of fabric into rectangles 5 by 3½ inches. Next, tack fabric at each corner onto the wooden board so it is stretched taut.

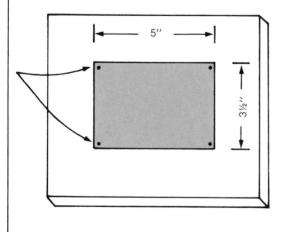

## Heating and applying the wax

Heat batik wax in an enamel saucepan on a hot plate at 350 to 375 degrees. Dip the tjanting tool or brush into the melted wax and rub it across a wire to remove excess or lumpy wax.

With a tjanting tool, you can use the needle-like tip to control the dripping wax. Conversely, you can paint or spatter a loose pattern with a paintbrush.

## Coloring the fabric

Dyeing is done in cool dye baths so that the wax pattern does not melt. Wetting the fabric before dyeing improves absorption of the dye. Household dyes are good for this technique, but be sure to mix these dyes, as directed, in boiling water. Mix at three times the recommended strength, then cool the dye to luke-warm. Prepare the lightest-colored dye for the first bath. When the wax design is dry, untack the fabric from the board and immerse it in the color bath. Let the fabric stay in the dye

### Multiplying the colors

If you want to add another color, retack fabric on board. Paint on more wax to add to your design. Cover dyed areas with wax where you want the previous color to remain.

Dip fabric into next color of dye until the shade is correct. Rinse thoroughly again and hang up to dry. Repeat the entire process for each new color that you want to add.

until the shade is the intensity desired. Remember that colors look darker when wet.

Rinse dyed fabric under running lukewarm water until no dye runs out, then hang fabric on a rack to dry.

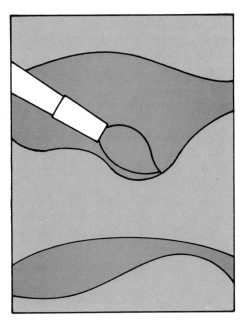

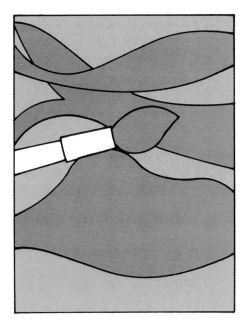

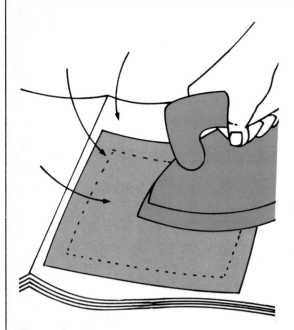

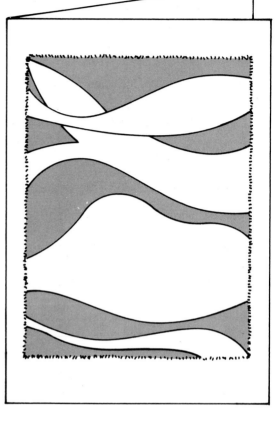

### Removing wax

To remove wax, place fabric flat on a pad of newspapers and cover with paper towels. With the hot iron on the paper towels, absorb wax to remove it from the fabric. Use dry-cleaning fluid in a well-ventilated room to remove the last traces of wax.

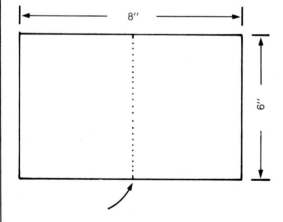

### Decorating stationery

Cut pieces of notepaper into rectangles measuring 8 by 6 inches. Fold each sheet in half like a greeting card. Using fabric glue or rubber cement, center and secure the batik to the front of the card.

Now that you have mastered this art, try making gossamer scarfs, decorative batik mobiles, and original batik designs of your own.

# Linoleum and woodcut place cards

Do you remember the simple linoleum block prints you made in grade school? They may have been somewhat primitive, but charming nonetheless. Basically the same technique is applied in creating these distinctive prints with linoleum or woodcuts.

Woodcuts are among the oldest forms of graphic arts. The idea of using incised wood to print a picture dates from at least the ninth century, when the Chinese began to stamp images on walls with wood blocks. The picture you cut on the wood surface is the negative of the picture you will print. With tools as common as a spoon and a kitchen knife, you can try your hand at making both a woodcut and its first cousin, a linoleum cut called a linocut. Either one will print fine place cards you can reproduce in quantities. Linoleum has no grain and can be cut with ease in any direction. Wood, on the other hand, has a natural grain which creates interesting surface texture when printed, but it can inhibit your cutting freedom.

Materials: a printing block; one color of printers' ink; solvent; a sheet of glass; a brayer (ink roller); printing paper, such as rice paper or other papers recommended by your local art supply store; a burnisher or large tablespoon; and a linocut tool (a sharp knife will do). A stack of blotter sheets is an optional extra. Art supply stores can be most helpful in your selection. Note: For easy cleanup and for working with children, use water-base inks and linoleum blocks rather than oil-base ink.

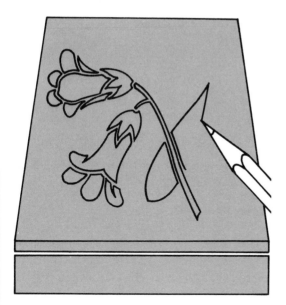

### Making a linocut
Heavy linoleum can be bought in quantity at a flooring store, but it is better to start with a linoleum block. This is a piece of linoleum already bonded to a wooden block, so it lies flat and is suitable for printing. Art supply stores generally offer several sizes. Wash off the linoleum so that it is free of any dirt that might interfere with the ink. Should there be any scratches, scrape the surface lightly with the flat of a single-edged razor blade until it is completely smooth. Wash surface again and dry.

Draw a simple design on a piece of paper the same size as the block. The beginner is advised to avoid designs with fine detail, and to work in bold images, to make the cutting less difficult. If you are including any lettering, remember to cut the mirror image of the letters, as they will print in reverse.

When the sketch is completed, transfer design to the block. Place a piece of carbon paper on the block, carbon side down. Then place the sketch on top of the carbon paper

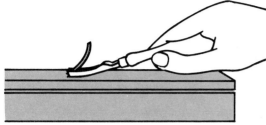

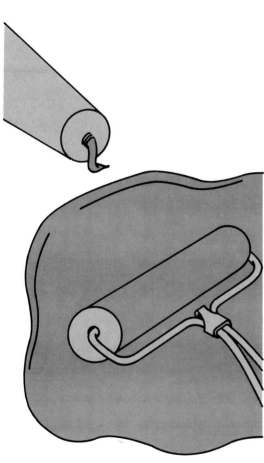

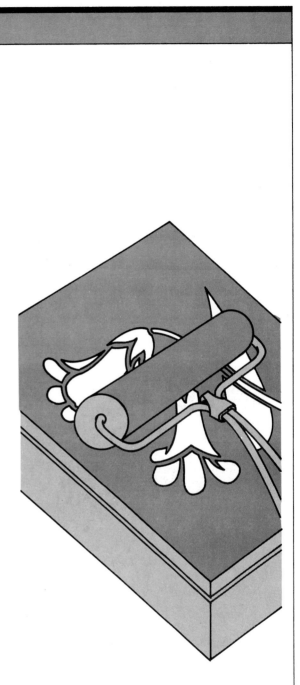

and tape to the block with masking tape. With a sharp pencil, trace the design onto the linoleum surface. Be sure to go over the carbon impression with a pencil so the details show up clearly on the linoleum to facilitate cutting.

With sharp cutting tools (see CRAFTNOTES) cut out the areas that you do not want to print. The ink will be picked up by the remaining linoleum surface, so cut away all the spaces around the images for the clearest print.

**Testing the print**
To get a preview of how your print will finally look, put a small amount of printers' ink on a sheet of glass. Spread the ink until there is a film at least 4 inches square. Roll the brayer across the ink film several times until it is coated evenly with ink. The consistency of the ink should be tacky. Roll the inked brayer across the linoleum block, leaving a thin film of ink on the linoleum surface.

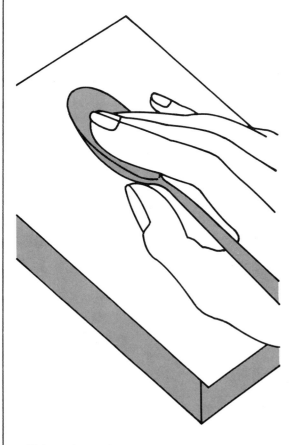

Take a sheet of your printing paper and, holding by two diagonally opposite corners, center it over the linoleum block. Place it face down squarely on the inked surface, being careful not to move the paper once contact is made.

Holding a large spoon firmly with your fingers in the bowl and your thumb under the handle, rub the bottom over the back of the paper. If the paper is thin, the image will show through to tell you when you have rubbed enough. If not, experience and an occasional peek under one corner should guide you.

Remove the paper, being careful not to smudge the image as you lift it. Set the print face up to air-dry, and study it to see that all parts of the design are printing as they should. If not, make bolder cuts or press the paper against the ink more firmly, depending upon what this first proof shows. If more work must be done on the linoleum, clean the surface with solvent before you cut again.

## Printing in quantity

When you are satisfied with your design and technique, print the rest of your cards. Set each aside to air-dry or place them in a stack with sheets of blotter paper between.

## Cleaning up

When you have finished the series, clean the block, brayer and ink slab with solvent. The brayer should be powdered with talcum afterward to draw out any remaining moisture, and stored so that it hangs free from the handle. Hang the roller by the handle or it will lose its perfect roundness.

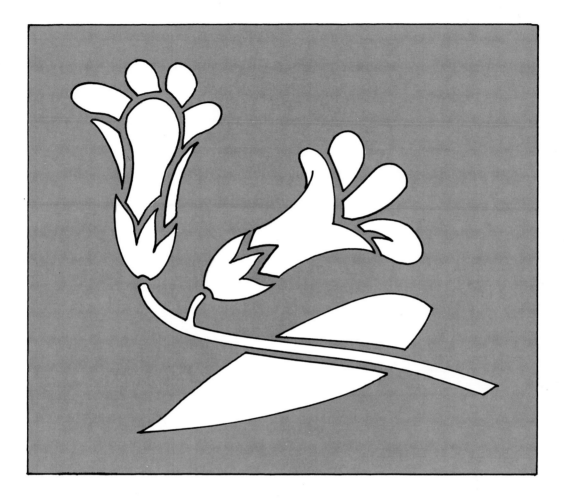

### Making a woodcut

For the skilled artist-craftsman, any piece of wood can be adopted; but the beginner will find certain woods easier to cut than others. Pine is excellent, as are fruitwoods, basswood, beech, poplar and sycamore. Use a sharp knife to cut away areas with V-shaped incisions. Do not undercut the printing surface as it might chip off when printing pressure is applied (see CRAFTNOTES).

As you make your drawing, remember that designs which run predominantly with the grain of the wood are easier to cut. Proceed through the printing steps as in a linoleum cut.

# Costumes

Costuming is one of the most important elements in theater success. For family and community productions, or for costume parties, they need not be elaborate. Simply start with basic clothing items and create the desired effect with materials available at home. The technique in making costumes look authentic is to create accessories that immediately identify the character, the national origin of the costume, or the animal or object being portrayed. The costumes shown—a pirate, an American Indian and a bumblebee—may not be exactly what you need; however, the techniques used in making these costumes are easy to adapt to other characters. As far as possible, everyday clothing is used for the costumes. The addition of the appropriate accessories makes the clothing take on the appearance desired.

Materials: a tape measure; pencil or chalk; dressmaker's pins; cellophane tape; needle and thread; staples and stapler; glue; scissors; and an assortment of felt-tip markers. For the pirate costume, you need: a pair of dark trousers; a striped T-shirt; a bandanna; black construction paper for the eyepatch and mustache; a shoelace; a large earring; a wide solid-color sash; two 24-inch-square pieces of black felt for the boots; and cardboard and aluminum foil for the sword. The American Indian costume requires 2¼ yards of 48-inch-wide cotton fabric; about 3 yards of 1½-inch-wide felt for fringe; and about 1 yard of ¾-inch-wide elastic for the waistband; colored posterboard for the war bonnet: two 10-inch-by-12-inch red sheets, two 10-inch-by-12-inch yellow sheets, and three pieces 3 by 24 inches—one red, one blue and one brown. You will also need a pair of moccasins or loafers. The bumblebee body requires a pair of black or yellow tights; a sleeveless black knit turtleneck shirt; three pairs of yellow knee socks; polyester batting or clean rags for stuffing two pairs of the socks; and transparent nylon thread or fishing line. Also needed, for the wings: a piece of white illustration board 24 by 24 inches; 1½ yards of black string or ¼-inch-wide ribbon; for the hood: a piece of black fabric 12 by 26 inches; two pairs of snap fasteners; a pair of pipe cleaners; and yellow tissue or crepe paper.

### Creating the pirate costume

Start with dark trousers, a striped T-shirt, and a bandanna to tie on the head. Make an eyepatch and mustache, drawing the outlines of each on black construction paper, then cut out. Punch two ¼-inch holes in the paper eyepatch and attach a shoelace to fit around head. Tape the construction paper mustache in place, and attach a large earring to one ear. Tie a wide, solid-color sash around the waist.

Make boots to fit over the tops of ordinary shoes. Measure the distance from the floor to where the boot top will be on the leg (in the example shown, 16 inches); add 4 inches for the top cuff of the boot and 2

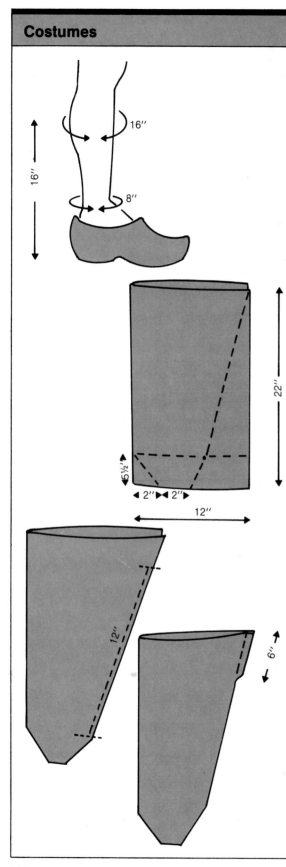

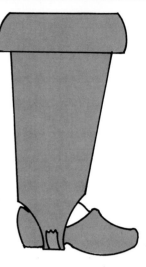

inches for the underfoot tabs (making the total length 22 inches). Measure around the widest part of the calf of the person's leg (16 inches in the example shown), add 8 inches (for total width of 24 inches) and divide in half (12 inches). Measure loosely around the ankle (8 inches in this case), divide in half (4 inches) and add 2 inches (for a total of 6 inches). For each boot, fold the felt in half, and cut the piece to arrive at the desired height and width (22 inches and 12 inches, respectively, in our example). Measure, mark and draw a line across the folded felt, 5½ inches up from the bottom. Make a mark on this line the distance of the ankle measurement from the folded edge (6 inches in our example). On the bottom edge of the felt, mark a point 2 inches from the folded edge and then another one 2 inches past that. Draw a line from the top corner of the raw edge to the 6-inch mark, and from this mark to the second mark on the bottom edge. Draw another line from the 6-inch line at the folded edge to the first mark on the bottom. Cut felt along these lines. Stitch a ¼-inch seam along the felt edge from the ankle line to a point 4 inches from the top. Turn boot right side out. Sew the cuff seam to the top. Fold down cuff. To wear, remove shoe, slide boot over leg with seam to back, put shoe back on, pull boot flaps under bottom of shoe and tape flaps together.

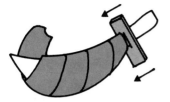

To make the fierce-looking cutlass worn in the pirate's sash, trace a pattern on cardboard and cut out. Cut a 1½-by-4-inch cardboard blade guard, and make a slit in the center to slide over the handle. Tape guard to blade at base of handle. Color handle and guard with felt-tip marking pen. Wrap the blade with aluminum foil.

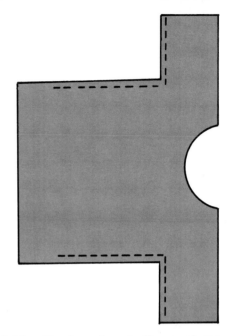

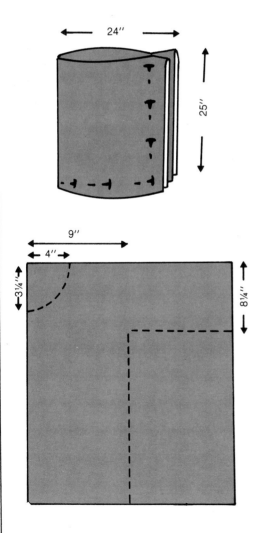

**Making the American Indian costume**

This consists of cotton fabric. For a boy or girl approximately 5 feet tall, cut a piece of cotton fabric 48 inches wide by twice the desired length of the blouse (in our example, 25 inches doubled = 50 inches). Fold the long dimension in half, with right sides together. Fold in half along the other dimension, making the folded piece 24 by 25 inches. Pin layers together around edges to hold in place, with folded edges at left and top. Mark a point along the left fold 3¼ inches below the top edge. Mark a point along the top fold 4 inches from the left edge. Cut out curve between the two marks. Mark a point at the top fold 9 inches from the left edge, and another point at the bottom edge 9 inches from the left edge. Draw a line between these points. Along this line, mark a point 8¼ inches below the top fold. Mark another point along the right edge 8¼ inches below the top fold. Draw a line connecting these two points. Place several pins just inside these lines to hold the layers together. Cut along lines to form blouse. Remove pins and unfold. Sew together sides and arms of blouse, using a ¼-inch seam. Do not sew bottom 4 inches of side seams. Turn blouse right side out.

To make the fringe, mark a line ⅜ inch from

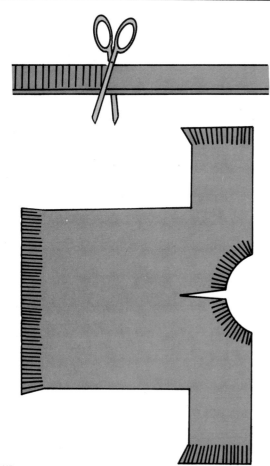

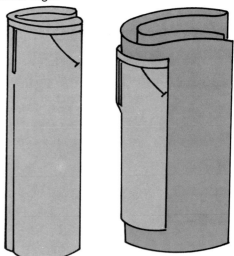

to the top of the trousers. Cut out the material. With right sides together, sew each leg together up to crotch marks, allowing a ¼-inch seam. Sew around the crotch seam between front and back waistlines. Fold over 1 inch at top and sew a casing, leaving a small opening. Cut a piece of ¾-inch elastic the size of the wearer's waist and thread through the casing. Sew ends of the elastic together and close the casing with slip stitches. Turn pants right side out. Trim the bottoms of the legs with felt fringe or cut fringe directly from trouser legs.

the edge of the 1½-inch felt strip. With scissors, make cuts from the edge to this line, spacing the cuts approximately 2¼ inches apart. Make a 2¼-inch-deep slit in the middle of the front neck opening of the blouse. Cut pieces of fringe to fit around the neck opening, sleeve cuffs and bottom of the blouse. Pin fringe in place on the blouse, then sew.

Use a pair of trousers belonging to the person who will wear the costume as a pattern for making the Indian pants; fold the trousers in half with one leg on top of the other. Using 1 yard of cloth 48 inches wide, fold the material in half across the 26-inch width, then fold it in half again in the same direction. This will give you four 12-inch layers. Pin the material around the edges. Place the trousers on the folded fabric, with the front edge of the trousers along the double-folded edge of fabric. Mark the outline of the trousers. Make a mark for the location of the crotch. Add 1 inch

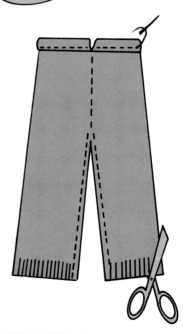

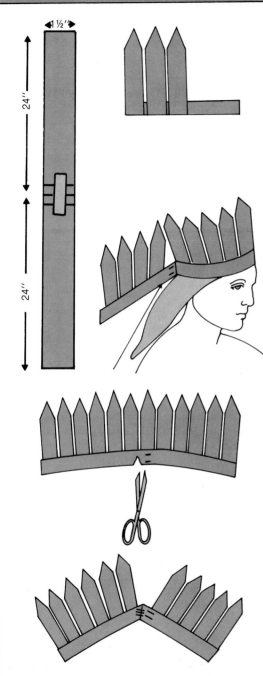

flush with the bottom of the band, with approximately ⅜ inch between feathers. Cut triangles and circles out of the red and blue posterboard, and glue to front of headband in a symmetrical design. Wrap headband around the wearer's head, with the middle of the headband in the center of the forehead. Fit snugly and staple the two sides of the headband together in the back. Notch the bottom of the headband behind the staples, leaving approximately ⅜ inch of board at the top. Pull down end of headband so that it hangs down the wearer's back. Staple together notched area.

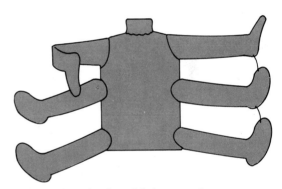

### Assembling the bumblebee costume

This dramatic outfit is ideal for fantasy plays. It is worn with yellow or black tights. Sew one yellow knee sock over each armhole of the turtleneck shirt for sleeves (if the wearer's arms are longer than the socks, cut out the toes for hand holes). Stuff the two remaining pairs of socks with polyester or rags. Sew open ends to sides of shirt for bumblebee legs. Tie outer ends of legs on each side together with thread or fishing line and connect to elbows so that they will move in unison when the actor moves his arms.

Draw wing pattern on the 24-inch-by-24-inch illustration board and cut out. Decorate wings with yellow and black felt-tip pens. Poke two holes about 2 inches apart through the center of the wings. Thread a length of black string or ribbon through the holes. Place wings on wearer's back and tie string or ribbon in front of his chest. Hold string in place by pinning in the front and the back.

The war bonnet is made of posterboard: brown for the headband, yellow and red for the feathers and red and blue for the decorations. Cut two strips of brown posterboard 1½ inches wide by 24 inches long and tape together to make one long strip. Cut sixteen feathers out of the red and yellow posterboard. Glue feathers to back of headband,

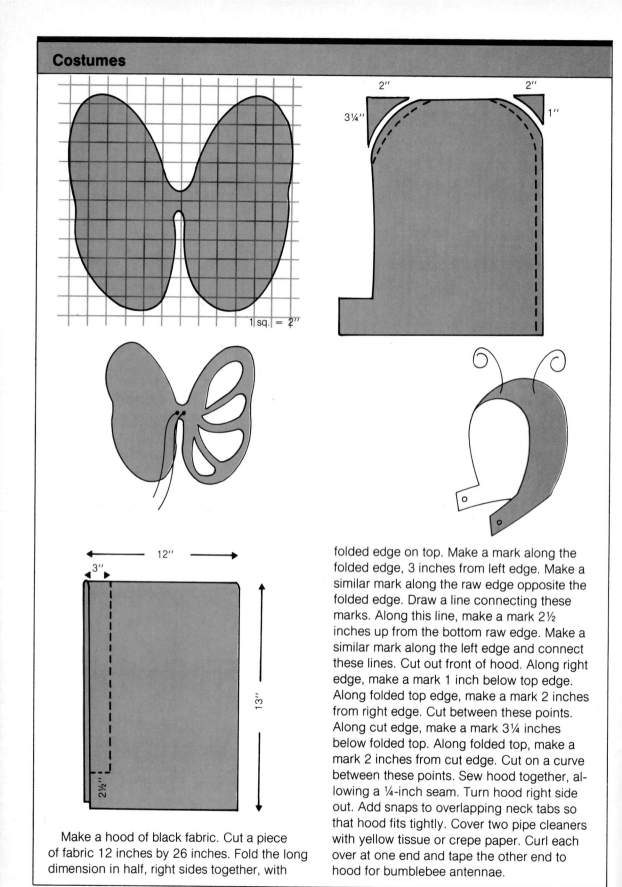

1 sq. = 2"

2"  2"

3¼"  1"

12"

3"

13"

2½"

Make a hood of black fabric. Cut a piece of fabric 12 inches by 26 inches. Fold the long dimension in half, right sides together, with folded edge on top. Make a mark along the folded edge, 3 inches from left edge. Make a similar mark along the raw edge opposite the folded edge. Draw a line connecting these marks. Along this line, make a mark 2½ inches up from the bottom raw edge. Make a similar mark along the left edge and connect these lines. Cut out front of hood. Along right edge, make a mark 1 inch below top edge. Along folded top edge, make a mark 2 inches from right edge. Cut between these points. Along cut edge, make a mark 3¼ inches below folded top. Along folded top, make a mark 2 inches from cut edge. Cut on a curve between these points. Sew hood together, allowing a ¼-inch seam. Turn hood right side out. Add snaps to overlapping neck tabs so that hood fits tightly. Cover two pipe cleaners with yellow tissue or crepe paper. Curl each over at one end and tape the other end to hood for bumblebee antennae.

# Makeup

In the professional theater, application of makeup is an art, but to the amateur actor, it is a large part of the fun of partaking in a theatrical production. Makeup helps the actor take on the appearance of the character being portrayed on the stage. Convincing makeup persuades the audience and the other actors to react to the character, rather than to the actor. Effective makeup can also make you the star attraction at a costume party or win you the prize on Halloween. Children love to use makeup, too, for playacting. For most amateur productions or just for fun, ordinary cosmetics are quick and more than adequate.

Materials: shades of face powder; lipsticks in shades of pink and red; rouge; eye shadow in blue, green, gray and white; eyebrow pencils; false eyelashes; mascara; flesh-colored tape; and talcum powder or cornstarch to make gray hair. Other items for special effects include old mops, rug yarn, wool, pipe tobacco and spirit gum.

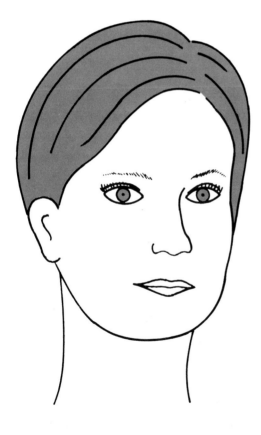

## Applying makeup

A common error, among both professionals and amateurs, is to apply theatrical makeup like everyday beauty makeup. Remember that the makeup is not intended to bring out your own good points, but to make you appear to be someone else. If, as a lovely young lady, you can succeed in completely transforming yourself into an old woman or a rag doll, then you can be proud of your makeup job.

Another frequent error is to apply too much makeup. This not only creates a problem of believability, but the weight of heavy makeup makes it difficult for you to vary your facial expressions. Experiment with your makeup and practice putting it on and wearing it for a length of time.

## Using cosmetics

Basic cosmetics are used as follows: face powder (light, medium, dark) to remove facial shine; lipstick (light, medium, dark shades of red and pink) to change lip lines; rouge to highlight cheekbones; eyebrow pencil to darken eyebrows (all but the darkest, bushiest eyebrows usually disappear in the strong stage lighting) and to draw wrinkles and character lines; white and gray eye shadow spread below and in corners of eyes to exaggerate the eye size; blue eye shadow spread under

the eyes to give a haggard look; green eye shadow around the eyes to give a sinister expression; and mascara and false eyelashes to accent eyes and eyelashes. Flesh-colored tape is also helpful to pull skin outward and upward to change facial expression.

## Becoming an old person

Makeup will vary according to the person wearing it as well as to the character being portrayed, but the techniques are basically the same. In general, try to follow the contours of your face. For example, to become an older person, sit in front of the mirror and wrinkle your forehead, purse your lips, suck in your

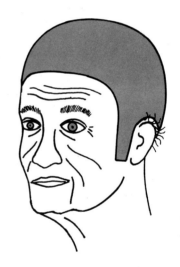

cheeks and tuck in your chin. Then use eyebrow pencil to draw the lines where the wrinkles occur. Use rouge on the cheeks, to make them appear sunken; deepen the eye sockets with gray eye shadow. To make a man bald, paint a tank swim cap the color of his head and cut out ear holes. For gray hair, brush cornstarch or talcum powder into the hair; don't forget to gray the eyebrows, too, as well as a mustache or beard. In portraying a historical or fictional character, study a picture or drawing of the character and copy the strongest features.

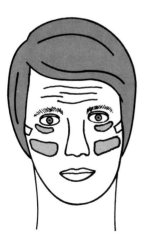

## Making a clown face

To create a clown face, begin by patting white highlighter cream on your face, leaving blank spaces on your cheeks. If you rub the highlighter in, most of the color will fade. To

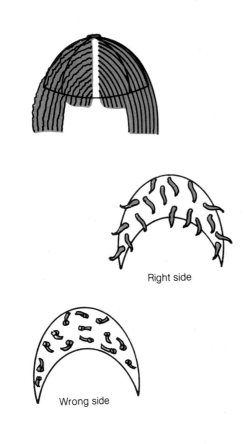

Right side

Wrong side

achieve the best effect, treat your face like an Impressionist painting and use your fingertips like paintbrushes to dot the color over the surface of your face. Next, draw solid circles on your cheeks with lipstick and use the eyebrow pencil to exaggerate eyebrows and to draw a smile. Then, don a wig.

## Making a rag doll face

Lots of fun and simple, too, the rag doll face requires only white highlighter, red lipstick and an eyebrow pencil. As with the clown face, begin by patting the white highlighter (or a *very* light makeup base) over your entire face, excluding your nose. Be sure to cover your eyebrows well. (White powder may be helpful here.) Outline your nose with the eyebrow pencil and draw semicircular eyebrows high on your forehead, lower eyelashes high on your cheekbones, and an exaggerated smile curving upward from the corners of your mouth. The last step is to color your lips and fill in the outlined area of your nose with red lipstick. To complete your image, do your hair in a multitude of tiny braids to create the effect of yarn hair. (Try looping a few braids and pinning them up for a comic, rag doll look.) If your hair is short, set it in tight curls. Or you can make yourself a wig.

## Making wigs

Wigs can be made of many materials. For a clown or a rag doll, dye an old but clean mop a bright color and tie onto the head with string. For a more elaborate wig, sew wool, twine or raffia to the crown of an old hat, or poke holes in a swimming cap and pull pieces of wool, rug yarn or raffia through the holes. Tape bits of dyed wool or twine to the face for mustaches, beards and sideburns, or draw them on the face with eyebrow pencil or burnt cork. For beards and sideburns, first draw outlines, then fill in. For a rough, unshaven appearance, apply pipe tobacco to your face with spirit gum.

The right makeup, properly applied, lets you be just about anyone you want to be.

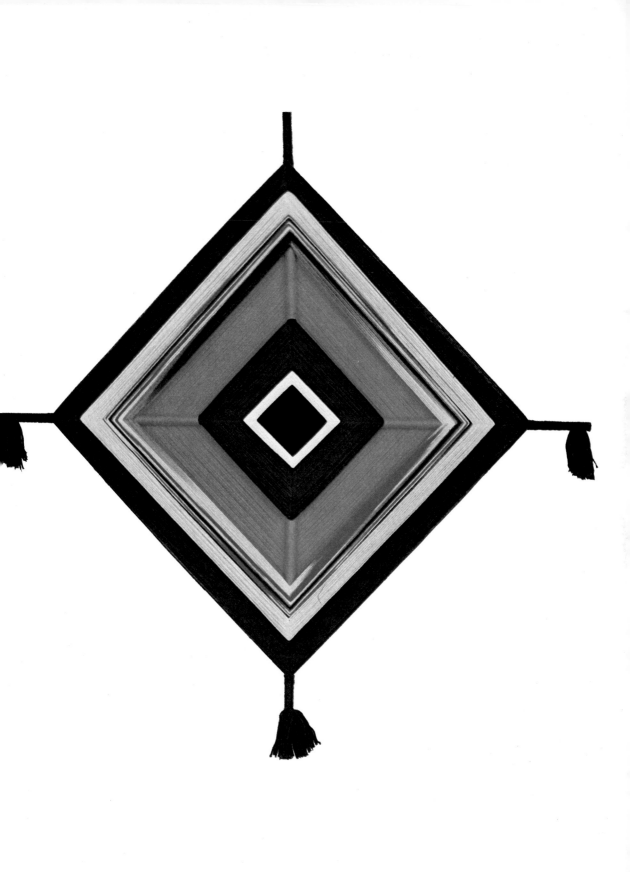

# Ojo de Dios

This colorful wall hanging, inspired by the Mexican *Ojo de Dios,* is relatively simple to make by weaving yarn around two dowels joined at the center axis. For the Huichol Indians who live in the Sierra Madre mountains in west-central Mexico, the *Ojo de Dios* (Eye of God) is a religious symbol, used to petition for luck and good fortune, and to secure good health and long life for children. It is the eye through which the eye of God will see the supplicant. The Huichols make the hanging 3 feet across in five basic colors: red (representing courage); yellow (for wisdom); blue (for beauty); green (for love); and rainbow colors (for happiness). Free-standing, smaller versions of the "eye" are made by these Indian craftsmen specifically for export and for the tourist markets in Mexico City and in the boutiques of Mexico's Gold Coast resorts. These unusual miniatures make charming party favors.

Materials: two 3-foot lengths of ¼-inch-diameter dowels; one skein (4ounces) each of black, white and three different colored yarns; household glue; sharp penknife or small saw; tape measure; scissors; and a 1-by-4-inch piece of cardboard.

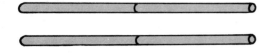

Measure and mark the midpoint on each dowel.

Put the dowels together to ascertain tight fit. Take them apart and put a drop of glue into one of the notches and fit the dowels at right angles to each other. This is very important. Allow dowels to dry.

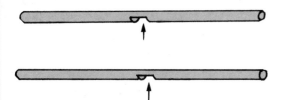

**Making dowel axis**
Using the penknife or small saw, carve a notch ½ inch wide and ¼ inch deep at the midpoint of each dowel.

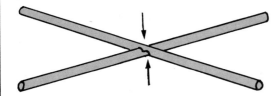

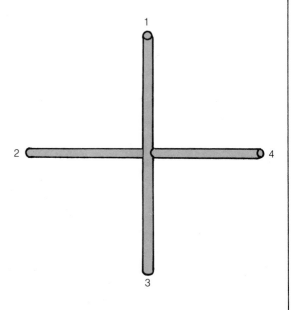

Number each of the dowels counterclockwise. This will make winding the yarn easier.

# Ojo de Dios

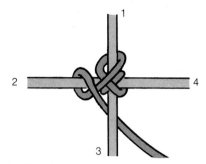

## The starting knot
Using the black yarn, tie a tight knot across the joint of the dowels, with the knot at the back. Wind the yarn clockwise around dowel 1, stretch the yarn to dowel 2 and wind clockwise, stretch the yarn to dowel 3 and so on.

## Weaving the black pupil
Start with dowel 1 in your left hand, stretch the yarn to dowel 2 with your right hand, transfer dowel 2 to your left hand and wind the yarn around it using your right hand, stretch the yarn to dowel 3 and so on. As you wind, the "eye" will be turning in a clockwise direction. After six or eight winds you will notice the basic diamond-shape pattern emerging. Keep the yarn taut while weaving around staves and be sure yarn strands do not overlap.

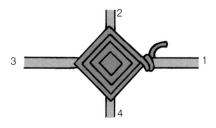

## Finishing the pupil
Keep winding the black yarn until the diamond pattern measures 3 inches across. To finish this part of the hanging, put a drop of glue on the back of dowel 1 and wind the yarn through the glue twice, holding the yarn in place until the glue sets. Snip the yarn off 1 inch below the glue spot, leaving a tail.

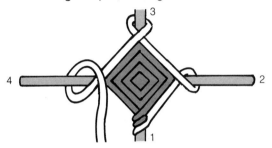

## Weaving the white iris
Using the white yarn, tie a tight knot around dowel 1 right over the glue spot. Make a half wind around the dowel and stretch the yarn to dowel 2, wind clockwise tightly and stretch to dowel 3 and so on. As you wind the white yarn, cover the tail of the black yarn left hanging from the glue spot. Keep winding until the second diamond forms and the white band of yarn is about ½ inch wide. Close the white section as instructed for the black. This completes the pupil (black) and iris (white) of the *Ojo de Dios*.

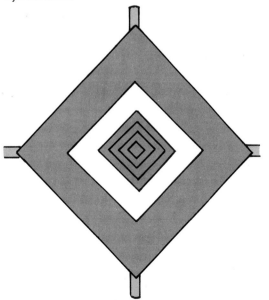

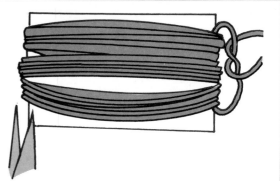

### Completing the eye

To complete the rest of the "eye," repeat the winding and tying process as directed for the black and white parts, using two to three other colored yarns. Hangings of this size usually contain between three and five colors. For additional variety, alternate wide and narrow bands of color.

As the yarn is added to the "arms" of the hanging, the diamond pattern will get wider and wider expanding along the dowels and filling the spaces between them. Remember to wind the yarn tightly so it won't unravel. When the dowels are completely covered with the exception of the last 3 inches, close off the last band.

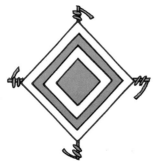

### Finishing corners

To complete the hanging, cover the last exposed part of the dowels with yarn, winding the yarn evenly around each dowel. Use either the same color yarn or a contrasting color for the last band. Then make three tassels (see below), and tie one to each of three dowels, about 1 inch from the end. For the fourth arm, make a 1-inch loop, using the same color yarn used for winding the last 3 inches of the dowel, and tie it around the dowel about 2 inches from the end. This loop is for hanging the piece.

### Making tassels

To make the tassels, use the same yarn used to wind the dowel endings. Cut a 4-inch piece of yarn and place it along the 1-inch side of the 1-by-4-inch piece of cardboard and, using the remaining yarn, wind it 40 times around the cardboard. Tie the 4-inch piece of yarn at the top of the cardboard into a double knot, then cut the yarn along the bottom of the cardboard.

### Variations

There are a number of variations on the above instructions. Use dowels of smaller diameter and shorter length to make smaller hangings, or vary the design of the "eye" by weaving the yarn around the dowels in different ways.

Instead of winding all the bands in a clockwise direction, alternate by weaving one band of colored yarn counterclockwise, creating one band that runs under rather than over the dowels.

**Petal patterns**

Wind yarn around dowel 1 and 3, skipping 2 and 4, then alternate. Wind yarn around 2 and 4, skipping 1 and 3. This creates a petal shape and leaves an open space between dowels to see through. Weaving this way uses much more yarn, and bends dowels, giving a 3-dimensional appearance to the "eyes". The

Alternate winding dowels 1 and 3 clockwise and 2 and 4 counterclockwise, to create an over-and-under pattern.

petal pattern must be done immediately after the iris part of the eye, and can be made 4 or 5 inches high before returning to the usual method of winding all four dowels. To hang, run a length of yarn from either dowel 1 to 3 or dowel 2 to 4, to provide more support for the heavier hanging.

# Dough whimsies

Sculpturing with dough is similar to working with modeling clay. The dough, specially prepared with flour, water and salt, is colored, rolled, then cut and twisted or shaped into a variety of forms. The sculptures are baked and then lacquered to insure a degree of permanency. These baked dough whimsies are for display only and are not edible.

Materials: 4 cups of unsifted flour; 1 cup of salt; 1½ cups of lukewarm water; a large mixing bowl and spoon; a roll of aluminum foil; a large cookie sheet; a rolling pin; an oven; several paper clips or hairpins; clear shellac or clear water-base acrylic; a ½-inch bristle paintbrush; a variety of food colorings or opaque acrylics; and an assortment of cookie cutters, tongue depressors, shells, butter knives, tools, and other implements which will add unusual textures to the surface of the dough shapes.

### Preparing dough
Preheat oven to 350 degrees Fahrenheit. To prepare the dough, place 4 cups of unsifted flour, 1 cup of salt, and 1½ cups of lukewarm water into a large mixing bowl. Mix the ingredients well with a spoon for five minutes. The consistency of the mixture should be pliable (do not allow the dough to become soft and flat). Place a large sheet of aluminum foil on a flat countertop. Remove the dough from the bowl and proceed to knead it by repeatedly drawing out and pressing the mixture together. To color the dough, divide the dough, cutting into as many sections as the number of colors desired. Add food coloring to the dough, kneading each separately. Set aside.

### Shaping the dough
Use a rolling pin to flatten the colored dough into circular or rectangular sheets, approximately ¾ of an inch thick. Cut individual shapes from the dough with a butter knife or with a cookie cutter to form a flower, fish,

clown face or whatever the imagination dictates. To create a basket, a frame for a small mirror or cylindrical container, cut strips of dough and build these objects with the flat or rolled dough strips, twisting or coiling the dough.

To build a relief, moisten both flat sides to be joined and press together firmly with fingers. Attach rolled balls of various sizes or coils to increase the height of the surface. Also use fingers to push and pull the dough or use kitchen household utensils to create definite lines and features.

### Drying and finishing
For sculptures to be hung on a wall, push a

bent hairpin or paper clip into the middle of the top edge of the piece to act as a hook. Paint diluted food coloring directly on the shape before it is placed in the oven. Place each sculpture on a cookie sheet that has been lined with aluminum foil. Bake the sculptures at 350 degrees Fahrenheit for approximately one hour. Pieces that are thicker than ¾ of an inch will require longer baking time. When one hour has elapsed, remove the cookie sheet from the oven and set on a rack to cool. Use shellac, clear acrylics, or opaque acrylics to brush on the surface of the sculpture. This last step is important to insure the permanence of the art forms.

# Bread flowers

Soft fresh bread is transformed into sculpturing dough with a few drops of glycerin and glue. The dough can be shaped into flowers or into decorative pieces from pop art to traditional objects. Color is added to the dough before sculpturing. To make the miniature flowers illustrated, use a wide variety of colors if you plan to create a floral centerpiece. You may decide to make a purple cow or a turquoise fish once you get a feel for sculpturing in this medium. Children and young adults usually outperform their elders, but don't let this inhibit you.

Materials: three slices of white bread; a small amount of glycerin; white glue; a box of small, thin black hairpins; a can of clear varnish spray or clear acrylic spray; ¾-inch-thick foamed plastic about 10 inches square; tempera paints in as many different colors as desired for the flowers; small plastic bags, as many as the number of colors; plastic foliage; floral clay; and a small planter.

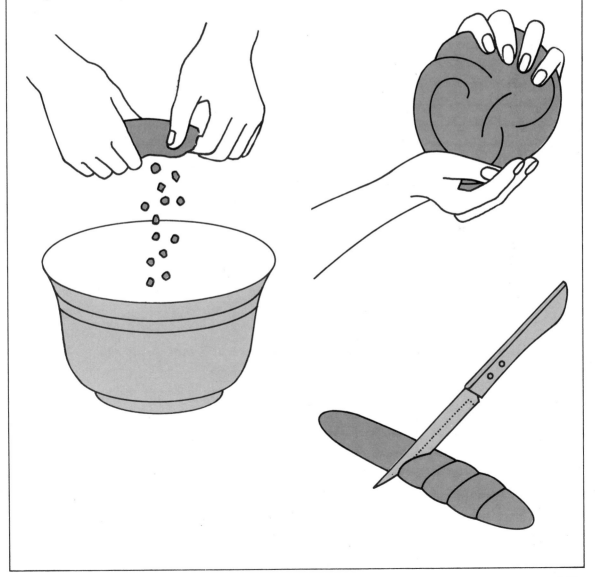

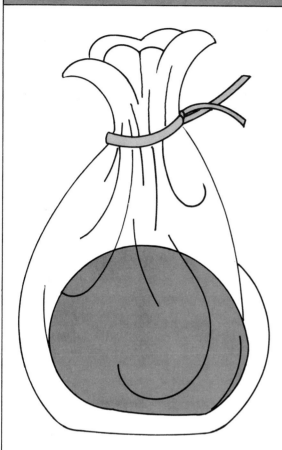

### Preparing dough for sculpture

Remove the crusts from the slices of bread.
Crumble the bread into a mixing bowl. Add
three drops of glycerin and one ounce (two
tablespoons) of white glue. Knead into a ball,
then flatten out dough into a thick, flat roll.
Cut the roll so there is one piece for each
color desired. Knead each piece into a ball.
Place each one into a separate plastic bag,
close the bags, and put them into the refrigerator. This will help keep the bread dough soft
and pliable, and prevent it from drying out.

### Coloring the dough

Take one of the bread balls out of the plastic
bag and mix in one color of tempera paint, a
teaspoon at a time, until the desired shade is
attained. Place the bread back into its plastic
bag and put into the refrigerator. Repeat the
coloring process with all the bread balls.

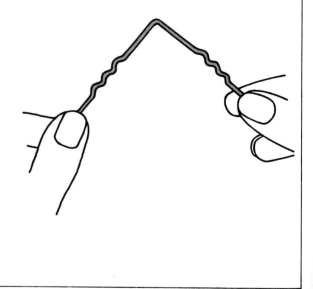

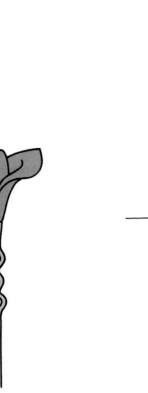

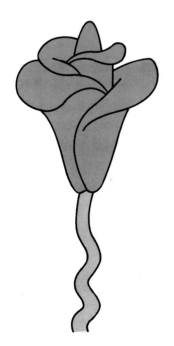

### Creating flowers

Straighten the hairpins. Take out one of the colored bread balls, and remove a small pinch of dough from the ball. Roll it between your fingers and place it on the tip of a hairpin. This is the pistil, the center of the flower, to which the petals are attached. Pinch off four more pieces of dough, slightly larger than the first, and roll them to the size of tiny peas. Flatten one of these small balls between your fingers, then wrap it around the pistil on the hairpin, folding the top back slightly to make the first petal. Flatten and place the second petal opposite the first, again folding it back. Place the third and fourth petals at right angles to the first two. When the flower is completed, push the end of the hairpin, which is the flower stem, into the foamed plastic to dry.

### Varying the bouquet

Continue to form flowers in the same manner, working with one color before going on to another. Vary the sizes slightly to add interest to the arrangement. Mix colors (a pistil of one color, petals of another), but make sure you wash your hands thoroughly between colors. Do not let the flowers touch one another during the drying process. Allow them to dry at least eight hours.

### Arranging the permanent display

Spray the flowers with acrylic or varnish. (This can be done while they are still in the foamed plastic.) Let them dry completely. Then place floral clay in a flowerpot or planter and set the flowers in place, arranging them with the plastic foliage.

# Batik scarfs

Striking silk scarf originals can be made by the batik process. Read carefully the batik instructions in Batik place cards and check the basic materials needed.

Materials: an old picture frame or canvas stretcher 15 inches by 40 inches; or make one with four lengths of ¾-inch stock lumber (two lengths 15 inches and two lengths 40 inches); four wooden bars about 3 inches by 1¼ inches to brace each corner; a hammer; one dozen nails 1½ inches long; thumbtacks; a piece of silk 16 inches by 44 inches; a fine needle and thread; and dyes in desired tints and hues.

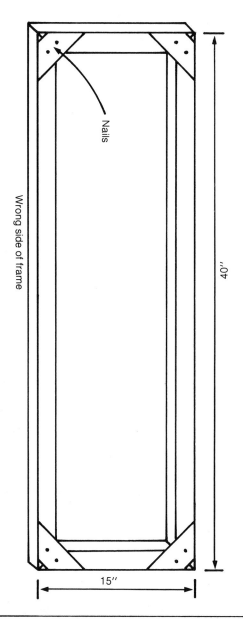

## Stretching and dyeing the silk

To make a frame from the four lengths of ¾-inch stock lumber, assemble them to form a rectangle, then nail a wooden bar in each

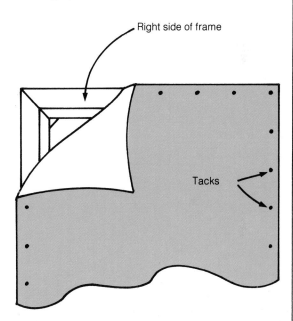

corner for support. Thumbtack material to the frame, stretching it evenly.

If scarf is large, wax one portion at a time. To achieve spattered effects, hold a white lighted household candle downward and let the wax drip on the fabric. Stamp other inter-

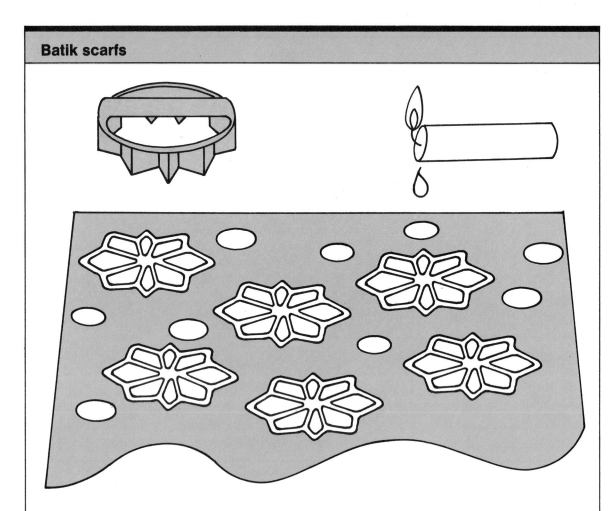

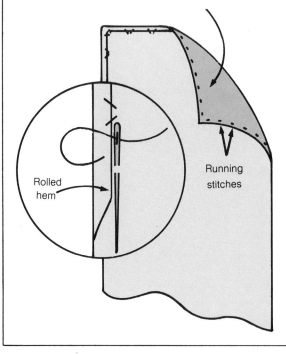

Right side

Running stitches

Rolled hem

esting motifs on the fabric by dipping cookie cutters or other kitchen tools in the wax and then holding them against the cloth. By pleating the fabric or folding it several times (forming a small rectangle), you can dip the corners and edges. Following the instructions for Batik place cards, proceed to dye.

## Completing the scarf

When you have completed dyeing the silk and it is dry, press it to remove the wax. Hem the edges with fine needle and thread. Roll under approximately ⅛ inch from the edge of the scarf (one section at a time) and sew running stitches along the entire outline of the scarf at ¼-inch intervals. These batik scarfs provide unusual fashion accents for sports clothes and high-styled ensembles, and they are distinctive as gifts for that someone special. Once you design and process a batik scarf, explore the other crafts utilizing this fascinating dye method.

# Bracelet and pendant

Jewelry crafting requires patience and an orientation in the metals most suitable to the different types of jewelry. There are numerous metals and alloys that are not prohibitive in cost, but gold, platinum, and silver are expensive. Purchase small quantities of several different metals with which to experiment. When choosing a metal for a project, remember that the specific characteristics of the metal will adapt more easily to certain techniques than to others, as noted below. Most metals are alloys. As the percentages of the components vary, the characteristics vary. Most alloys have been developed over years and centuries with the specific purpose of making certain characteristics available to metalworkers.

Since metals are heavy and can become uncomfortable, metal used in jewelry should be the thinnest piece that will retain its shape without bending under normal wearing and handling conditions.

A few of the many available alloys are described here, with some of their characteristics:

*Aluminum* is soft enough to shape, yet sufficiently hard for application of designs by chasing or engraving; stippled or textured backgrounds may also be applied with a hammer. An especially light and strong alloy, called duralumin, is made with 4 percent copper and small amounts of magnesium, manganese, iron and silicon.

*Brass* possesses a golden-yellow color, and can be pierced, hammered, chased and engraved. Brass is an alloy of copper and zinc, the zinc varying from 10 to 40 percent for varying degrees of hardness.

*Copper,* as a craft metal, offers the most possibilities; all kinds of shaping and decorative processes can be employed.

*Bronze,* which is harder than brass or copper, can be hammered, pierced, and etched. Bronze is an alloy of 90 percent copper and 10 percent tin.

*Nickel silver,* or German silver, which actually contains no silver, is an alloy of 18 percent nickel, 65 percent copper, and 17 percent zinc. It can be pierced, etched, or hammered. It closely resembles silver, and is a good working metal for beginners. Note, however, that it is not suitable for jewelry that is to be worn against the skin.

*Silver* is very soft when in a pure (fine) state; however, it is alloyed with copper to harden it, thus making it highly adaptable and easily manipulated. Silver is an excellent choice for the more experienced worker.

The delicate pendant and bracelet illustrated are made using techniques of piercing and sawing. These techniques are used to remove areas of metal, resulting in an openwork effect.

Materials: a sheet of metal (18 gauge); cleaning solution; 5-inch jeweler's saw; hand drill; jeweler's files; rouge and polisher; tongs; tracing paper; and rubber cement.

## Bracelet and pendant

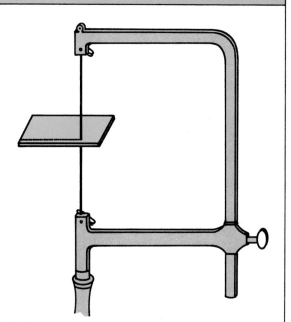

### Tracing design on metal

Clean the metal with fine steel wool and cleaning solution. On paper, trace the actual-size patterns below, shading the areas to be cut out. With rubber cement, affix the tracing to the metal sheet.

### Cutting out shape

Support the metal on a bench pin, then, using the jeweler's saw (held in a vertical position), cut the shape out along the outline. Saw exactly on the line to eliminate bumps, which require correction with a file. Make quick, short strokes with the saw, using about 2 inches of the blade length.

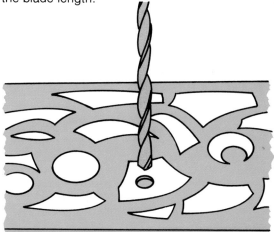

### Cutting out design

Drill a hole in each area to be removed; make sure to use a drill-bit larger than the saw blade.

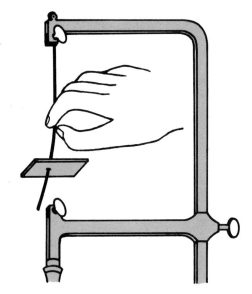

### Antiquing the pieces

Place each piece in a saucer containing a solution of about four parts powdered potassium and two parts lukewarm water (the solution should cover the piece). After fifteen minutes, remove the pieces with tongs. Buff only those areas of the piece you wish to shine to offset the black antiquing. Attach a jump ring around and through the hole illustrated, and thread a purchased chain or thin leather strip through the jump ring.

Loosen the saw blade from the frame and insert it (with the teeth pointing downward) into the hole drilled. Replace the saw-blade end in the frame and tighten the screws. Carefully cut out the shape, turning the metal with the left hand while cutting. Repeat this procedure for each area to be removed.

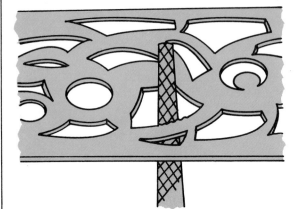

When the sawing is complete, remove the tracing paper and file rough edges. Curve the bracelet and pendant by shaping them over a dapping block or rolling pin. Then buff the pieces, using rouge and polisher, polishing cream, or treated polishing cloth. This finishing touch imparts a lovely shine, as well as a professional look to the jewelry.

After getting a feel for metal working, try your hand at simply designed rings, earrings, cuff links, collar-type necklaces, belt buckles, hair ornaments or a set of matching buttons for a blazer.

# Silkscreen T-shirt

Silkscreen is a printmaking technique similar to stenciling, in which a piece of silk or other fine mesh screen is stretched over and stapled to a wooden frame, and a stencil affixed to the screen for printing. The fabric acts as a support for keeping all the integral parts of the stencil in place without any of the ties or connectors that the older type of stencil requires. Silk is ideal because it has the right degree of porosity and will not sag or warp with repeated use. Fine muslin, organdy, and even nylon can be substituted for short-run projects.

Materials: T-shirt; silkscreen inks, known as process oils; a squeegee to apply them; thin white bond paper; a pencil; ruler; T-square; compass; stencil knife or razor blade; solvent; and a silkscreen frame. The silkscreen equipment and materials are available at art supply stores. Frames come ready-made or in precut pieces with hardware for assembling. An old picture frame can also be used for this purpose. To convert the frame, you need a simple unadorned one that measures roughly 14 inches by 22 inches on the outside; a single strip of wood the thickness of the frame; a sheet of fiberboard several inches larger than the frame in both dimensions; a pair of hinges with removable pins; some masking tape; a piece of silk or muslin; a staple gun; some waterproof glue; shellac; and a piece of fine sandpaper.

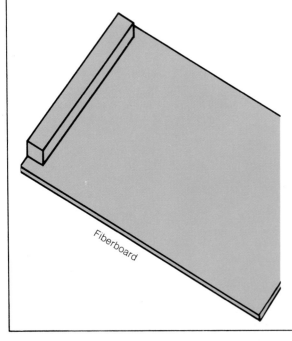

Fiberboard

### Assembling the frame

Cut a piece of wood the length of one of the short sides of the frame. With waterproof glue, fix the strip of wood along one of the short sides of the fiberboard. Allow to dry as directed on the label of the glue, until bonded.

Lay the frame on top of the fiberboard with a short side of the frame butted against the wood strip. Take two hinges with removable pins and place them along the joining (see illustration), so that one side of each hinge is squarely on the strip and the other on the frame. Position hinges approximately two inches from each end. Secure the hinges with screws. Give the frame a light sanding.

# Silkscreen T-shirt

Remove the hinge pins and detach the frame for easier handling. Cut a piece of silk or muslin that is 4 inches wider and 4 inches longer than the outside dimensions of the frame. Place the frame, hinged face down, on a table and center the fabric over the frame.

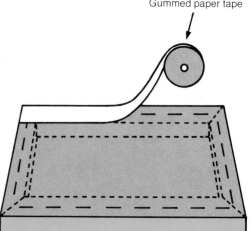

Gummed paper tape

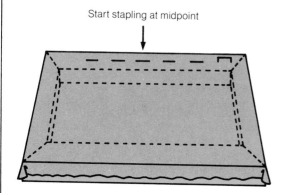

Start stapling at midpoint

Line up the fabric so that the threads run exactly parallel to the frame, and there are no gaps or wrinkles. Now, start stapling (or tacking) the fabric along one of the long sides. Begin in the middle and staple alternately on either side of the starting point until the corners are reached.

## Mounting fabric on frame

With one side completely fastened, stretch the fabric as tight as possible (be careful not to tear), from the opposite side. Staple this side as before, alternating on either side of the midpoint, watching that the silk remains straight on the frame. Stretch the third and fourth sides similarly. The fabric should be as taut as a drum head. Trim the excess fabric extending beyond the frame. Finish off the frame by covering the staples or tacks with strips of masking tape.

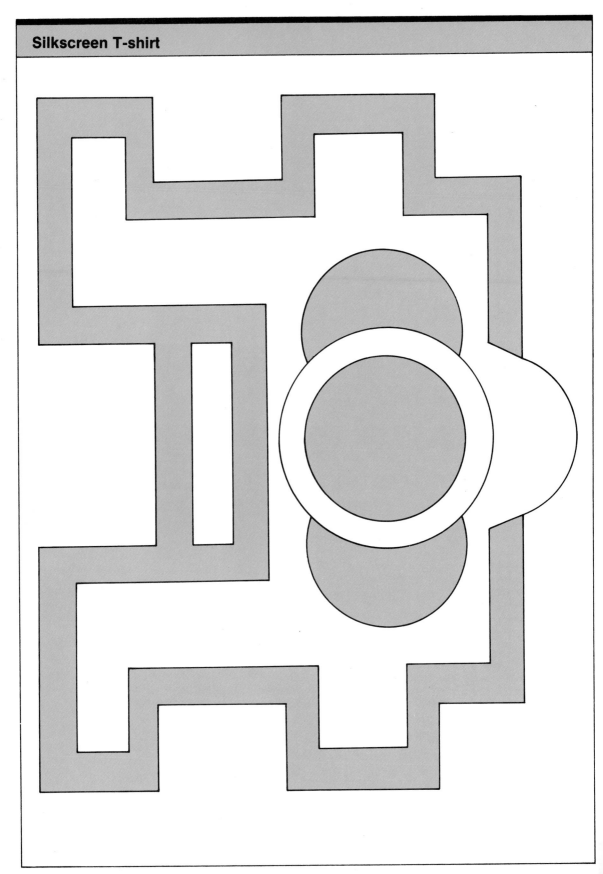

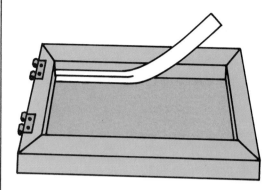

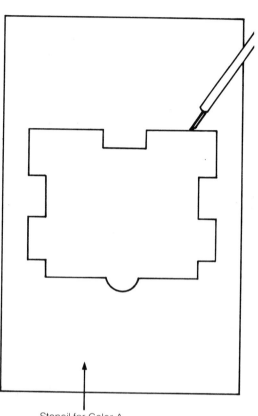

Stencil for Color A

### Waterproofing the silk on inside of frame

Turn the frame over so that the hinged face is up. Cut four strips of tape equal in length to the four inner sides of the frame. Place the strips of tape, folded in half, lengthwise, on the inside edges of the frame; with half of strip on the fabric and half on the wood. This will help hold the fabric and also keep paint from seeping under the frame during printing. Brush a coat of shellac or polyurethane over the tape to make it waterproof. If any shellac falls on the screen, wipe clean with solvent. Using household detergent and water, wash fabric clean of any sizing which might clog the mesh.

### Making the stencil

The stencil is a mask; the holes you cut in it will determine where the colored inks will print. A different stencil is required for each color to be printed. Before cutting the stencils, plan the design on a sheet of plain paper. The design must be smaller than the inside dimensions of the frame by at least an inch on all sides. Color the design as it is to appear on the finished T-shirt; determining the number of ink colors to be used. The example shown is printed in four colors, requiring four stencils. To create a geometric motif similar to the illustration, first draw a rectangle 8 inches wide by 6¾ inches high. With ruler, T-square, and compass (or the bottom of a glass), draw additional rectangles and circles. Color in the spaces as desired.

### Cutting stencils for each color

Cut as many sheets of paper as there are colors, to the exact size of the screen area. Center one of the sheets over the original drawing, tape down and trace the outline of Color A (the color which will be printed first). Use drafting tools for exact results. Remove the sheet of paper and trace a different color stencil on each remaining sheet. You will then have a separate stencil for the printing of each color. Because the inks are opaque, you can superimpose one color over another without bleeding the colors. In the case of the design shown, the green circle in the center will be printed on top of the magenta, eliminating the need to block out an area for the green on the magenta stencil. Cut out the stencil for Color A, running the knife along the lines you have drawn. Set the remaining sheets of paper aside.

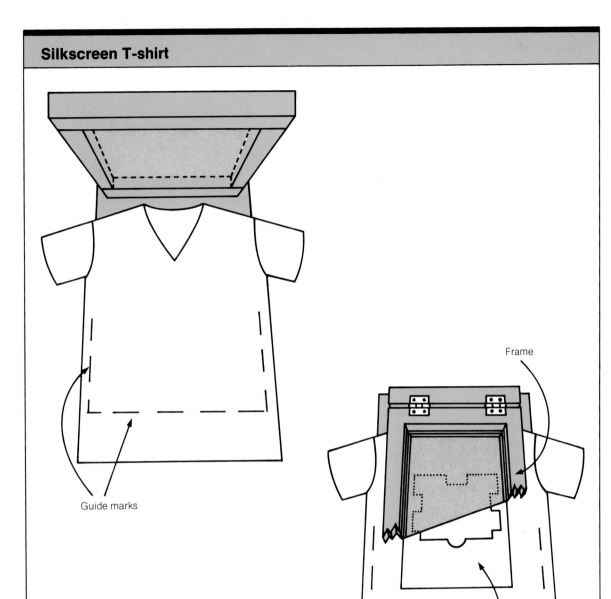

Guide marks

Frame

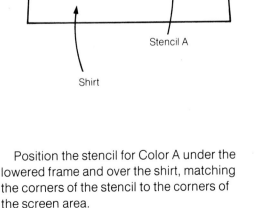

Stencil A

Shirt

## Aligning stencils on screen

Attach the screen to the base, inserting the hinge pins. Take the T-shirt, iron if wrinkled, and lay it under the frame so that the stencil will print on the upper front of the shirt. Insert a sheet of cardboard inside the shirt to keep the ink from penetrating through to the back of it. The shirt should remain in the same position through the printing of all colors. With tailor's chalk or needle and thread, mark the sides and bottom of the shirt, indicating the edges of the fiberboard. These guide marks are essential to keep the shirt in position and thus insure proper registration (the precise aligning of color areas). If the shirt is smaller than the baseboard, mark the guides indicating the two edges of the shirt on the base.

Position the stencil for Color A under the lowered frame and over the shirt, matching the corners of the stencil to the corners of the screen area.

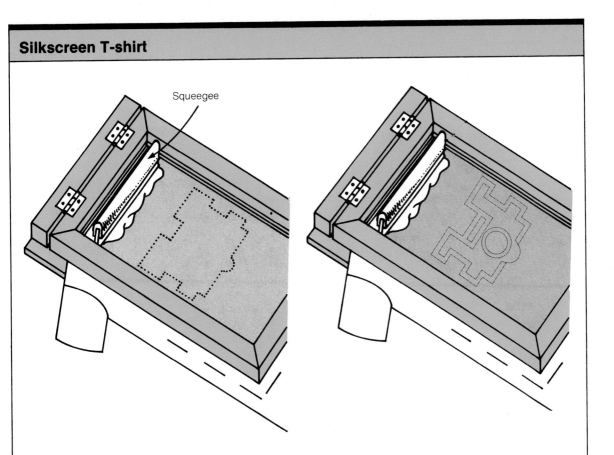

Squeegee

## Printing the design

Spoon out the ink for Color A along the hinged edge of the screen. When you pass the squeegee across the screen, the ink will adhere the stencil sheets to the underside. With the squeegee angled so that the edge of the rubber blade is on the screen, slowly draw the ink across the screen. Be careful to apply even pressure on the squeegee. At the opposite end of the screen, lift the squeegee over the ridge of ink and pull the ink back toward the starting point. The return trip should be done with enough pressure to clean the excess ink off the screen as you go.

Lift the screen and remove the hinge pins. Remove the stencil. While waiting for the ink to dry on the T-shirt, wash the screen with turpentine or some other solvent. Hold the screen up to the light to be sure it is entirely clean. Cut the stencil for Color B as previously described.

When you are sure the ink is dry on the T-shirt, attach the frame, position the stencil and apply the ink for Color B. Follow the printing steps explained for Color A and repeat for all other stencil colors until the entire design is executed.

To make several shirts of the same design, print them in sequence, so that all are stenciled, first in Color A, then Color B, and continue until all colors are applied. This will mean less-frequent changes of the stencil sheets.

# Silver neck ring and pendants

It is easy to create a simple neck ring made of sterling silver wire to display a treasured medallion or the handmade clay beads and pendant illustrated. Silver is sold by weight, therefore a piece such as this is quite inexpensive.

Materials: 7 feet of sterling silver wire (round, 14-gauge); a ball-point pen; a ball-peen hammer; a small pair of round-nosed pliers; wire cutter; and a fine-gauge jeweler's file. Also needed for the clay pieces: 1 cup of salt; ½ cup of cornstarch; ½ cup boiling water; food coloring; a plastic straw at least ¼ inch in diameter (or a pencil with the eraser removed from the metal end); aluminum foil or waxed paper; a cookie sheet; and a spatula.

## Making the neck ring

Before cutting the wire to the desired length, test the measurement around your neck with a length of string, allowing an extra 5 inches to make the two hooks that fasten the ring. For the neck ring illustrated, we cut a length 20 inches long.

If you have decided to use some large beads or a pendant that has a small jump ring that will not slip over the hooks after they are fashioned on the ends, these should be threaded on the rod before it is shaped. However, if you plan to make the clay beads and pendant illustrated, proceed as directed here.

Lay the wire rod on a metal or wooden surface. Using the ball-peen hammer, flatten out 2½ inches at each end of the rod.

Gently bend the rod in a circular motion, using both hands, so that it will conform to the shape of your neck. Work slowly so you can bend the rod into an almost perfect circle.

|←—2½″—→|

## Silver neck ring and pendants

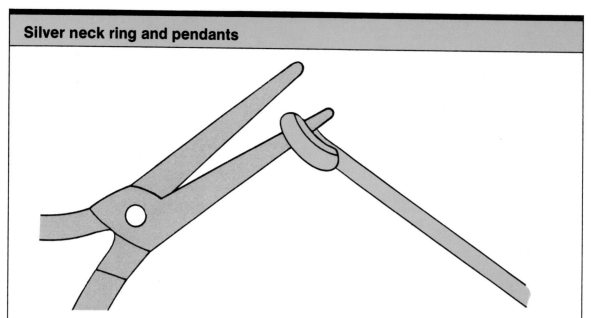

### Forming the hooks

With the pliers, bend one of the flat ends back so it is inside the circle. Bend the other flat end back on the outside of the circle. The two ends, held against each other by tension, latch together to hold the ring in place.

Use the file to round off and smooth the edges of each hook, working carefully. Place the hoop about your neck and latch the hooks together to check the fit. If necessary, adjust. Set the ring aside and make the clay beads and pendant.

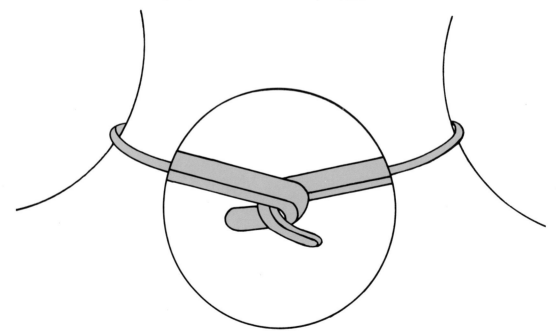

### Preparing the cornstarch clay

Mix the salt and cornstarch, add boiling water, and stir. Add the food coloring, a few drops at a time; the color of the clay will become a paler shade once it dries. When the mixture is cool enough to handle, knead it by hand until it is firm and not sticky. You may have to add a little more cornstarch.

### Forming the clay shapes

Roll the clay into a ball with your hands and place it on waxed paper or aluminum foil. Flatten the clay with the palm of your hand and then your fingers until you have a sheet of clay, ½ inch in thickness. Use a glass or empty juice can, about 3 inches in diameter, to cut out the large disk for the pendant. Use a straw or the metal end of a pencil with the eraser removed to cut out at least 9 clay disks, about ¼ inch in diameter.

### Drying the clay shapes

Line a cookie sheet with aluminum foil and, with a spatula, place the clay disks on the foil. Do not place the shapes too close to one another. Place in the oven at 350 degrees Fahrenheit to dry. When the tops appear to be dry, turn the disks over carefully with the spatula

### Forming the holes in disks

Use a piece of the silver wire to make holes in the disks. Insert the wire through the diameter of each of the small disks, as illustrated. Rotate the wire slightly to enlarge the hole so the wire does not fit snugly. This is done because the holes will shrink during the drying process and the wire must pass through these holes later.

Insert the wire through the large disk across its diameter. While the wire is in the clay, use small objects (paper clips or screwheads) to imprint a design on the top surface. When finished, remove the wire carefully.

and allow the other sides to dry. You may have to turn the pieces over a few times to be sure the clay is dry all the way through. Keep a close watch during this process. Remove disks from oven when you see that all the moisture is removed, but do not touch disks until they are cool.

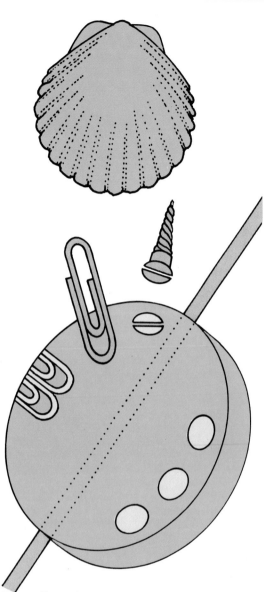

### Bending loops on each wire length

Use the pliers to form a loop at the unflattened end of each wire piece, as shown in the illustration. This loop should be large enough for the hooks of the neck ring to pass through, since these pieces are threaded on the ring. The wire pieces with the beads and pendant are threaded on the ring alternately with 30 unadorned wire lengths.

### Finishing the ring and pendants

On the remaining wire, measure off and mark 30 pieces about 1¼ inches in length. Cut with wire cutters. Flatten one end of each piece about ½ inch as instructed for the other wire pendants. Use the pliers to form a loop on the other end, large enough for the neck ring hooks to pass through.

Thread pendants on neck ring so the large pendant is at the center of the ring and the other beaded lengths are graduated in sizes on either side of the center pendant. Thread three unadorned wire pieces between each two beaded pendants.

### Threading clay shapes with wire

Cut the remaining silver wire into short lengths. Measure and mark the wire with a ball-point pen into the following lengths: one, 6 inches; two, 3 inches; two, 2½ inches; two, 2¼ inches; and two, 2 inches. Use wire cutters to cut pieces.

Using the ball-peen hammer, flatten one end of each piece to about ½ inch. This flattened end will keep the bead from slipping off.

Slip a small bead (disk) on each wire piece. On the 6-inch length, thread a small bead and then the large disk.

# Knitted shawl

Knitting needles and a ball of yarn are all the beginner needs when learning to knit. The most important fact that every potential knitter need know is that there are only two basic stitches in knitting. These are the knit stitch and the purl stitch. For this project, only the knit stitch is used. This triangular mohair shawl, which works up quickly on large needles, helps the novice to become familiar with casting stitches on the needle (to start any knitting project), with the knit stitch and with the technique of decorating a knitted edge with fringe.

Materials: 5 ounces of mohair yarn; a pair of No. 15 knitting needles; a crochet hook (any large size); and scissors.

## Casting on stitches

Begin by casting-on 4 stitches as follows: Unwind from the ball of yarn 4 inches or 1 inch for each stitch. Fold the yarn at this point, forming a loop, then pull another small loop through it. This is called a slip knit or slip loop. Using only one needle, held in the right hand, slip the loop on pointed end of needle and tighten by pulling one end of the yarn. Holding both strands of yarn in left hand, slide left thumb and forefinger between the two strands to form a triangle of yarn, with your thumb holding the yarn from the ball. Bringing the needle toward you, slip the point under the front strand of the loop on your thumb. Catch the strand of yarn on your forefinger with needle and draw it through the thumb loop. You have just cast the stitch on the needle. Now, slip the loop off your thumb and pull on yarn to tighten stitch. Repeat until there are 4 stitches on needle.

## Knitting first row

Knit row 1 as follows: hold needle with cast-on stitches in left hand, the other needle, or working needle, in your right. The knit stitch is worked with the yarn kept at the back of the work and brought forward for each stitch. With yarn wrapped over right forefinger and under middle finger, insert point of right needle, right to left, through front of first stitch on left needle. Loop yarn around point of right needle with forefinger (as for casting-on), and draw loop through stitch on left needle. Slip stitch you have just formed off left needle and onto right needle. As you knit, stitches should slide easily, neither tight nor loose. When you have knitted all the stitches from left needle to right,

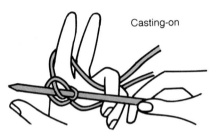

Casting-on

change needles so that the one holding the stitches is in your left hand, the empty needle in your right. Each time you start a new row, the needles should be in these positions.

## Knitting row 2 to the end

Start row 2 by increasing one stitch. To do this, knit twice into the first stitch by knitting as described above through the front loop, but before dropping stitch from left needle, knit another stitch on the same loop, this time inserting needle into the back of the stitch. You now have 2 stitches on right needle. Knit next 2 stitches. Increase last stitch on this row in the same manner as you added the stitch at the beginning of the row. You now have 6 stitches on your needle. With the empty needle in your right hand, start row 3 by increasing a stitch and knit as you did row 2. Each

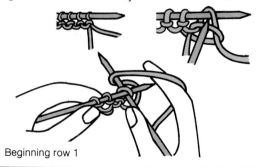

Beginning row 1

## Knitted shawl

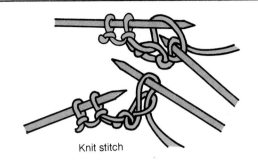

Knit stitch

come to last stitch. End off by cutting a 6-inch end of yarn and passing the cut end through the loop of the remaining stitch on the right needle, and pull snugly.

### Tying on the fringe

To make each fringe, cut 4 strands, each 10 inches long. Fold in half and attach to shawl. Pull through with crochet hook along one of the two shorter edges of shawl. Repeat at 1-inch intervals on these edges. With each 4 strands tie an overhand knot 1 inch away from shawl edge. Repeat for all fringes. To make second row of knots, take 4 strands from one knot and 4 from the adjacent one, and tie another overhand knot an inch below the first one. Repeat for all fringes. One group of 4 strands will be left free at each end. Then tie

consecutive row is knitted in the same way. Increase 1 stitch at the beginning and end of row, until you have 76 stitches on your needle. Then, increase 1 stitch at start and end of every other row, until you have 110 stitches on needle (or reach desired size). Then, knit one more row and do not add any stitches. To finish, bind off as follows: knit 2 stitches, then lift first stitch over second with tip of left needle and drop it off tip of right needle, leaving one stitch on right needle. Knit next stitch onto right needle and, with point of left needle, lift lower stitch on right needle over upper stitch and off tip of needle. Repeat until you

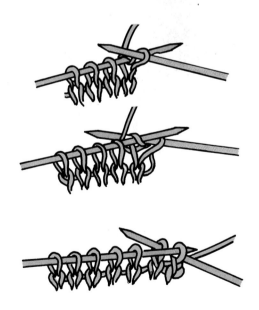

Knitting row 2

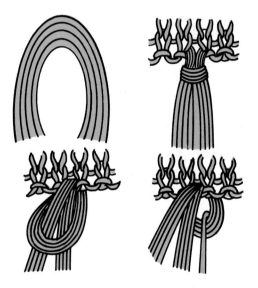

a third row of knots 1 inch below second row of knots. Start with the group of 4 strands left free at the right end of shawl and work across fringe tying knots in the same manner as the other two rows. Trim ends evenly. To finish, lay shawl out on a large towel or blanket and pin to size. Using a warm iron and damp press cloth, block by pressing carefully.

# Tie-dyed shirt

Tie dyeing is a marvelous way to turn ordinary monochromatic clothing, such as work shirts, T-shirts, cotton jackets, jeans and blouses into unique, multicolored garments. The technique is equally effective in creating colorful bedsheets, pillowcases and draperies. As the name implies, tie dyeing is achieved in two basic steps: the tying of the garment into knots, and the dyeing. Because the dye does not penetrate the knotted or tied fabric, the garment becomes randomly patterned with undyed patches on a dyed background. Cotton, rayon, nylon, silk, and other fabrics tie dye sucessfully. There are exceptions. Polyesters, acrylics, metallic-fiber fabrics, and fabrics treated to resist stains and wrinkles do not dye successfully with this technique.

One to three colors can be used but the lightest shade is dyed first, then progressively darker shades can be used. Keep in mind that you must tie off any area that is to remain white or a light shade, otherwise the darker shade will cover that area. Dyes will blend like paints to form other shades (e.g., red and blue produce purple; blue and yellow, green; red and yellow, orange), so you can produce a third shade with only two dye immersions.

For a more interesting effect, vary the size of the areas gathered. The larger the area sectioned off, the more white will be preserved. Sleeves can be gathered with rubber bands, knotted on themselves or both at once. Knot tightly. Gather the back of the shirt separately, for better control over the placement of the circles to achieve the effect desired.

Materials: a white shirt or blouse made of one of the acceptable fabrics; liquid or powdered dyes (light blue and navy blue were used here, but other compatible colors may be substituted); rubber bands in different colors and of assorted thicknesses and/ or string; a small quantity of noniodized salt; rubber gloves and an apron; a pot large enough to immerse the garment comfortably (glass, iron or enameled pots are recommended; aluminum or teflon-coated pans are not acceptable); another pot or bowl to carry the dyed garment between stove and basin; large spoon to stir the solution; and a plastic paint cloth or other disposable plastic sheeting to protect the work area (a large flat surface such as a kitchen counter).

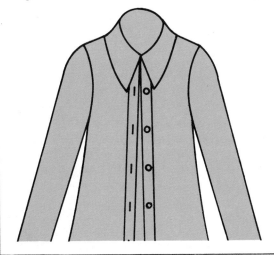

### Preparing garment for dyeing
Wash the shirt or blouse thoroughly in hot, soapy water to remove the sizing in a new garment and to make sure that a used garment is clean for dyeing. Allow to dry thoroughly since it is easier to tie knots tighter when the fabric is dry.

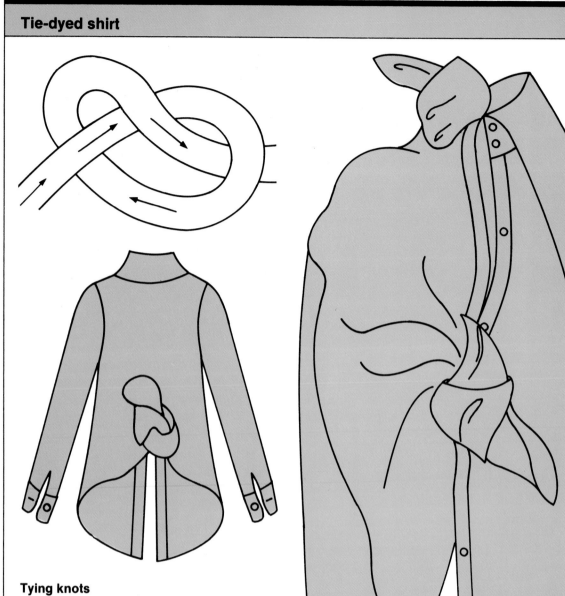

## Tying knots

Decide which areas are to remain white; which are to become light blue or navy. Use rubber bands of two different colors to gather the fabric. Use a dark rubber band to gather the areas that are to stay white throughout and a light-colored one on knots that you will be repositioning after the first dye bath. Pull a section of the garment out and wrap a rubber band around it. Wrapping tightly assures that the garment section will remain white.

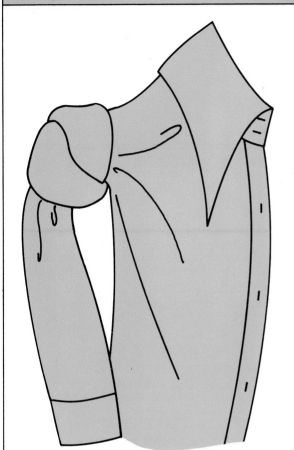

Knot the shirt using ordinary knots. Tie the knots as tightly as possible in the following manner: in the back, at the center, take a section of fabric 8 inches in diameter and knot it on itself. Do the same with a scattering of smaller knots around the larger knot until the back of the shirt is all knots. Similarly, in the front, on each side, tie the largest knots at the top and bottom, with smaller knots between, until the front is virtually all knots. On the sleeves, make large knots at each sleeve cap and continue knotting down to the cuffs.

Secure the knots by covering them liberally with tightly twisted rubber bands (the larger bands for the larger knots), to insure that the dye remains inside the knots. String may be used as an alternative.

## Tie-dyed shirt

### Dyeing with the first color

In the large pot, mix one bottle of liquid light blue dye or one package of powdered light blue dye according to package directions. Add 2 teaspoons of noniodized salt (to fix the

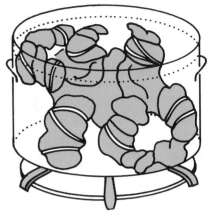

color) and stir again. Immerse the garment, still knotted and banded, in the light blue dye solution and simmer for 30 minutes. Do not allow to boil. Remove the garment and rinse thoroughly in cold running water until the water runs clear.

### Knotting garment for next dye bath

Remove the rubber bands and untie the knots

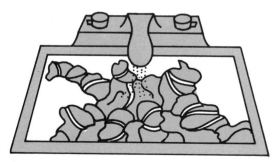

unless they are on areas that you want to stay white until the end. Rewrap the areas that are to stay light blue, because any areas that are not rewrapped will become navy in the next dye bath. Gather sections that are part white and part light blue and wrap with rubber

bands. Gather sections that are solid light blue and wrap tightly. Areas that you left wrapped will remain white. If you follow these steps, the finished garment will have a full range of monochromatic tones in blue.

### Dyeing with the second color

Prepare the navy dye bath according to the directions on the package, using either powdered or liquid dye. Add salt, stir. Immerse the garment, stir, and let simmer for 30 minutes. Do not allow to boil. Remove the garment and

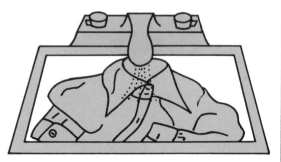

rinse thoroughly in cold running water until the water runs clear. Now, remove the rubber bands. Each gathered section will be slightly different in size, shape and color, making each garment unique. Let the garment drip dry and then press, if necessary.

For extra durability of colors, have the garment dry-cleaned and treated for water and stain repellence. Or apply a fabric protector, which is packaged in aerosol cans and available in notions supply stores or supermarkets. Then launder separately by hand or machine wash in cold water.

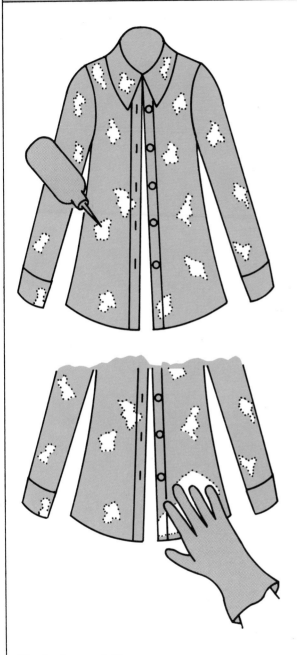

Squeeze droplets of fuschia dye and then purple dye at random all over the front of the garment. Rub the dye into the fabric with fingers. The dyes will seep through to the back as well, but for even fuller color saturation, also squeeze-dye the back.

### Knotting garment
Knot the garment, using ordinary knots, tied as tightly as possible as instructed for the blouse. Secure the knots with tightly twisted rubber bands (the larger bands for the larger knots), to insure that the dye remains inside the knots. String may be used instead.

### Immersing in color remover
Prepare a solution of color remover. If the powdered type is used, in a large pot, mix 1 ounce of the powder with 1 gallon of water brought to simmering. If liquid bleach is used, use ½ ounce of bleach mixed with 1 gallon of water. Immerse the garment in the solution and stir until the exposed parts of the garment appear completely white again.

Remove the garment from the solution. With the knots still tied, wash in hot, soapy water, and then rinse again in cold water until the water runs clear.

### Immersing in dye
In the large pot, mix one bottle of liquid tangerine dye or one package of powdered tangerine dye with about 1 gallon of boiling water and stir. Add two teaspoons of noniodized salt (to fix color) and stir again. Immerse the garment, still knotted and banded, in the tangerine dye solution and simmer for 30 minutes. Do not allow to boil. Remove the garment and rinse thoroughly in cold running water, until the water runs clear.

### Finishing the garment
Remove rubber bands and untie knots. Rinse garment in cold running water and hang to damp dry. While garment is still damp, press it with a steam iron.

### Tie-dyeing variation
Prepare the garment for dyeing as instructed previously for the blouse. Put on rubber gloves and apron. If liquid dyes are used, fill a plastic squeeze bottle with fuschia and another with purple, using dyes full strength. If powdered dyes are used, mix one package of each of these two colors with one cup of hot water and pour into the squeeze bottles.

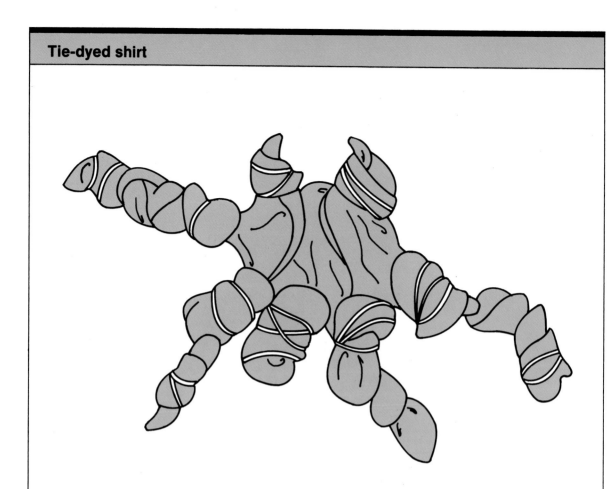

## Tie dyeing sheets and pillowcases

Plain old sheets and pillowcases may be elegantly renewed and transformed by the tie-dyeing process. Subtle changes in hues and shades are achieved by untying all the knots and reknotting between dye baths. Use two to four dye baths of colors which mix and blend well; for example, blue and yellow, which make green. (Three dye baths of the three primary colors produce all the colors of the rainbow.)

To tie dye a sheet, begin by pinching the center and pulling it up about 30 inches. With other hand, grasp the bottom of this gathered portion. Tie the first knot tightly here. Tie additional knots every 6 inches until you reach the top of the gathered portion. Tightly roll the entire gathered portion from the top toward the bottom until you are left with a ball in the center of the sheet. Wrap string around this ball very tightly several times and knot it.

Prepare the first dye bath, immerse the sheet in it, and rinse it well, all in the same manner as described previously for the blouse. Untie all the knots and allow the sheet to dry. (Drying sheet between dye baths prevents dyes from running into one another and makes it easier to tie knots.)

For the second, third and fourth (optional) color dye baths, repeat the process used for the first one, decreasing the diameters of the gathered portions as you proceed. Plan your knotting so that some areas of the sheet will be dyed only once, others twice, others three times, and so on. (This will create the rainbow effect.) Use your imagination to plan the spacing of the differently colored circles to produce an interesting design. The same process can be repeated on a smaller scale for matching pillowcases.

# Embroidered clutch purse

Bold and simple, embroidered designs are being used with more frequency on contemporary accessories, particularly hand-embroidered border decorations. Embroidery threads and yarns, available in almost every color of the rainbow and in a wide range of textures, open up a whole new vista of design possibilities. Loosely woven fabrics are particularly well suited to decorative stitching since they provide a natural grid on which to plan and execute designs. Many embroidery stitches are surprisingly easy and fast to work, such as the two that form the border for this homespun textured clutch purse. The coarse weave of the fabric makes it easy to stitch accurately, and the neutral shade is a good foil for the bright colors and smooth texture of the thread. The purse is a rectangular shape requiring a minimum of skill to sew.

Materials: a rectangle of cotton homespun or heavy natural linen and lining fabric, each approximately 10 by 24 inches; medium-weight or heavy-duty cotton thread to match handbag fabric; a spool of medium-weight cotton sewing thread to match lining; tailor's chalk; 6-strand embroidery thread in two colors (we used two 9-yard skeins of brown and two of light orange); a blunt-tipped embroidery needle; an embroidery hoop or canvas stretchers; and masking tape.

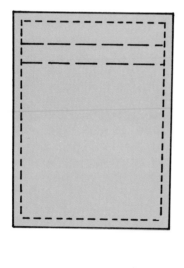

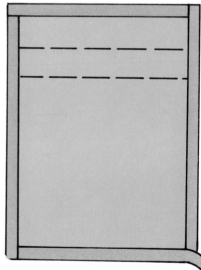

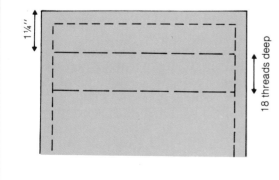

## Preparing fabric for purse

Mark the purse fabric with the specified dimensions and cut out, allowing an additional ½ inch on all sides for seam allowances. Mark the lining fabric in the same manner, with seam allowance, and cut out. Mark the ½-inch seam allowance with tailor's chalk on wrong sides. Also mark a band 18 threads deep on wrong side of purse fabric for placement of border, allowing 1¼ inches from top edge and ½ inch from each side edge. Bind all edges of purse fabric with masking tape to prevent edges from unraveling while embroidering.

## Embroidered clutch purse

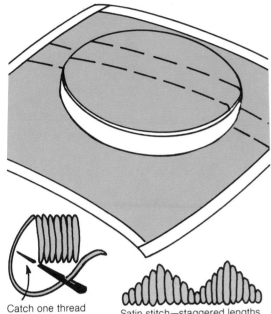

Catch one thread at end of each stitch

Satin stitch—staggered lengths

### Beginning the embroidery

Work embroidery before sewing bag together. Stretch fabric between rings of embroidery hoop or across canvas stretchers. Thread needle with two strands of brown embroidery thread by crimping through the eye of the needle. Start the border with one row of vertical surface satin stitches, three threads deep and one thread wide. (The reference to thread here is to the thread grid of the fabric.) For the first stitch, bring needle up at left edge of area to be covered, insert needle at opposite edge and return to starting line of threads by carrying needle underneath fabric. To conserve thread, don't carry the needle in back of the fabric for the rest of the stitches in the row, but instead catch one thread of fabric adjacent to the last stitch before starting next stitch. Keep stitches close together. Complete row 1.

### Stitching row 2

Row 2, worked in light-orange embroidery thread, consists of a band of triangles formed by surface satin stitches of staggered lengths. The stitches graduate as follows: for the first half of the triangle, start with the satin stitch covering 2 threads of the fabric, then 3

threads, 4 threads, to 5, to 6, to 7 threads; then for the second half of the triangle the stitches decrease in length from 7 threads to 6 to 5 to 4 to 3 to 2. The row begins and ends with a half triangle.

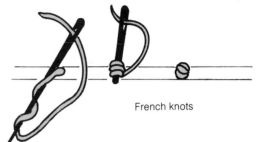

French knots

### Stitching row 3

Row 3 consists of French knots, attached over 2 threads of fabric, and spaced 2 threads apart. To make a French knot, simply bring needle up where knot is to be worked. Wind thread 2 or 3 times around point of needle. Insert needle in fabric as close as possible to, but not at, spot where thread emerges. Pull needle through to wrong side to form knot. Work one knot right after the other, without tying each off separately.

### Stitching rows 4 and 5

Row 4, worked in light-orange thread, is a mirror image of row 2. Row 5 completes the border pattern and is worked in brown thread, repeating the stitches in row 1. Leave one unworked fabric thread between rows 1 and 2 and between rows 4 and 5. There are no unworked threads between rows 2 and 3, and 3 and 4. Secure thread ends by backstitching and weaving underneath stitches.

# Embroidered clutch purse

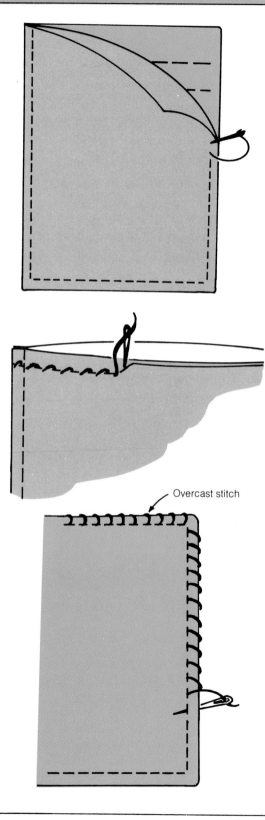

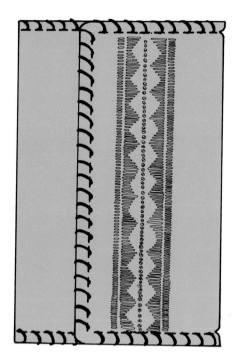

Overcast stitch

## Assembling purse

To assemble purse, remove masking tape, stitch 3 sides of fabric with medium-weight cotton thread to lining, right sides together, leaving top edge open. Trim seams to ¼ inch, turn purse right side out and press. Turn purse fabric and lining seam allowances at top under to wrong side and slipstitch lining to fabric so that no stitching shows on fabric side of purse. Fold rectangle in half, embroidered side out. Backstitch sides together with medium-weight or heavy-duty thread, ⅛ inch in from edge. Backstitch along the two open top edges, ⅛ inch from edge. Overcast side edges together, then overcast along each top edge, stitching through each backstitch. Fold bag 4 inches from top to form flap. Lay a press cloth over purse and press well. Finish, if desired, by treating with a fabric-protector spray to repel stains and water. To create variations of this purse, select different color combinations and fabrics, and design your own patterns.

## Leather bag

Once you have gained leathercrafting skill and practice by fashioning the tooled leather belts, this smart, versatile handbag is an excellent second project. Leather remnants and supplies left from the belt project are a start in assembling your materials. A leathercraft store, however, will have what you need.

Materials: a vegetable-tan leather skin (usually 1 square yard), about $\frac{1}{16}$ inch thick; a pen; a mat knife; straightedge metal ruler; revolving punch for making holes; brown beeswaxed linen thread; harness needle; compass; an old piece of wood or heavy-duty cardboard for a cutting surface; and rubber cement and brush.

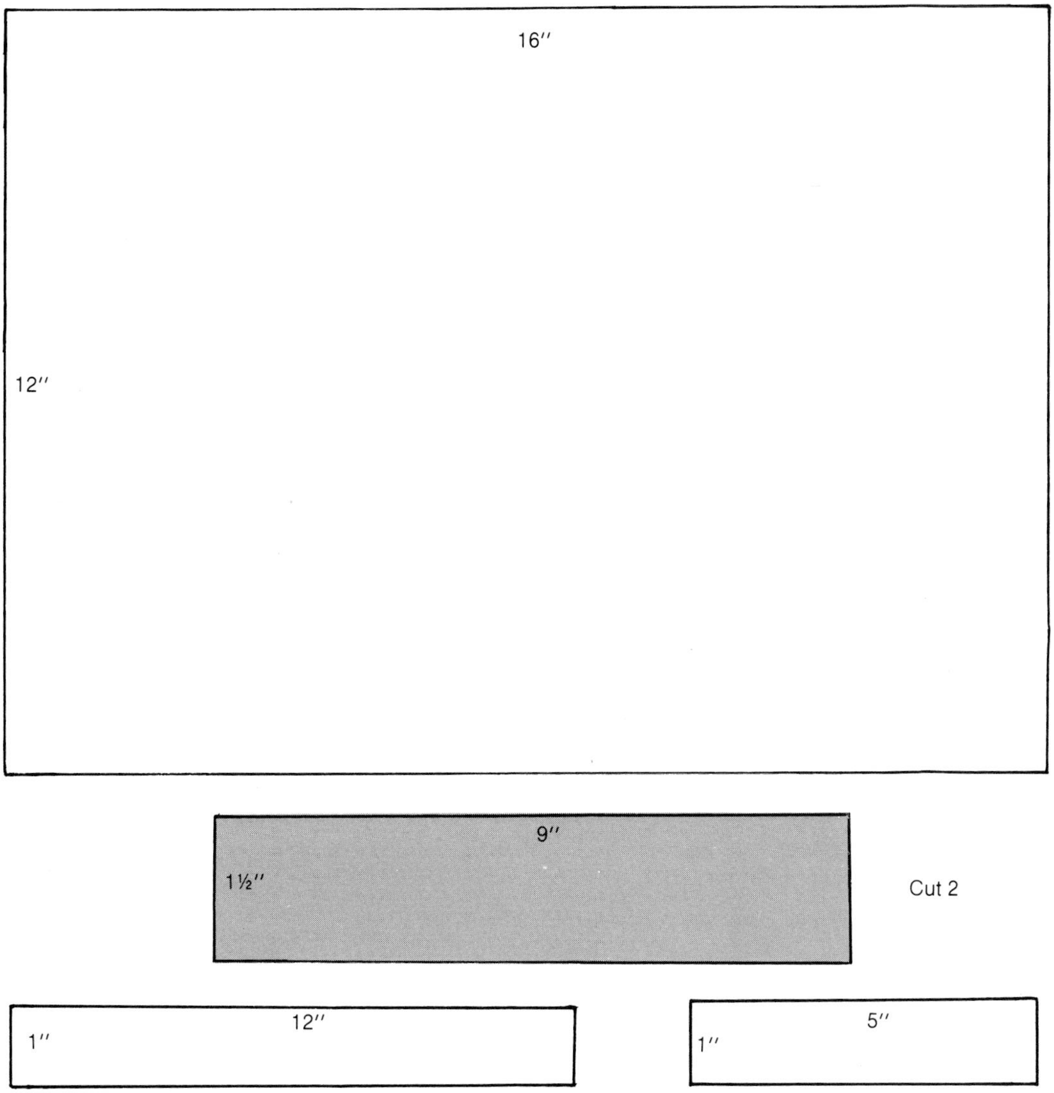

16"

12"

9"

1½"

Cut 2

12"

1"

5"

1"

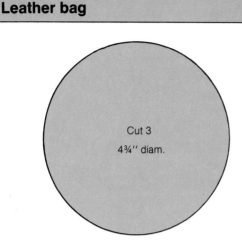

Cut 3
4¾" diam.

ameter, and reserve for later. (You will have three circular rings and three circles). Also cut one tongue piece for the closing, measuring 1 inch wide and 5 inches long; and one piece 1 inch by 12 inches to reinforce the bottom of the bag.

On the ungrained side of the leather of the body piece, mark the halfway point on each of the 16-inch edges. Then, mark off a band 1¼ inch wide, ⅝ inch on each side of the mid-point marks. This band will form the bottom of the bag. With a mat knife, score the 1¼-

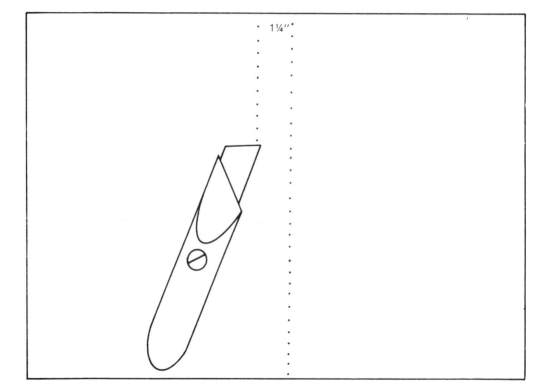

1¼"

### Cutting out leather parts

Mark all pattern pieces directly on the un-grained, soft side of the leather skin, which is placed flat on your working surface. With mat knife and ruler, cut one piece for the body, measuring 16 inches by 12 inches; two 1½-inch-by-9-inch pieces for bag sides; and three leather circles, each 4¾ inches in diameter. Then within each circle, mark and cut with a mat knife a concentric circle with a 3½-inch di-

inch band on the ungrained side of the leather. Do not press hard when scoring or you will cut through the leather. (Try scoring on leather scraps first, to get the knack of it.) Then fold along the two score lines, leaving a uniform 1¼-inch width along the bottom of the bag. Bend both sides upward, reinforcing the scored line with your fingers. Take the 1-inch-by-12-inch piece of leather that you cut and apply rubber cement to the raw side of

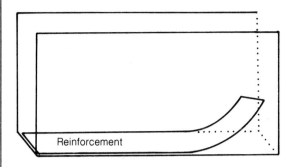

Reinforcement

cle with a 1¾-inch radius, as illustrated. At top, punch holes in a semicircle (for circular handles to be attached later) with a 2½-inch radius, then a 2-inch-radius concentric semicircle for the handle on each side of the bag. (The semicircle midpoint will be 6 inches from each side.)

it. Also apply rubber cement on the raw side of the 1¼-inch-by-12-inch bottom band that you scored. When the glue on both pieces has dried, position the reinforcement piece over the scored band on the bottom of the bag and bend together for a strong bottom to support the shape of the bag.

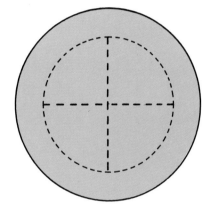

## Finishing the bag

Take one of the three 3½-inch leather circles you cut earlier and, on the raw side, mark with a compass the center of the circle. Then with a ruler mark the diameters on the raw side in a cross "X" shape to divide the circle into quarters. Cut out the inner circle along the dotted lines with a mat knife, as shown. (Discard the two remaining circles.)

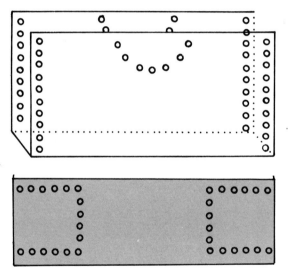

## Punching holes for laces

With the revolving punch set at the small notch, make holes ¼ inch apart and ⅛ inch from edges for all pieces where instructions for holes are given. Start by punching holes along the sides of the bag body. Then place six holes along the 1¼-inch bottom band at ¼-inch intervals, 1½ inches inward from the edge, on both sides and across the width of the bottom. Then punch holes in each of the four lower corners of the bag in a quarter cir-

# Leather bag

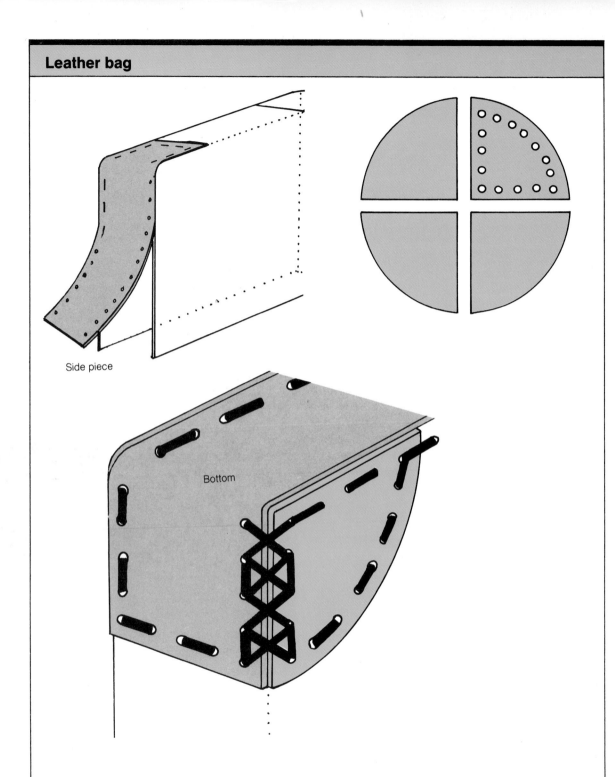

Side piece

Bottom

Punch holes along the bottom and both sides of the two 1½-inch-by-9-inch pieces (sides of bag). Stitch them in place as shown, using a running or basting stitch at the bottom of the bag only. Then, take the four quarters cut from the circle and punch holes along all sides of each quarter-circle piece. Line these holes up with those made on the front and back of the bag with an "X" shape, or cross stitch, and seam bottom edges together. Secure the curved part of the circle in place with running stitches.

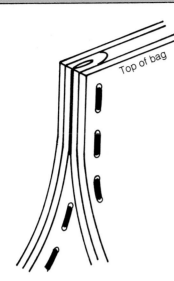

Top of bag

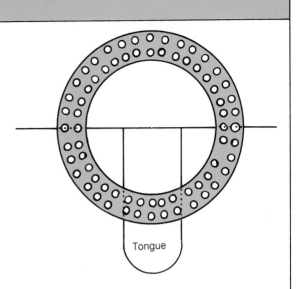

Tongue

Fold both sides of the bag upward, tucking bottom flaps up from the inside. Sew with a running stitch up both sides of the bag. Sew bag flaps and sides together 1 inch from the top of the bag, much as you would gather-stitch a clothing seam. This will make the bag close better at the top and leave substantial bottom width.

Then punch holes around the inner and outer circumferences of both rings, 1/16 inch from each edge. Align these rings on the front and back of the bag and sew in place, leaving a 1 1/4-inch opening at the bottom center of each ring. Sew the tops of the rings with a saddle stitch for a finished look.

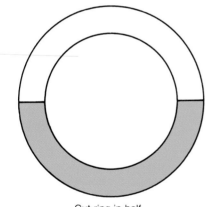

Cut ring in half

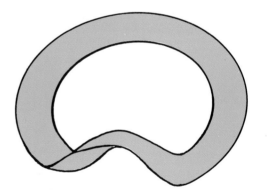

The three circular rings are used for the handles. The lower half of two rings will be sewn onto the bag, with the other half of each extending above the top of it. The third ring is cut in half and used to reinforce the two handles extending above the top edge of bag. Glue one half of the third ring to the wrong side of what will be the upper portion of each handle ring.

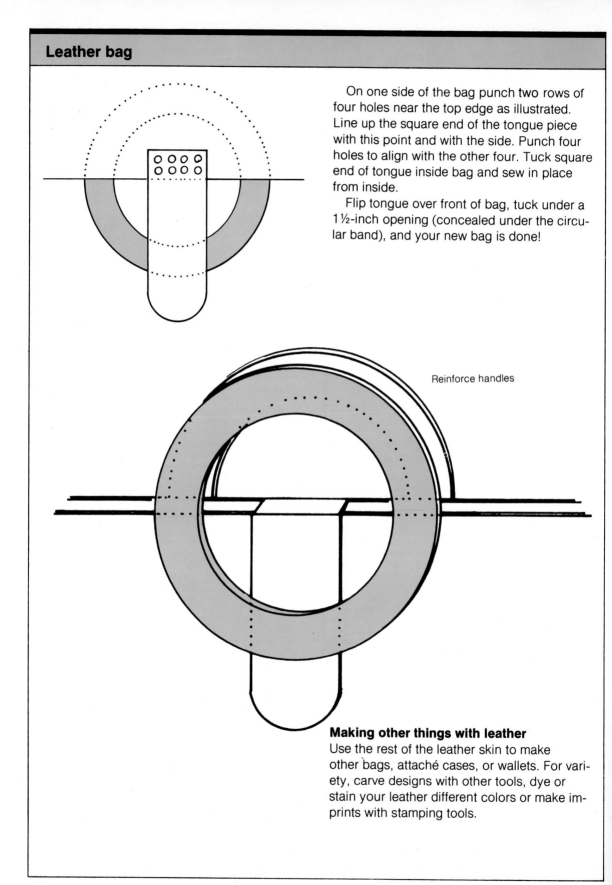

On one side of the bag punch two rows of four holes near the top edge as illustrated. Line up the square end of the tongue piece with this point and with the side. Punch four holes to align with the other four. Tuck square end of tongue inside bag and sew in place from inside.

Flip tongue over front of bag, tuck under a 1½-inch opening (concealed under the circular band), and your new bag is done!

Reinforce handles

### Making other things with leather
Use the rest of the leather skin to make other bags, attaché cases, or wallets. For variety, carve designs with other tools, dye or stain your leather different colors or make imprints with stamping tools.

# Macramé vest

The striking lacy design is made on this custom-fitted vest by a simple series of alternating square knots. You can be sure it fits perfectly by working it on a dress form. You can also cut out a cloth or paper pattern and pin it onto a foam cushion or bed to serve as a guide as you knot the cords.

To familiarize yourself with the technique, and to determine the exact amount of cord and decorative beads needed, make a sampler following the directions below. Calculate the amount needed according to the desired finished body measurements and length. The technique of macramé is that of joining several doubled cords onto a holding cord with mounting loops and then knotting them. Remember that each cord is doubled, and that you will need multiples of four strands to work out the square-knot pattern evenly. Each cord must be 4 times the finished vest length.

Materials: the dummy or pattern guide; white silken-textured rayon or nylon macramé cord; clear plastic beads; T-shaped pins, to keep knots in place as you work; a ruler to check measurements; and scissors.

## Making the sampler

The first step (and this is important) is to make a pattern for the finished vest according to your body measurements. This is easily done by outlining the vest pattern on an old piece of sheeting. Cut out pattern and check fit on body; adjust wherever necessary (see CRAFTNOTES). Determine the number of square inches in the finished area. (Do not count the space which will be covered by the dangling cord fringe.)

To determine the amount of cord needed for the vest, make a 4-inch-square sampler. Begin by knotting a 6-inch mounting cord at each end and pinning it to your working surface (see CRAFTNOTES). Attach working cords with mounting loops until work measures 4 inches

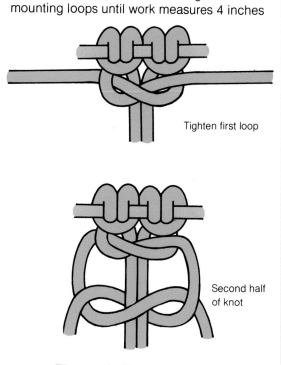

Tighten first loop

Second half of knot

across. Then work alternating square-knot pattern described below, until the work is 4 inches long.

The alternating square-knot pattern, a basic macramé technique, combines two or more groups of square knots, using a minimum of

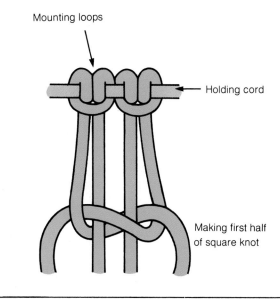

Mounting loops

Holding cord

Making first half of square knot

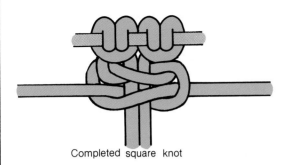

Completed square knot

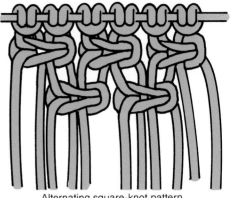

Alternating square-knot pattern

8 cords. Separate cords into groups of 4 each. Cross right outer cord of each group over both center foundation cords and under the left outer cord. With cords in this position, pick up outer left cord, place it under the 2 center cords and up through the loop. Draw outer cords up and tighten. Step 2 of the square knot follows the same procedure, but from opposite sides. Cross left outer cord over 2 center cords and leave it in this position. Pick up right outer cord, place over left outer cord, under 2 center cords and up through left loop formed. Pull tightly.

Second row

As you work the sampler, note the amount of cord it takes you to complete the 4-inch square. Then multiply the amount of cord used for the sampler by the number of square inches of the finished vest pattern; then divide that number by 16 (number of square inches in the sampler). Finally, add the length you want your dangling cord fringe to be, multiplied by the number of working cords you will be using. (You can estimate the number of working cords needed by counting the number it took to work the 4 horizontal inches of the sampler and dividing that into the total width of the vest pattern, for both back and front pieces.)

To determine the length of each working cord, take the number of inches one working cord (after doubling and mounting) in your sampler used up to reach a 4-inch length and multiply that number by your desired vest length (excluding fringe). Divide by 4. Add desired fringe length and double the total. Then add two feet for a safety margin. (You can estimate working-cord length roughly by multiplying finished vest length, including fringe, by 4.)

For example, if one working cord used up 10 inches to reach a 4-inch length in the sampler and you want your alternating square-knot pattern to reach down 16 inches, multiply 10 by 16 (giving you 160) and divide by 4. You need 40 inches of cord for the knotting. You want a 12-inch fringe, so you add 40 to 12 to get 52; double that for 104 and add 2 feet (24 inches) for a total of 128 inches (or 10 feet, 8 inches). An estimate would have told you: 16-inch vest plus 12-inch fringe = 28; 28 x 4 = 112 inches, or 9 feet, 2 inches.

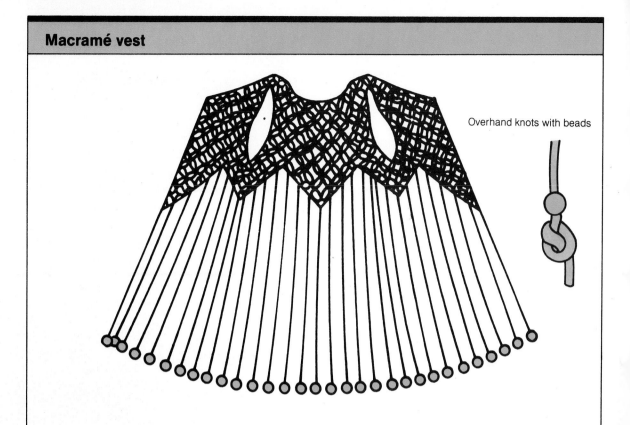

Overhand knots with beads

## Making the vest

Cut a holding cord long enough to fit around the back of neck and across tops of shoulders. Pin cords in the center of the top of shoulders so that one half the cord length serves as a working cord for the front and the other half length for the back of the vest. Proceed as for the sampler, pinning your work to the form to keep it taut.

To make the large number of cords easy to handle, while you are knotting, you wrap excess length into bobbins around your hand and secure with rubber bands.

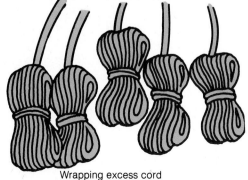

Wrapping excess cord

Work in pattern across all cords for back, adding doubled cords at both edges as needed to form underarm. Work each half of front separately, adding doubled cords at armhole edges as needed until you reach curve of underarm at bottom of armhole. Then, join each front section to back by working a row of square knots across all cords.

Continue working alternating square knots evenly all around vest until point where you wish to begin zigzags. Shape each zigzag by simply omitting first one knot, then an increasing number of knots in each row, at right and left front edges and at points equidistant from each side of armhole curve in front and back. Continue until you have a single knot forming the point of zigzag at center of each side of the front, the center of the area under the armhole, and the center of the back. At this stage, each zigzag is complete.

Finish vest by trimming each free cord evenly to desired length, threading a bead over it, and tying an overhand knot to prevent cord end from fraying.

# Macramé necklace

A handsome companion to the Macramé vest, this delicate macramé necklace is worked with fine linen thread in a detailed pattern utilizing the basic knot learned for the Macramé vest and Macramé wall hanging projects. For this project, you learn how to work double half hitches on the diagonal and how to tie a tassel.

Materials: fine linen cord or button and carpet thread; 6 wooden beads, ⅜ inch in diameter; four wooden beads, ¼ inch in diameter; a board; T-shaped pins; a necklace clasp with 2 jump rings; and scissors. Each necklace band requires four 14-foot cords, doubled; and the pendant requires 14 cords, each 7 feet long. (To determine the length of cords to be tightly knotted, multiply the length of the completed item by 10 for each cord.) The necklace measures 16½ inches long, with each necklace band 8½ inches long; a 6-inch-long pendant; and a 2-inch tassel.

## Mounting the cords and beading

Start each necklace band by mounting 4 doubled cords through clasp jump ring with reverse double half hitches; or simply pull each cord through ring, if it is small enough, and double at center of cord. Work alternating square-knot pattern, 2 knots wide, as shown, until each band measures 8½ inches long.

(Review knot instructions given for Macramé vest.)

Thread the 4 smaller beads onto a 2-strand holding cord, which will also serve as outside knotting cords in completing the necklace. Mount 2 doubled cords with reverse double half hitches onto holding cord between each 2 beads, and one doubled cord on either side of right and left beads. Attach neckbands with reverse double half hitches onto holding cord. There are now 36 strands on holding cord.

## Knotting the pendant

To begin pendant, work a chain of 9 sennits of 4 square knots each, as shown. Then divide each group of 4 strands in half, and make 8 chains of square-knot sennits, 4 knots long. Chain knot the 2 free outside cords on each side to the same length as the sennits with half knots. Pass left cord under right cord at each edge, then pass right cord up through the loop formed and tighten gently. Start each half knot in the chain with the left cord.

Continue pendant pattern with a 9-sennit row of 7 square knots each, replacing some knots in the third, fifth and seventh sennit chain with ⅜-inch beads. Divide cords and work a row of 8 sennits, 2 square knots long, leaving 2 outer cords on each side free. Then make another row of 9 sennits, 7 knots long, replacing some knots in fourth and sixth sennits with ⅜-inch beads. Divide and work another row of 8 sennits, 2 square knots per sennit, leaving 2 outer cords free on each side. Work one more 9-sennit row, 7 knots long, replacing some of the knots in the center sennit with the last ⅜-inch bead.

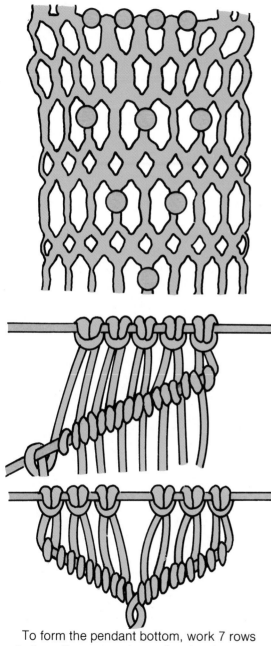

make a diagonal double half hitch, lay each outside cord at a slant over other cords and tie a row of double half hitches to it, making 2 half-hitch loops for each cord and pulling tightly, as shown. After tying each diagonal to center, wrap right anchor cord over left anchor cord and lay them at an outward slant. As you work each diagonal double half hitch, add the last cord used to the holding cord, thus taking up all ends within the diagonal, so that they come together at the center.

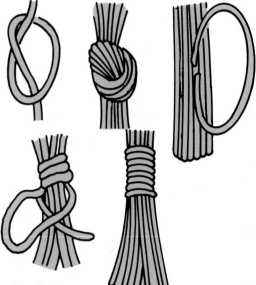

### Tying the tassel

Gather all center cords to form a tassel. There are two simple methods of tying tassels. The first is to tie an overhand knot by picking up all cords, bringing them over themselves at the top of a loop, then behind and out through the loop. Holding overhand knot at top, pull cord ends gently to tighten.

The second method is to cut 2 feet of extra cord and form it into a large loop around the top of the group of cords, with one pointing downward, the other end upward. Starting at top of tassel, wrap cord around tassel cords about 5 times, pulling tassel cords back through loop after each turn to prevent tangling. Tighten wrapping by pulling hard on ends of wrapping cord until secure, then cut excess cord at top and bottom of wrapping. Trim tassel ends evenly to a 2-inch length to finish.

To form the pendant bottom, work 7 rows of alternating square knots, leaving 2 cords free at beginning and end of each row, then ending with a single square knot for the point. Using the 2 outside cords on each side as holding cords, work a row of diagonal double half hitches from sides to point in center. To

# Wrap-around skirt

This chic wrap-around skirt, perfect for casual wear at home or on a holiday trip, can be fashioned many ways. Here it is seen at ankle length, but the design is so versatile, it can be almost any length, below or above the knee. If you can use a sewing machine, you can make this skirt with ease because of its simplicity in design. The bright red color with lace trim is very attractive, but the skirt can be made in a print or any combination you desire. As described, the skirt will fit a waist of approximately 24 to 27¼ inches. Adjust dimensions, as necessary, to fit your measurement, adding to or subtracting from the sash piece length and the skirt width.

Materials: 1¾ yards of 48-inch-wide fabric (1¾ yards of 36-inch fabric if the skirt is not to be ankle length): two sash pieces 7¼ inches wide, one 56 inches long and the other 46 inches long; two pieces of 3¼-inch-wide press-on interfacing, one 55 inches long and the other 45 inches long. For hems, you will need one piece of color-coordinated seam binding 58 inches long by ⅝ inch wide, and two pieces of lace trim each 44 inches long and 1¼ inches wide.

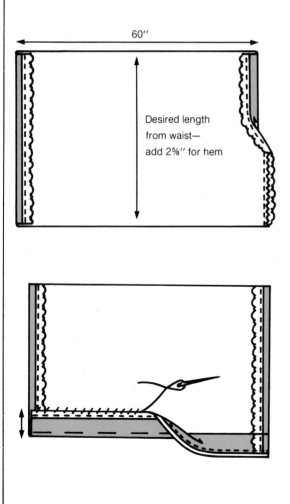

60″

Desired length from waist— add 2⅝″ for hem

### Attaching sash to skirt

Turn sash right side out and press. Stitch two sash pieces together at top of fold only, leaving a slit in the sash.

Fold under ¼ inch of raw edges of open section of sash and gather the waist seam of the skirt inside of the opening. On right side, topstitch along the open edge of the sash, enclosing the waist seam.

To wear, pass the longer end of the sash through the slit, wrap around your waist, and tie.

### Preparing skirt piece

Determine the finished length of the skirt by measuring from your waist to your ankle, knee, or wherever you want the hem to fall, add 2⅝ inches to this dimension, and cut off excess length. With pinking shears, cut vertical edges. Sew lace binding to cover pinked edges. Fold the fabric 1⅜ inches from the pinked edges to form facings on the inside of the skirt.

To make a decorative hem, fold up the additional 2⅝-inch length and baste along the inside of the skirt close to the fold. Neatly sew or machine stitch the matching binding over the raw edge. Then slip-stitch the hem to the skirt.

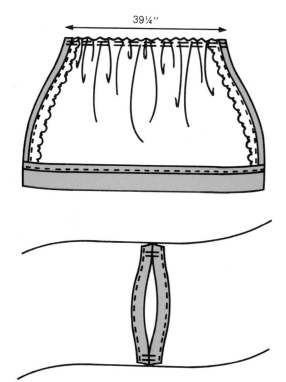

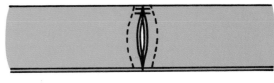

Press on or machine-baste interfacing to wrong side of sash pieces, ¼ inch from one of the long edges.

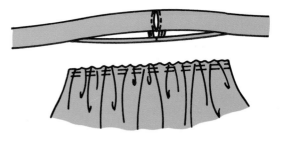

### Gathering waist of skirt

Run two close rows of gathering stitches across the full width, ⅜ inch below the top edge. Gather the material to 39¼ inches (or to the measurement of your waist, plus 12 to 15¼ inches for overlap). Secure the gathers by machine basting.

Fold sash in half lengthwise, right sides together. Stitch at each end, allowing a ¼-inch seam, and along the length of the sash from each end as shown, leaving open a 39¼-inch section (or width of the gathered skirt). Trim seams.

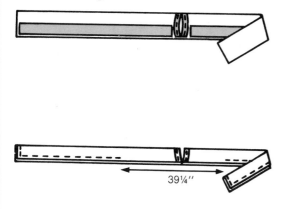

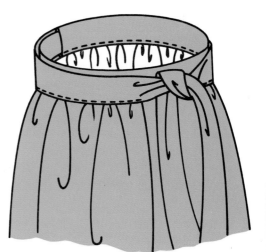

### Stitching the sash

Fold under one end of each of the sash pieces ¼ inch, and hem with a straight stitch. Trim seam. Tack the two sash pieces together at top and bottom of hemmed ends only.

# Kite caftan

After thousands of years and as many variations, the loose-fitting caftan is still a popular fashion for both casual and formal wear. This kite-shaped caftan, Oriental in feeling, is designed so that it is more full at the top and narrower at the hem; just the reverse of the classic caftan. There are no side seams, only front and back seams.

To make this kite caftan, use a soft fabric that drapes easily, such as crepe or jersey, in a vivid solid color or a bold all-over print. If a striped fabric is used, the stripes will miter at the center front and back. Do not use a plaid or a print that requires matching. If you wish to underline the garment with a very light or sheer fabric, cut lining pieces exactly as outer pieces, baste together, and handle as one throughout.

Materials: to determine the yardage of 36-inch-wide fabric needed, measure length from shoulders to the floor, double that amount and add 4 inches for the hem. To give the neckline and sleeve edges an attractive finish, you need 2 yards of flexible braid trim.

## Marking the fabric pieces

Place fabric on flat surface to avoid stretching. Fold, right sides together, first across the width and again lengthwise so that there are four layers. Be sure all edges are even. Pin together if fabric is slippery. Keep the folds on the left side and top edge, with open edges at right and bottom.

## Marking diagonal

Make all markings with soft chalk, pins or very small snips in the fabric. From the long fold on the left side, measure 8½ inches along open bottom edge, and mark. From the long fold on left side, measure in 17 inches along folded top edge, and mark. With a ruler or other straight edge, join these two points. This diagonal line is the center front or center back. On this line, mark a point about 22 inches up from the bottom edge for the back slit. (If desired, vary the depth of this slit in proportion to height.) On the diagonal line, mark a point about 8 inches down from top edge for neckline slit.

## Marking neckline

For the neckline, measure down the center back or front 2 inches and across the top edge 3 inches from the diagonal line. Join these two points in a gentle curve. At the side fold, mark two points, 7 inches and 15½ inches down from the top edge for the beginning and end of the sleeve slits. Join these two points with a line. For the shoulder, join the mark at the top of the sleeve with the outer point of the neckline curve.

# Kite caftan

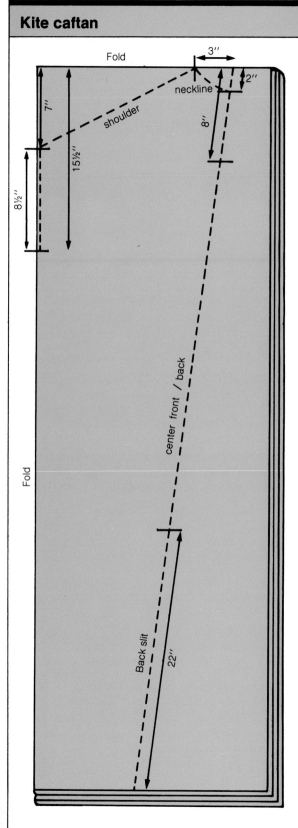

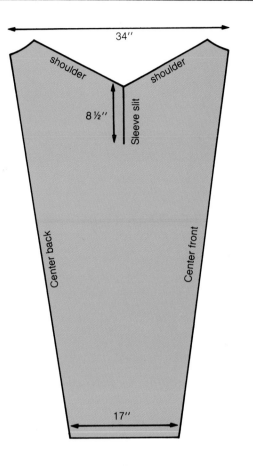

## Cutting caftan pieces

Cut out caftan pieces on lines marked. *Do not cut the side fold,* except for the sleeve slits.

## Sewing caftan

Open fabric pieces out flat so the open edges are on the right and left sides, leaving them together with right sides on the inside. Now the caftan is ready to be sewn. Use a ½-inch seam allowance throughout. Seam center front from top to bottom. Use either open edge; pieces are identical.

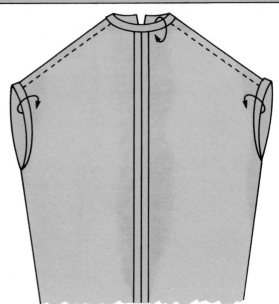

Refold caftan so that seams just sewn are in the center and sleeve slits are at sides. Keep right sides together and stitch shoulder seams. Hem sleeve slits and the neckline curve as instructed for back and neckline openings, tapering ½-inch hem to nothing at bottom point of sleeve slits. Try on caftan, pin up bottom edge and hem.

Seam center back (other edge) between mark for back slit and mark for neckline slit. Press seams open. Turn under raw edges of neckline and back slits ½ inch and hem. (For a fabric that ravels easily, add a piece of bias tape to the edges as a hem facing.)

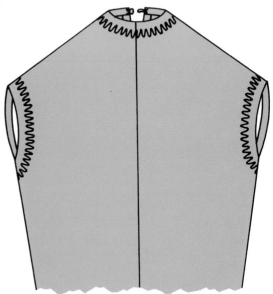

Tack flexible braid trim in place around neckline and sleeve edges. Sew hook and eye at top of neckline slit.

LEF

256

# Appliquéd pillows and wall hanging

The art of appliqué, like many forms of embroidery and needlework, has recently been enjoying a renaissance. The variety of contemporary fabrics, in both natural and synthetic fibers, as well as the wide range of colorfast prints and bold colors, is a boon to appliqué work. With appliqué, the novice can achieve exciting visual effects with fabrics, starting with simple and large designs, such as the flower and ladybug patterns, for the pillows; and the free-form grass and sun pattern appliqué on linen or canvas, for the wall hanging.

Materials: a pencil, construction paper and colored pencils, for the preliminary design and paper patterns; brightly colored and print fabric remnants; scissors; needle and thread; heavy linen or cotton canvas for the wall hanging (size desired, plus a 2-inch allowance for stretching or binding); a set of 4 canvas stretchers, the same size as wall hanging, or 2 dowels, the width of the hanging; 2¼ yards washable fabric in solid color, for pillows, cut to size desired, plus ½-inch seam allowances; and two ready-made muslin-covered pillows, size to fit pillow covers when complete, or make pillows (see Patchwork pillow for instructions and materials needed).

## Making the patterns

Measure and cut 4 equal pieces of fabric, 2 for each pillow, allowing ½ inch on all sides for seams. Measure and cut fabric for wall hanging to desired size, allowing ½ inch on all sides for stretching or turning under hanging edges. To make design patterns, draw the preliminary designs on construction paper, for each pillow and the wall hanging, following patterns illustrated. Make shapes large enough to fit within the finished size selected for each item. Fill in the shape on the paper rendition of the design with colored pencils,

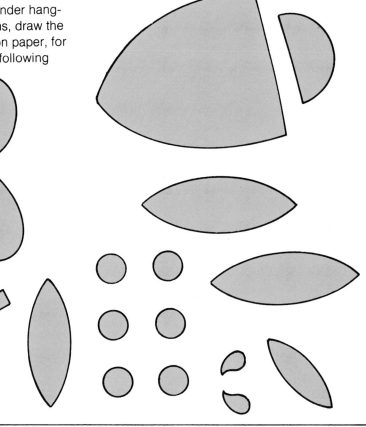

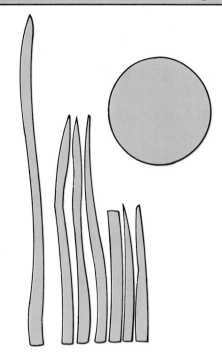

to help stimulate your awareness of fabric colors and surfaces as design elements.

Cut out paper shapes for the three designs and pin them onto the fabric remnants selected for each part of the appliqué design. Cut out fabric shapes along pattern outlines. Remove pins. Lay fabric shapes directly on fabric background, for each appliqué design, right side up, according to design scheme, making any necessary adjustments. When satisfied, pin fabric in place and press carefully. If iron-on interfacing is used, pins are not necessary. Simply cut pieces of interfacing the same size as fabric shapes, using paper patterns, and arrange on fabric background following design. Then, lay corresponding fabric shapes in place over interfacing and press carefully.

### Appliquéing the designs

Secure edges of appliqué pieces for each pillow and for the wall hanging to background fabric for each item. Use any of several decorative hand or machine stitches, so the stitches become decorative accents, such as the legs of the ladybug. Use straight stitches, such as the running stitch or backstitch, to secure fabric edges that do not ravel easily. If your fabric tends to ravel, as many wovens do,

use an overcast or simple zigzag stitch to cover the entire edge of each appliqué piece. Fabrics that tend to ravel badly can be secured with a satin or surface satin stitch. (See Embroidered clutch purse for instructions.) When all shapes have been stitched to background, press entire piece well.

### Finishing the pillows

Attach appliqued piece to back piece of cover. Place right sides together and seam all around 3 sides, using ½-inch allowance. Turn on right side and stuff with pillow. Close fourth side by turning each edge ½ inch and sew together with an overcast stitch.

### Finishing the wall hanging

Stretch hanging over canvas stretchers, aligning design corners with stretcher corners, and tack to back of canvas. Or, turn side with slipstitches, then turn top and bottom edges under around dowels, taking up 2-inch allowance, and secure with slipstitches to wrong side. For protection against fading, stains and dust, treat finished pieces with a spray fabric finish.

# Needlepoint place mats

The pleasures of needlepoint, the art of creating embroidered designs on canvas with yarn and a tapestry needle, have been familiar to women for centuries. Today, men are discovering this absorbing craft as a means of relaxation. The classic needlepoint designs for footstool and chair covers, although still popular, have given way to a whole new vista of interesting accessories, home furnishings, and some very striking wall hangings. Designs vary from classic patterns to unique originals.

Needlepoint canvas is available in single (mono) or double (penelope) thread mesh, and the canvas mesh varies from coarse to fine, depending on the number of threads per inch. Blunt tapestry needles used for stitching come in different eye sizes to suit the canvas and yarn used. Yarns come in a rainbow of colors and a range of thicknesses to accommodate the mesh size of the canvas. A set of needlepoint place mats, as shown, is a unique and serviceable table accessory. You can duplicate the place setting design illustrated, or copy your own silver and china pattern for the place setting design on the mat.

Materials: 15-inch-by-20-inch penelope or mono canvas, 10 mesh per 1 inch; a knife, fork and spoon; a dinner plate; set of waterproof felt-tipped markers, if possible, in the same colors as the design; roll of masking tape; No. 17 tapestry needle; and 40-yard skeins of Persian (3-ply) or tapestry (4-ply) needlepoint yarn in the following colors and quantities: 6 skeins pale gray, for the silver; 1 skein dark gray, for silver highlights; 10 skeins white, for the plate; and 1 skein each dark green and gold, for the china pattern and rim of the plate (or 1 skein of each color to duplicate your china pattern; estimate 2 ⅙ yards for each square inch of 10-mesh canvas to be covered).

You also need the following colors and quantities of yarn to duplicate the background: 9 skeins dark blue; 18 skeins light blue; 9 skeins bright green; and 5 skeins light green. If desired, substitute other colors of your choice in the same quantities listed above.

Also required are: a piece of linen, felt, or other woven fabric, 14 by 19 inches, for the backing of each place mat; a needlepoint frame or two 15-inch and two 20-inch canvas stretchers; sharp, pointed scissors; a board; rustproof pushpins; and a terry-cloth towel. Check with your hardware dealer to be sure the pushpins are rustproof.

## Marking designs on the canvas

Needlepoint can be worked in your lap. However, since the Continental stitch tends to pull canvas out of shape, it is recommended that the canvas be kept squared by tacking it to a needlepoint frame or tacking it to canvas stretchers with pushpins. Apply masking tape around the raw edges of canvas to prevent raveling. Copy your design directly on the canvas with waterproof felt-tip pens, as shown on diagram. Finished dimensions for each place mat will be 13 by 18 inches, with a customary 2-inch allowance of unworked canvas on each of the four sides. This allows for turning edges under when finishing the place mats. Work an additional 2 rows to finished dimensions. To trace outline of dinner plate, turn plate face down in approximate center of canvas, and outline it with felt-tip pen. Measure and mark a 1½-inch rim inside plate edge. Place silver in the proper positions on each side of plate, then with pen trace around the outline of knife, fork and spoon. Mark on canvas the light and dark accent areas of silver, using actual pieces as guide.

# Needlepoint place mats

Mark rows of vertical stripes from each 13-inch edge to center in the following sequence, starting at one side and working toward the center of the place mat: Band 1: 5 rows dark blue, 1 row light blue, 3 rows dark blue, 8 rows light blue, 2 rows dark blue. Band 2: 4 rows bright green, 2 rows dark blue, 3 rows bright green, 4 rows light green, 2 rows dark

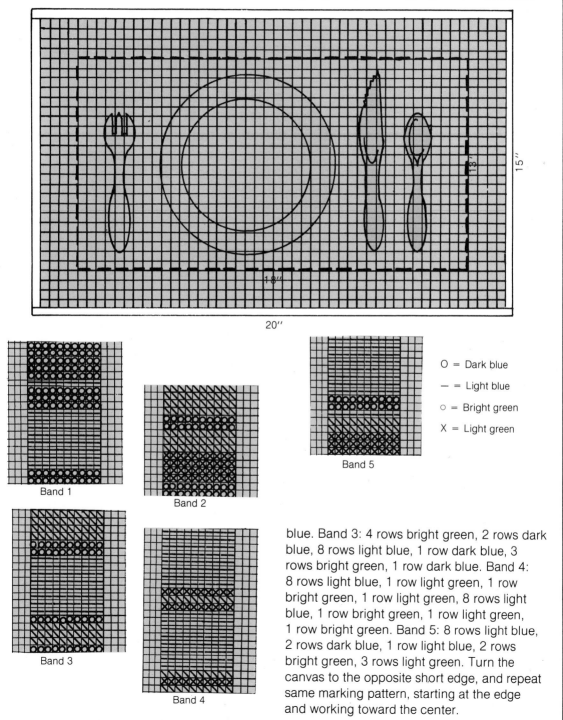

Band 1

Band 2

Band 3

Band 4

Band 5

O = Dark blue

— = Light blue

○ = Bright green

X = Light green

blue. Band 3: 4 rows bright green, 2 rows dark blue, 8 rows light blue, 1 row dark blue, 3 rows bright green, 1 row dark blue. Band 4: 8 rows light blue, 1 row light green, 1 row bright green, 1 row light green, 8 rows light blue, 1 row bright green, 1 row light green, 1 row bright green. Band 5: 8 rows light blue, 2 rows dark blue, 1 row light blue, 2 rows bright green, 3 rows light green. Turn the canvas to the opposite short edge, and repeat same marking pattern, starting at the edge and working toward the center.

# Needlepoint place mats

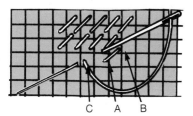

Continental stitch

## Doing the Continental stitch

The entire canvas is worked in the same basic diagonal stitch, the Continental. Following the diagram, bring needle from wrong side of canvas through A, down through B and out at C. You can work the Continental on penelope (double mesh) or mono (single mesh) canvas, always right to left. When you complete the last stitch of a row, turn canvas around clockwise and work the following row again from right to left.

## Stitching design and background

Work Continental stitch as described above. Stitch silverware pieces and plate first, using 1- to 2-foot lengths of yarn. (Longer lengths will fray and pull.) Work yarn ends through and between stitches on wrong side as you stitch. Stitch background bands of stripes next, starting at one end and working toward the center. Stitch the other half of mat background by starting at the opposite edge and working toward the center. With shorter sides horizontal, stitch right to left, turning work at end of each row. Block finished place mat following instructions given in CRAFTNOTES.

## Backing and finishing the mats

After blocking, trim unworked edges of canvas to ½ inch for place mat seam allowance. Trim backing fabric to measure 18½ by 13½ inches; fold under raw edges of fabric and baste. Do the same with raw edges of the canvas. Notch corners (see illustration) to turn under neatly.

Then slip-stitch canvas to backing, mesh by mesh. (If any exposed canvas shows, cover with a needlepoint Continental stitch.) Press.

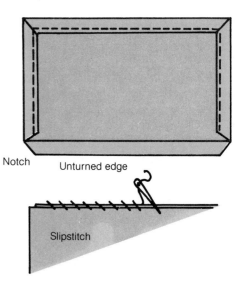

Notch    Unturned edge

Slipstitch

If your dining table has a glass top over wood, position place mats on table beneath the glass top. The mats need not be removed until they need some freshening. Soaking or sponging with a cold-water detergent solution helps keep needlepoint clean, soft, and bright.

# Crocheted afghan

This handsome crocheted afghan is worked in one piece with thick yarn, a large crochet hook and basically one stitch, the double crochet stitch. Considering its size when complete (52 inches by 58 inches), it works up rather quickly. The increases and decreases in working across each row, producing an undulating chevron design, keep it interesting for both the beginner and the more advanced crocheter. There are four yarn colors used in making the afghan and these colors change frequently in the work to create wide and narrow stripes.

Materials: size J crochet hook; tape measure; safety pins; and knitting worsted in the following colors and quantities: A (Medium green), 8 ozs.; B (Peach), 4 ozs.; C (Jade), 16 ozs.; and D (Cranberry), 8 ozs.

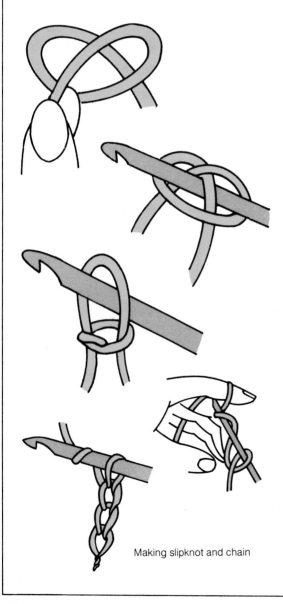

Making slipknot and chain

### The pattern colors

Using the colors indicated in materials needed, or substituting your own choices, the color pattern will run as follows: Rows 1 to 3, A; row 4, B; row 5, C; row 6, D; row 7, A; row 8, D; row 9, B; rows 10 to 11, A; row 12, C; and row 13, A. Rows 14 to 18, C; rows 19 to 20, D; rows 21 to 25, C; rows 26 to 36, repeat colors used for rows 2 to 11. Repeat rows 14 to 35, two more times plus rows 14 to 25. For the border, repeat rows 1 to 13 in reverse color order beginning with row 13.

The afghan is crocheted on a foundation chain of 196 stitches and will be worked in 8 panels, each of which should measure 6½ inches.

### Making the foundation chain

Start with color A, and make a slipknot on the crochet hook about 6 inches from the end of the yarn. Pull one end of yarn to tighten knot. Place crochet hook between right index finger and thumb, holding hook as you would a pencil. Thread a strand of yarn over ring finger, under middle finger, and over index finger, holding short end between thumb and middle finger. If more tension is desired, wrap yarn around little finger. Now you are ready to chain stitch. Insert hook under and over strand. Catch yarn with hook and draw it through loop. Make 196 chain stitches to form the foundation chain. The entire afghan will be crocheted on this chain, and when complete, it will measure approximately 52 by 58 inches.

# Crocheted afghan

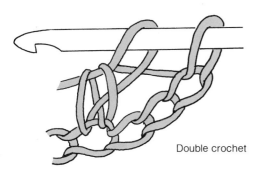

Double crochet

## Doing the double crochet

The double crochet stitch is used throughout. To make a double crochet, start with the loop from the last chain stitch still on the hook, yarn over hook, insert hook into the 4th chain from hook. Draw up a loop. There will be 3 loops on hook. Wrap yarn over hook once again and draw yarn through the first 2 loops on hook, yarn over again, draw through last 2 loops on hook, completing the double crochet.

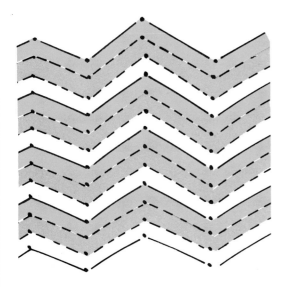

## Crocheting row 1

Double crochet in each of next 10 chain stitches, 3 double crochets in next chain. Work 1 double crochet in next 10 chains, then work 1 double crochet in the next 3 chains as follows: yarn over, insert the hook in the next 3 chain stitches, catch yarn and pull

through first two loops on hook, yarn over, catch yarn, pull through remaining two loops, thus completing 1 double crochet in 3 chains. This pattern of 24 stitches is repeated across, ending with 10 double crochets in each of the next 10 chain stitches, and 1 double crochet in the last 2 chain stitches. Chain 3 and turn the work.

## Crocheting row 2

(The 3 chains you made before turning work are considered the first stitch.) Begin working in the second stitch and work only the back loop of each stitch. Make one double crochet in next 10 stitches, 3 double crochets in next stitch, 10 double crochet stitches, 1 double crochet in next 3 stitches, repeat across. Repeat this sequence of stitches across the entire row to within 2 stitches from the end of the row, then make 1 double crochet in last 2 stitches, chain 3, and turn work.

## Crocheting rest of afghan

Repeat row 2 exactly for the next 94 rows, always making 10 double crochet stitches, increasing 3 double crochets in one stitch; then making 10 more double crochets; then decreasing by making 1 double crochet in next 3 stitches; ending the row with 10 double crochets, 1 double crochet in last two stitches and making 3 chains before turning work to begin the next row.

## To change yarn colors

To change to a different color yarn, following the pattern at the beginning of this project instruction, cut off the yarn that is being worked, leaving a 2-inch tail, attach new color, and continue to work the pattern stitches as directed.

## To finish afghan

Finish off by cutting yarn a few inches from hook, drawing end through loop on hook, then removing hook and pulling end tightly to close loop. Weave ends through last few stitches of the last row. Block as directed in CRAFTNOTES or have it done professionally.

# Macramé wall hanging

As a contemporary art form, macramé, the ancient art of decorative knotting, is becoming increasingly more popular, especially in the creation of fashions and jewelry. The availability of new fibers, in a wide variety of textures and colors, is in part responsible for this current interest in knotted designs. Macramé started as a functional form and later it appeared most frequently as a hand-knotted fringe decoration. British and American seamen referred to the craft as "square knotting." Contemporary macramé is used for chair seats, plant hangers, bedspreads, necklaces and wall hangings. The macramé wall decoration shown, worked from sisal and beads, is one a beginner can complete successfully in a short time.

Materials: heavy 2-ply sisal; two 18-inch wood dowels; nylon thread; working board or surface; T-shaped pins; ruler; scissors; and 22 large glass beads (6 coral, 16 green). Be sure the beads have openings large enough to thread easily yet snugly over the sisal. Depending on the type of sisal used, calculate amount required by making a small sampler of the knots used in the design (see Macramé vest).

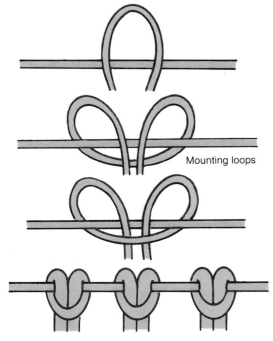

Mounting loops

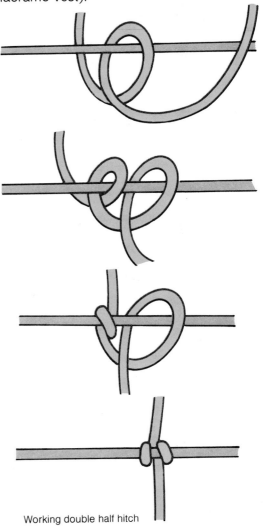

## Mounting the cords

To mount cords and make mounting loops for a hanging measuring 12 inches wide by 54 inches long, cut 10 lengths of sisal, each length 7 to 8 times longer than the length of the completed piece. Double each length in half, forming a loop. Mount the 10 doubled lengths of sisal around top dowel with a holding row of mounting loops. Take each double cord to form a loop over dowel. Reach up through the loop with your thumb and index

Working double half hitch

# Macramé wall hanging

finger and bring both the free ends back down through the loop. Tighten knot. When all 10 doubled lengths of sisal are mounted, there will be 20 working cords.

## Knotting the cords

Make 2 rows of horizontal double half hitches, using outside cords as holding cords. The principle of this knot is that you work the two outside cords to the center of the work by making a series of double half hitch knots on each side. Starting on the right side, take the last cord (holding cord) and place it horizontally across the other cords, pinning it taut.

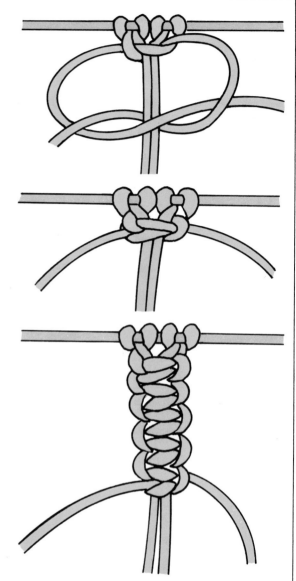

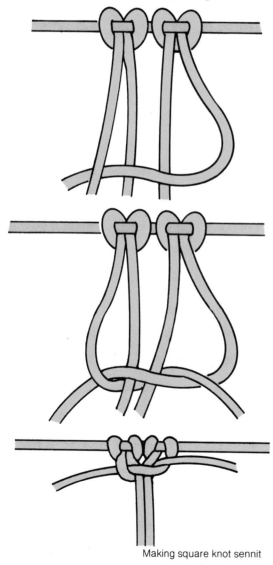

Making square knot sennit

Then, starting with adjacent cord, lay each free length of sisal under the horizontal cord, bring end up and loop it over horizontal cord. Drop free end behind horizontal cord and pull loop tight. Again, pass same free length behind anchor or holding cord and through the loop formed. Pull knot tight. Continue from edge across row to center of working cords, making 2 loops with each knotting or working cord. Take the holding cord on the left edge and, in the same manner, work to the center. At center of row, cross holding cords and work outward to edges again.

## Macramé wall hanging

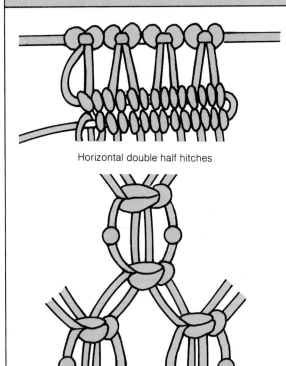

Horizontal double half hitches

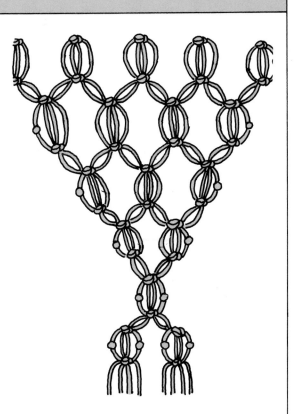

Alternating square knots and beads

When first 2 rows are completed, divide ends of sisal into 5 groups of 4 strands and make 5 sennits with 2 square knots in each. A sennit is a 4-strand chain of square knots. The square knot is worked with 4 cords; the two outside cords are the knotting cords, and the two center cords are used as foundation cords that lie flat and give body to the square knot formed. To tie a square knot, cross right outer strand over 2 center strands and under outer left strand. With knot in this position, pick up and place outer left strand under 2 center strands, and up through right loop. Next, cross left outer strand over 2 center strands in same group. With cords in this position pick up right outer strand and pass it over left outer strand, under 2 center strands and up through left loop. Pull tightly.

### Lacing in a diamond star of beads
After the row of square knot sennits, repeat 2 rows of horizontal double half hitches. Then, starting with center 4 lengths, work 2 square

knots, threading beads on each of the 4 cords between the knots. Separate cords below second square knot and pick up adjacent cords. Make 2 square knots, threading beads between the knots and placing colors as pictured. Continue to divide groups of 4 cords in half and pick up adjacent cords, thus working diamonds within a diamond star, from center outward to edge, then inward again, from edge to a double-pointed center. All done with square knots.

### Hitching to the bottom dowel
Reversing sequence of rows of top knots, make 2 rows of horizontal double half hitches, then 5 sennits of 2 square knots each from 5 groups of 4 cords. Repeat 2 rows horizontal double half hitch pattern. Finally, knot a row of double half hitches around bottom dowel, using dowel as a holding or anchor cord. Trim ends of sisal evenly and ravel out each sisal cord. Attach and tie a loop of clear nylon cord to center top of the wall piece for hanging.

# Woven-yarn wall hanging

You don't have to invest in expensive equipment to learn weaving. Among the several types available, the frame loom is one you can make yourself from a picture frame or a set of four canvas stretchers, a hammer and some nails. One free horizontal thread (the weft) is laced over and under a taut set of vertical threads (the warp). From this basic principle, an infinite variety of textures and color relationships can develop. You can use just about any thread, yarn, rope, string or any pliable fiber you choose. The weaving process has an immediacy that inspires novices to try individual experiments in fiber design. The rich hues and thick, soft textures of this miniature hanging are achieved by weaving the colors at random with a darning needle.

Materials: a picture frame or set of four canvas stretchers in dimensions close to finished size of hanging (this one measures 7¾ by 14 inches); 32 nails; a hammer; cotton carpet warp yarn or a ball of heavy crochet cotton in a neutral color; large blunt tapestry needle; large comb; craft, rug or quickpoint yarn in shades of bright and burnt orange, red, yellow, coral, deep purple and white (about ½ ounce for each color); two wood dowels, about 10 inches long, for hanging; a package of thumb tacks; spray starch; and clear-drying white glue.

### Making frame loom
Prepare the frame or stretchers on the wrong side by marking 16 nail positions ½ inch apart on each of the two shorter sides of the rectangle. With hammer, drive nails halfway into frame at each of the marked positions. These sides of the rectangle will become the top and bottom of the loom.

### Winding warp yarn around nails
Lay warp, vertical threads, of carpet yarn or crochet cotton by taking one end of yarn and winding one complete turn around lower left corner nail and tie securely. Draw yarn up to the first top left corner nail and half turn around nail, then draw yarn down to second lower nail from left, and wind a half turn around nail. Continue winding up, then down around the nails, working across the frame, pulling yarn taut but not too tight. End by tying yarn to top right corner nail and breaking off.

### Starting to weave weft yarn
Cut weft yarn into 18-inch lengths. Thread one length through tapestry needle, leaving a 2-inch tail. Starting at bottom left corner, weave the weft yarn over and under each warp thread, working across from left to right end of row, then work the weft across right

to left, in an interlocking darning motion. Space rows closely by pushing work toward bottom with teeth of a large comb. Do this at end of every row. Be sure to keep both edges of the work straight, so the width of the woven piece is the same for the entire length, from bottom to top. Do not pull yarn too tightly; this will change the width. Rethread needles as needed, working strand ends into the work on wrong side. Change colors as desired, at any place in the weaving. The pattern in the photograph looks like cloud formations and peninsulas, jutting across the warp and disappearing into points. The deeper bands of solid

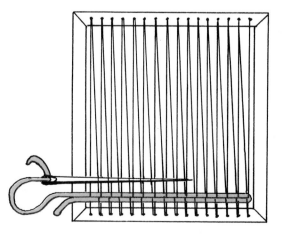

## Woven-yarn wall hanging

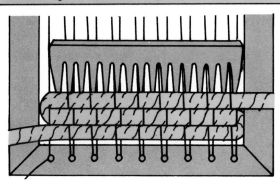

color toward the edges provide a provocative accent to the design. Weave some areas loose or leave some unwoven, as shown, if desired.

### Creating textural accents

To achieve additional texture accents, make a few rya-type knots along a woven row, around warp threads. Thread needle with one strand, or as many as will fit through the eye. Working across the same row, starting at any warp thread, bring yarn through warp, then up to form a loop of height desired; skip one warp. Bring yarn down through the next warp and out through the warp before it. Working with the needle heading right to left, continue this backstitch motion, pulling up loops to form knots at every other warp thread. Leave loops uncut, unless a cut pile effect is desired. When you have finished the desired number of knots, cut end of yarn on right side the same length as the loops and work it across warp to blend with other strands.

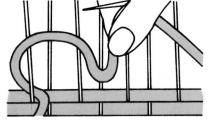

### Finishing the hanging

To finish, weave into work all loose ends on back. Spray piece with a few coats of spray starch to stiffen. Brush a coat of glue along the top and bottom rows of weaving on wrong side of work, but do not glue weaving to frame. Allow to dry, then pull out nails along top and bottom of frame, replacing them as you go with thumbtacks. This is done to keep the edge in line until all nails are withdrawn from the frame. Then remove tacks to free weaving from frame. Lay dowels along top edge and overcast with yarn around dowel and through top loops (heading) of warp. Break off yarn at end of overcasting, tie an overhand knot and work end through over-casting on wrong side. Repeat to fasten bottom dowel. Tie two equal lengths of yarn to each top corner and then to each other. The rainbow weaving is ready for hanging.

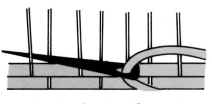

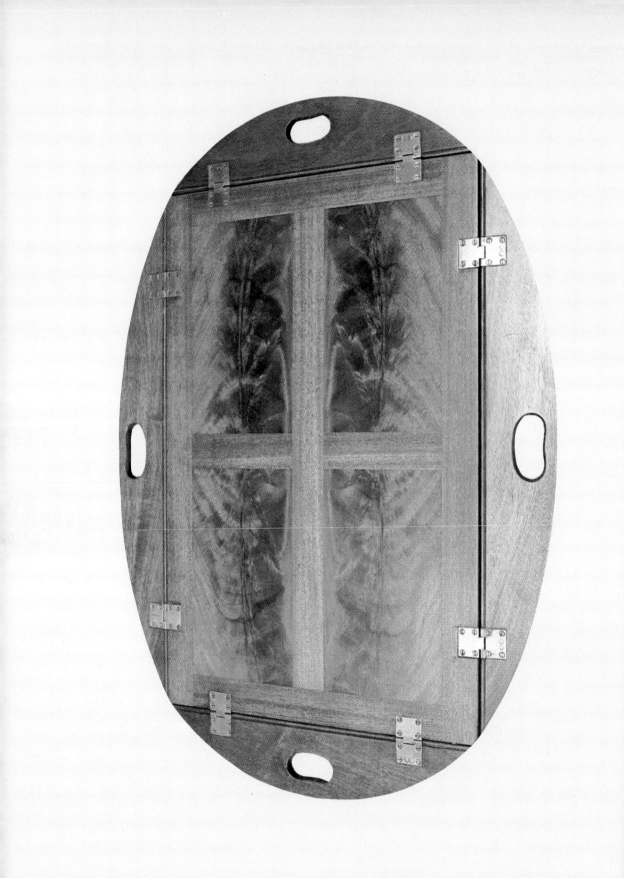

# Inlaid tabletop

The inlaid design on this tabletop appears to be wood inlay work, but it is surface inlay made of veneer, which is wood sliced very thinly from logs. Because it is cut from around the log, rather than through it, face veneer often has very distinctive and striking grain patterns. Look for these when buying veneer. The tabletop shown measures 20 by 30 inches. The veneer is glued to a base of ⅜-inch plywood; the plywood's raw edges may be covered with wood tape or molding.

Materials: four 8-by-12-inch panels of wood veneer (select those with grain patterns that match or complement one another); 12½ feet of 2¾-inch-wide wood veneer strip; stain; clear shellac; and casein or liquid hide glue. Tools needed are: sharp thin-bladed knife; rule; roller; straightedge ruler; glue brush; paintbrush; rags; coarse abrasive paper; and two grades of sandpaper, fine and very fine.

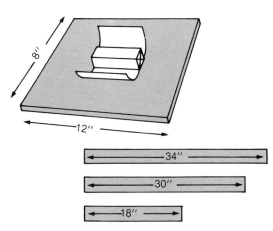

### Preparing plywood and veneer
Use the coarse abrasive paper to roughen the plywood in order to make a good bonding surface. For best results, wrap the paper around a block of wood that fits comfortably in the hand. Cut two 2¾-inch-wide veneer strips 34 inches long, one 30 inches long and three 18 inches long. If the veneer's thicknesses are wavy, moisten them on both sides and stack flat between boards a few hours to straighten.

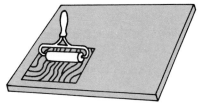

### Gluing veneer panels
Mix hide glue with water according to manufacturer's directions. Brush a thin coat of glue on the roughened plywood surface and let

dry. On a dry surface, arrange pieces of veneer as you wish them to be laid, using the grains as design elements to achieve a pleasing effect. Start with the 8-by-12-inch panels. All veneer pieces are cut a fraction of an inch oversize; they will be trimmed after they are in place to insure a tight fit.

With a pencil, carefully mark on the plywood the exact location of the four corners of each of the four panels of veneer as they are to be placed. Spread glue on the plywood where the first panel is to be attached, 2 inches from the narrow end of the tabletop and 1½ inches from the long edge.

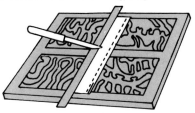

Spread glue on the back of the veneer panel and press it into place. Rub the panel with the roller, working out bubbles toward edge, until it is firmly bonded. Repeat the procedure with the remaining three panels.

### Trimming and placing the strips
Mark one of the 18-inch strips ⅜ inch in from each long edge. Place it on top of the veneer panels across the middle of the tabletop; measure from both ends to make sure it is perfectly centered. Set a straightedge ruler along one of the marks and with a knife, cut through both the veneer strip and panels.

Move the straightedge ruler to the line along the other edge of the strip, and again cut through both strip and panels. Remove waste and apply glue to the plywood and the back of the strip. Press the strip in place between the panels. Move the roller heavily over the joints, pressing toward them from both sides to close them tightly.

Mark the 30-inch-lengthwise center strip, ⅜ inch in from each long edge, and set it in place, overlapping the panels and the center strip. Measure to make sure the lengthwise center strip is equidistant from the sides. Place the straightedge ruler along one edge mark and use the knife to cut through the lengthwise center strip, panels, and cross strip. Then move the ruler to the other edge, mark and repeat the cutting operation. Remove scraps, apply glue, and press in place, rolling firmly.

Roll firmly to close joint. Repeat with the other end of the strip. Similarly measure and cut the two strips for the long edges of the tabletop and glue in place. Trim the ends of the long strips flush with the ends of the tabletop.

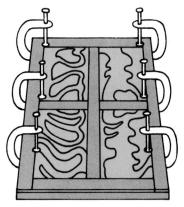

### Staining and shellacking

Apply pressure to the veneered surface by clamping lumber or plywood across it or by weighting it with books or other heavy objects. Allow glue to dry for two to three days. Sand the surface of the tabletop with fine, then very fine, sandpaper. Apply stain to the veneered surface; rub off with a soft rag. Repeat the stain application and rub off stain as before. Repeat until the desired shade is achieved. Sand the surface lightly. Apply at least two coats of shellac, sanding lightly with very-fine-grit sandpaper between coats.

Mount tabletop on a wood or metal base with screws, dowels, or screws and angles, depending on the type of base you choose. If desired, you may wish to cut and stain four fold-up sides, the same measurements as the sides of the finished tabletop, and attach them with hinge plates to the underside.

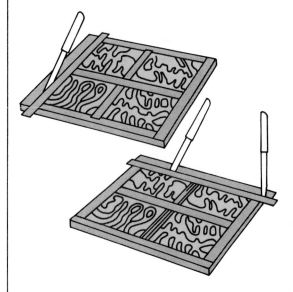

Mark the two remaining 18-inch strips to a 2 inch width. Place one strip along one of the short edges of the tabletop, flush with the outer edge, and overlap the panels and the center strip. Set the ruler along the marked line on the strip and cut the same way as the other strips, as described above. Remove waste, apply glue and press strip into place.

# Button mosaics

Buttons are a unique medium for mosaic work, providing great versatility in design. Unlike the angular appearance of stone and marble, used in traditional mosaics, the contour and textural variations of buttons create a jewel-like illusion, particularly when the mosaic is displayed in the proper light. Use buttons with flat backs, and select to suit the design. Odd buttons collected from old clothing are satisfactory to start a project, but you will have to supplement them with buttons of a specific color, size or shape to complete the design as planned. This button mosaic portrait of a lady is reminiscent of the Byzantine mosaics of the Greek and Russian Orthodox Churches. The finished size is 30 by 40 inches.

Materials: two sets of canvas stretchers, 30 and 40 inches (or, for a smaller size, use a 3:4 ratio, such as 15 and 20 inches); canvas tacks; unprimed cotton or linen canvas, 32 by 42 inches (or similar proportions to accommodate size of canvas frame); picture hooks and wire; white gesso primer; large paintbrush; clear-drying white glue; large, flat work surface; sheet of paper the same dimensions as the canvas; dressmaker's carbon paper and a pencil or tracing wheel; 10 inches of beige fabric for the lady's dress; an assortment of flat-bottomed buttons; and muffin tins or small dishes, one for each size and color button you are using.

To determine the exact sizes, shades, texture and quantities of buttons needed, study the pattern, assembling buttons on it. The buttons used for the background of the mosaic illustrated are: two shades of large, blue buttons for each corner; a large, blue button for the center of each flower near corners; medium or small deep blue buttons for the flower petals; alternating shades of blue in large and medium sizes, for the inner row of the oval frame; alternating large and medium-sized buttons in two other shades of blue for the next row of the frame; small, deep blue buttons for the third row of the frame; and alternating blue and white small buttons for the outer row of the oval.

The lady's hat requires buttons of any assorted shades and sizes, including: white, beige, blue, brown, gold and green. For the hair, eyebrows and eyes, use assorted sizes of black and brown buttons (the pupils are two large, dark buttons). Three small red buttons form the mouth, and assorted sizes and shades of white and light beige buttons fill in the face and neck. The necklace is of large beige buttons, enclosed by two smaller beige buttons, and a light brown, medium-sized button for the pendant. For the dress, use small beige buttons and small and medium-small light brown buttons, placed on the beige fabric background in six alternating rows.

## Drawing design

Draw the design on the paper cut to the size of the frame, following pattern illustrated. Adapt button quantities and sizes to the size canvas you are using. To transfer the design to the canvas, place the dressmaker's carbon paper, carbon side down, between the canvas and the design; then trace design with a pencil or tracing wheel. Mark placement of rows of buttons or outlines of shapes with dotted lines, and centers of circular shapes with "X" marks. With experience, you can dispense with the paper pattern and design directly on background, using only a few pencil marks for guidance. Using the pattern and dressmaker's carbon paper, transfer the dress outline to the beige fabric, cut out and set aside.

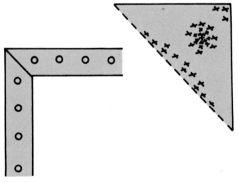

### Priming canvas

Brush the unmarked side of canvas with a coat of white gesso primer and allow to dry in a well-ventilated area for 24 hours. This gives the canvas body. Stretch dry canvas tightly, unprimed side out, over stretchers, checking alignment of design's corners with the stretched canvas. When satisfied, tack canvas securely to back of stretchers. While canvas is drying, separate buttons into dishes or muffin tins by size and color.

## Button mosaics

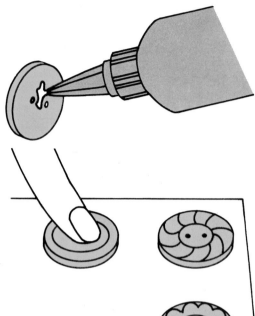

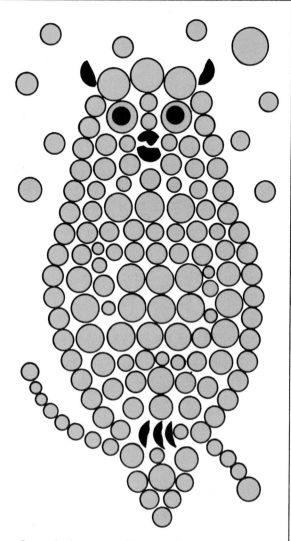

### Mounting buttons on design

When the canvas is dry, spread a thin coat of glue on the back of the cut-out dress fabric and position on canvas. Then start to apply buttons to canvas, working one at a time. Spread glue on the back side of button, then press into position. You can work from the center of the design to edges of canvas; or begin with the frame, then place buttons to form the neck, face, hair and hat. To complete, apply corner buttons. Work in the way that is most comfortable for you. The glue dries quickly, so apply buttons at a steady pace. As you work, the mosaic takes shape quickly. When all buttons have been applied, wait 15 minutes before hanging.

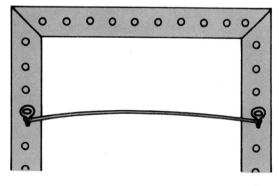

### Completing mosaic

This mosaic is designed so the canvas frame is unadorned and serves as a frame for the work. To hang, insert screw eyes into back of the side pieces of the frame, about 10 inches from the top of frame. Thread screw eyes with picture wire and fasten wire ends to screws. Hang mosaic in a well-lighted area, where the light plays on the button surfaces.

Create bolder designs and experiment with buttons broken in two or three pieces. The sharp edges of the pieces provide accents in the design in contrast to the rounded shapes of the other buttons, as illustrated in the owl design above. You can also design a mosaic entirely of broken buttons.

# Juice-can hassock

A child's hassock made of recycled juice cans, old socks and nylon stockings may not seem like much, but after it is covered with a handsome piece of upholstery fabric, it looks quite impressive. The hassock is approximately ten inches high and fifteen inches in diameter.

Materials: seven 46-ounce juice cans with tops left on (punch holes to pour out juice, rinse thoroughly, and dry); seven large athletic socks; several old clean nylon stockings cut up for stuffing; two 16-inch squares of corrugated cardboard; one yard of 54-inch upholstery fabric; 1 ½ yards of cording; a spool of heavy upholstery thread; a strong needle; scissors; and a tape measure.

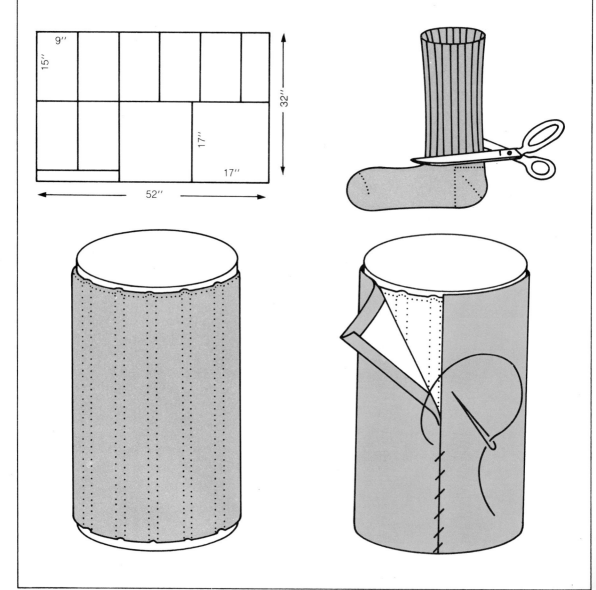

# Juice-can hassock

### Covering cans

From the upholstery fabric, cut two pieces 17 inches square and seven pieces 9 by 15 inches. Cut off the socks at the heels and pull the upper part of socks over each can, smoothing them out carefully. Cover each can with a 9-by-15-inch piece of fabric, wrapping the fabric around the cans over the socks. First fold under the raw edges along the 15-inch dimension, wrap around can, then fold over the

raw edge where they meet at the middle of the can, and sew together with an overcast stitch.

### Assembling cans

Place the seven covered cans together, with one in the middle and the rest surrounding it. Fabric seams should all be turned to the inside so they are concealed. With an overcast stitch, sew together where the cans touch. When all are joined, turn the assembly over and sew together on the other side, in the same fashion.

### Cutting corrugated cardboard pieces

Place the can assembly on one of the pieces of corrugated cardboard and trace around the outside of the cans. Repeat with the other piece of cardboard. Cut the two pieces of cardboard along the traced lines; they should look like flowers.

### Cutting top and bottom fabric pieces

Use the cardboard as a pattern to cut out the two larger pieces of fabric, allowing an extra 1 inch of fabric all around. Place one of the cardboard pieces on the can assembly, then place

Fabric: allow 1 inch beyond cardboard.

Cardboard

one of the pieces of cut fabric over it. Turn under the excess material. Join the surface fabric to the fabric covering the cans with an overcast sewing stitch. This will form the bottom of the hassock.

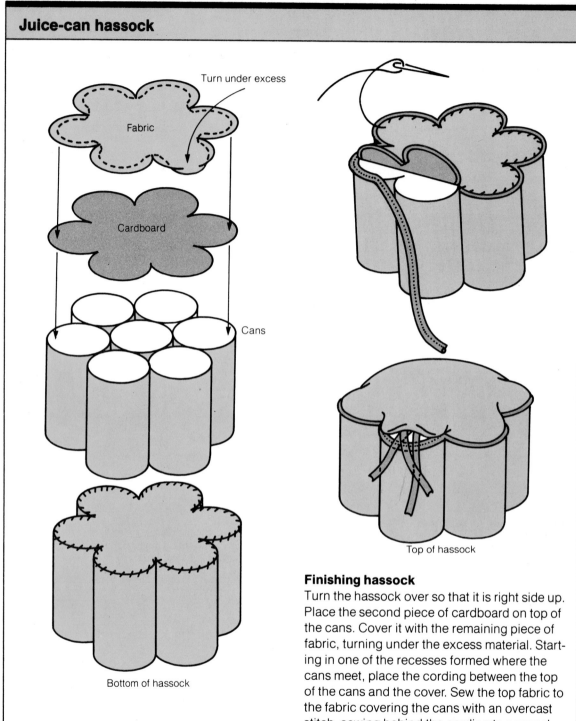

Turn under excess

Fabric

Cardboard

Cans

Bottom of hassock

Top of hassock

## Finishing hassock

Turn the hassock over so that it is right side up. Place the second piece of cardboard on top of the cans. Cover it with the remaining piece of fabric, turning under the excess material. Starting in one of the recesses formed where the cans meet, place the cording between the top of the cans and the cover. Sew the top fabric to the fabric covering the cans with an overcast stitch, sewing behind the cording to conceal the stitches. When approximately three-quarters of the top is sewn, stuff the cut-up nylon stockings between the cardboard and the fabric. Use plenty of stuffing; the top will flatten out if there is not enough.

When the top is sufficiently stuffed, close the opening, sewing with an overcast stitch.

# Ceramic chess pieces

Handmade chess pieces have always been coveted by princes and chess buffs, and these handsome ceramic chessmen are no exception. The pieces are formed by rolling and layering coils of clay, in a fashion similar to that used for the Ceramic lamp project. When fired and glazed, the chessmen serve not only as game pieces, but as lovely decorative objects when they are not in play.

Materials: high-fire red clay; slip or slurry (a binding agent made of clay and water); a metal kidney-shaped tool, for smoothing; a shaving tool with a triangular wire at one end and an oval wire at the other end, to remove excess clay from the surfaces during the drying process; several layers of newspaper, to cover the work surface; several small plastic bags (one for each chess piece); powdered ferric oxide, to make the stain; a ½-inch paintbrush; and ingredients to duplicate the high-fire turquoise glaze (2% copper carbonate, 5% tin oxide, and 93% water), and the lavender glaze (2.5% rutile, 2.5% tin oxide, 2.5% manganese dioxide, and 92.5% water). All items are available at craft or hobby stores. Also needed are: wooden spoon and containers, to mix stain and glazes; a sponge to remove excess water from the working area; and a large, flat working surface (preferably wood, which will absorb the seepage of water). It is recommended that the pieces be fired professionally at a local pottery or porcelain studio.

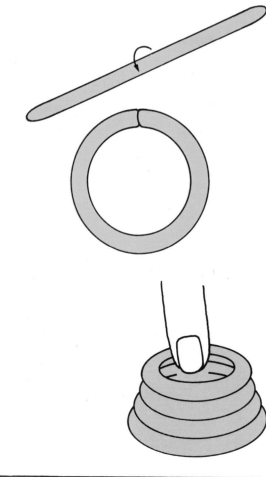

**Building chessmen with coils of clay**
Begin by spreading several layers of newspapers over your work surface to absorb moisture as you work. Mix a pastelike binder called slip or slurry, combining clay and water. Roll several lengths of clay coils about ¼ inch thick. Take a small ball of clay and with the palms of your hands, roll the clay on a flat surface to form the rope-like clay coil. Be sure the thickness is the same for the entire length. Cut into 2-inch or 3-inch pieces.

# Ceramic chess pieces

Lay a length of coil on the newspaper surface and form a small circle, the diameter of which is equal to the measurements given below for the piece you are making. Lay more coils in a spiral over the first circle, smoothing with slip after every few layers and smoothing piece on the inside with slip, the kidney tool, and your fingers.

Follow this procedure in building each chess piece, varying widths and heights of coiled layers of clay to shape each chessman.

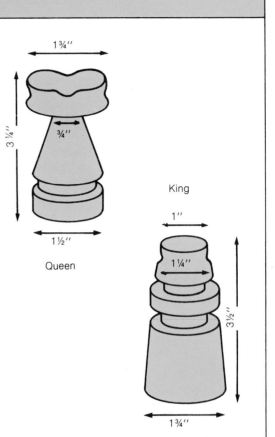

King

Queen

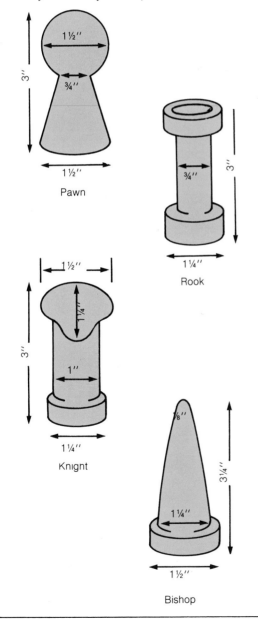

Pawn

Rook

Knight

Bishop

If newspaper sticks to clay, simply peel it off. When you have completed the layering process, smooth the outside of the piece and define indentations with the kidney tool, the shaving tool, and your fingers. As you work, support pieces by placing one or more fingers inside the base and holding the bottom with your thumb.

## Sizing the pieces

Measurements of each chess piece are detailed in the listing that follows. Total height of each pawn is 3 inches. The 16 pawns have a base tapering from 1½ to ¾ inches in diameter and 2 inches high; and heads are 1½ inches in diameter at the widest part and 1 inch high. Each of the 4 rooks is 3 inches tall, with a base 1¼ inches in diameter and ¾ inch high: a midsection ¾ inch in diameter and 1½ inches high; and a top 1¼ inches in diameter and ¾ inch high. The 4 knights stand 3 inches tall, with a base diameter of 1¼ inches and base height of ¾ inch; their heads are 2¼ inches tall and 1½ inches across at top of head, 1¼ inches long at the forepart of the head and ¾ inch wide at tip of nose. The total height of each bishop is 3¼ inches. The 4 bishops have bases 1½ inches in diameter and ½ inch tall, tapering in a cone from 1¼ inches in diameter at bottom to ⅛ inch in diameter at tip. The cone is 2¾ inches tall. The 2 queens are a regal 3¼ inches tall, with bases ½ inch high and 1½ inches in diameter; indentations ⅛ inch and ¼ inch long between base and a midsection 1¾ inches high with a diameter tapering from 1⅝ inches to ¾ inch; and crowns 1¼ inches in diameter, slightly indented along midpoint of crown circumference, and ¾ inch high. Last, but certainly not least, our 2 kings stand on bases 1¾ inches in diameter and 1½ inches high; a ¼-inch-high and ⅛-inch-deep indentation separates base from the midsection, which is ½ inch high and 1⅝ inches in diameter; another indentation ¼ inch high and ⅛ inch deep separates midsection from crown. They are 1 inch high from neck to tip of crown and 1¼ inches across at the widest part of the crown, tapering to 1 inch in diameter at the very top. In all, the kings are 3½ inches tall. If you wish, you can vary the specific measurements of the pieces to suit the size of your chessboard, keeping approximately the same proportions.

## Drying and bisque firing the pieces
It takes about a week for clay to dry slowly and thoroughly. Enclose each piece tightly in a plastic bag and let stand 24 hours. Then

open the bag to allow air to circulate around clay piece. After additional drying, test with a moist finger; if it sticks slightly to the clay, the clay has reached a leather-hard stage. Remove plastic, give each piece a final smoothing with the kidney, and let pieces stand for a few days, until they are bone-dry (no moisture present). Have pieces fired to bisque temperature, indicated by a light pink color.

## Staining and second firing
Stain the newly fired pieces with a liquid mixture of ferric oxide and water; using the ½-inch paint brush, apply the stain to the inner

and outside surfaces. Let dry until your wet finger sticks slightly to surface. Then have them fired a second time.

## Glazing and final firing
While your chess pieces are firing, mix the glaze ingredients together for each color. Firing temperatures are measured by the melting points of clay cones placed inside a kiln. These particular glazes have a high firing temperature of 5 plus cone. Therefore, it is important that clays and glazes have compatible firing temperatures. Your clay supplier can help you select the right match. After the chess pieces have cooled from second firing, apply the glaze liberally. Brush half the chessmen with turquoise and half with lavender glaze. Do not glaze the base, or it will fuse to the inside of the kiln. Let dry until glaze sticks slightly to your wet finger. The colors of these glazes will thin during firing, allowing some of the stain to show through. Have pieces fired a third and final time.

# Acrylic game table

This strikingly modern game table is made of acrylic sheeting, a relatively new material for the amateur craftsman. It is a simple second project to attempt, after working with a small-dimensional cube such as the Acrylic cube planter project. In this project, you learn how to apply paint to the acrylic surface.

Materials: four square pieces of plastic ⅛ inch or ¼ inch thick, each 15¾ inches square, for the sides of the cube; and for the top, one piece 16 inches square (¼ inch thick) or 15⅞ inches square (⅛ inch thick). Have your dealer cut the pieces to size. You can cut the ⅛-inch thickness yourself, as described below. You also need: solvent cement in a needle-nose applicator, or solvent cement and a small paintbrush (available from the same dealer); masking tape; acrylic spray paint; 80-grit sandpaper; and a sanding block. Tools required are: sharp knife or razor blade; hooked plastic cutter resembling a penknife, called a scriber (optional); large flat board or worktable; wood blocks or heavy books to support pieces while you cement them; rubbing alcohol; anti-static plastic cleaner and polisher; and some soft towels.

## Cutting sheet plastic
The plastic sheet comes covered with a protective paper. Leave this paper in place on the 15¾-inch-square piece for the top. If you are working with ⅛-inch-thick plastic, score and break the plastic in the following manner. Mark dimensions first. Place the point of the sharp scriber at one edge of the material, and applying firm pressure, draw the tool along a straightedge the full length of the plastic. Repeat if necessary. To break large pieces such as these cleanly and easily, place the scored line over a ¾-inch dowel or pipe running the length of the intended break. Hold the larger side of the sheet with one hand and apply downward pressure on the short side of the break with the other hand. Sand all cut edges smooth with 80-grit sandpaper wrapped around a sanding block.

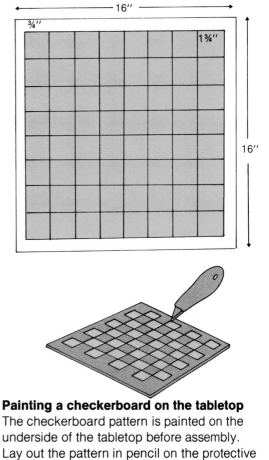

## Painting a checkerboard on the tabletop
The checkerboard pattern is painted on the underside of the tabletop before assembly. Lay out the pattern in pencil on the protective paper covering the plastic. The squares are 1¾ inches each, with a ¾-inch border all around the pattern. Outline only the squares

that are to be painted. Use a sharp utility knife or razor blade to score the outline of these squares on the paper, but do not press too hard or the knife will score the plastic. Then carefully cut out and remove these squares of paper, exposing the plastic in these squares. Cover the top border and edges with masking tape for protection. Spray a coat of acrylic paint on the exposed plastic. After 30 minutes,

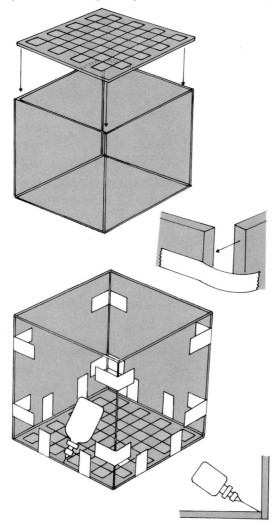

apply a second coat. Allow to dry completely. When paint is dry (not sticky to the touch), remove masking tape from the top border and edges.

### Joining all the parts
Assemble the table temporarily with masking tape, with one edge of each of the four side pieces overlapping the thickness of the edge of the matching side piece. With the painted side of the top facing the floor, place this top piece above the four-sided square. Carefully turn the assembled table upside down, so the top rests on a board or flat work surface. Using wood blocks or heavy books for vertical support, cement the four sides to the top, applying the solvent along the inside edges of the cube with the special applicator or a fine brush. Cement each edge in one continuous motion; avoid interrupted or erractic movements. Allow each edge to set for 10 minutes before cementing the next edge, so that the cement establishes a bond between matching parts. (Small pieces will set in a much shorter time.) Carefully lay the game table on one side, with the top buttressed by a wood block or book. Then cement along one lower inside edge, to the corner. Allow each side to set for 10 minutes, then turn the table to the next side and cement the next edge. Repeat until all joints are cemented, then allow the table to set for three hours to make sure the cement is thoroughly dry. Remove tape and protective paper. If you wish, you may assemble the table without preliminary taping, using the method described for the Acrylic cube project.

### Cleaning and polishing the table
Clean the game table thoroughly by applying rubbing alcohol with a towel, using short, even strokes. (Do not use detergent and water, or unwanted streaks will appear on the table surface.) When alcohol has dried, apply the plastic cleaner and polisher to give the table a brilliant antistatic finish and protect it against fingerprints. (Make sure the solution is at room temperature.) Shake container well and spray generously, wetting all surfaces. Then rub gently with a towel. While still wet, polish the table surfaces with a dry towel until they feel icy smooth. Now get out your chessmen or checkers and invite a companion to play with you.

# Tufted footstool

Tufting adds a decorative design to an upholstered piece, but its very practical function is to hold the stuffing of the piece firmly in place and prevent it from shifting. This project is a cushion for a small footstool, 9 by 13 inches, and 3½ inches thick.

Materials: fabric 20 by 24 inches (footstool shown covered with gold velvet); a piece of muslin the same size; ½ pound of horsehair stuffing, or substitute 3-inch-thick rubber or synthetic foam covered by 1 inch of cotton felt, cut to the size of the cushion; a piece of ⅜-inch plywood 9 by 13 inches; staples or upholstery tacks; twine; five shank buttons covered with the upholstery fabric; 48 inches of flat ornamental braid or round cord; white glue; and a footstool pedestal. Also needed are: scissors; stapler or tack hammer; ½-inch bit drill; and a tufting needle, which is a double-pointed needle with the thread hole near the end. Similar techniques can be used with a webbing base in re-covering an existing cushion, but plywood's rigidity makes it easier to work.

### Positioning of the tufts
Prepare the pattern, determining the five tuft positions on the cushion. There are many pos-

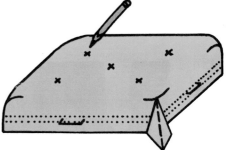

sible variations, but the outside rows should always be the same distance from the edges of the cushion, with other buttons spaced equally in between. Lay out the tufting pattern on the plywood base. Mark the position of each button on the base, and drill a ½-inch hole through the plywood at each mark. In the cushion shown, one button is located in the center of the cushion, with four others, each 2 inches in from the long edge of the base and 3 inches in from the shorter edge.

### Getting it all together with muslin
Arrange the horsehair or foam rubber piece (covered with cotton felt) on the base. Cover with the muslin, allowing it to overlap the base equally on all sides. Stretch the muslin gently until the stuffing is firmly packed, then fasten the muslin to the base with one staple or tack in the middle of each side. Using the pattern, mark the positions of the tufts on the muslin.

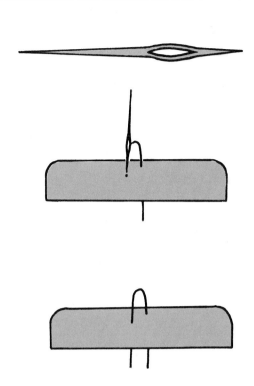

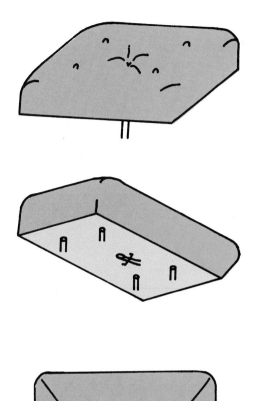

## Tufting the muslin cover

Cut ten 14-inch lengths of twine. Make sure that they are all the same length; this is important to assure uniform depth of tufts. Thread the tufting needle with a piece of twine and push the long end of the needle through the center hole in the base and up through the muslin where it is marked for the center tuft. Pull needle through, then bring the short end of the needle down through the muslin approximately ⅛ inch away and pull back down through the base. Remove the needle and pull the twine through so that both ends are of equal length. Repeat the process in each of the other tuft holes.

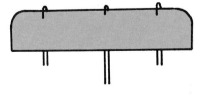

Again starting with the center tuft, pull the ends of the twine down, depressing the surface, until you are satisfied with the depth of the tuft (experiment to see what depth looks and feels best). Measure the length of the twine below the base, then tack or staple the twine to the bottom of the base. When all tufts have been formed, finish stapling the muslin to the base, spacing staples approximately 2 inches apart along all edges and folding over neatly at corners. Trim off excess muslin all around the base.

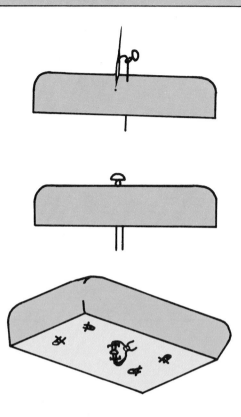

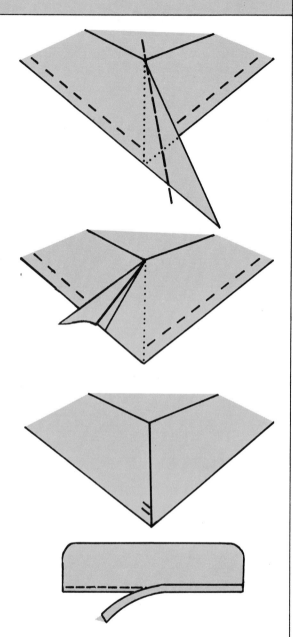

### Tufting the upholstery fabric

Place the upholstery fabric over the muslin, allowing it to overlap the base equally on all four sides. Fasten by stapling or tacking to the base at the midpoint of each side. Cut five more 14-inch lengths of twine, again making sure that all are the same length. Thread the needle with one of the lengths of twine and push the long end of the needle through the center hole of the base, through the muslin tuft and through the cover fabric. Pass the twine through the eye of the button shank, then push the short end of the needle back down through the fabric and the hole in the base. Pull twine through. Repeat with all other tufts. Then, starting with the center button, pull down twine until the button is at the depth of the tuft in the muslin. Staple or tack and tie the twine securely. Cut off excess. Repeat with all other buttons.

### Completing and decorating the footstool

Finish stapling or tacking the cover fabric to the base, working from the center outward along each edge and spacing staples approximately ¾ inch apart. At corners, notch and cut away excess fabric, then fold one side over and fold under the raw edge of the other, and fasten at the bottom with tacks or staples. When all sides are secured, trim excess fabric.

Cut braid or cord to fit around the lower edge of the fabric. Glue in place to conceal tacks or staples. Mount completed cushion on the footstool pedestal with heavy-duty glue used for wood, or use screws or dowels.

# Mahogany table

This teakwood and mahogany table appears to be the work of a superb craftsman, but it was built and finished by an amateur with little woodworking experience.

Materials: a ⅝-inch-thick teakwood top, 17 by 25 inches (substitute teak-veneered hardwood plywood if teakwood is unavailable); a piece of teakwood veneer 6 by 3 inches, and four ready-made 18-inch mahogany legs. Other mahogany pieces needed are: two side aprons ¾ by 3 by 23 inches; two end aprons ¾ by 3 by 14½ inches; and 8 feet of molding ⅝ by ⅝ inch. You also need a 6-inch length of ⅜-inch dowel; four 2-inch metal corner braces with screws; white glue; ½ pint of ready-mixed mahogany stain; 1 pint of satin-finish varnish; and four furniture glides (rolling feet). Tools and equipment required are: rule; carpenter's square; ½-inch drill; screwdriver; sharp knife; miter box; backsaw; paintbrush; rags; sandpaper in three grades: medium, fine and very fine; and a power saw. If you do not have a power saw, you may be able to rent one from a do-it-yourself shop, or have the difficult cuts, such as the end and side aprons, made at a cabinetmaker's shop or lumber yard.

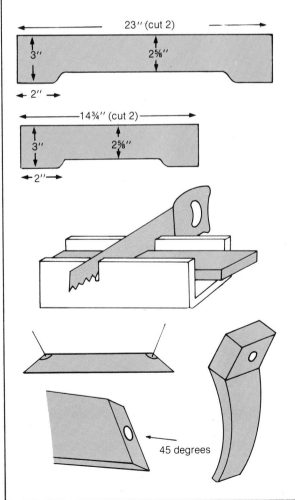

23″ (cut 2)

3″  2⅝″

2″

14¾″ (cut 2)

3″  2⅝″

2″

45 degrees

## Preparing the aprons

Cut the four aprons to size: 2 inches in from each end, the middle portion of each apron is ripped to a width of 2⅝ inches (you may prefer to leave this operation to the professional). Each end of the apron pieces is cut at an angle of 45 degrees; do this by holding the piece tightly in the miter box and cutting with the backsaw. In the center of each beveled or mitered face, drill a ⅜-inch blind hole, ¼ inch deep. Be careful not to penetrate the other side of the apron with the drill bit. Align the apron with the drill bit. Align the apron pieces accurately with the corresponding leg faces and mark dowel hole locations on legs. Drill ⅜-inch blind holes, ⅜ inch deep, in legs.

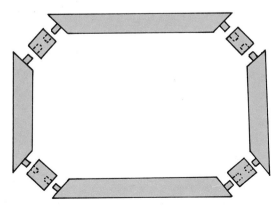

## Mahogany table

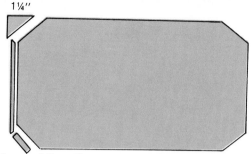

1¼″

### Assembling the aprons and legs

Cut the dowel into eight pieces, each ⅝ inches long. Glue one dowel into each of the blind holes in the apron pieces. Assemble aprons and legs with glue and dowel joints, making certain that the assembly is perfectly squared. Cut back the corners of the teakwood top 1¼ inches on each side. Carefully measure and cut pieces of molding to fit around the edge of the top; ends of the molding should be mitered at an angle of 66 degrees. If you do not have an adjustable miter box, use the top as a guide for making angle.

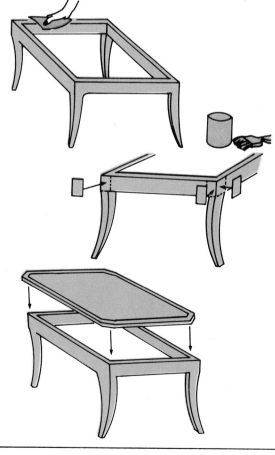

### Completing the woodwork

Sand the leg-apron assembly and the molding pieces. Apply mahogany stain, then rub it off with a rag. Repeat the procedure until the wood is the desired shade; make sure that all pieces are the same shade. Attach the top to the legs with metal angles held securely with wood screws. With a sharp knife, cut four pieces of teak veneer to fit the outside surfaces at the tops of the legs; glue in place. Glue edge molding around the top.

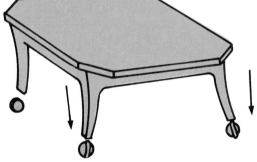

### Finishing the surface

Sand the entire unit, using progressively finer grades of sandpaper. Wipe away all dust with a soft rag, and apply the finish in as dust-free a room as possible. Apply at least two coats of varnish, sanding lightly between coats with very fine sandpaper. When the final coat has dried, tap the furniture glides onto the bottoms of the legs to complete the table.

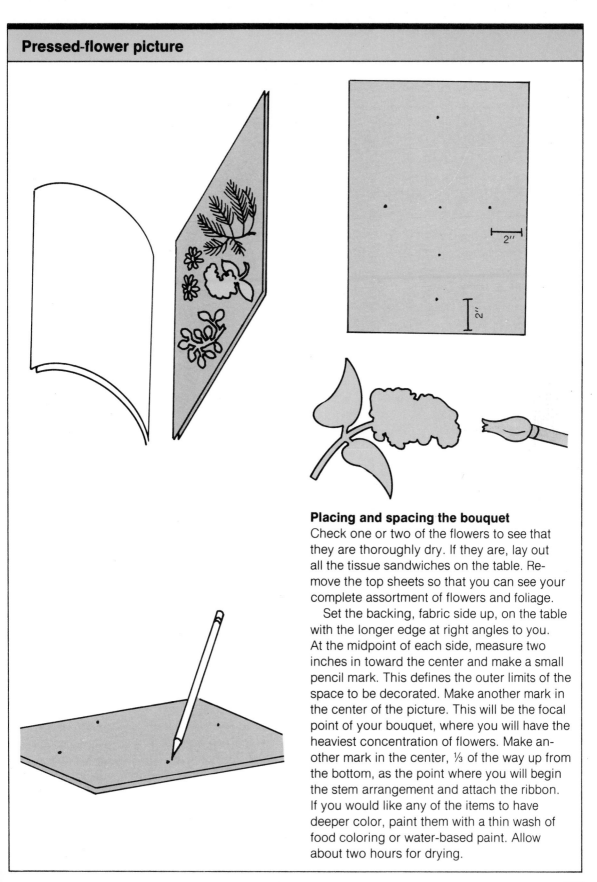

## Placing and spacing the bouquet

Check one or two of the flowers to see that they are thoroughly dry. If they are, lay out all the tissue sandwiches on the table. Remove the top sheets so that you can see your complete assortment of flowers and foliage.

Set the backing, fabric side up, on the table with the longer edge at right angles to you. At the midpoint of each side, measure two inches in toward the center and make a small pencil mark. This defines the outer limits of the space to be decorated. Make another mark in the center of the picture. This will be the focal point of your bouquet, where you will have the heaviest concentration of flowers. Make another mark in the center, ⅓ of the way up from the bottom, as the point where you will begin the stem arrangement and attach the ribbon. If you would like any of the items to have deeper color, paint them with a thin wash of food coloring or water-based paint. Allow about two hours for drying.

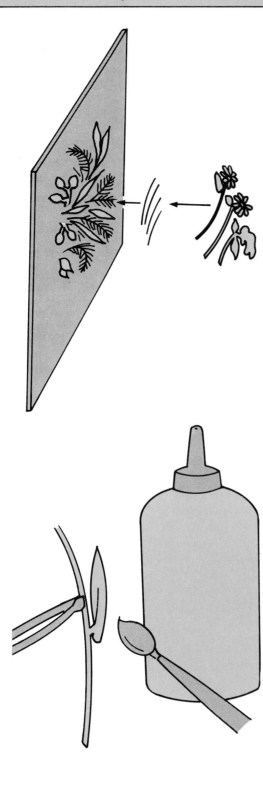

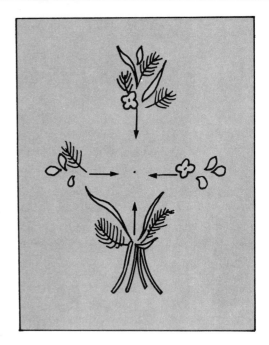

### Attaching the bouquet to the backing

Add a few drops of water to your glue to make a thinner solution for attaching the flowers and leaves to the fabric. Lay out grasses and greens on fabric first, then a second layer of stems, then your tall and outline flowers, building up thickness. With tweezers or a straight pin to hold the materials as gently as possible, brush on the adhesive with a water-color brush, applying it to the backs of items. Work with a very light stroke. Place each piece in the composition as soon as you have applied glue to it, starting from the outer edges of the picture space and working to-ward the center, making the concentration of plant materials heaviest at the center. If you are using flowers such as daisies, you will not need to simulate stems except at the bottom of the picture. When arranging flower petals to form a fantasy flower, you should also use one of the tiny dried stems you have prepared as a stalk. As you are making your composi-tion, don't forget that color and texture are also important. All flowers in the bouquet should rise on their stems from a central point to the left and right. The foliage should appear to lead the eye from left and right to center.

## Pressed-flower picture

Using the length of bright ribbon, arrange loops and streamers running from the point where the flowers end and the stems begin. Do not actually tie a bow, as it would be too bulky under the glass. Instead, cut a 2- or 3-inch strip of ribbon and fold a bow or rippled streamer by gluing a looped or upward folded piece of ribbon, and pinning in place to dry. Continue folding at 1-inch intervals, gluing and pinning along the length of the streamers. Glue remainder of ribbon in place.

When all the flowers and leaves are glued in place, take a few of the dried stems and arrange them in a natural manner as they would look if you had just picked a bunch of fresh flowers and tied a ribbon around them. Glue the stems as you did the flowers.

## Pressed-flower picture

### Assembling the framed bouquet

After the entire composition has been completed and a few minutes allowed to let the glue dry, assemble the frame, glass and flower-covered backing. Seal up the entire unit to prevent moisture from damaging the flowers. Run a strip of adhesive tape around the space between the backing and the frame. You are now ready to hang the picture.

### Using dried plant parts for other projects

Do not throw away any leftover petals, stems, or greens. Make a file of each by type and color and save for future compositions. Other projects that can be made from the pressed greenery include: notecards, place cards, and stationery with pressed leaf, stem, floret, or petal designs protected with a sheet of rice paper. You can also make a vase arrangement of pressed flowers, forming the vase by penciling an outline onto the background and working upward from the bottom of the vase, petal points facing upward toward the top of the vase. You may also try pressing and drying other natural materials from gardens and fields, such as toadstools, and make many other unique designs.

# Knotted plant hanger

For plants that naturally send off trailing vines, a hanger provides a natural way to encourage proper growth and to display the plant. Indoors, plant hangers are usually placed near a window or at head height in the corner of a well-lighted room. Ready-made simple hangers that are directly affixed to the pot are not nearly as attractive as handmade holders. This macramé sling, for instance, adorned with tassels and beads, surely furnishes a more interesting and more personal way to exhibit a lovely plant. Outdoors, plant hangers are often used to decorate a balcony or terrace.

The designs possible with macramé are varied, depending upon the degree of skill in knotting, upon the string or yarn, the bead materials used, the size and shape of the pot, and the plant you select. Hanging plants live in the upper part of the room where the temperature tends to be warmer, so select a nonporous pot to slow down evaporation. Since the hanger may discolor and possibly rot under a pot that throws off moisture, choose one without a hole in the bottom, or design your hanger so it does not come in direct contact with the base of the pot. In this case, simply place a plastic ring or disk between the bottom of the pot and the hanger. As for the plants which will do best in your climate and room location, your gardening center can give you the best advice. Some of the possible choices are grape ivies, several types of sedum, staghorn fern, fuchsia, and philodendron.

Materials: plastic or metal rings; beads of various colors; scissors; flat knotting surface; jute, a natural twine, or heavy rug yarn; T-shaped pins; and a nail in the wall or on a table edge to anchor the work as you knot the hanger. To duplicate the plant hanger illustrated, use 4 ounces of yarn or 38 yards of twine and 4 beads with holes ¼ inch in diameter. Materials are available at craft supply or upholstery shops.

### Preparing the top ring and cords
Cut a 3-yard length of yarn. Wrap the entire length of yarn around ring, tying ends together and tucking them underneath the yarn

wrapped around the ring. The metal ring should be completely covered with yarn.

Measure and cut 36 lengths of yarn, each 3 yards long. Pull the lengths halfway through the ring and fold around the ring, thus giving you 72 even working strands for your hanger. Cut a new strand of yarn 1 yard long and wrap it securely around all 72 strands, just below ring. Tie ends of the wrapped strand together and trim, then tuck under wrapping.

Place ring around a T-shaped pin fastened to a board or edge of a table, to hold it in place as you work.

### Knotting groups of cords
Divide your 72 working strands into 4 equal groups of 18 strands. Work each group in the following manner: Leave 6 inches unworked below the ring, then tie a spiral chain of half

# Knotted plant hanger

knots, using 8 strands (the 4 outside strands on the left and right sides of each group) for the knotting cords. Bring the 4 left outside strands over the 10 center strands and pass them under the 4 right outside strands. Pass the 4 right outside strands under the 10 center strands and up over the 4 left outside strands. To complete the half knot, start with the 4 left outside strands again, bringing them over the 10 center strands and under the 4 right outer strands. Pass the 4 right outer strands under the 10 center strands and up over the 4 left outside strands. Continue in this manner, always beginning the knot with the left outer strands, until there are 12 half knots in the spiral. Repeat the procedure for the remaining three groups of cords.

When all 4 groups have been completed up to this point, divide each group of 18 strands

in half to form 4 new groups of 18 strands each as follows: add 9 strands from each adjacent group to the left of the 9 strands of the first group. This will leave 9 strands on right side of the 3 newly formed groups and 9 strands on the left of these 3 groups. Join these two 9-strand groups to form the fourth group. The work is now enclosed in a circular fashion. Tie one square knot in each group, using 8 outside strands (4 on each side) as knotting cords. Bring 4 left outside strands over and to the right of the 10 center strands. Place 4 right outer strands over the 4 left outer strands and pass them under and then to the left of the 10 center cords, bringing these 4 cords up through the loop formed between left outer strands and center strands. Pass the 4 outer strands now on the left under and to the right of the 10 center strands, placing it over the 4 outer cords on the right. Bring the 4 right-hand cords up and over the 10 center cords and pass them through the loop formed by the left outer cords. Now pull the outer cords tight to complete the square knot.

## Completing the hanger

Divide each group of strands in half again and join with half the strands in the adjacent group to form 4 new groups of 18 strands (in same manner as previously). Tie one square knot in each group, using 8 outside (4 on each side) strands for knotting cords. Leave 4 inches below this square knot, then tie another square knot in each group, slip a bead onto center cords, and tie one more square knot. Now bring all 72 strands together, 4 inches below the last square knots. To complete, tie one spiral chain of 12 half knots, using 8 strands (4 on each side) as knotting cords around a 64-strand center. Finish the plant hanger by trimming ends neatly and evenly.

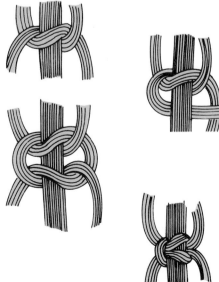

Square knot

# Acrylic cube planter

Hard as rock and crystal clear, acrylic sheeting has revolutionized contemporary home furnishings. This durable material is especially well suited to the creation of small or large objects assembled in almost any geometric shape. For example, a cube becomes a planter, sculpture stand, mail holder, or container for bath salts. Made to larger measurements, a cube serves as a coffee table, wastebasket or the base of a chair. Work on a small scale until you are familiar with the plastics medium. A four-inch cube is recommended for an initial project; the plates are small enough to be easily worked.

Materials: plastic sheeting; plastic cutter; solvent cement; antistatic cleaner and polisher; rubbing alcohol; ½-inch paintbrush; paper towels; and a woodblock. All are sold at plastic supply stores. Plastic sheeting, known as acrylic, and under various trademarks, comes in several thicknesses. The most popular are ⅛ inch and ¼ inch. It also comes in different colors. If you work with the ¼-inch thickness, have a plastic dealer cut the sheeting to the desired dimensions. If you work with ⅛-inch thickness, use the plastic cutter, which is a small, hooked tool resembling a penknife. A large book or smooth-surfaced woodblock (a cutting board is excellent) is used to support the vertical sections of the cube as they are cemented in place.

### Forming the acrylic cube

The cube will be 5 sided. Using ¼-inch plastic sheeting, have your plastic dealer cut one piece 4 inches square for the base and four sides 3¾ inches square. If you use ⅛-inch sheeting, adjust dimensions of 4 side pieces to 3⅞ inches square. Mark the dimensions on the sheet, then score along the marked lines with the plastic cutter. Pieces break apart cleanly and easily.

Place the 4-inch square in a horizontal position on a smooth, level surface. Place one of the 3¾-inch squares in an upright position, on top of and at a right angle to the first square. Be sure the corners of the pieces are flush. Support firmly with book or board as illustrated. With the paintbrush, apply cement to the inside of the angle formed by the two squares. Allow one minute drying time. Fit another 3¾-inch square in an upright position, on top of the base at a right angle to the first upright square. Buttress firmly with the book or board, apply cement on the 2 inside joints (horizontal and vertical), and let dry one minute. Fit the third 3¾-inch piece to the assembled squares in the same way, and apply cement to the 2 inside joints. During the assembly process, the 4-inch square remains in a horizontal position and the four 3¾-inch-square pieces in an-

upright position as they are affixed to the 4-inch-square base.

To form the fourth upright side of the cube, place the last 3¾-inch-square piece in the open space between two mounted sides. Apply cement to the 2 inside joints. If it is difficult to use the brush to apply cement, invert the cube so that one of the edges of this side points 45 degrees downward on the bottom of a diamond shape, as illustrated. Run cement directly from container downward to the edge. The cement will seep through and penetrate the joint. Set the cube upright and let cement dry one minute.

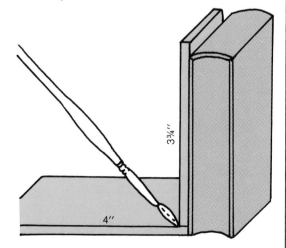

3¾"

4"

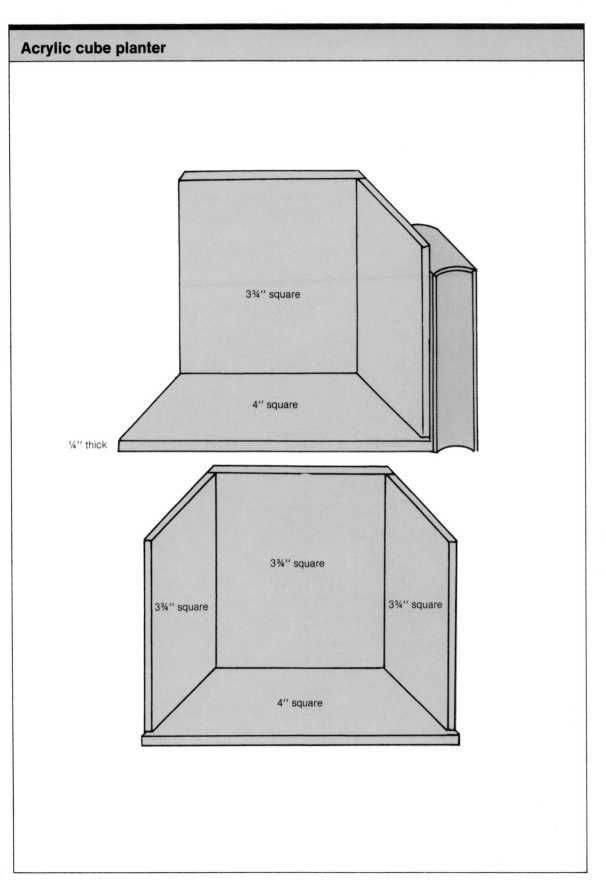

3¾″ square

4″ square

¼″ thick

3¾″ square

3¾″ square

3¾″ square

4″ square

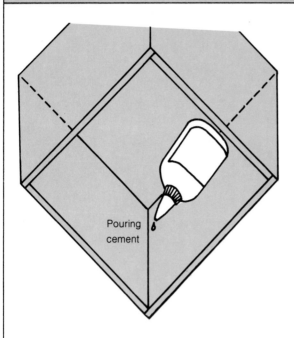

Pouring cement

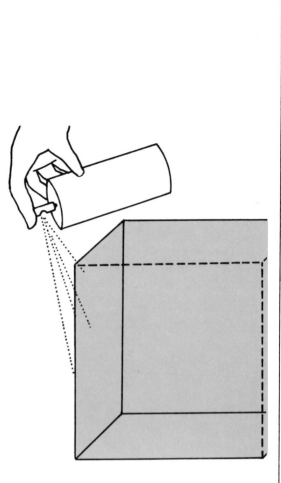

### Cleaning and protecting the surface
To remove excess cement and to give the cube a thorough cleaning, apply rubbing alcohol with a towel, using even strokes. Set cube aside until dry. Do not substitute detergent and water for the alcohol; this will leave faint but unwanted streaks on the cube surface. Alcohol will do the job much better, without harming the plastic.

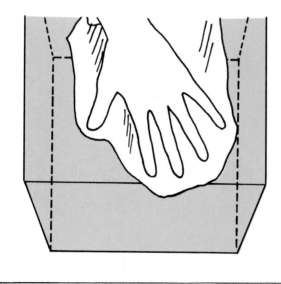

To give the cube a brilliant antistatic finish and protection against finger marks, use the plastic cleaner and polisher. Make sure the solution is at room temperature. Then shake container well and spray generously, covering all surfaces. Rub gently with a towel. While still wet, polish cube with a dry towel until all surfaces feel icy smooth. The piece is ready for use and its simple beauty protected from surface scratches and marks.

### Building bigger and brighter forms
Having successfully completed this small cube, make a larger one. Then as your skill increases, cut and join plastic sheets into various shapes and forms, experimenting with a range of color combinations, as well as paints, to create textural variety.

# Terrarium

To have a fascinating miniature rain forest of humidity-loving plants, create a terrarium. Plants that thrive in the environment of a covered glass container need very little attention once they are properly established in the planter. This method of growing plants under glass, developed and popularized in the late nineteenth century, is specially recommended to the beginner who may not have been too successful in growing house plants.

Materials: a large glass container (anything from a brandy snifter or a goldfish bowl to a 20-gallon fish tank will do, but it must have a close-fitting lid so that the moisture in the enclosure cannot escape; in a rain forest, the lush treetops act as an almost airtight lid); pebbles or gravel and charcoal chips for proper drainage; and an assortment of the proper plants. Garden supply stores carry some of the following flowering plants: begonia, gloxinea, Boea hygroscopica, Sinningia pusilla, Sinningia concinna, Streptocarpus cyanandrus, Koellikeria erinoides and Columnea. For foliage, choose a few examples from among these plants: Arcorus gramineus variegatus, Adiantum bellum, Calathea, Carex variegata, Helxine soleiroli, Pellionia pulchra, and Pilea depressa, as well as moss and small ivy. Complete the landscape with a selection of pretty stones from a tropical fish supply store or create a design using colored sand, available at craft suppliers and variety stores. Artificial light is more reliable than sunlight for a terrarium. We recommend a fluorescent unit, described more fully in Indoor light garden.

### Landscaping the terrarium

To assemble a terrarium in a fish tank, spread 1 inch of pebbles as drainage material on the bottom of the tank. Pour the colored stones or a multilayered design of colored sand around the edges of the tank and fill in the central portion with pebbles. Then pour in a 1-inch layer of charcoal chips.

Prepare a soil mixture consisting of one part peat moss, two parts perlite, and two parts vermiculite. Be sure to blend all three thoroughly—especially the peat moss. Build a ''landscape'' on top of the charcoal. The con-

tours of the landscape should be designed to display the plants advantageously. Arrange the soil so that the lowest part of the garden is in the front, with hills rising gradually to the back and sides. The more levels you provide, the greater the illusion of a natural landscape.

### Planting and completing the garden

If they are not in pots, place each of the plants in a small plastic or terra-cotta container. Dig holes for the pots and set the plants in place, angling the pots into the hillsides to facilitate their disguise. Pots used should be in proportion to the size of the tank. If you use a brandy

snifter, or small tank, it is not necessary to keep your plants in pots. Do not allow your plants to touch the sides of the terrarium and do not crowd them,as they need room for the roots to grow. Choose a few choice plants to provide good color and interesting shapes. Between the pots and directly in the soil, insert a few tiny plants like Sinningia pusilla and Sinningia concinna and small ivy, which do not develop large root systems.

Cover the pots with soil and a few flat stones. Experiment with placing your smaller stones toward the back of the terrarium. Rocks in a natural landscape seem smaller in the distance. Stones, thus arranged, will add to the illusion of real hills and valleys. When the pots, plants and stones are placed, finish the low foreground with a few more flat stones. If desired, add a small glass or ceramic animal or figurine. Brush the sides of the glass clean of any specks and brush off any debris that has fallen on the stones. Clean the leaves with a sprinkle of water. Spray the landscape with a fine mist, using one of the small devices sold in gardening shops. Place the glass lid on top of the terrarium.

### Lighting and heating the terrarium

The terrarium will grow best under artificial light, preferably a two-unit fluorescent fixture suited to the size of your tank. Suspend the fixture about 6 inches above the lid. Use one tube of cool white, and one of warm white, both commonly available in hardware and electrical supply stores, to give the ideal light balance. You can also purchase fluorescents especially designed for indoor light gardening, but these tend to be more expensive, and are not necessary. The fluorescents create a small amount of heat, and a healthy terrarium requires a fairly consistent temperature of 65 to 70 degrees Fahrenheit. You should make some adjustments in hot weather unless there is air conditioning in the room. On warm days move the lid so that a little air is permitted to enter. In very hot weather turn off the light for a day or so. Of course, when the lid is opened, moisture will escape, so give the terrarium a misting before the lid is closed. During periods when the terrarium is growing nicely with the lid closed, you should mist every three or four weeks. If plants grow too large or are not thriving, simply replace them.

# Indoor light garden

Your garden can have 365 sunny days a year, if you garden with artificial light. Deprived of sunlight, plants grow slowly, flower little or not at all, and often die of starvation. With the aid of fluorescent lights, however, plants become healthier than they do in the sun. Indoors under artificial light, plants have no seasonal limitations. There are no temperature changes, droughts, or months of short daylight hours. A host of previously finicky plants have adapted to common indoor usage, and new strains have been developed. Indoor light gardens can be set up in the darkest corner of the house, bringing a spot of greenery to a once cheerless area. If you have been frustrated as an indoor gardener, make this simple light garden and your plants will reward you with a burst of new life. You can build a freestanding light box, using ½-inch plywood for the enclosure, but it is simpler to use a bookcase. One or more shelves can be adapted for the purpose with less effort, and the resulting unit will look custom built. Also needed are ½ pint white paint; two fluorescent fixtures; an electric timer; and a selection of light-hungry plants. Tools for assembling the unit are a hammer; drill; a few nails; and the usual gardener's materials, soil mixtures, and pots or other containers.

### Preparing and lighting the box

A bookcase or similar shelving is suitable for a light garden. The ideal dimensions are based on the length and light-spreading capabilities of standard fluorescent lights. Use a box or bookshelf space 18 to 20 inches high, 12 to 16 inches wide, and 30, 42, or 54 inches long. The length should accommodate standard fluorescent tubes of 24, 36, or 48 inches, plus the additional space required by the light fixture.

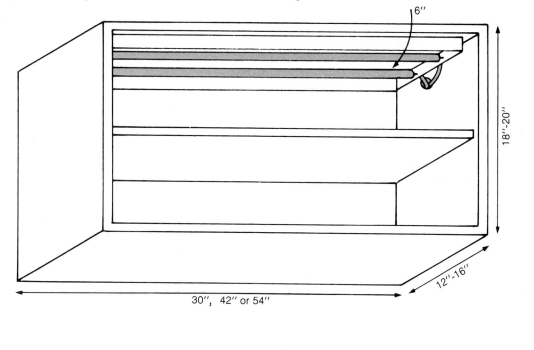

6″

18″-20″

12″-16″

30″,  42″ or 54″

## Indoor light garden

Paint the inside of the box white. Install two fluorescent fixtures above the garden space. The fixtures should be mounted 6 inches apart in a parallel position, and centered left to right and front to back. If the shelf is considerably wider than 16 inches, mount a third tube, as the spread of high-intensity light is only 3 inches on either side of the fixture. For most purposes, and in the standard bookcase, two tubes are adequate. To get the broadest pos-part perlite for plants like African violets which require a very rich soil. Less demanding plants, including foliage plants, should be given less humus—about two parts humus to the rest of the mix. Then place a layer of pebbles for drainage on the bottom of each pot, cover with the proper soil mixture, anchor plant roots, and fill pot with same soil. Arrange the plants in the light garden with the tops of the flowering variety about 4 inches below the

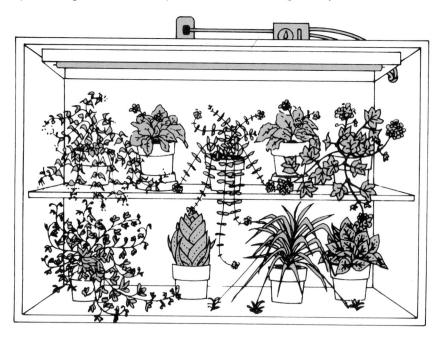

sible spectrum of light and to give your plants maximum nourishment, combine one cool white and one warm white tube (40 watts). Drill a hole at the back of the shelf to run the electric cords through.

light sources. Set the shorter potted plants on inverted saucers.

Plug the fluorescent fixtures into an electric timer that is plugged into an outlet. Set timer for 16 hours a day for flowering plants; 14 hours for foliage. Arrange the turn-off hours during the night, enabling the plants to enjoy a period of darkness; plants need a rest. Water the individual plants as required. Since the indoor humidity levels are usually very low (especially in steam-heated apartments), it is a good idea to give your plants a daily misting with a spray bottle made specifically for plants. An empty window-cleaning spray bottle, thoroughly rinsed, will also serve.

### Planting and maintaining the garden

Select your plants. Choose relatively compact growers that will fit comfortably in the 20-inch-high space. African violets, gloxinias, fuchsia, colomneas, Sinningias, Streptocarpus, Oxalis regnelii, and Cuphea hyssopifolia are among the great performers. You can also use cuttings from your outdoor garden, rooting them in moist vermiculite in the light garden. To pot rooted cuttings and to repot plants, first mix a quantity of soil. Use three parts humus to two parts vermiculite and one

# Miniature gardens

There are so many ways to create table-top gardens with interesting planters and miniature plants. Search for tiny ferns, mosses and seedlings in the woods and apply imagination in the choice of a planter. Shown here is an example of a miniature garden planted in a chunk of tufa. Tufa is a very porous and soft sedimentary rock, which is formed by nature around hot springs and geysers. Its particular appeal to the gardener is the ease with which it can be shaped with nothing more complicated than a spoon. Many garden supply houses have tufa in stock. To start this project, select a chunk of tufa and a few small succulents of a nonflowering variety purchased from a florist or nursery. They have a capacity to store water and are rather sturdy. As a second project, create a tiny forest garden in a wooden box or a shallow ceramic dish and select plants found in the woods or meadows.

Materials: a chunk of tufa; miniature plants (most suitable because they should be close to the surface of the rock, rather than rising high above it) including huge prickly cactus and tiny velvet-leafed plants; a soil mixture (equal parts of perlite, vermiculite and peat moss); and a long sharp instrument such as an icepick or spoon.

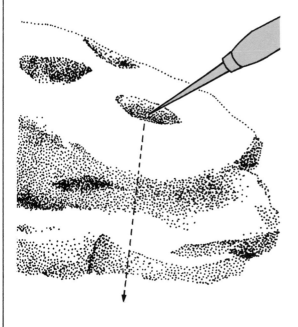

### Boring into the tufa

Dig a number of separate holes along the top of the tufa with a heavy spoon or chisel. The size and depth of the holes should vary according to the sizes of the plants you are going to use. Placement of the holes is a matter of design, but following the rock's natural contours will generally produce the best results. Using a sharp instrument (an ice-pick, a long thin nail, or a drill), pierce a tiny drainage channel from the bottom of each hole through to the underside of the rock. Prepare a soil mixture, blending equal parts of perlite, vermiculite and peat moss, stirring and sifting until all the lumps are pulverized. Put a little of the soil mixture in the bottom of each hole.

### Planting the garden

Place one succulent with its roots and soil ball on top of the soil in each hole. Fill in and around it with more soil, and pack it firmly into place. Put the tufa garden in a shallow holder, such as a tray filled with pebbles, to collect any water that may drain through. Give the planter sufficient water to bond the old soil to the new. Succulents are an excellent type of plant for experimentation by the new gardener. They are reasonably comfortable in the hot, dry atmosphere found in most households, and will thrive with minimum care. They do like plenty of sun, but water only when the soil feels dry to the touch.

If you are creating the planter as a gift, prepare it a few weeks in advance, to give the plants time to settle into the rock. The plants

should be watered with a bulb-type sprayer so you can be sure the soil does not wash away.

### Making a tiny forest garden
There are many objects that take well to table-top plantings. A shallow ceramic dish that is round or rectangular in shape will do nicely. Or perhaps you prefer a redwood box that can be made or purchased from a garden shop. There should be good drainage in the planter, no matter what the choice. A layer of small pebbles (purchased at a tropical fish shop) at the bottom of the dish will aid drainage. Spread a thin layer of soil mixed with peat moss over the pebbles, then place the plants in position with their roots and soil balls on top of the soil layer. Fill in with more soil and peat moss and pack it down around the plants. Water with a bulb-type sprayer.

To make a truly authentic woodland garden in miniature, go out into the woods to select mosses, grass and weeds, very tiny seedlings of trees and shrubs and any non-flowering plants that seem to require a minimum amount of tender loving care. Should you find moss growing on a small rock, do not remove the growth; instead, take the rock and place it in the center of the planter and arrange the plants around it. Should you discover after two or three weeks that one of the plants or weeds is not suitable because it is growing too rapidly, simply remove it from the garden and replace it with another choice. Half the joy in planting a miniature woodland garden is in the experimentation with various finds from the woods. It is not practical to mix plantings gathered in the woods with plants cultivated in your garden or in a greenhouse.

# Simulated bonsai

Over the centuries, the Japanese have developed a rare skill in growing dwarf trees, especially evergreens. They call this technique bonsai; and though it is studied by Japanese amateurs as a hobby, the great masters find it takes a lifetime to perfect the most subtle refinements. Often a dwarf tree represents the work of several generations of gardeners, and it is not uncommon to find examples over two hundred years old. The object of bonsai is to stunt the growth of the tree so that it can be kept in a small pot, but still allow it to attain the shape and proportions characteristic of the species grown to full size. You can derive great rewards in a relatively short period of time from the simulated bonsai described, designed for indoor gardening.

Materials: a dwarf variety of some woody-stemmed plant; an 18-inch length of 14-gauge copper wire, for the trunk; two 12-inch lengths of 18-gauge copper wire, for the branches; pruning clippers; a sharp knife; a decorative planting pot; and potting soil mixture.

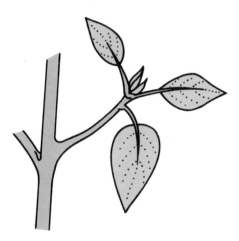 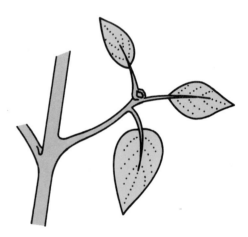

### Starting the plant

At your local florist, ask to see the selection of dwarf plants with woody stems. A stem that resembles a miniature tree trunk, with bark, is part of the effect desired. Evergreens, such as cedar, take nicely to bonsai. Pomegranates do very well, also, and might even produce some fruit and flowers. Whatever you select should be healthy and nicely shaped. Replant the dwarf in a decorative pot and let it grow for several weeks until a new crop of lush green growth has leafed out. Pinch off the new leaf growths at the bases of their tiny stems. Nature provides every plant with a defense mechanism. When you pinch off the growing part of the plant, a dormant leaf bud, located at the axil of the new leaves (where the leaf stalk is connected to the stem), will begin to grow. This will affect your plant to make it grow taller, as it seeks the sunlight. Whenever a crop of new growth appears, pinch it off.

# Simulated bonsai

## Trimming the roots

The plant will continue to grow roots, even though you have been cutting back the foliage, so once a year you must trim the roots. Invert the plant. Tap the bottom of the pot gently until the soil and plant slide out. Put the root ball on a newspaper and free the roots from the soil. Using a sharp knife, cut off one third of the length of each root, then replant.

## Shaping the plant

Now you can begin to shape the plant, keeping in mind that your goal is to create a tree-like effect. Bonsai traditionally required bending the stems to create interesting branch and trunk formations. You can force your tree to bend by wrapping the stem where you wish it to bend with fine, flexible copper wire. The wire should be put on in a spiral, each turn being about ¼ inch above the previous one. Wrap it so that it stays firmly in place but is not so tight as to cut the stem. Good young plants will respond to this wiring by bending naturally. If you want to force the stem into more severe formations, you can tie one end of the wire to a securely anchored object.

# Fresh and dried herbs

Growing herbs is less troublesome than most gardening efforts and the results are twice as rewarding. Herbs are easy to cultivate indoors or outdoors in a backyard garden, in pots or boxes on kitchen windowsills. The formal English herb garden, planned in a circular or rectangular shape, is usually quite elaborate; however, an informal plot is quite adequate and probably much more practical. Herbs also grow nicely with vegetables. They resist pests and disease and thrive in light, fertile, well-drained alkaline soil containing some small particles, humus and sand. They benefit from an annual feeding with lime fertilizer.

During the growing season, most herbs need six to eight full hours of sun a day, though some exceptional herbs flourish in shady areas, in poor soil, or even in little or no soil. The illustrations of garden layouts suggest the more formal herb gardens, combined with footwalks. However, to start an herb garden outdoors, it may be more advisable to use a small area or corner of your vegetable garden. The information that follows covers the preparation of the soil, germination of seeds, transplanting seedlings, harvesting and preserving herbs.

Materials: You need the usual collection of garden tools, adapted to the size of the garden you undertake. Either a small plot of land, or pots and window boxes will hold your plantings. Soil conditioners, pH testing kits, manure, plant sprays, and other needed chemicals are specified in the following sections. Also required will be seeds or cuttings of various herbs.

### Planning the herb garden

In selecting the garden location, consider first the amount of sunlight available in relation to the plant requirements. A vitally important consideration is good drainage. Herbs require frequent watering, yet their environment must be fairly dry. Another consideration is the growing season. Outdoor herb gardens are started from seed in spring and grown in summer, except for slow-germinating perennials, which are started in fall and recultivated or transplanted in spring.

Annuals produce new seeds for future planting, while perennials increase by division, stem cutting, or layering. To determine the number of plants to grow, consider the space available for the herb garden and the quantity of fresh herbs desired for use during the summer. Also consider the quantity of herbs you plan to dry or freeze for use during the non-growing season, as well as the number of plants you wish to use for next year's seeds.

If fresh and preserved herbs are desired, plant about a dozen annuals and choose the number of perennials according to germination period and the winter climate in your area. (The colder the winter, the more perennials you plant.) However, for a first herb garden, the following popular culinary herbs are suggested: sweet basil, chives, dill weed, sweet marjoram, oregano, parsley, and savory.

### Sweet basil (Ocimum basilicum)

This bushy annual of the mint family is grown for its clove-scented, shiny green leaves. The plants require moderately rich, moist unfertilized soil and full sun or a semi-shady area. Sweet basil grows fairly erect, to about 12 to 18 inches, bearing spikes of white or purple flowers at the tips of the stems. To promote full, attractive growth, pinch stem tips frequently. Germination period is a week or less.

### Dill weed (Anethum graveolens)

This drought-resistant, single-stemmed annual reaches up to 2 feet high and spreads 9 to 12 small yellow flowers in umbrella-shaped clusters that go to seed in fall if left unharvested. Dill needs full sun and moist, well-drained soil. Germination takes two weeks. Since dill has a tap root, which can hinder transplantation, sow seeds to propagate during spring and allow them to sow themselves in fall. Its sharp, pungent flavor is fullest as flowers open.

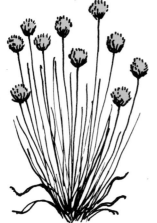

### Chives (Allium schoenoprasum)

These are hardy, slow-germinating perennials. The round, hollow leaves, with an onionlike flavor, grow from bulbets in grassy clumps 12 inches tall, with an 8¾-inch spread. The leaves replace themselves when snipped off. Cloverlike red-violet chive flowers appear in midsummer. To promote new growth, remove the blossom before it is in full bloom. Medium rich, moist soil and full sun are best for chives. Clumps of chives can be propagated every 3 to 4 years by root division.

### Sweet marjoram (Majorana hortensis)

This tender, fragrant perennial of the mint family grows from semi-woody stems branching upward to 2½ feet, with a spread. The bushy plant has small, velvety oval leaves clustering at the stem tips, and small white flowers. Marjoram likes full sun and moderately rich, slightly alkaline, well-drained soil. Marjoram increases by stem cutting or root division. Trim and cut blossoms occasionally to prevent stems from becoming too woody. When flowers ripen, gather seeds, and sow in a nursery flat or cold frame, since marjoram can be temperamental when germinated outdoors.

### Oregano (Origanum vulgare)
This sharp-tasting perennial is treated as an annual, with new seeds sown annually. It averages 2 feet high outdoors, but cutting keeps it shorter and bushier. Oregano has rounded, blunt-tipped dark green leaves with small, mauve-colored blossoms. It grows best in fairly rich, well-drained soil in full sun. Propagation is from seed or by dividing a plant.

### Parsley (Petroselinum crispum)
A popular garnish and seasoning herb, parsley likes rich, moist, well-drained soil and full or partial sun. It grows about 1 foot tall and

spreads 12 to 18 inches. The curly French variety illustrated has wrinkly, tufted basal leaves, deeply divided. A biennial that flowers in its second year, parsley can be treated as an annual and started from new seeds each year. Harvest parsley before flowering, otherwise the leaves taste bitter. To keep a fresh supply, pinch new flowering stems.

### Summer savory (Satureia hortensis)
A graceful, shrublike annual with small, narrow bronze leaves, savory has a height and spread of about 12 inches and delicate, pale lilac flowers. It grows best in full sun and light, rich soil. Savory has a delicate, spicy taste, somewhat like pepper.

### Preparing the soil, sowing, and thinning
Before planting the garden, determine soil pH (acidity or alkalinity) by consulting a regional agricultural agency or using a test kit available from garden centers. Add lime to correct alkaline deficiency. Dig site during winter thaw to a spade's depth, about 1 foot, removing large particles, stones, and debris. Lighten heavy soil with 2 buckets of compost, peat, or sand per square yard. To make soil medium rich, add cow manure. A small amount of peat moss increases humus.

If plants are potted, the potting soil or vermiculite should be porous and well-drained. After the winter frost, seeds can be sown outdoors. Make sure soil is well drained, not constantly moist. Before sowing, treat seeds with special disease-resistant dressing recommended by your nursery. Turn soil with spade and break up clods. Till finely with a rake,

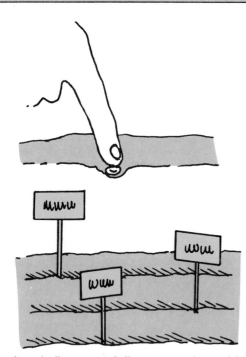

minators can take longer, but you can speed the process by soaking seeds overnight prior to sowing. Germinating in pots or containers indoors allows more control over the atmosphere and soil conditions during winter. Transplant properly germinated seeds outdoors in the spring. Keep soil moist, not soaking wet, by watering with a fine, low-pressure mist. You can soak bottoms of pots in a dish or basin of water for an hour to let soil draw moisture by capillary action.

using shallow scratch lines as sowing guides.

Place seeds in furrows, ½ inch deep and 8 to 12 inches apart, according to expected root spread. When seedlings are large enough to handle, thin to 3 inches apart in rows, and later, thin again for final spacing. In pots and containers, the distance between seeds should be twice the diameter of the seed. Perennials planted in spring should be sown in a separate bed and remain there after thinning, then transplanted to a permanent site in autumn or the next spring.

Cover seeds over lightly and evenly with ½ inch of soil, marking and labeling rows, and separating herbs of different types, heights, and growing patterns. Firm soil down with board or hand and moisten gently with a fine mist, being careful not to dislodge seeds or make soil soggy. If your garden has seed-eating birds, cover herb bed with a fine-mesh screen. To insure proper drainage in pots and containers, there should be holes or slits on the bottom. A board or saucepan placed underneath will catch water.

### Transplanting

Annuals generally germinate in 12 to 14 days, while perennials take 3 to 4 weeks. Slow ger-

If tapping on the side of a pot or container makes a hollow sound the roots are too dry to absorb water and their balls should be loosened with a stick and soaked thoroughly for several hours. Cover pots with wet burlap or newspaper. In larger containers and outdoors, use plastic mulch to help preserve soil moisture. The ideal germinating temperature range is 65 to 75 degrees Fahrenheit. Lift containers 1 to 2 hours a day to air soil surface.

When seeds have germinated, remove covering, transfer containers to a location with 60 to 70 degrees Fahrenheit and good indirect sunlight, and turn daily, always in the same direction, for even light exposure.

When two pairs of true leaves sprout, it is time to thin and transplant. Herbs transplanted to larger containers need a richer soil mix of ½ garden soil, ¼ finely sifted peat moss or ground bark, and ¼ coarse sand. To minimize transition shock, place plants in flats or in new pots indoors in the shade for a few hours a day one week before transplanting. When placing plant in new container, make sure you have sufficient soil around roots to form a ball, which should come within 1 inch of container

snaps when bent sharply. Cut just below joints with a sharp knife. Keep cuts moist and shaded between two damp cloths or paper towels for a week before planting. Propagate a small number of cuttings in a clay pot or empty coffee can. For large quantities, strip lower leaves from ½ to ⅓ of each stem, cutting before inserting in equal parts of peat and sand in a frost-free frame, where they can remain until transplanted the following spring.

Fill moistened and drained containers with soil of ⅔ sand, ⅓ vermiculite, allowing for good drainage. Firm soil well, and level surface. Dip cut ends in hormone powder to stimulate root growth and place in soil at depth equal to length of defoliation. Water soil gently. To maintain a moist environment, cover cuttings with an inverted glass jar or plastic bag, allowing fresh air in for an hour or two a day to prevent mold or fungus.

Growth can take 4 weeks to several months. Bright green foliage, but no new leaves, indicates that roots have formed. Transplant to ¾-inch-diameter pots, leaving some original soil mix around roots. Keep soil moist and cuttings out of sun until new roots emerge through drainage holes. Transplant to permanent locations the next spring. To check growth of invasive roots, sink metal sheets or tiles vertically into soil around plant.

rim. Firm soil well around root ball and water thoroughly and evenly.

To transplant prestarted seeds planted in tiny containers made of a growing medium, place container directly in the ground once seeds are ready to set out and keep cups moist. The container decomposes to provide plant food and to permit root expansion.

### Planting shoot cuttings
Perennials can be propagated during spring or summer growing season by cutting and rooting side shoots. Choose strong, new tip growth with good upper end foliage that

### Layering
The object of layering perennials is to bring branches into contact with soil, causing them

to root without detachment from parent plant. Select a section of a vigorous, flexible branch growing near the ground and bend it about 1 foot below stem tip, just below leaf node.

Directly below this point, dig a shallow hole and mix soil with equal parts of peat moss or ground bark and sand. Make a slanted cut halfway through thickness on underside of section to be buried (scrape away only outer layer of slender stems) and apply hormone growth powder to cut or scrape to stimulate root growth. Anchor stem in hole with heavy wire loop or staple. Bring branch end to vertical position and stake upright.

Fill in hole with firmed-down soil, and water thoroughly. Keep soil firm and moisture-retaining with a brick or stone placed on surface directly above layered stem section. If layering in fall, cover layering with plastic mulch, leaving only tip and several leaves exposed. Roots may form as early as 6 weeks. Check root growth by carefully removing soil from around stem. When roots are well established, sever stem from parent plant and transplant to garden or container.

### Planting root cuttings

To propagate by root cuttings, cut a few ¼- to ⅜-inch-diameter roots into pieces ⅓ inch

long when the herb plant sends up new stems. Place cuttings horizontally, 2 inches apart, in box or nursery flat, filled up to 1 inch from top with light garden soil. Cover cuttings with another ½ inch of soil, water thoroughly, cover with glass or newspaper, and place in shade until new growth and leaf buds appear. Remove covering and transplant each cutting into its individual pot, or deeper flats, about 6 to 8 inches apart. New root growth can be cut or pulled from parent plant in autumn or early spring, when no new growth is forming. Dig herb up and pull or cut root clump into sections. Replant sections in garden or containers immediately, keeping soil moist until plants have adjusted.

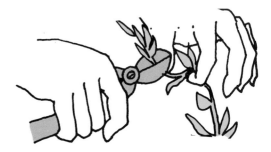

### Mulching and spraying

To keep herb plots moist and weed-free, and maintain vigorous growth, apply a mulch of peat or compost in the spring. Prune shrubby herbs annually in spring or fall. Cut back straggly plants to encourage bushy growth from base. If plants become infected with blotches, rust pustules or white rot, they should be cut down or dug up and destroyed. Spray parsley leaves that start to show discoloration (leaf spot or mild virus) immediately with a chemical pesticide like captan.

### Harvesting

Harvest leaves to use fresh, just before flowering, and gather seeds in late summer before they turn yellow or brown. You can harvest herbs to use fresh almost any time during the growing season, but if you wish to preserve them for future use, gather leaves when their flowers start to open. At this stage in growth, the oils in the leaf glands, which give herbs flavor and aroma, are most concentrated. Choose a dry, sunny morning after the dew has evaporated, before heat of day, to harvest.

Cut green shoots carefully to avoid bruising and to preserve the aroma. Remove damaged or discolored leaves, then strip from the stem the large leaves to be dried, and leave small-leaved shoots whole for drying. Wash grit and dirt off in cool water, and allow to dry off. (Cut seed heads or stems into a paper bag when capsules are almost ready to drop off.) The herbs are ready to be preserved by any of three methods: drying, freezing, or salt curing, depending on the particular herb.

### Drying

Drying involves exposing herbs to warm, dry, freely circulating air, but not directly to sun-

light (which will damage leaves and impair the flavor). There are several drying methods. For instance, you can dry basil, summer savory, dill and parsley by placing leaves on a cookie sheet in a hot oven for a few minutes. Do not let herbs burn. Store the oven-dried herbs in a tightly closed glass or glazed pottery jar.

To dry herb leaves or seeds on screens or trays, spread one layer on each screen or tray, allowing room for air to circulate. The

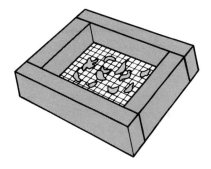

drying process should be done indoors, in a dry atmosphere of even temperature. Seeds, large-leafed herbs like basil, or short stem tips dry easily this way. Two small wood strips placed underneath the screen frame or tray provide for free air passage. Turn herbs carefully once a day for four days to one week, till they are brittle to the touch to insure even, thorough drying. To check for dryness, store herbs in clear, airtight glass containers in your refrigerator for a week. If moisture appears inside containers, remove and dry for 2 days more in trays; otherwise herbs will decay.

Before drying seeds, rub capsules carefully through your hands before placing on screen.

## Fresh and dried herbs

During the drying process, the capsules will blow away with a breeze, leaving the seeds.

Dry long-stemmed herbs like marjoram and savory in bunches, tying stem ends together with string, and hanging upside down in a warm, dry, roomy area, away from walls and direct sunlight. Herbs to be dried in bunches should be harvested with branches and leaves whole, rinsed in cold water and trimmed of dead or discolored leaves. To keep herbs dust-free, tie paper bags around tied ends of

stems. Make sure leaves can hang freely inside. Cut or punch holes for ventilation. Allow up to 2 weeks for herbs to dry to crackling before taking them down. Remove leaves from stems carefully, avoiding breakage.

### Freezing

To freeze fresh herbs, harvest and wash as for drying, but do not strip foliage. Tie string or

thread around stems, blanch in unsalted boiling water for 50 seconds and remove quickly. Cool in ice water for a few minutes. Snip or chop leaves and place small quantity (enough for one recipe) in plastic bags or containers. Be sure to seal tightly and identify each by name and date packed on label. Herbs can be stored up to 6 months this way.

### Salting

Salt curing is done by rinsing leaves in water and letting them air-dry or blotting them between 2 paper towels. Remove leaves from stems. Pour a layer of noniodized salt into a jar, then a layer of leaves, followed by another layer of salt. Fill jar in this manner, press

leaves and salt down firmly, cover tightly and store in the refrigerator. Rinse salted leaves in clear water before using for cooking. Always use airtight containers of glass or clear plastic to store dried or cured herbs. Do not break herb leaves up before using. Always store in a cool, dark, even-temperatured place, such as the refrigerator.

Remember when cooking with dried herbs that their flavor is concentrated. A tablespoon of dried herbs equals about ¼ cup fresh or frozen herbs, so use them sparingly.

# Patio blocks

It is relatively simple to create a patio or terrace surface with lightweight concrete blocks cast in a manageable size, then assembled in a bed of sand. The concrete pieces or blocks are cast in different shapes and sizes to lend a more decorative design to the floor pattern. The blocks shown were cast in square and circular forms, but the shapes are easily changed to free-form pieces by altering the shape of the forms. Square blocks measure 1 foot by 1 foot; the rounds are 1 foot in diameter.

Materials: (to make approximately 29 square blocks or 40 rounds) one bag of cement; 220 pounds of clean, dry sand; 330 pounds of fine aggregate (¼- to 1¼-inch gravel); and 21 quarts of water. Add strength to the blocks, if desired, by reinforcing them with pieces of wire coat hangers, straightened and cut into 8-inch lengths. To color the blocks, add concrete pigments; the round blocks are colored with black oxide of iron, the squares tinted with yellow oxide of iron. Other colors are also available.

It is best to build several forms so that you can make a number of blocks at the same time. For each square form, you need four pieces of 2-by-2-inch lumber 20 inches long and for each round form, a piece of ⅛-inch hardboard 2 by 38 inches and some heavy duty metallic tape. You also need tarpaper 16 inches square for each form and grease to coat the inside of the forms so the concrete does not stick.

After the blocks have cured, they will be laid in a bed of sand. For each 32 square feet of patio surface, you need 35 cubic feet of sand. Spaces between the round blocks are filled with white gravel; approximately 13 cubic yards are needed for each 32 square feet of patio surface. In addition, you need 2-by-6-inch lumber to form a border around the patio (determine the outside dimensions of the patio, to estimate quantity needed); 1-by-2-by-12-inch stakes (allow two stakes for every yard of lumber used for border); 2-inch common nails; and pentachlorophenol or other wood preservative.

Tools required to make the patio blocks and to prepare the patio foundation are: hammer; saw; tin snips, to cut the coat-hanger reinforcement; shovel; strikeboard or any straight-edged piece of lumber at least 20 inches long; steel trowel; rake; any tamper to tamp down the sand, if necessary (make one by nailing a 10-inch length of lumber to a 2-by-2-inch piece of wood for the handle); tape measure or folding rule; carpenter's level; string; and broom.

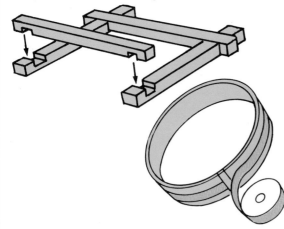

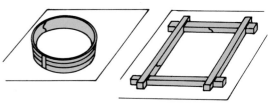

**Making the forms for the concrete blocks**
For the square blocks, cut notches halfway through each piece of 2-by-2-inch lumber, 2 inches in from each end and the width of a piece of 2 by 2. Fit the pieces together; they will come apart easily for reuse. For a form

## Patio blocks

for the round blocks: with the smooth side turned inward, bend the 38-inch length of hardboard, so that both ends meet, forming a circle. Where the ends meet, wrap securely with heavy-duty tape, then wrap the outside

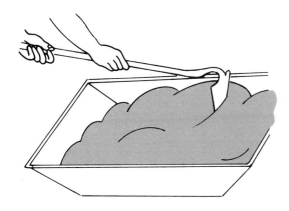

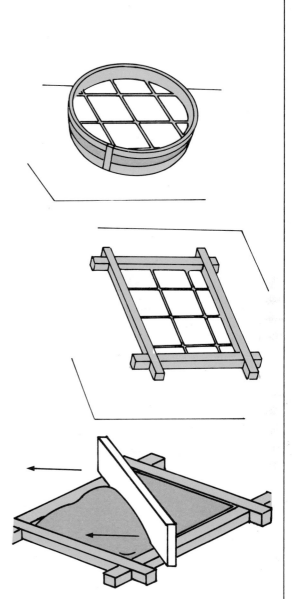

of the circle with tape to make a sturdy form. Grease the inside of each form, then place on tarpaper on a flat surface, either a concrete walk or flat stretch of ground.

### Mixing the concrete

Mix the concrete in a wheelbarrow, on a piece of plywood or on a concrete surface. The formula is one part cement, two parts sand, three parts aggregate. You can measure the amount with the shovel; mix only enough to fill a few forms at a time. Place cement on the mixing surface, then add the appropriate amount of

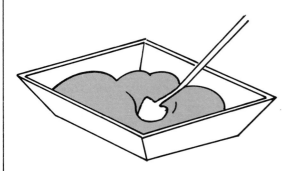

sand. Blend thoroughly, turning over with the shovel. Add the gravel to the mix, and again blend thoroughly. Complete mixing is essential if the resulting blocks are to be the proper strength.

When the ingredients are fully blended, scoop out a small depression in the middle of the pile to form a basin for the water. Add water a few quarts at a time, and mix in with the shovel. Keep adding water until the mix is of a medium-stiff consistency, with all parts thoroughly and equally wet and the aggregate completely covered by the cement. If you are coloring the concrete, add pigment at this stage, and mix. Add more, if necessary, until you achieve the desired shade.

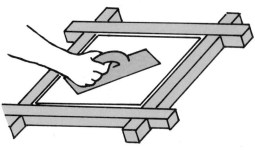

## Making the blocks

Use the shovel or wheelbarrow to pour concrete into the forms, roughly level with the tops. When you have finished pouring the concrete, immediately wash off the mixing surface with plenty of water so no concrete residue will harden on the surface. Imbed the cut and straightened coat-hanger wire into the middle of the concrete, several pieces at right angles in each form. Remove excess concrete

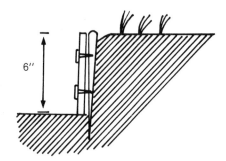

6″

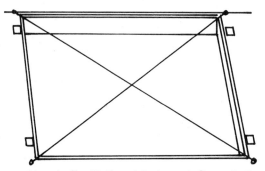

and level off with the strikeboard. Smooth the surface with the trowel, moving it over the concrete with a slight pressure in a half-arc motion. Allow concrete to set for a half hour. Wash off tools thoroughly to prevent concrete from sticking.

When the concrete has begun to set, finish the surface by moving the trowel over the patio blocks, with the leading edge slightly raised. The curing concrete should be kept damp for a week, either by covering with wet burlap or by frequent spraying. Forms may be removed after the first few days, regreased and reused if additional blocks are needed.

## Laying a bed of sand

To lay the patio blocks, excavate the area of the patio to a depth of 6 inches. Treat the wood borders with preservative and set in place inside the excavation. Check to make certain that they are level, then drive shar-

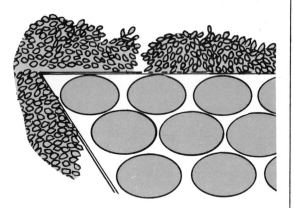

pened 1-by-2-inch stakes at intervals around the outside of the border and nail the 2-by-6-inch boards to the stakes. Tie strings tautly across the excavation, between opposite corners of the border. Fill the lower 4 inches of the excavation with sand, spreading it evenly with a rake. Tamp it down firmly. Measure from the strings to the sand level to make sure there is exactly 2 inches of space; level off high spots and fill in low ones.

## Placing the blocks

Lay blocks on the tamped sand bed in any pattern you wish. Leave about ½ inch between square blocks. When all blocks are in place, sweep the sand from the surface of the blocks into the ½-inch gaps. Spray the surface with water to compact the sand, then sweep on more sand to fill any low spots. Fill spaces between the circular blocks with gravel.

# Tire planter

Take a useless automobile tire, a worn and ugly object, and transform it into a unique outdoor planter that adds a bright spot to lawn or garden.

Materials: a tire; a discarded wheel rim (available in any auto junkyard); outdoor latex paint; a paintbrush; a piece of chalk; a sharp heavy-duty utility knife; a scrubbing brush and heavy-duty detergent.

Scrub the old tire with a solution of detergent and water, then rinse well and allow it to dry.

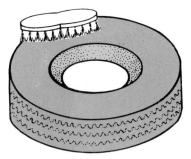

### Cutting the tire
With the chalk, draw a zigzag pattern freehand around one side of the tire. With the heavy-duty knife, cut the tire along these lines, from just inside the lip (be careful not to cut

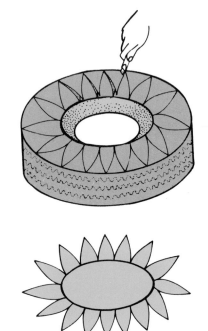

through the lip, since it holds the cut-outs together) at the tire opening out to the first tread. The cut-away part is lifted out and becomes the base of the planter.

### Painting and finishing planter
Turn the larger remaining part of the cut tire inside out. Paint both tire pieces and the rim, using the same color for all three pieces or use a contrasting color for the tire rim. When

the paint has dried, assemble the planter. The base is placed on the ground; the wheel rim fits over it, and the inside-out tire is centered on the rim. Fill the planter with soil and set in the plants. Flowering annuals, small leaf ivy and variegated leaf plants make a pleasant arrangement.

# Hemp hammock

Sailors are used to sleeping in hammocks as are many peoples in warm climates who live in primitive homes, such as the Cuna Indians living in the San Blas Islands of the Caribbean. Hammocks are usually hung outdoors in the shade between two trees or posts. Canvas or woven hammocks are comfortable for napping and might also be hung indoors in a play-room or solarium. The hammock illustrated is woven from flat strips of vinyl and it assembles rather quickly.

Materials: 48 yards of jute webbing 4¼ inches wide from an upholstery shop or the same amount of the vinyl webbing used for outdoor furniture; 50 feet of sisal rope ¼ inch in diameter; several additional feet of sisal rope for hanging the hammock, available at hardware stores; two lengths of hardwood lumber each 40-by-2-by-1 inches; two heavy metal rings 3 to 4 inches in diameter; several feet of heavy-gauge household wire; a pair of pliers; and several feet of colored adhesive tape. Also needed are: a heavy-gauge needle and thread; a sewing machine; and a drill with ¼-inch bit.

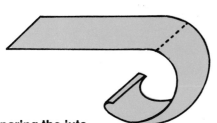

## Preparing the jute
Cut the 48 yards of jute webbing into 27 strip lengths: 8 measuring 8 feet 10 inches long and 19 measuring 3 feet 10 inches long. Take one of the longer strips and fold one end under 1½ inches; then fold down another 9½ inches to form a loop. Machine stitch through the triple thickness of the jute, making two or three rows of stitching. Repeat this process at the other end of the strip. Fold and stitch loops in the same manner on each end of the remaining 8-feet-10-inch strips.

## Weaving the hammock
Take one of the looped strips and lay it on the floor. Starting just below the loop, place each of the short strips across the long strip, alternating one over and one under, as shown below left. Space the short strips about ½ inch apart across the long strip, and be sure the end of each strip extends 5 inches beyond the long strip. Tuck each extended end under or over the long jute strip and, with needle and thread, tack each strip into position. Machine stitch short strips to long strips.

Lay out another long strip of jute on the opposite side, parallel to the first long strip. Take each of the loose ends of the short jute strips and repeat the process described above, laying them across the second long strip. This time alternate the short jute strips in the op-

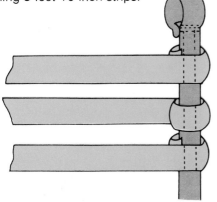

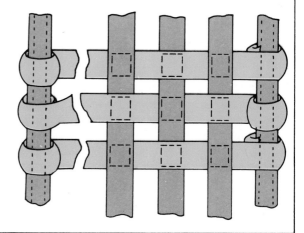

posite direction. For example, if one short strip lies over the first long strip, it should lie under the second long strip, and vice versa. Space strips, fold extended ends under, tack into position. Machine stitch, as on other side.

Stitch the long and short jute pieces together, both at the inside and outside edges of the long jute strips on both sides.

To weave the remaining eight long strips, draw each through the short cross strips, weaving them over and under, all the way through, pinning the intersections. Machine stitch strips at intersections.

### Adding wooden supports

Sand the two pieces of hardwood to remove any roughness which might cut into the jute

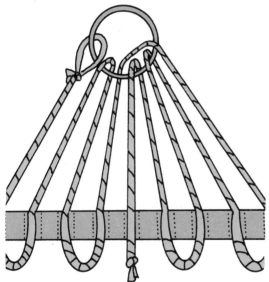

webbing. Start 2 inches from the end of the wood strip, drill nine ¼-inch holes, spaced 4 inches apart. Slip the wood supports through the loops at each end of the long jute strips.

### Connecting to metal rings

Cut two 25-foot lengths of sisal rope. Tape one end of each of the two lengths of rope so the rope will pass through the wood easily.

Push one untaped end of the rope through the center hole, tie a knot at the end and pull tightly so the knot is against the wood. Then take the taped end of the rope and pass through one metal ring and then take the rope back to the first hole to the right of the center hole, pass through this hole and then into the second hole to the right of the center and through the metal ring. Pass the rope from the ring to the third hole right of center, through it and into the fourth hole right of center and back through the metal ring. Now pass the rope through the first hole to the left of the center hole, then through the second hole to the left of the center, then back through the ring again and from there to the third hole left

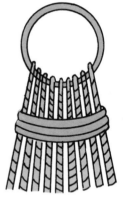

of center, through that hole and through the fourth hole left of center, ending back at the metal ring. Tie a knot at the ring, closing the rope off. Repeat process for other end, following the diagram at right.

### Securing with wire

Pull the metal ring away from the wood support, spreading the rope evenly between metal ring and wood. With the household wire held between pliers, make eight or ten turns around the rope about 1 inch below the metal ring. Hide the wire by wrapping and tying sturdy fabric or leftover rope around it. Repeat at the other end.

Hang your hammock from hooks in trees or in posts by slipping rings over hooks. Or stretch a length of rope from the hooks to the metal rings. Make sure hooks are firmly in place, and knots are very securely tied.

# Birdhouse and feeder

Give your feathered friends a happy home. Hung from a tree branch, or set upon a post or on a shelf outside your own dwelling, this cheerful birdhouse will attract small bird species such as the bluebird, nuthatch, chickadee, swallow, titmouse, prothonotary warbler, wren, and downy woodpecker. For larger birds, make a proportionately larger house. Instructions for a companion feeder are also given.

Materials for the birdhouse: 60 inches of ½-by-8-inch lumber; 8 inches of ⅜-inch dowel; wire nails; a large screw eye; and paint. Decorate your birdhouse to your taste. Ours has tiles painted on the blue roof, curtained windows with flower boxes, and a pink door with a border of flowers. But do not paint the inside; most birds object to the odor of paint.

Materials for the feeder: 68 inches of ½-by-8-inch lumber; 48 inches of ¼-by-1½-inch lattice; four 2-by-1⅜-inch roundhead wood screws with 16 flat washers; 1-inch wire nails; a hook and eye; a large screw eye; and paint. The tools you need are hammer; crosscut saw (a power saw will make the job easier, but a handsaw will also do perfectly well); rule; screwdriver; paintbrush; scissors; pencil; a 1⅜-inch drill and a ⅜-inch drill for the birdhouse; and a No. 5 pilot drill for the feeder.

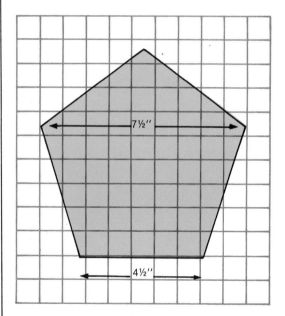

the 3¾-inch radius of the circle. Open the compass slightly and mark five equal segments on the circle. When you have divided the circle equally, draw the five sides of the pentagon. Cut out the pattern, and use it as a guide to cut the two pentagon-shaped end pieces from ½-by-8-inch lumber.

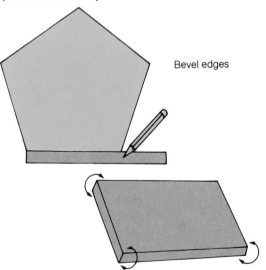

Bevel edges

### Cutting out parts for the birdhouse
The ends, sides and roof pieces are the same for both the birdhouse and the feeder. The ends are equilateral pentagons. Make a full-size paper pattern of the pentagon as shown. Or lay out the paper pattern by using a compass to draw a 7½-inch diameter circle, then inscribing the pentagon within the circle. One leg of the pentagon will be slightly longer than

Cut the two side pieces 7 inches long. Use an end piece to mark the exact width of each side piece (it should be the exact width of one of the legs of the pentagon). Cut the sides to this width, then bevel both 7-inch edges of each side piece outward, so the bevels are cut in opposite directions. If you are using a power-saw, set the guide fence to 72 degrees. If you are using a handsaw, mark the angle of the cut on the end of the lumber, using the pentagon-shaped piece as a guide, and hold the saw at that angle as you cut. The roof and base pieces will hide any slight imperfections.

Cut the roof pieces 6 by 8 inches to allow for an overhang all around. Roof pieces are also beveled along both long edges at the same angle as the side pieces, except that both bevels on each roof piece are cut in the same direction. The two bevel angles on one side of the roof are identical but they are cut in the opposite direction to the two identical bevels on the other side of the roof.

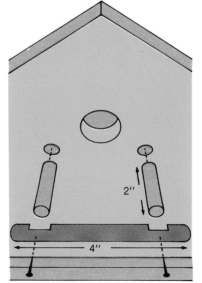

### Assembling the birdhouse

Cut a 6-by-8-inch base. With a pencil draw a line on top of the base, along the two 6-inch ends, ⅜ inch from the edge of each end. Then take one of the pentagon-shaped ends, and drill a 1⅜-inch-diameter hole in the center of the piece. This will be the entrance to the house. Place each of the two end pieces on the base, inside the pencil lines, so the end is equidistant from each side of the base. Join the end piece to the base by driving three or four nails through the base and into the ends.

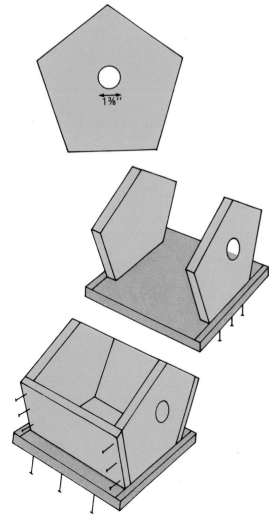

Mount the two side pieces on the base and join the pieces by driving nails, first through the sides to the ends and then through the base. Nail the roof pieces to the ends and sides, allowing equal overhang at front and back. Be sure the two beveled edges of each roof piece match and fit neatly at the pitch before nailing into position.

Cut a 4-inch length of ⅜-inch-diameter dowel. Measure ⅜ inch in from each end of the dowel, then cut ⅜-inch-wide notches halfway through the dowel. Cut two 2-inch lengths of dowel to fit into the notches; nail the longer dowel to these pieces. In the end with the entry hole drilled in it, drill two ⅜-inch-diameter holes, one on each side of the entry hole, and 1⅜ inch below it. Insert the perch into these holes, allowing it to extend from the house approximately 1⅝ inches. After the birdhouse has been painted and has dried, put a large screw eye in the roof and hang the house with wire or cord in a partially

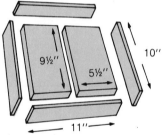

shaded area, with the doorway lightly shielded by foliage. Birds are very protective of their privacy, and do not like to be observed coming and going. To entice prospective tenants, provide food and bits of straw or string for the birds to use in building a nest.

### Cutting out parts for the feeder

Cut two 5½-by-9½-inch base pieces from the ½-inch lumber. Cut two 11-inch lengths of lat-

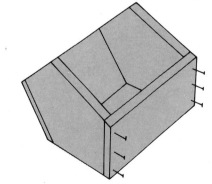

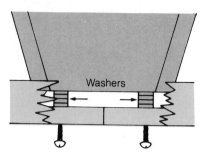

Washers

tice and use them to join together the base pieces, nailing the lattice flush with the bottom of the ½-inch side of the lumber. Cut two 10-inch lengths of lattice and nail along the edges of the base. The lattice serves as both a perch for the birds and a retainer for birdseed.

### Assembling the feeder

Nail the sides of the feeder to the pentagonal end pieces, marked and cut as directed for the birdhouse. Center this assembly on the base and mark the outline with pencil, then remove the assembly. The base is not fastened directly to the sides; it is screwed on, with washers used as spacers to allow the seeds to pass through. Drill two pilot holes at each end of the base, approximately ¼ inch inside the pencil outline drawn. Pass the screws through from under the base, place four washers over each of the four screws, then drive the screws into the ends of the assembled feeder.

Nail on one half of the roof. Attach the continuous hinge to this half, then screw the hinge onto the remaining half. Install the hook under the overhang of the movable roof piece and the eye on the side of the feeder. Paint the outside of the feeder. Either mount the feeder on a post or suspend it with a screw eye and cord from a tree branch.

# Silkscreen prints

The silkscreen process is a versatile technique for producing multiple copies of a design. Sometimes, as in the Silkscreen T-shirt project, a paper stencil is affixed to the silkscreen to print the design. But the more widely practiced method for making silkscreen prints is the block-out method, in which a film of glue on the silk acts as the stencil.

The silkscreen print shown here is of particular interest because it manages to combine a background color with three design colors, using only two color applications. You can achieve this effect with an original design, or duplicate the one illustrated.

Materials: a silkscreen frame and squeegee; ruler and pencil; 4-ounce bottle of mucilage; masking tape; silkscreen paints or tubes of artist's oil paints for the colors planned; a 1-pint can of silkscreen binder; one or more sizes of watercolor brushes; soft cloth or paper towel; turpentine; soap; and enough paper to make the desired number of prints plus one extra for a preliminary sketch.

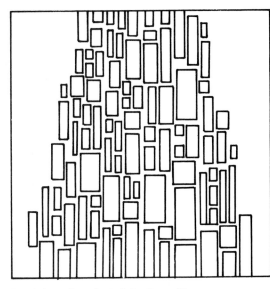

angles on the screen where the corners lie, so you will have a guide for positioning all subsequent sheets of paper. These are register marks which assure correct registration of colors later. Trace the drawing onto the silk, being careful to catch every line and shape that you want to print. Remove the original design sketch.

**Applying the sketch to the silk**

The maximum size of your silkscreen design is determined by the size of your printing screen. The design must be smaller than the screen by at least 1 inch on each side. Determine your maximum dimensions and measure them out on a sheet of printing paper. Pencil in the boundaries with a ruler. Within that space make a color sketch of the print as you plan to make it.

Insert the sketch in the silkscreen frame. Again allow at least 1-inch margins between frame edge and print edge on all four sides. When the paper is correctly lined up, tape it lightly in place and with pencil mark the right

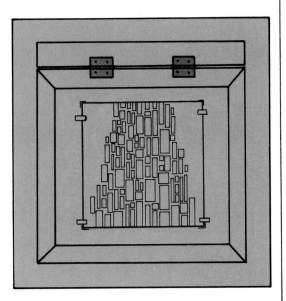

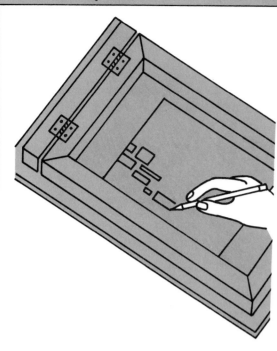

blue-green have been blocked out in the first color application. Let the glue dry for an hour. Hold the screen up to the light to check for pinholes (where the glue has failed to take). Retouch any holes with the glue solution and allow to dry again.

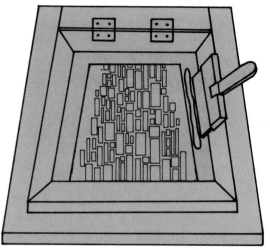

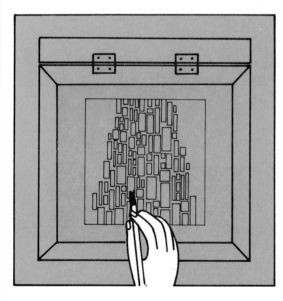

**Blocking and printing the first color**
Make a glue solution, diluting the glue to a consistency suitable for brushing on the silk. About two parts glue to one part water are the right proportions.

Before applying the background color, you must block out with the glue solution all the areas that are to be part of the foreground motif. In the example shown, all parts that are

Put a clean sheet of printing paper under the silkscreen frame, aligning all the corners with the register marks. Tape the paper lightly to keep it from slipping. Prepare the print for the background color, in this case black. Use prepared silkscreen paint, or mix one teaspoon of artist's oil paint with one cup (8 ounces) of binder. Spread the paint along the right side of the screen. Start with a few spoonfuls, and see how many impressions or prints you can get. Once you have learned to control the paint, you can use larger quantities.

Place the squeegee along the right side of the screen, parallel with the reservoir of paint. Holding the squeegee firmly in the right hand, pass it across the screen to the left side, pushing a ribbon of paint in front of the rubber blade as you go. When you reach the opposite edge, pull the squeegee back ½ inch to release the paint. Do not pull squeegee back too far into the actual printing area.

Lift the screen, remove the paper, and pin the impression up to dry on a clothesline or hang it over a towel rack.

Repeat the procedure, reversing the movement direction of squeegee each time across the screen. Hold squeegee in left hand to

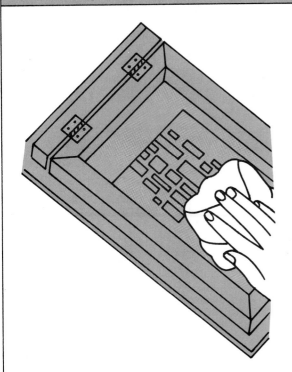

### Printing the other colors

Place the original sketch under the screen, in the proper register position, and trace the design onto screen. Remove drawing. Brush on a coat of glue wherever the background color appears. This is to block out background during the printing of the design portion of pattern. Use a small brush to apply glue in and around small areas. Turn the silkscreen over and brush a second coat of glue onto the

move it across to right and then reverse, until you have printed all the copies you will want plus a few spares to allow for error. Remove the background paint and glue from the screen with turpentine. Then wash it with soap and water, using a soft rag. Blot dry.

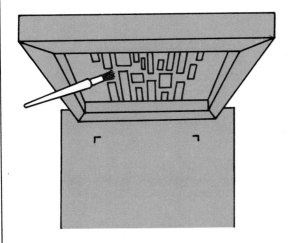

underside. Check to be sure there are no pinholes in the glue stencil. Allow to dry. Check again.

Take down the first of the silkscreen prints that you hung to dry and place it under the silkscreen in proper position. Spill a line of three colors (yellow, blue and green created the effect in illustration) along the right side of the frame; do not mix them; allow them to bleed into one another. Do not use a large quantity of paint at one time because many swipes of the squeegee will cause the colors to mix entirely rather than to float next to each other. Instead, replace paint frequently. Spill additional paint as before, along the right side of the frame. Use the squeegee as previously instructed. Hang each of the finished prints to dry.

Because the colors mix in random fashion with each swipe of the squeegee, no two prints will be the same. This is the advantage of this method of applying paint. If you desire a still greater accidental appearance in the design, lay some of the papers slightly off register during the second printing process.

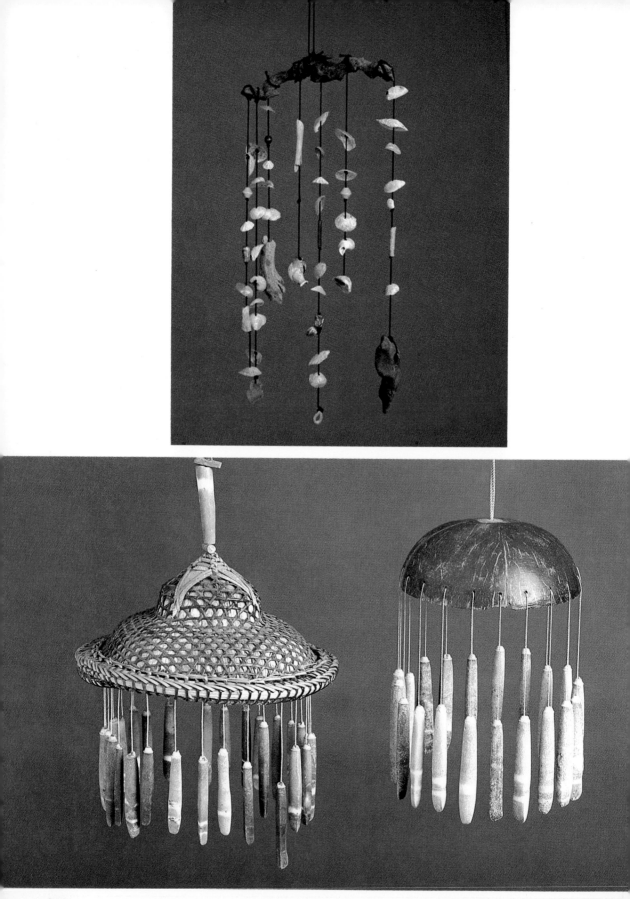

# Wind chimes

What could be more relaxing on a warm, sunny day than to sit or work in one's garden to the music of softly tinkling wind chimes! Hang these graceful mobiles from an open window, your front door, a tree branch or any location where they can catch a passing breeze. Wind chimes can be fashioned very easily from a variety of common materials. The possibilities are limited only by your imagination. The basic components of a set of wind chimes are: a holding piece or sculptural object with appendages from which chimes can be hung and strung (an odd-shaped, gnarled piece of wood, a dowel, or a twisted coat hanger); string or nylon, silk or cotton thread, compatible with the weight and structure of the objects to be strung; and visually appealing objects of varying sizes and thicknesses that will produce interesting sounds when struck together (hollow pieces of wood, shells, keys, colored glass pieces, ceramic shapes, coins, or metal shapes cut from tin cans or aluminum sheeting).

Materials: clear-drying non-water-soluble glue; string or thread; wire coat hanger; gnarled piece of wood; hammer; hand or power drill; awl; scissors; and an assortment of keys, shells, ceramic pieces and tin pieces. To make the ceramic chime pieces you also require: scraps of clay; a kitchen knife or nail file; a rolling pin; glaze and/or iron oxide (left over from other ceramic projects); newspapers; a ¼-inch paintbrush; plastic wrap; and pearl beads for the bell chimes. For the metal-shaped chimes, you need: an assortment of bottle tops, tin can tops and bottoms or aluminum sheeting; sandpaper or emery board; and outdoor spray paint, if desired. The shells used for the chimes in the photograph come from an area where a variety of colored shells are plentiful, but clam or mussel shells are suitable.

### Making clay chimes
To make ceramic chimes from scrap clay, cover a large, flat work surface with newspa-

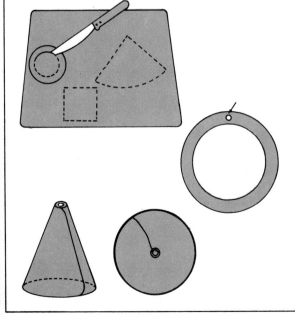

per. With rolling pin, roll clay into flat pieces at least ⅛ inch thick and not thicker than ⅝ inch. (The thinner the piece, the higher the pitch, and vice versa). Cut out geometric shapes with a nail file or kitchen knife. Also, cut a small hole near the edge of each shape for stringing. To form bells, roll flat rectangles of clay slightly more than 5 inches on the longer side. Starting from the bottom, shape the rectangle with your fingers into a cone of

about 5 inches bottom circumference, tapering to a top opening circumference of about
⅛ inch. Cut out a small rectangle of the same
clay for bell ringers. Cover each shape tightly
with plastic wrap and let dry for 24 hours until
stiff, but not totally dry. Remove plastic and
let clay dry uncovered for 4 more days until
it is bone-dry (no moisture, at about room temperature). When bone-dry, clay is ready to fire.
Depending on the type of clay used, firing
generally takes at least 8 hours, plus cooling
time. Since kilns are costly investments, have
your pieces fired professionally. First firing will
be to a "bisque" temperature, indicated by a
light pink color. If you wish, you may string
the shapes at this stage, or stain the pieces.
Brush a stain mixed from powdered iron oxide
and water into all surfaces and let dry one
hour before having pieces fired again. In addition, you may brush glaze left over from other
projects on each piece and have them fired
a third time. (See Ceramic chess pieces.)

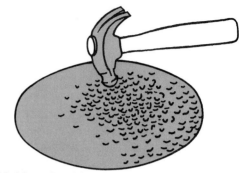

### Making tin chimes

To make tin chimes, gather an assortment of
bottle tops, tin can tops and bottoms, or
scraps of aluminum sheeting. Use shapes as
they are, or cut your own designs with tin
snips or kitchen utility shears. File edges of
shapes with sandpaper or emery boards.
Place awl near edge of each shape and hammer a tiny hole through thickness of tin.
(Shells can also be pierced this way.) To flatten bottle tops or add textural interest, tap the
head of a nail against the surface of the tin
with a hammer for a stippled effect. Tin
catches the sunlight strikingly and may be
strung unadorned. However, if you desire
more color, spray each piece with outdoor
spray paint and let dry according to the manufacturer's instructions.

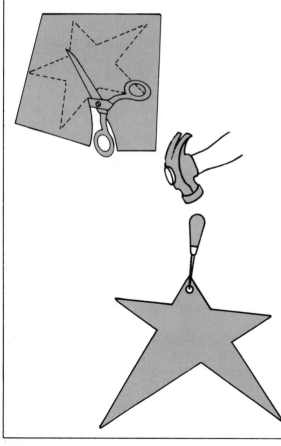

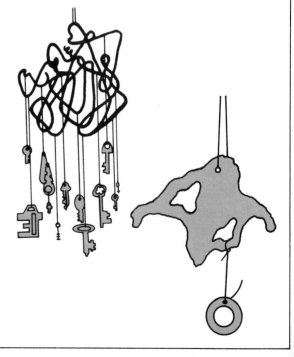

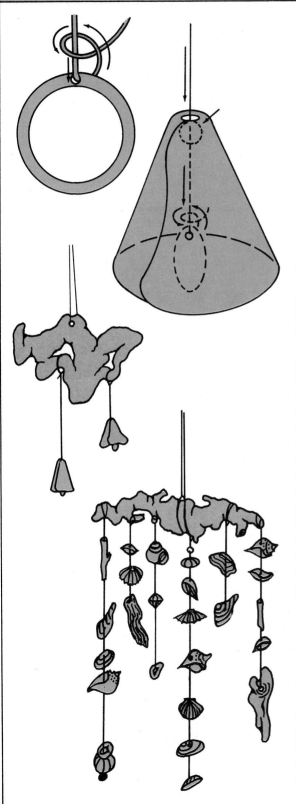

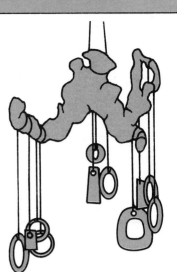

### Making holding piece

To make a holding piece from a wire coat hanger, use hands or pliers to bend wire into interesting shapes, then suspend chimes from it, or if desired, first spray-paint the holder. If you are using soft wood for your holding piece, use a hand drill to make holes in the wood for suspending chimes. Make holes in hard wood with an electric power drill. Saturate string or thread with glue before threading around and through the holes in the appendages and chimes. Make sure you have a hole in the center top of the holding piece, both for hanging and for establishing a focus of balance for the finished chimes. When the suspended chime is at desired length from holding piece, tie overhand knots around and through holes. (Do not tie or thread through center top hole.) Cut away excess string or thread. Chimes should hang fairly close together at varying heights, so that they touch when they are set in motion by a flow of air. They should not be spaced so closely that they tangle excessively. Bells are strung first through top opening of the bell, then through the pearl, around and through the ceramic ringer, and then tied with an overhand knot. When you are satisfied with your arrangement, pass matching thread or string coated with glue around and through the center top opening of the holding piece. Tie ends of string with an overhand knot around a hook, tree branch, or a beam to hang the chimes.

# Dipped, rolled and molded candles

Candlemaking requires no special skill, but the results provide a rewarding experience for both children and adults. There are three basic methods of making candles; molding, rolling, or dipping, each method adapting easily to variety in shapes, size, and color combinations.

Materials: specific candlemaking items needed are available in craft and hobby shops. Candlewicks are made of braided cotton yarn, treated with a thin coating of wax. They are available in two or three widths and are sold in lengths. A flat, loosely braided wick curls as it burns, causing the flame to be slightly off center, while the tightly woven or square-shaped wick does not curl. Wicks are also available with a supportive metal core to use in heavy candles that are more than 2½ inches wide to prevent the wick from falling over and being extinguished in a pool of wax.

Paraffin, or commercial wax, comes in white blocks which are easily cut up for melting. Stearic acid, a component of animal fats, is added to the wax to make candles burn more slowly and to increase the durability of delicate candles. Use about 10 percent stearic acid by weight of the wax. Paraffin candles without stearic acid burn fast and unevenly, but they have a beautiful translucence; whereas the acid gives the candle an opaque quality. Polyethylene, another additive, either alone or combined with the stearic acid, gives a candle a longer burning span and makes it white and glossy. There is one drawback: it may clog the wick, because polyethylene burns more slowly than paraffin. To compensate, a larger wick than normal is used. Polyethylene must be melted separately from the wax, and added only when both are completely dissolved.

Dyes are available in powder form or in slabs. The powder is preferable because it can be measured and the colors duplicated as needed. Slabs, which are heavy concentrations of dye in wax, are not as controllable. Crayons, melted with the wax, are also good coloring agents; but they contain a sediment which will accumulate at the bottom of the liquid wax. If crayons are used, allow this sediment to settle before pouring. Pour carefully, leaving a small amount of wax in pan to discard with the sediment.

Scent oils, if used, are added to the melted wax just before pouring or dipping. Use a modest amount; too much will not blend completely with the wax, and thus the finished candle will have an undesirable dappled effect. Use cardboard tubing or a paper milk container as a mold, or purchase ready-made candle molds of metal, plastic, or rubber.

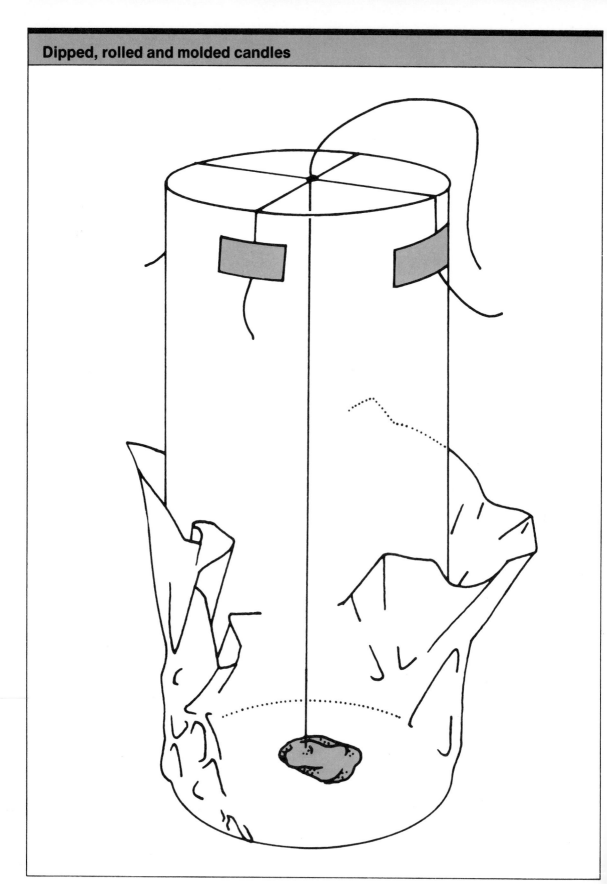

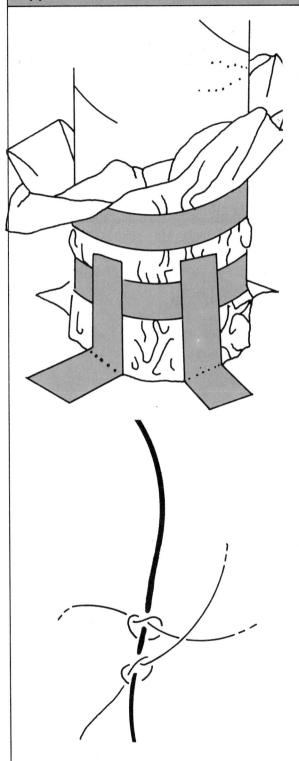

## Molding candles

To prepare the working area, tape a protective layer of newspapers on the surface. Heat the wax in a double boiler over low heat. Wax is flammable and should not be melted over a direct flame. Keep a box of powdered baking soda handy, as a precaution, to extinguish a wax fire, should one occur. The wax pours best at about 30 degrees above its melting point, which may range from 125 to 160 degrees Fahrenheit. Use a candy thermometer to measure temperature, or judge it by noting that the temperature will rise 30 degrees above the melting point approximately ten minutes after the wax has been completely melted.

Using a paper towel, coat the inside of the mold with cooking oil. This will provide a smooth surface for the candle and an easy release when the mold is removed. To prepare a mold that has no bottom, cut a wick at least 6 inches longer than the height of the mold. Tie two strings around the wick, 3 to 4 inches from one end. With a sticky, nonflammable, non-melting substance, such as clay or chewing gum, attach the other end to a large piece of heavy-duty aluminum foil. Pull the end of the wick with the strings around it through the mold, and looking through the mold, adjust the foil so that the bottom end of the wick is centered in the mold. To keep the wick centered, wrap the aluminum foil around the mold. Pull the top of the wick taut and adjust the strings so that the knots line up with the mold's top rim. Tape the ends down tautly on the outside of the mold just below the rim so the excess dangles outside the mold. Wrap the bottom of the mold with another piece of foil, and tape tightly around the outside of the mold. Then tape the mold securely to your work surface.

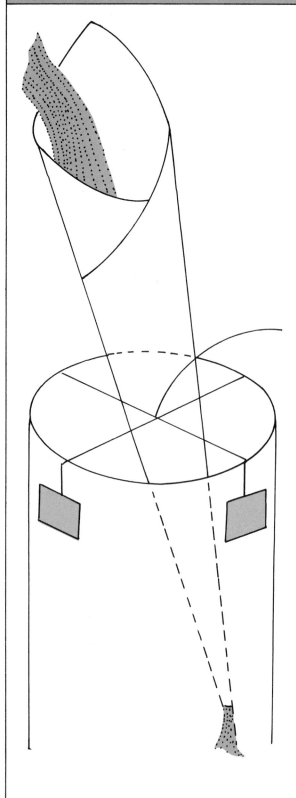

To mold a candle in layers of different colors, for a striped effect, pour each color of melted wax through a funnel made of rolled newspaper. This will prevent wax splashes on the inside walls. Let each layer dry until it is solid, but still warm to the touch, before the next pouring. If the wax is too soft, the hot wax poured on this surface will blend with the previous color. Sometimes this effect is desired. If the wax is too hard, the layers will not fuse properly and the joining edges will be rough.

As each layer dries, a well forms at the base of the wick. It can be filled before the next pouring, or after the pouring is finished. In either case, as the depression forms, pierce the candle along the wick with a sharp tool, such as a knitting needle or skewer, to prevent cave-ins due to the inner tensions created in the candle during the shrinking process. As the wax hardens, fill in the well. Allow 6 to 8 hours for the wax to set, cooling slowly. Do not cool in the refrigerator, or the candle will crack. When the wax is completely hardened, peel the mold off gently. If necessary, run warm water over the wax to remove remaining paper.

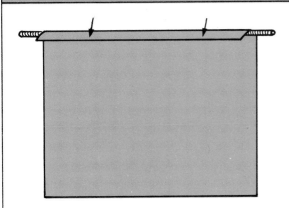

## Rolling candles

Rolling is the simplest method of candle-making. There is no melting, no waiting for wax to harden, and there are no molds to remove. Beeswax is used because it has clean burning characteristics and a lower melting point. You need a sheet of honey-combed beeswax 8 by 16 inches, a length of candlewick, scissors, a straightedge, a pencil, and a cutting surface. Cut the wick several inches longer than the desired length of the candle. Mark the wax sheet with the pencil, and cut to the desired length and width. This standard-size sheet of beeswax makes one 9-inch candle when rolled length-wise, or a 17-inch candle rolled across the width of the sheet.

Secure the wick along one edge of the wax by pressing the two together with fingers. This will soften the honeycomb to permit a fairly

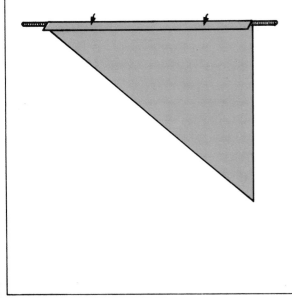

solid fusion. Roll the sheet of wax away from you with the wick inside, making careful, tight turns and keeping the edges even. The tighter the candle, the better and longer it will burn.

For an unusual effect, cut the beeswax sheet into a triangle and roll with the slanted edge spiraling downward. The wax, as it burns, will drip around this slight edge, creating an interesting configuration. Roll two triangular beeswax sheets of different colors in one candle for a striped effect. One sheet should be larger than the other, and one right angle should lie on top of the other. After candles are

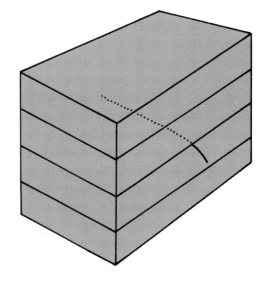

rolled (if different configurations are desired), candles can be softened in hot water, near a household heating unit, or in the sun, then twisted or bent into odd shapes.

### Stacking beeswax to make candles

Stacking small (2 inches by 3 inches) rectangles of beeswax creates a thick, four-sided candle. Cut out 12 to 14 rectangles, 2 inches by 3 inches, from beeswax sheets of different colors. Stack them on top of each other, laying in the wick (so it extends beyond the edges) at the middle point on top of the sixth or seventh rectangle, and continue to stack the remaining rectangles. Place a heavy weight, such as a book, on top of the stack to press the beeswax leaves together to form the candle. Do this in a warm place so the leaves will fuse.

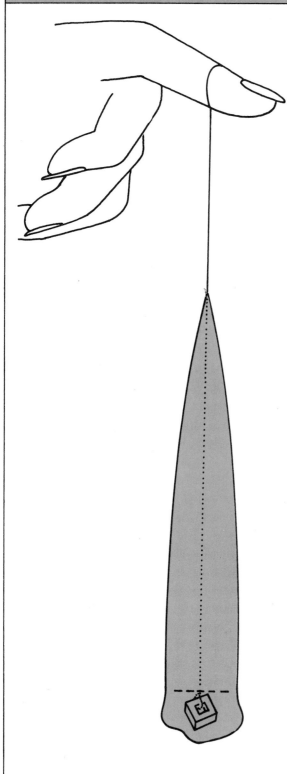

## Dipping to make tapers or candles

The hand-dipped candle or taper is a traditional form of candlemaking. Use paraffin, beeswax or a mixture of both. Suspend weights (nuts, bolts, fishing sinkers) at the bottom of pre-waxed wicks (soaked in hot wax and straightened when dry). Use the flat braided wick if a dripping candle is desired, or square wick for a dripless taper. Hang a wick or a number of wicks from a holder (broom handle, wire coat hanger, stick) and lower them into melted wax time after time until the desired thickness is attained. The top of the container holding the wax should be at least 2 inches above the wax level, to accommodate the increasing size of the taper. The wax must not be too hot, or the taper will dissolve rather than grow. Since wax cools quickly, it may be necessary to skim or even reheat it at intervals. To taper the candle, make each successive dip shallower than the previous one. Dipping too quickly may cause air bubbles to form, leaving blotches. About 30 dippings are required to produce a taper with a 1-inch-base diameter. With a sharp knife, trim off the bottom of the candle containing the weight, and finish it with a final dip.

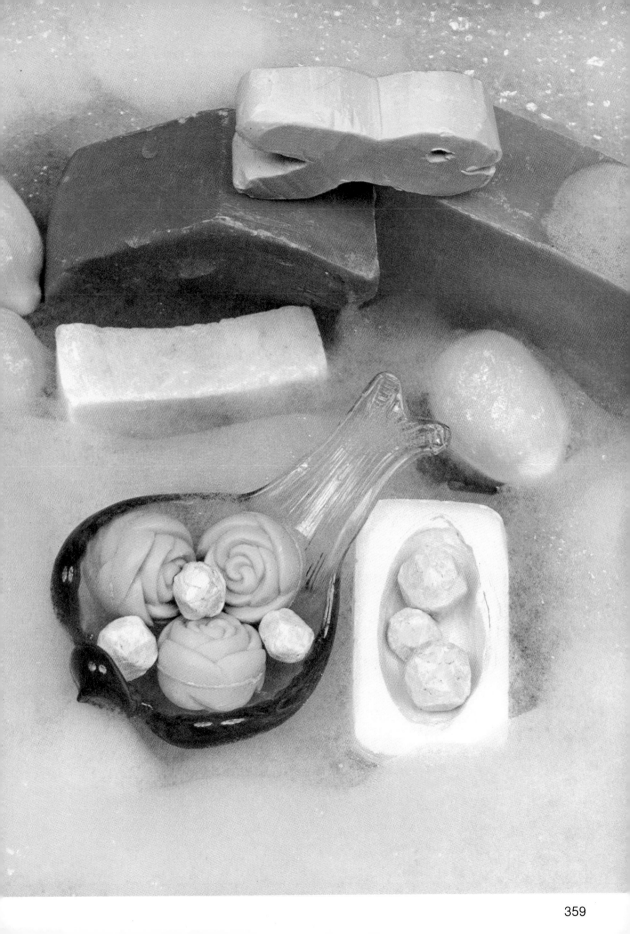

# Scented soaps

From lemonade stands to more enterprising efforts, children and especially teenage boys are intrigued with any recipe or simple chemical formula that can be turned into a moneymaker. Homemade soap, for instance, is easy to prepare with relatively inexpensive materials. While the homemade product is no match for some of the imported specialty soaps that may boast of cucumbers, rose petals or other exotic ingredients, it has its own charm manifest in color, shape and scent.

The basic recipe calls for liquid animal fat and lye. To make the product unique, experiment with color as well as scents. Try essence of cloves and color the soap brown, or experiment with oils of mint and create a bright-green color for the soap. You might take small quantities from the first batch prepared and use it for testing scents and colorings. Part of the fun in working with this project is creating a product that is your very own, and if you plan to shape the soap into a fish or an Easter egg, tint the soap brilliantly with whatever color your imagination suggests. Should you decide to make up the soap in the more traditional pastel colors, give the product originality in its shape. Factory-made soap, with its artificial scents and predictable shapes, doesn't begin to have the appeal of the handmade product. We offer simple instructions for making a batch in your own kitchen.

Materials: 12-quart enamel or stainless-steel pot for rendering the fat; measuring cups; shoe box or similar container to mold the liquid soap; lye (sodium hydroxide) in pure, concentrated flake form; essential oils; and vegetable coloring. Also needed: meat thermometer; safety goggles; rubber gloves; and apron.

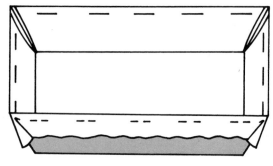

Mold

### Making a soap mold
First prepare one of two containers to serve as molds. We suggest, until you become more proficient, a shoe box; later you can experiment with other handmade or household molds. The formula given here will yield enough liquid soap to almost fill a shoe box, which is also ideal for cooling the liquid until the soap sets.

To prepare the shoe box, line it smoothly and completely with a sheet of plastic; a plastic garbage bag can be cut to do the job. After you have smoothed it down as much as possible, staple it around the top of the box, and put it aside.

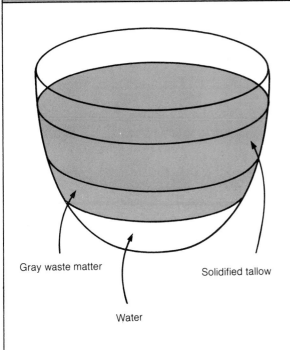

Gray waste matter

Solidified tallow

Water

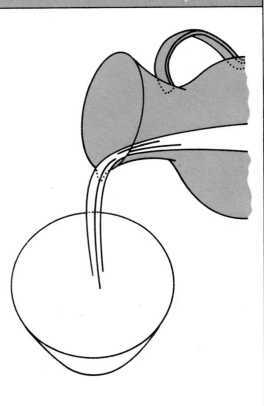

### Rendering the tallow

Cut 6 pounds of animal fat and cut it into small pieces or put it through a meat grinder. Place in a large pot with 10 ounces of water and simmer for several hours over low heat, stirring occasionally. When the cracklings or nonmelting parts of the fat that will not render have separated, and the rest of the fat is liquefied, strain and discard the cracklings. The remaining liquid is tallow and will be the basis for your soap. Allow the liquid to cool and then refrigerate. This chilling process will cause water separation, and the solidified tallow will rise to the top. Discard the water and the gray waste layer beneath the tallow. In order to ready it for soap making, the tallow has to be liquefied over heat.

### Preparing the lye solution

Be sure the lye (sodium hydroxide) is in pure, concentrated flake form, and prepare according to package directions. It is generally sold in 13-ounce cans. Before working with lye put on safety goggles, rubber gloves and an apron. Lye is activated by the slightest amount of moisture, even perspiration, and can cause severe burns if allowed to touch the skin. Keep a bottle of vinegar nearby as an antidote. Mix the can of lye with *cold* water in a 2-quart bowl. Add the lye, a small amount at a time, to the water. *Never* add water to the lye. Combining lye with water produces intense heat (be very careful). You may have to wait several hours for the solution to cool down. It should be between 95 and 98 degrees Fahrenheit before you proceed. Before using, set the bowl of lye solution into a larger bowl containing warm water in order to raise the liquid temperature slightly above room temperature. Use the meat thermometer to check this rise.

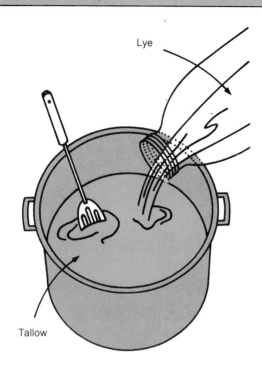

Lye

Tallow

### Mixing tallow, lye, scent, and color

When the lye and the tallow both reach the same temperature, 95 to 98 degrees Fahrenheit, place the tallow in a 6-quart pot. Add the lye *very slowly* and carefully, stirring with a slotted spoon, until the mixture is thick and creamy. The odor may be unpleasant at this stage, but it will dissipate. Again, if any spillage occurs, wash with vinegar. Add a tablespoon of an essential oil (lemon, bay, verbena, or your choice) for scent, and a few drops of food coloring to tint the soap delicately. Stir the mixture well until the scent and the color have both been assimilated.

If you wish to make several colors, pour the soap mixture into two or more bowls before adding the coloring. Each color of soap is poured into a separate mold to set. This is an extra step you may wish to try when making your second batch.

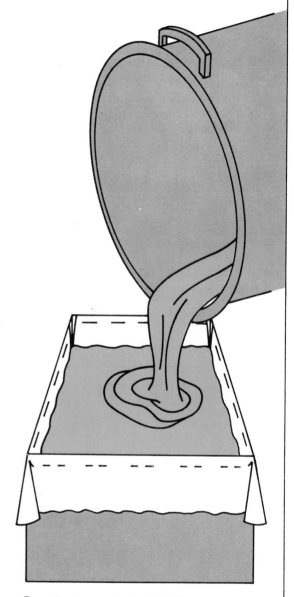

Pour the soap solution into the prepared mold. Cover the warm soap with a sheet of cardboard and place a towel or some other insulation over the cardboard to slow the cooling process.

# Scented soaps

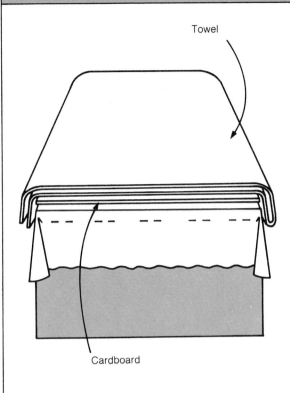

Towel

Cardboard

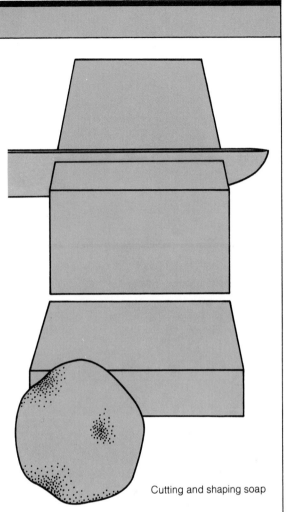

Cutting and shaping soap

When the soap has set for a day, remove it from the box, cut it into cubes, and mold soap balls in your hands. Or leave the soap in the box until it has cured for another day, cut it into cakes, and carve it so the sharp edges are nicely beveled. In either case, set the soap cakes aside to air-dry for a month. If you are using the soaps as gifts, wrap them separately in imaginative ways — in pretty papers or with an attractive soap dish.

After you have made a batch of soap, you will be able to try innovations in color, scent and shape. In fact, the first batch might well be used for testing colors and scents. Take a small quantity of the liquid soap and experiment with the vegetable coloring. When you obtain a shade you like, record the number of drops of coloring used and the quantity of soap. Then when you wish to make a batch

of that color you can refer to your notes. This method is also advised in the addition of essential oils to provide the scent for the soap. It is important to note that a few drops of these concentrated scents will be sufficient for a complete recipe.

You might also try variations in the mold used for curing the soap. For example, to create disk shapes, pour liquid soap in a shallow container such as a rectangular foil pan, or use an empty cylindrical cereal box. Also experiment with individual dessert molds or muffin tins. In shaping blocks of soap into animals, fruit or whatever whimsical object you wish to make, work with the soap before it has completely cured so it will be more manageable. For simple oval or rectangular shapes, only beveling is required and this can be done when soap is completely cured.

# Calico flowers

This arrangement of calico flowers and babies' breath is created especially for a kitchen or breakfast room. The spritely fabric flowers are sewn and assembled with a button for the pistil and wire for the stems.

Materials: 50 inches of calico or gingham fabric remnants; 9 small buttons about ½ inch in diameter (the shank type is best); 3 ounces of cotton wad stuffing or a sheet of polyester fiber fill, 30 by 40 inches; 9 feet of thin wire; 1 roll of green floral tape; a block of foamed plastic; dried sphagnum moss; dried statice or babies' breath; a small basket or similar container; heavy paper or cardboard; pencil and compass; scissors.

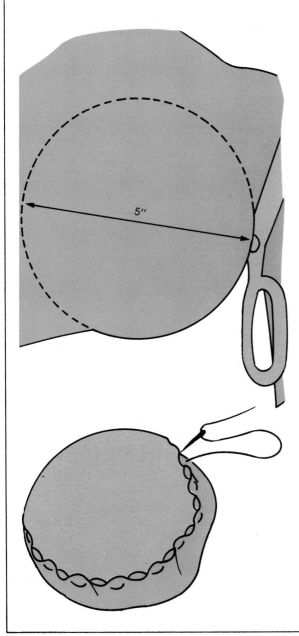

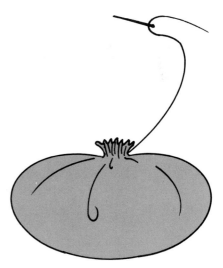

5"

### Making flower heads
To make the pattern, use a compass and pencil to draw a circle 5 inches in diameter on the paper or cardboard. Cut out circle and use as a pattern to draw nine circles on the fabric. With needle and thread, sew a line of small

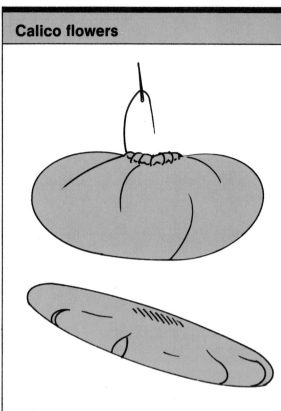

running stitches around the outer edge of each circle, gathering the fabric loosely to form flower. Place a small amount of cotton or polyester stuffing inside each circle. Draw together the gathering stitches, and secure tightly with several overcast stitches. Flatten flower, with stitched opening in middle.

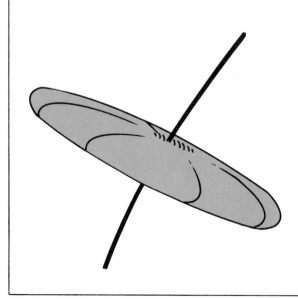

### Adding stems

Pass a 12-inch length of thin wire through the stitched opening of each flower, and push it through the fabric on the opposite side. Take the end of the wire on the gathered side of each flower and thread it through the shank or holes of the buttons to form the pistil of the flower. Fold the wire at the midpoint, then draw the end down through the flower. Twist the wire ends to form the stem. Wrap green floral tape on stem and shape as desired.

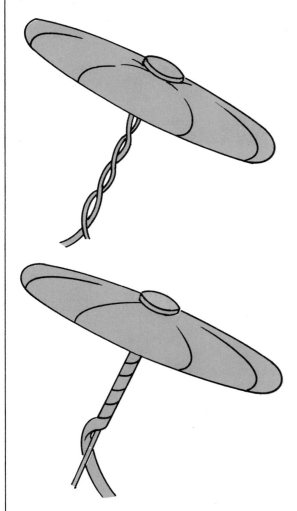

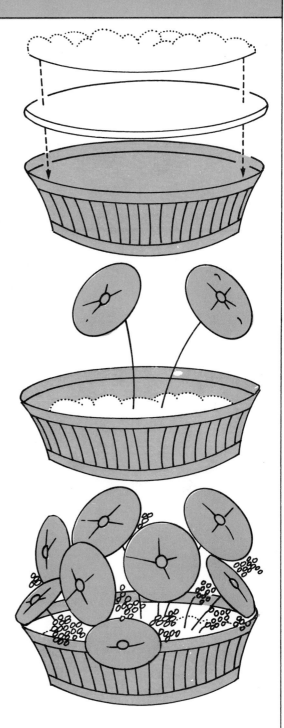

### Completing the bouquet

Cut the foamed plastic to fit snugly in the bottom of the basket or container. Arrange sphagnum moss on top to conceal the foamed plastic, then insert the flower stems into the plastic. Fill in the bouquet with dried statice or baby's breath.

# Cut-bottle tumblers

Unusual glass tumblers, vases, even planters, can be made from glass bottles. If you have a bottle with a pleasing shape and color, set it aside and try the technique described below.

Materials: there are two types of cutter kits on the market; the kit that uses a tapping device to sever the top of the bottle from the bottom, and the kit that uses a combination of hot and cold temperatures (a candle and ice cubes, for instance) to complete the job. The first is more reliable (instructions are for that type), but either one will do. In addition to the cutter kit, you need emery paper or silicone paper (a type of paper available in hardware stores), and goggles or some other protection for your eyes. The selection of bottles depends on the project. Some are better suited for vases, while others make fine ashtrays. To make a set of tumblers, look for a wine or fruit bottle, with a diameter small enough for comfortable holding. Since you will probably want to make a set of six or eight tumblers, it is necessary to buy that many bottles. When you have emptied the bottles, you can begin. Bottles 2 to 4 inches in diameter make good tumblers; smaller ones are good for fruit juice glasses. Bottles should be round, of normal thickness, and free of embossing (unless the embossing happens to be above or below the space where you will make your cut).

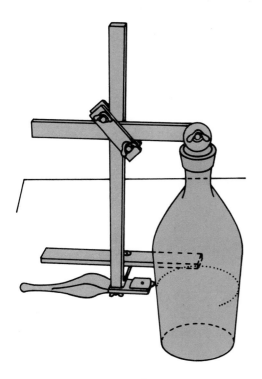

### Scoring the bottle

Wash the bottles, removing the labels and the glue, and clean the insides thoroughly. Allow the bottles to dry, as dampness may cause the cutter to slide. Prepare for cutting by spreading a newspaper on your work surface. Place the bottle standing upright on the paper. Assemble the various parts of the kit, usually a scoring device and a tapper. Put a drop of lubricant on the cutting blade (cooking oil, sewing machine oil or baby oil). Set the scoring device so that its top is in the mouth of the bottle and the cutting blade is touching the side of the bottle at a height appropriate for a tumbler. Five to six inches is conventional, but you may want to compare the bottle with one of your regular glasses and adjust up or down. Tighten all the thumbscrews on the scoring device. Put on your goggles. Lead the scoring device around the bottle in a smooth, firm motion, using one hand to press down on top of the rig and the other hand to press the cutting wheel on the side of the bottle. The pressure should be enough to produce a slight grinding sound. Keep turning until you see the fracture line of the glass completely around the bottle. At this point the scored line is causing light refraction. You can see it by holding the bottle up to a lamp.

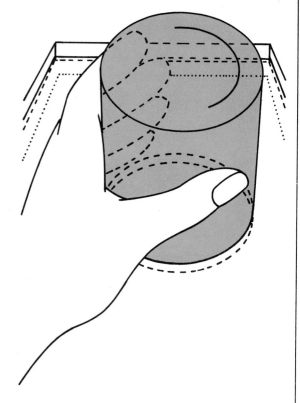

## Tapping to divide the bottle

When the bottle is scored evenly, remove the scoring device. Put the tapping device inside the bottle and adjust the length so that the tapping end touches the scored line exactly. Tap along the line, moving about ⅛ inch at a time. As you tap, the sound of metal against glass will change from a clear "ping" to a dull "pong," which indicates that the glass has been cut through at that point. Continue tapping around until the top and the bottom parts of the bottle separate. Do not force the separation, as a crack can form. Remove goggles.

## Smoothing the lip of the glass

Smooth down the sharp lip of the tumbler with a sheet of medium-weight emery or silicone paper. Finish the edge with a sheet of fine-grade waterproof emery or silicone paper. Put the paper right side up in a shallow dish (or frying pan) and add ¼ inch of water. Invert the glass on top of the paper and rotate it until all traces of sharpness have been removed. Repeat these steps on the remaining bottles. Be sure to wear goggles while cutting.

## Cutting a jug to make a planter

After having mastered the bottle-cutting technique, consider making a planter by cutting off the top of a gallon jug. Pebbles in the bottom for drainage, topped off with several inches of soil, will make it a fine planter.

# Gingerbread sculpture

Making gingerbread cookies, or lebkuchen, is a holiday ritual dating back to the fourteenth century, when German monks first adapted recipes for honey cakes to include exotic spices brought to Europe from the Middle East. Lebkuchen was the pride of the medieval Bakers' Guilds in Germany and other European countries. The spice cake was baked in different shapes and molds, some of which were beautifully carved to point up the smallest detail. The shape depended on the festive occasion, for these were luxury cakes, too expensive to enjoy any day of the year. The Bakers' Guild of Nürnberg, which had access to the finest native honey and foreign spices, produced the most prized gingerbread in Europe. It was valued highly enough to be acceptable as tax payment and was presented by diplomats to each other as gifts.

For years, gingerbread ornamented the fairs of the past and punctuated special events. By the nineteenth century, the repertoire of shapes included the characters from Grimm's "Hansel and Gretel" and the now-classic gingerbread house that appears in pastry shops throughout Europe and the United States at Christmastime.

Today, almost all European countries have their own version of lebkuchen, and gingerbread cookies in various shapes and forms hang from Christmas tree boughs.

Gingerbread dough is rolled, shaped by fingers, or cut out with a knife to make almost any image desired. To decorate, use a thin sugar glaze and dried fruits or peppermint candy for accents. A thick butter frosting can also be used to decorate the shapes and outline the details of the image.

Materials: To make the gingerbread cookie dough, you need: 1 cup shortening; 1 cup sugar; 1 teaspoon salt; 1 cup unsulfured molasses; 4½ cups sifted flour; 1 teaspoon baking soda; 1 tablespoon ground ginger; and 1 teaspoon ground nutmeg. (Makes about three dozen cookies, four inches in diameter.) For the glaze frosting, you need: 2 cups (a 1-pound box) confectioners' sugar; 4 teaspoons water; food coloring; and a pastry bag or decorating tube.

## Making the gingerbread dough

Measure sifted flour, add soda, salt, nutmeg, and ginger, and sift together. Melt shortening in a large saucepan. Add sugar and molasses and mix well. Gradually stir in about 3½ cups of the flour mixture. Then work in remaining flour mixture with hands.

## Cutting and shaping cookies

Roll out a small amount of dough at a time, ⅛ to ¼ inch thick, on a *lightly* floured board. Cut into gingerbread people, houses, circles, mushrooms or anything else you fancy. The cookies in the color illustration were cut in circles with the rim of a 1-pound coffee can. To make the cookies look more sculpted, press hollows for the eyes with your thumbs and use extra dough to form a nose and hair. If cookies are to be hung on a Christmas tree, make a hole at the top center of head with a beverage straw, and insert a short length of the straw in hole to prevent it from closing during baking.

Bake on greased baking sheets in a moderate oven (375 degrees Fahrenheit) for 6 to 8 minutes. Cool on a wire rack. Transfer the cookies from pastry board to cookie sheet and from cookie sheet to cooling rack using an extra-large spatula, since the cookies are very soft and fragile until they are completely baked and cooled.

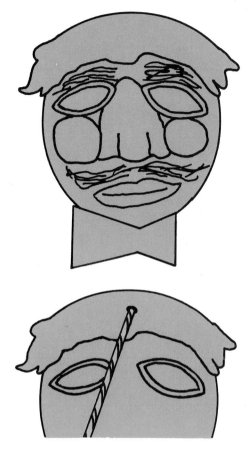

### Decorating the cookies

Combine ½ cup confectioners' sugar and 1 teaspoon water at a time. Add food coloring to small amounts of frosting for each color you desire. Use the colored frosting and your imagination to make eyes, nose, mouth and hair for the gingerbread people or to decorate the other designs you have cut or sculpted. Allow frosting to set for 15 minutes, then thread the hole at the top of head with ribbon or heavy waxed cord and knot so it can hang from a Christmas tree bough.

### Shaping a large gingerbread face

For a children's party, shape and bake a larger sculpted gingerbread face. Preheat oven to 375 degrees Fahrenheit. Dust dough with flour and roll out dough into a large circle about ¼ inch thick. With a sharp knife, cut a large circle for the face. (Exact dimensions are not necessary, since part of the charm of this

sculpture is its childlike unevenness.) The features of the face are shaped with pieces of the rolled-out dough that remain after the circle is cut out. With fingers, shape a large, wide-bottomed nose (approximately in the center of the circle) and form a thick, curved strip for hair at the top of circle. Take another two pieces of dough and build a round cheek on each side of the nose, one slightly higher than the other. Form almond-shaped eyes and place on either side of bridge of nose (again, one slightly higher than the other). Bottoms of eyes should touch tops of cheeks. Place a piece of dough below the nose (about ⅓ the distance between bottom of nose and bottom of face) and shape lips. Carve gingerbread eyebrows and mustache lightly with knife. Form a gingerbread bow tie and join to bottom of circle, centering below nose and lips. Sides of the tie should be unequal. Baking time is 8 minutes on a lightly greased cookie sheet. When done, remove cookie from oven and cool for 15 minutes on a wire rack.

### Preparing frosting

While gingerbread is baking, prepare frosting as described for the cookies or (if a buttercream frosting is preferred), as follows: Blend 1 cup softened shortening with 1 pound sifted confectioners' sugar. Add ½ tablespoon vanilla and ¼ cup milk gradually, beating after each addition until frosting is smooth, but stiff enough to force through a pastry bag. If frosting becomes too dry as you work, add about

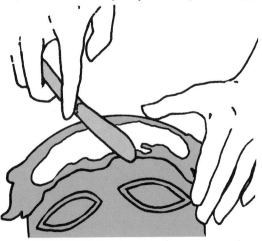

## Gingerbread sculpture

½ teaspoon of hot water and beat. Divide frosting and tint about one half with yellow food coloring; about one fourth with a few drops of red food coloring to tint frosting pink; and to the remaining frosting, add green coloring. (Use your judgment to determine exact amount.)

**Frosting the gingerbread face**

Spread yellow frosting thickly onto hair with a small spatula or butter knife, and spread pink icing onto lips and cheeks in the same manner.

To the remaining pink frosting, add several drops of red coloring to tint it red or darker pink. Spoon red frosting into pastry bag or tube. (For easy filling, stand pastry bag in a glass.) Twist bag to remove air from inside. Squeeze bag to force frosting out of end and, with a ribbon of frosting, outline tie, and along outlines of each eye and center of mouth, between lips.

Spoon green frosting into a clean bag or tube and force frosting out to form three small circles inside bow tie to make polka dots. Set pecan halves in center of eyes and on the knot of the tie.

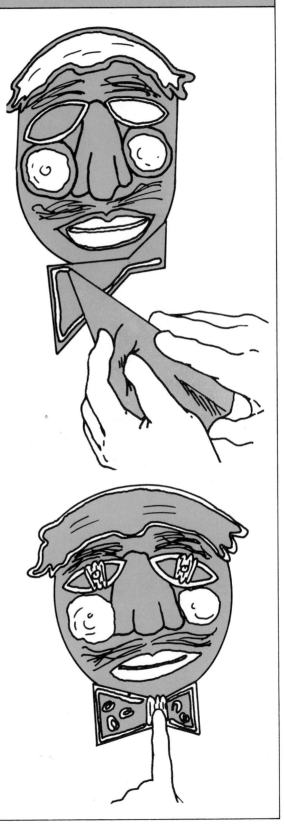

# Sachets, potpourris and pomanders

Sweet scented herbs, spices and flower petals have long been used as effective air fresheners, and some pungent combinations even discourage moths from nesting in woolens. Quaint and old-fashioned jars of potpourri, herbal pillows, sachets in different sizes and shapes and closet pomanders are as charming and practical in contemporary living as they were in the past. Experiment with the recipes that follow, then explore new combinations and search for some of the rare herbs in specialty shops or an apothecary. In recipes calling for drops of oils or essences, measure with an eyedropper.

### Citrus scent sachet

¼ lb. lemon peel
2 oz. tangerine peel
2 oz. lemon verbena
20 drops lemon oil
20 drops bergamot oil
5 drops lemongrass oil

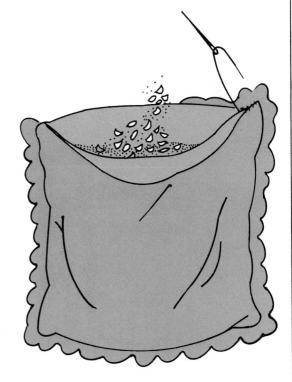

### Fragrant wood sachet

1 lb. rosewood powder      ½ oz. cedarwood oil
1 lb. sandalwood powder

For either sachet blend the ingredients together in a jar, then cover tightly and allow to sit for five days. Sew small sachet bags, made of small, tightly woven silk squares, about 2½ to 3 inches square. Fill with sachet and trim with lace or ribbon, if desired.

### Scented pillow

¼ lb. oak moss            2 oz. hops
¼ lb. peppermint          ¼ lb. wild thyme
2 oz. spearmint           1 oz. lemon verbena

Break up oak moss, then combine all ingredients and sew into a small but comfortable-size pillow. The refreshing scent is very restful and soothing.

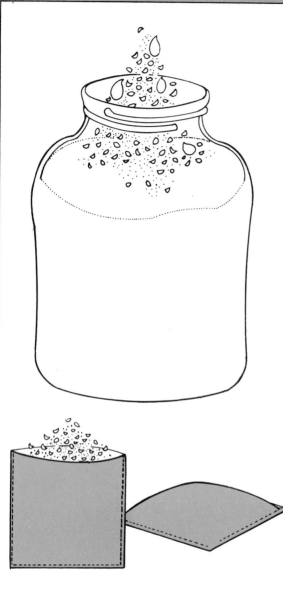

### Pomander ball

Take a ripe, unblemished piece of fruit. Thin-skinned oranges are most commonly used, but pears, apples, lemons and limes may also be used. Stud the fruit all over with whole cloves. You need about 2 oz. for each piece.

Put the fruit in a bowl containing a mixture of orris powder and a blend of ground spices.

### Herbal moth ball bags
Mix equal amounts of rosemary, tansy, thyme, mint, and southernwood, and a few pinches of ground cloves (too much cloves may dominate the mixture; use a small amount). Blend mixture and put into small sachet bags and tuck among sweaters and woolens in closets and drawers.

A traditional spice mixture includes cinnamon, allspice, and cardamom. For an Oriental woods scent, combine sandalwood, cedarwood and musk crystals. A blend of sassafras, star anise, ginger, anise, fennel and cinnamon produces a nostalgic candy scent. Use the orris powder in combination with any of the above mixtures. Leave fruit in bowl for five days, rolling it in the mixture once a day.

When the fruit is completely dried out, wrap a length of satin or narrow velvet ribbon around the circumference of the fruit, and tie with a bow and loop to hang in a closet. The pomander makes a lovely ornament for a holiday tree or several in a shallow bowl provide an interesting table centerpiece.

### Spice and flower potpourri

| | |
|---|---|
| 1 oz. bay leaves | 1 oz. lemon balm |
| ¼ lb. rosebuds | 1 oz. peppermint |
| 2 oz. cornflowers | 2 oz. spearmint |
| 2 oz. marigold flowers | 1 oz. calamus root |
| 1 oz. orange blossoms | 20 drops orris oil |
| 1 oz. oregano | 10 drops blue lilac oil |
| 2 oz. deer's-tongue | |

Break up bay leaves, then mix all ingredients together in a jar. Cover, and allow scents to blend for a week to two weeks before filling individual jars.

### Romantic potpourri

| | |
|---|---|
| ¼ lb. sassafras | 2 oz. cassia bark |
| 2 oz. orange peel | 2 oz. star anise |
| 2 oz. dill weed | 1 oz. oak moss |
| 2 oz. whole allspice | 10 drops pettigrain oil |

Break up sassafras, then mix all ingredients together in a jar. Cover, and allow to season for five days. To revive a fading scent, add 4 drops of French brandy.

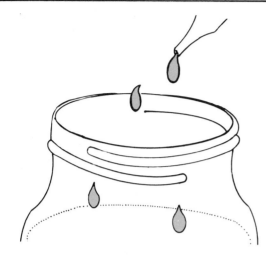

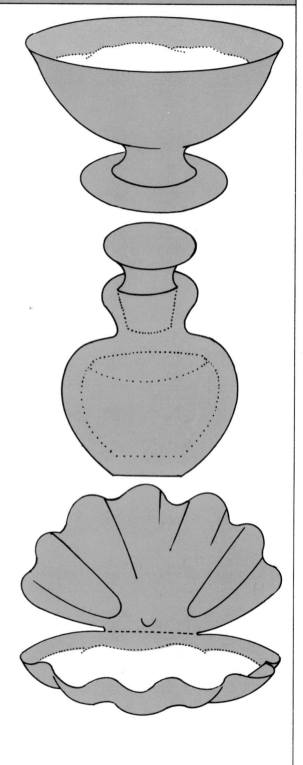

### Potpourri containers

Select an attractive china or crystal bowl or apothecary jar for the potpourri. A covered container is practical to maintain the scent when not in use. A wicker basket, silver bowl, crystal compote dish, or sea shells are equally attractive containers for a potpourri mixture.

# Enameled jewel box

A distinctive gift, this unique jewelry box is created by enameling on copper. In enameling, finely ground glass is fused to a metal surface. It is an ancient craft, dating thousands of years back to early Chinese and Egyptian times.

Materials: a kiln (a 4-inch-diameter kiln costs a relatively small sum; butane gas or Bunsen burner; a copper box (available from craft shops); a stock of opaque and transparent enamels; colorless, transparent flux; clean white paper for working surface; a fine (approximately 80 mesh) strainer; and a clear fire binder diluted with two parts water. Essential cleaning materials include: 1 ounce vinegar; ¼ teaspoon salt; fine steel wool; tweezers; and a clean cloth. Required firing utensils are: asbestos gloves; an asbestos board atop a brick on which to place the hot enameled box; a flat steel wire mesh to hold the box; and a small enamel stilt (to prevent box from adhering to mesh). You will also need an atomizer, brushes and a toothpick.

## Preparing box
Clean the copper box by submerging it in a pickling solution of 1 ounce vinegar and ¼ teaspoon salt for 1 to 2 minutes. Handle only with tweezers (natural skin oils adhere to metal surface). Rinse box in water, polish with steel wool, rinse again, and dry with a soft cloth. Pour some binder into a fine spray atomizer and spray all box surfaces evenly. Set wire mesh on clean white paper (rough side up), positioning stilt on mesh and placing the box on stilt. Paper catches excess enamel, which can be poured back into containers and reused.

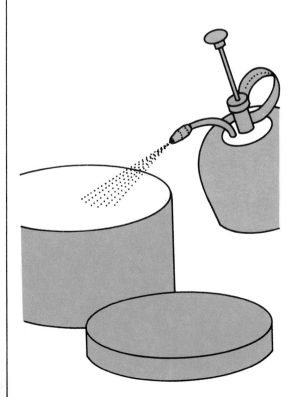

## Applying and baking the base coats
Apply a base coat of white enamel to box and cover, as evenly as possible. An even base

## Enameled jewel box

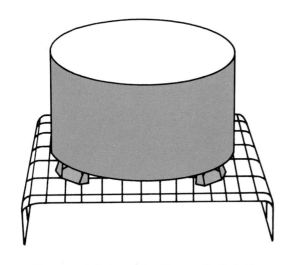

### Painting a design on the top

Plan a simple design for the box cover. Moisten enamel color to be used in the design with binder until it has a fluid, but not watery, consistency. Apply enamel with a brush and toothpick, much the same as for a miniature painting. Working this way lets you place your colors next to each other, and the binder prevents them from running together. Place on stilt to dry, then fire a third time.

coat is especially important for vertical shapes such as the sides of this box. The white base assures a soft but true final color.

Set pieces on the enamel stilt and allow to dry thoroughly. Then fire in the preheated kiln for two to four minutes at 1500 degrees Fahrenheit (when the kiln interior appears cherry red). Remove the box from the kiln when its surfaces look shiny and fluid and place on the asbestos block until cool. Repeat above steps for second coat, using pink opaque enamel (or other color of your own choice) over the white base coat.

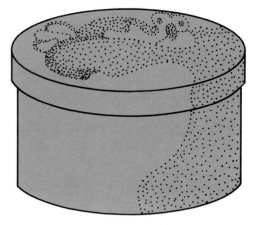

To finish, clean the edges with fine steel wool to remove fire scale. The result will be a truly personal, as well as serviceable, decorative object.

# Enameled cuff links

Old coins make wonderful designs for jewelry! If you save copper coins in your cookie jar for future rainy days, take two and make a handsome pair of enameled cuff links.

Materials: use coins or purchase copper disks, along with cuff-link findings, and epoxy, at a crafts store. If you have made the Enameled jewel box project from this chapter, you will have a kiln, enamel colors, tools and a working surface already prepared. If not, refer to the instructions for Enameled jewel box to assemble your equipment, which includes: colorless transparent flux; an 80-mesh strainer; clear fire binder diluted with two parts water; pickling cleaning solution; steel wool; a pair of tweezers; firing utensils; and a clean cloth.

### Painting and firing the background enamel

First clean the copper disks with pickling until the copper appears pink. Handle only with

tweezers, to avoid getting natural skin oils on the coins. Rinse, polish with steel wool, and dry with a soft cloth.

Apply binder to the back of each disk and counter enamel, using clear flux only. Use a light coat of binders, set disk on stilt; let dry thoroughly so piece will fuse correctly, and apply clear flux to front of disk. Allow front coat of flux to dry thoroughly.

### Adding a colorful design

Place disks in preheated kiln (interior will be correct temperature when it has turned cherry

red) and leave inside to fire for two to four minutes. Disk surface will appear shiny and fluid when fusing is complete. Remove disks with tongs and set aside to cool.

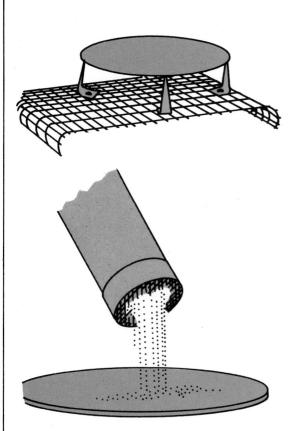

brush, pushing colors together with toothpick into areas you wish to emphasize. Let the enamel fall loosely and gradually onto other areas of the disk. Repeat this procedure for each color, working dry and with a gentle touch.

After each coat dries, fire, remove from heat and place on top of the asbestos board to cool. Clean the edges of the disk with fine steel wool.

Affix the cuff link backs to the backs of the two cuff link disks with epoxy or a lead solder.

Choose two or three transparent and opaque colors, in any combination. Using a mesh strainer, sift one color onto each area of disk. Then work enamel with a fine, dry

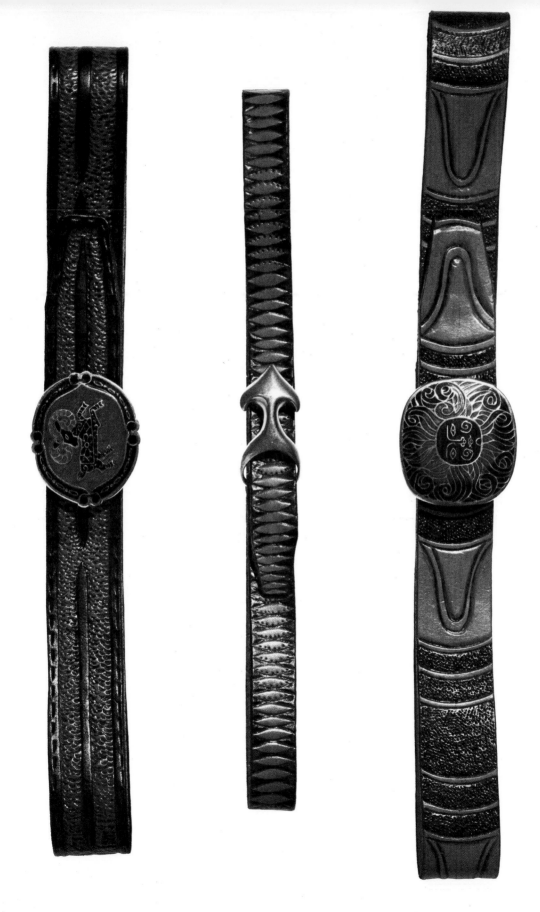

# Tooled leather belts

Leatherwork can be an easy hobby with a minimum amount of effort or it can be involved, depending upon the time and effort you are willing to put into your work. There are many tools available, but only a few are required for basic leatherwork. A carved belt can also serve as a shoulder strap for a purse.

Materials: leather; a bowl of water; a sponge; a metal ruler; a mat knife; and a No. 3 bevel file. For carving designs,you will need: a swivel knife; a stipple; a deerfoot; a balling utensil; stamps; and a revolving hole puncher. Dyes, finishes, and buffing cloths should be chosen according to the effects you desire. Fastening materials, such as belt buckles and beeswaxed linen thread (to be used with harness needles),should also be color-coordinated with the dyes used.

Leather comes in different thicknesses and surface textures. Cowhide ⅛ inch thick is the best leather for making a carved belt. Presized, precut leather belt straps may also be bought in any leathercraft store. Widths range from ½ to 2 inches (1 inch makes a narrow belt; 1⅜ inches is regulation width).

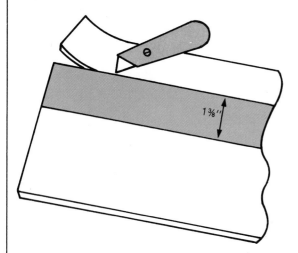

1⅜"

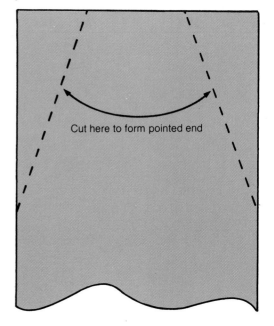

Cut here to form pointed end

## Cutting the strap

If you have not bought a precut belt strap, measure the desired width by marking two parallel lines on the smooth leather surface. For easier cutting, wet the rough side with a damp sponge until you see water bleeding through to the surface. Do not soak the leather. Using the metal ruler and mat knife, proceed to cut your belt strip from the hide.

For a more professional look, cut one end of the belt strap in a pointed-end shape with a mat knife. You should also measure the

waist or hips of the wearer to determine the desired length of the belt. Leave space for several notch adjustments and for overlap at the buckle, and cut off excess leather.

A No. 3 bevel file should be used to round off the edges for leather that is ⅛ inch thick. To bevel an edge, simply slide the bevel along the rough edge, pressing gently.

# Tooled leather belts

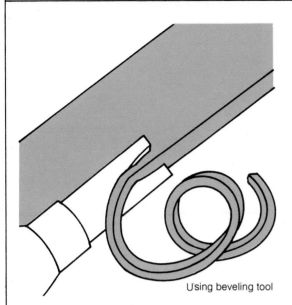

Using beveling tool

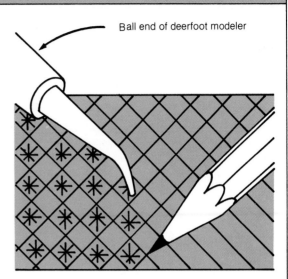

Ball end of deerfoot modeler

## Carving the design

Before you start carving, you must moisten the back of the leather with a damp sponge to allow flexibility. This is called casing. Now you are ready to carve your design onto the leather. Using a pencil or the tip of a deerfoot tool, sketch your design on the leather.

To carve with the swivel knife, place your index finger in the curved top and hold the stem with thumb and middle fingers. Pull the knife through the leather with an even stroke. If you have a scrap of leather, you should practice manipulating with the swivel knife, making circles and crosshatching. Once you acquire skill in using the knife, it will be a simple task. Do not force the tool, but let it float.

If you want to add depth to your carved lines, use the deerfoot or balling tool. Each has a scribe at the opposite end to make deeper carved lines. Since the leather is moist, it will remain quite flexible. You can press down some areas to make adjacent areas stand out. Applying pressure with the deerfoot tool will not injure the leather.

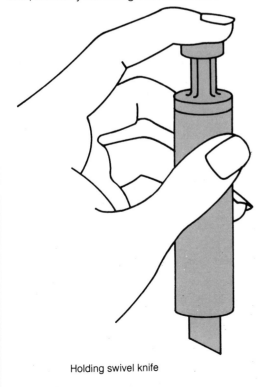

Holding swivel knife

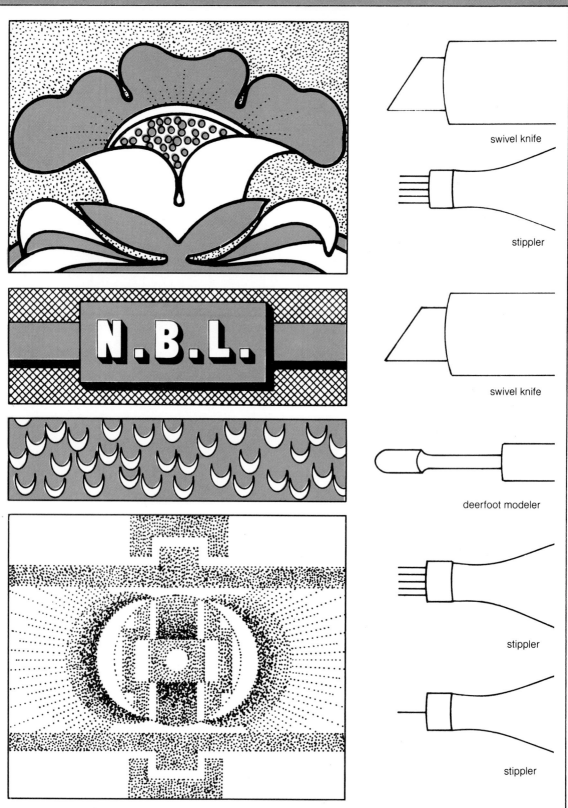

swivel knife

stippler

swivel knife

deerfoot modeler

stippler

stippler

# Tooled leather belts

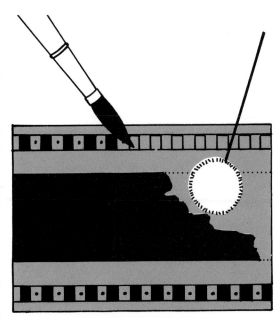

## Coloring and protecting the surface

Once your design is complete, you have the remaining tasks of dyeing, staining, waxing, and buffing your belt. Since dyes and antique stains come in various shades, the choice of coloring is personal. Dyes seem to adhere best to the leather when it is damp because there is less chance of streaking. Dyes should be applied with cotton swabs in long, continuous strokes. If detailed areas are being dyed, an artist's paintbrush is highly recommended. Once dyeing is completed, you can make the finished product more appealing by rubbing in a leather preservative. Shoe wax or mellow wax finishes can also be applied to give the leather a richer quality. After wax or cream is absorbed, buff the belt with a clean, soft rag.

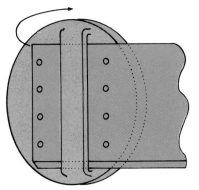

## Attaching the buckle

If the chosen buckle has a back bar, push 1⅛ inches of the face of the belt through it and bend it into place. With a small hole puncher, place four holes vertically spaced ½ inch apart on the tucked piece and also punch four holes vertically spaced ½ inch apart on the front of the belt where the flap touches, so that the columns of holes match.

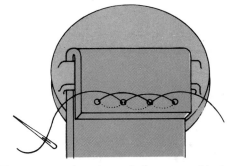

To sew together through the rows of holes, a simple backstitch may be used. Waxed thread with a harness needle should be used. To begin, insert needle from the front through the second hole, bring up through the first hole, down through the third, up through the second, down through the fourth, and up through the third. When the sewing is completed, make a small knot and carry the needle to a stitch in back to secure the knot.

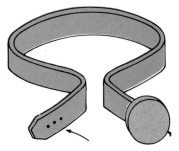

To adjust the size of the belt, punch holes in the leather for the prong on the back of the buckle to hook in snugly. Try making your own buckles out of leather or use old shoe buckles or welded metal for buckles. The more you practice carving leather, the more intricate your designs will become.

# Leaded-glass belt buckle

Leaded glass is commonly called stained glass because of its similarity in appearance to cathedral stained-glass windows. The leaded-glass technique adapts extremely well to contemporary designs in fashions and home furnishings, as you will see when you create this attractive belt buckle. With the technique described below, you can also make jewelry, lamps, and mobiles.

Materials: three sheets of colored glass; a glass cutter; scissors; pencil; paper; ruler; masking tape; a remnant of carpet; pliers; plaster bat or charcoal block; pumice stones; copper tongs; 24 inches of standard gauge copper foil (one side adhesive); kerosene; a spool of rosin core solder (10-gauge); a soldering iron; 5½ inches of 10-gauge nickel wire; 2¾ inches of 14-gauge nickel wire; a finished leather or suede belt strap 2¾ inches wide and 8 inches longer than the waistline of the intended wearer; a hole puncher; beeswaxed linen thread; and a harness needle.

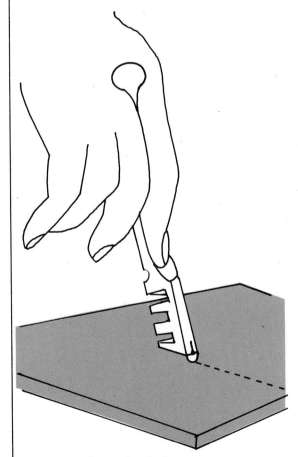

of each piece of colored glass, to serve as a guide in cutting the piece needed. Lay the sheet of glass to be cut on a flat, sturdy surface (an old remnant of carpet is excellent). Hold the cutter against the glass, with wheel pressed downward and the notched edge of the cutter toward you. Place the ball end of the cutter between your first two fingers. Your thumb and index finger should be in position to bear down on the shoulders of the cutter. If it is scoring properly, it will make an even, biting sound. Keep a small container of kerosene nearby to lubricate the cutter wheel.

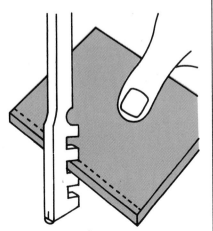

### Preparing the stained glass
For this particular belt buckle, start with 3 strips of paper: one strip ½ by 3 inches; one strip ¾ by 3 inches; and one strip 1¼ by 3 inches. Tape one strip of paper to the back

Glass should snap off evenly when the scored line is placed slightly beyond and parallel to the edge of the worktable. To cut off a narrow piece, tap along the scored line, using the cutter's ball-shaped handle, and hold the glass near the surface of the table to prevent shattering. To trim off a very narrow piece of glass, use the notch on the glass cutter that is nearest in size to the thickness of the glass you are cutting.

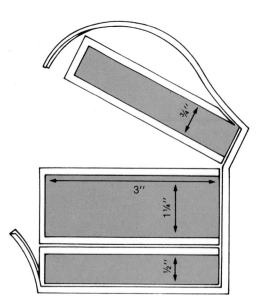

Carefully tape all sides of each individual piece of colored glass with the adhesive copper foil. Then, with masking tape, assemble the three pieces of glass together, forming a rectangle 2½ by 3 inches.

### Soldering the glass

How to use and care for the soldering iron: If the iron is new, the copper tip must be tinned before using. Heat the iron to "hot" (6-8 minutes). Sprinkle rosin on the flat copper side and rub the tip of the iron in rosin. Then melt the solder against the tip until the tip shines. After repeated use, the soldering iron tip may become rough and corroded. When this occurs, simply file down to the copper base and repeat this tinning procedure.

Here are some tips to remember: The temperature of the iron must be watched carefully. If the iron becomes too hot, the solder will melt uncontrollably; if too cool, it will not melt at all. Using a short piece of solder will risk burning your fingers. Keep the soldering iron unplugged and on its metal support when not in use. It is best to solder on a plaster bat or on a block of charcoal surrounded by pumice stones. Keep a basin of water and copper tongs within reach.

To solder the glass pieces for belt buckle: Bend a piece of solder on or around the glass shapes. Touch the hot tip of the soldering iron to the joint and simultaneously touch the solder in your hand to the tip. The solder will run across the joint, bonding it. With a little practice, you will use the minimum amount of solder necessary to form a bond while avoiding unsightly bubbles. Each of the separate pieces of glass may now be joined to the adjacent piece, with the solder filling the joint. Solder joints on both sides of glass rectangle. Remove masking tape and solder around the perimeter of rectangle on both sides.

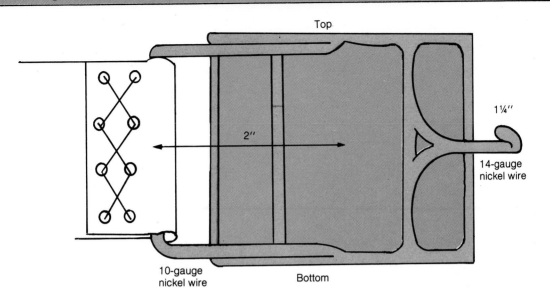

Top

1¼"

2"

14-gauge
nickel wire

10-gauge
nickel wire

Bottom

### Forming the buckle frame and tongue

When the joints have been soldered (both front and back), take the nickel wire needed for the belt holder, and bend the 5½-inch wire piece into a "C" shape (see illustration) the same length as the belt buckle. Bend both ends back, parallel to each other. The middle point of the "C" shape should be 2 inches from the middle of the belt buckle, allowing 1¼ inches of the flat ends to overlap the very top and bottom of the buckle. Cover these end points with copper foil, then proceed to solder them to the back of the buckle. Next, bend the 2¾-inch piece of nickel wire into a pointed "V" shape, bending the tip back ¼ inch to form a hook. Allow ¾ inch for each serif of the "V" so that the serifs and lower "V" can be soldered to the middle of the joint on the glass strip. Push the belt strip 1½ inches through the "C" shape. Bend the leather and punch two rows of small vertical holes through both thicknesses of leather where they over-lap. Using the beeswaxed thread and harness needle, stitch the leather together, enclosing the metal "C" shape. Put the belt on, mark positions for holes to close it, and punch several holes in the belt so that the tongue, which is the hook at the end of the "V" shape, fits into them.

# Carved walking canes

Slender rods of wood can be carved and finished to make handsome walking sticks. This project will generate a variety of activities, such as beachcombing to collect driftwood; searching the brush for fallen branches of redwood, pine, or oak; shopping to locate old canes that can be refurbished; observing walking-cane designs of other cultures; and exploring three-dimensional sculpture on wood. The techniques for finishing the cane, described here, can also be used to refurbish furniture.

Materials: Find a sturdy piece of wood in a comfortable length with the weight evenly distributed. You will also need small woodcutting tools; small wood rasps and files; gauges; garnet #80 sandpaper; #000 steel wool; carnauba paste floor wax; olive oil; shellac; alcohol; stain; and plenty of rags.

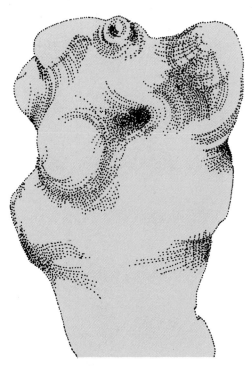 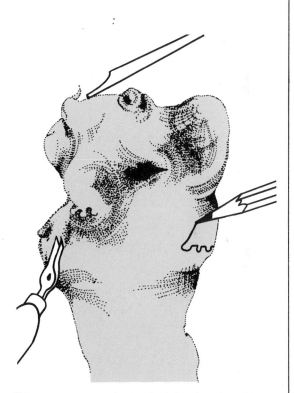

### Carving the design
Use a straight-grained wood, free of knots. Pine is the simplest wood to carve because it takes deep cuts. Lay out the design in pencil directly on the wood, or make a working clay model before you sketch. Perhaps the shape of the wood will suggest a free-form design.

Often you can make an incision in pine with only one stroke of a woodcutting tool, but with deep profiles make at least two cuts. Cut hardwoods such as chestnut, walnut or brittle fir ⅛ inch at a time, and the final cut even less, for smoothness. Turn the piece frequently, working it from different angles.

### Smoothing the wood

Rasps and files are used to define detail and to smooth the wood. First use coarse files, gradually working with finer-grained surface files. The surface is filed in one direction only, using short even strokes. Sand the piece when you have finished filing the surface, and round off the edges, using a grit file and coarse #80 garnet sandpaper. Grit #000 steel wool is used for smoothing. Rub a penetrative oil such as olive oil into the wood to preserve it as well as expose the grain.

### Staining or painting and finishing the cane

Select one of a variety of stains available at hardware stores and apply one coat of stain to the cane. Follow this by several coats of a clear quick-drying finish. Woods such as pine and fir do not take a light-colored stain, so finish with opaque paint of a dark color. Between coats, sand all finishes lightly to facilitate adhesion of the following coat. When

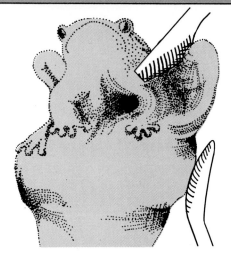

using a French finish, rub in the final coat of shellac with #000 steel wool, and wax with a paste floor wax (except on open-grain woods like Philippine mahogany where wax will turn white when it is absorbed). Personalized canes with engraved initials or expressive designs are unusual and appreciated gifts.

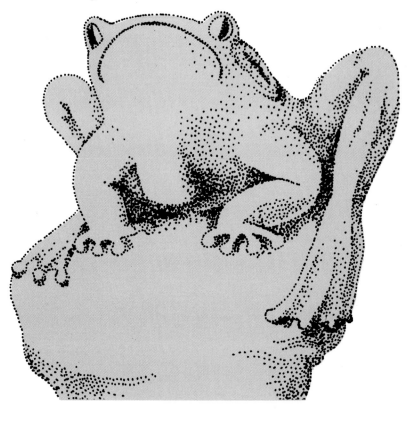

# Needlepoint acrobats

They fly through the air with the greatest of ease, these needlepoint men on their flying trapeze! An example of contemporary needlepoint ideas, these brightly colored daredevils of the air perform from towel bars, curtain rods, dowels, or any rodlike surface on which you can wrap their hands and feet. The acrobats are easily stitched on needlepoint canvas and backed with cardboard or chipboard and felt for durability. Thin household wire gives flexible strength to hands and feet. See Needlepoint place mats.

Materials: yarns you need are five 40-yard skeins each of royal blue, turquoise, bright-green, and black for the costume of the smaller acrobat; nine 40-yard skeins each of royal blue, turquoise, dark-red violet and red-violet for the taller acrobat's costume; 2 skeins of beige, one of dark green; one skein each of pink, blue, and black are needed for the hair, skin and faces.

You also need: one yard of penelope or mono needlepoint canvas, 10 mesh to the inch; a No. 17 blunt tapestry needle; a square yard of cardboard or 3-ply chipboard; 3 feet of thin household wire; scissors; 1 yard of felt; bottle of clear-drying glue; 2 dowels or towel bars; pair of shoelaces or a few feet of yarn or twine; masking tape; towel; sponge and water; board for blocking; rustproof pushpins; and, to keep the canvas taut as you work, a needlepoint frame, embroidery hoop, or 2 pairs of canvas stretchers assembled to fit the size of your canvas.

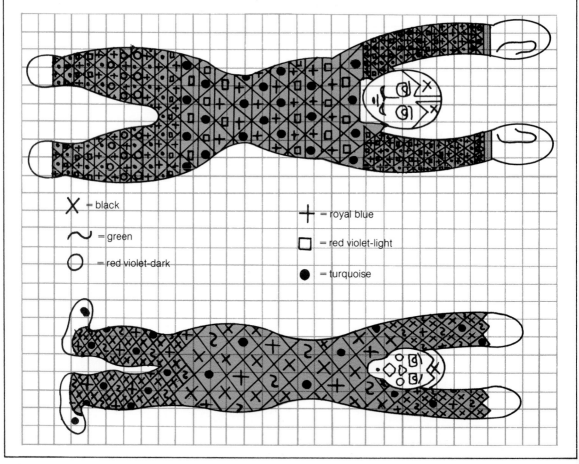

X = black

~ = green

O = red violet-dark

+ = royal blue

□ = red violet-light

● = turquoise

400

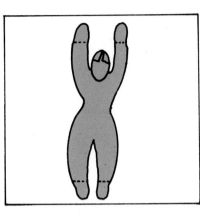

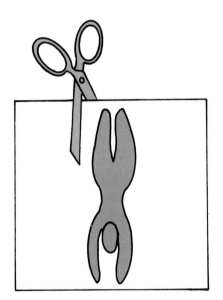

Legs are 2 inches wide at their fullest part and arms are 1⅝ inches at the widest part. The distance between top of head and neck of costume is 4½ inches. The designs of both costumes are largest at the midsection of the body and smallest at the wrists and ankles.

### Stretching the canvas

Trim canvas so there is a 2-inch rectangular border surrounding the figures. To prevent edges from raveling, bind them with masking tape. If you wish, stretch canvas in a needle-point frame or embroidery hoop, or make a frame from 2 pairs of canvas stretchers of suitable dimensions and tack the canvas over it. Stretching prevents your work from pulling out of shape as you stitch.

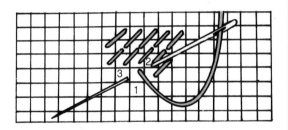

### Stitching continentally

The most basic stitch used in needlepoint is a slanting stitch that crosses one intersection of the canvas. The Continental stitch, an example of the basic diagonal stitch, is used for both acrobats throughout the design. Always work this diagonal stitch from right to left, turning canvas around one half turn clockwise as you complete each row. To work the stitch, bring the needle up from wrong side through 1, down through 2 and up again through 3. (See diagram). Continue in this manner throughout each row. Work with strands that are no more than 2 feet long, otherwise the yarn will start to fray from being pulled too often through the canvas. Secure yarn ends by stitching over them on the wrong side as you work. Follow the diagram and color key.

### Drawing the designs on the canvas

Draw figure on canvas according to the diagram shown. The taller acrobat measures 30 inches, with 2-inch feet and 1½-inch hands. The shoulders measure 7 inches in width, the waist 4 inches wide, hips 6 inches wide, wrists 1½ inches wide; arms and legs 2¼ to 2½ inches across at their widest points; and the ankles measure 1½ inches wide. The distance between top of head and neck of costume is 5½ inches. The costume consists of bands of triangles and inverted triangles that form diamonds. The shorter acrobat wears a costume with a diamond pattern. This figure is 26 inches long, with 3-inch feet and 2-inch hands. The shoulders are 5 inches wide, the waist 3 inches wide, and hips 4¼ inches wide.

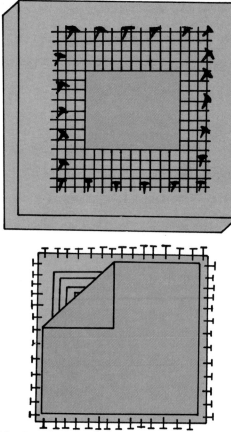

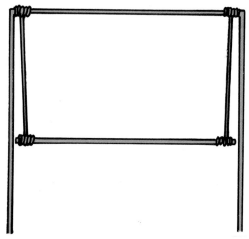

remaining two sides. Dampen wrong side again, and allow four days for work to dry. When dry, cut out each acrobat and glue a continuous strand of dark green yarn along the outline of the entire body. When glue is dry, lay each figure over felt, trace outline of body, and cut. Glue felt figures to cardboard or chipboard, except for hands and feet. Trace on the cardboard along body outlines once again, then cut out. Place thin wire ⅛ inch inside edges of hands and feet, between canvas and felt, bending and cutting it to conform to hand and feet contours. Glue each figure to cardboard or chipboard and then glue the figures to felt backing. Stitch open edges around hands and feet (canvas and felt) together with overcast stitches.

### Making the acrobats

When stitching is completed, block work to make sure it is straight. Tack a towel tautly over the surface of a wooden board and place work right side down on the towel. Always use rustproof pushpins or nails. Check with your hardware dealer if you are not certain. Dampen wrong side of the needlepoint with sponge. Tack one side of unworked canvas border in a straight line at even intervals. Gently pull and tack opposite side into shape, then the

### Swinging from bars

The acrobats need one stationary bar and swinging bar from which to hang. Use a towel bar or dowel for the swinging bar and any stationary rod that is supported on both ends for the top bar of the trapeze. If you have none, wedge a dowel between the sides of a window or door. Make trapeze ropes by wrapping equal lengths of yarn, shoelace, or twine around ends of both bars, tying an overhand knot at each end, and gluing the wrapped and knotted strands to both bars, rods or dowels. Allow glue to dry then place your performers in position to suit their audience by wrapping hands or feet around bars. For best results, hang the trapeze artists in an airy location, so they can move gracefully with the breeze.

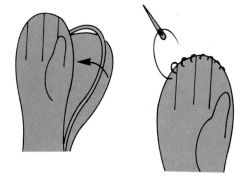

# Turtle pillow

This turtle is not only a lovable toy for your child; it is a decorative pillow, too. When playtime is over, place this cuddly pet on your child's bed to accent the room's décor.

Materials: a piece of cotton fabric 13 to 14 inches square for the body; a piece 12 inches square for the feet, head and tail; a bag of polyester fiberfill or old nylon hosiery for stuffing; two buttons for the eyes; embroidery thread; a needle; straight pins; pencil; compass; and scissors. Use the color scheme shown, or select other shades to complement the interior of your child's play area.

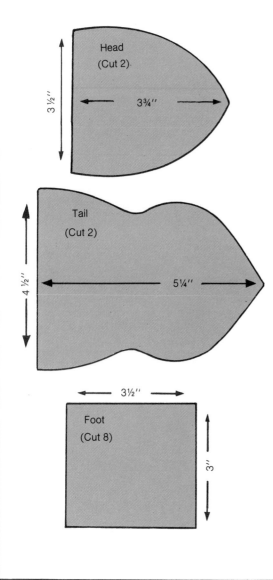

**Forming the head, legs, and tail**

Cut eight pieces of fabric to the dimensions 3 by 3½ inches. Pair off the material by placing the designs on the fabric facing each other. Stitch the two 3-inch sides and one of the 3½-inch sides with a simple running stitch. Leave a ½-inch seam all the way around. You will not stitch the last 3½-inch side closed now, because you will later turn each foot right side out, stuff, and attach each foot to the body. Following the next pattern, measure two trianglular pieces of fabric for the tail. Cut and sew the two sides of the tail in the same manner as the feet, leaving the wide end (4½ inches) open. In the same fashion, cut two pieces of fabric for the head, leaving the 3½-inch end open to be turned right side out and stuffed later. Carefully trim any snags on the seams. Turn all pieces right side out and stuff them with polyester filler until plump.

# Turtle pillow

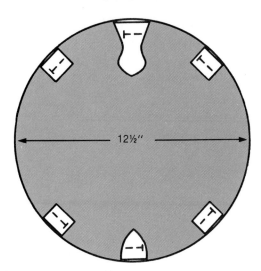

## Getting it all together

Use a compass or round plate to measure two circles, 12½ inches in diameter, for the body. Place one of the cut-out circles right side up and gently pin the feet, tail and head in place according to the diagram. Make sure that all of the trimmed edges of the feet, tail and head are even with the edge of the circle.

Place the other circle directly on top with the design side of the fabric covering the turtle layout. Sew the circles together, leaving a ½-inch seam all the way around. Keep one side of the turtle open between each of the two pairs of feet.

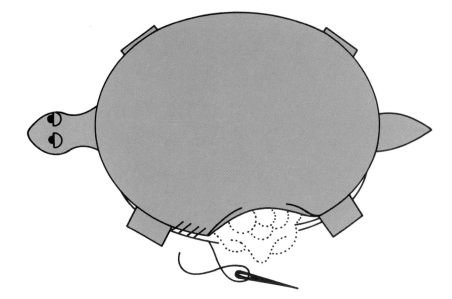

## Making him lovable

Turn the sewn circles right side out and stuff through the opening, using a decorative over-cast stitch to close. Remove straight pins. Now that you have completed the turtle pillow, give him a dash of character. Add twinkly but-tons for his eyes, and a piece of felt for his tongue. When you see how much your child loves this harmless pet, you will enjoy design-ing your own easy patterns to create other lovable creatures.

# Appliquéd shoulder bag

Appliquéd touches of color on jeans and shirts in geometric shapes, hearts, and flowers, have sparked a new interest in appliqué as a decorative medium for wearables and accessories. The technique of applying one fabric to another in contrasting colors or prints is most simply used as a decorative accent; however, an elaborate design applied to a banquet-size tablecloth or a bedspread is apt to be considered a fabric collage.

It is probably true that the art of appliqué evolved from the necessity of patching worn garments and household linens, and that with ingenuity in design and embellishments of embroidery, the attractive overlay effect developed into a folk art. Some of the best examples of American eighteenth and nineteenth century appliqué are heirloom quilts and bed coverings which have been preserved and are now displayed in museums. Many of these pieces, which may have taken a lifetime to create, depict a panorama of the countryside, family milestones, or the growth of a nation.

To begin working with appliqué designs, make simple cutouts of either printed or brightly colored fabrics, fold under the edges, and stitch the pieces by hand or machine to ready-made kitchen towels, aprons or T-shirts. Another way to practice the technique is to appliqué a border of embroidered ribbon or printed tape on a cardigan sweater or denim jacket. After you get into doing more elaborate designs, use fancy embroidery stitches to apply the pieces of appliqué.

The shoulder bag illustrated is handmade and decorated with appliqué cutouts and border appliqué strips. The patterns for the appliqué flower design are easy to enlarge and can be used for other projects as well.

Materials: 1 yard of 45-inch-width washable woven fabric in a solid color; contrasting colorfast fabric swatches for the appliqué flower design; ⅓ yard of printed fabric or 2 yards of embroidered or printed ribbon to make the border appliqué; needle and thread; dressmaker's pins; iron-on interfacing (optional); and scissors.

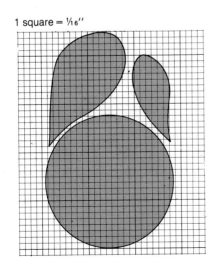

1 square = ¹⁄₁₆″

Appliqué design patterns

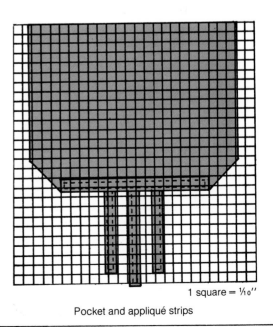

1 square = ¹⁄₁₀″

Pocket and appliqué strips

# Appliquéd shoulder bag

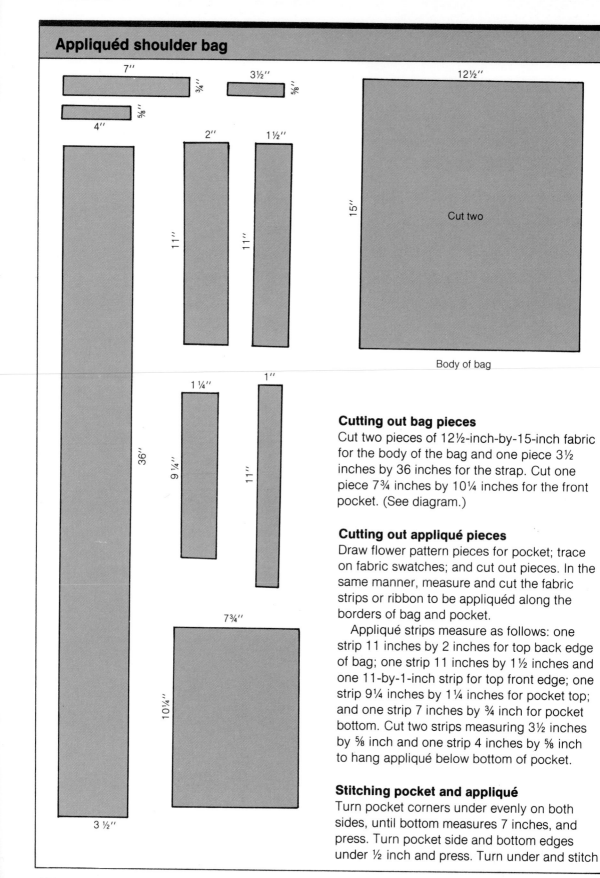

7″

¾″

3½″

⅝″

4″

⅝″

2″

11″

1½″

11″

12½″

15″

Cut two

Body of bag

36″

1¼″

9¼″

1″

11″

7¾″

10¼″

3½″

## Cutting out bag pieces

Cut two pieces of 12½-inch-by-15-inch fabric for the body of the bag and one piece 3½ inches by 36 inches for the strap. Cut one piece 7¾ inches by 10¼ inches for the front pocket. (See diagram.)

## Cutting out appliqué pieces

Draw flower pattern pieces for pocket; trace on fabric swatches; and cut out pieces. In the same manner, measure and cut the fabric strips or ribbon to be appliquéd along the borders of bag and pocket.

Appliqué strips measure as follows: one strip 11 inches by 2 inches for top back edge of bag; one strip 11 inches by 1½ inches and one 11-by-1-inch strip for top front edge; one strip 9¼ inches by 1¼ inches for pocket top; and one strip 7 inches by ¾ inch for pocket bottom. Cut two strips measuring 3½ inches by ⅝ inch and one strip 4 inches by ⅝ inch to hang appliqué below bottom of pocket.

## Stitching pocket and appliqué

Turn pocket corners under evenly on both sides, until bottom measures 7 inches, and press. Turn pocket side and bottom edges under ½ inch and press. Turn under and stitch

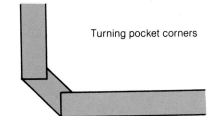

Turning pocket corners

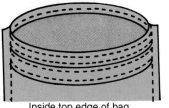

Inside top edge of bag

edges of the three strips to hang below pocket, then center them along the bottom edge of the pocket, ½ inch apart. Pin and stitch strips in position. (See pocket illustration on grid.) Pin and stitch bottom pocket strip in place along edge. Fold top pocket strip over top edge of pocket and secure both edges of strip to pocket, stitching through all thicknesses. Place flower design pieces in position on pocket with pins or iron-on interfacing and stitch to pocket along edges. (If desired, tuck edges under all around before pinning down.) Press well. Center pocket on front of bag, 2 inches from top and 1½ inches in from each side edge; pin, stitch pocket sides and bottom to bag, and press again.

### Stitching bag
Stitch bag front to bag back, right sides together, leaving a ½-inch seam allowance. Do not stitch top edges together. Turn bag right side out and press. Top-stitch edges of bag, then top-stitch sides and back ½ inch in from edges of sides.

### Stitching appliqué strips to bag
Take the two 11-inch strips for bag top and fold under ½ inch on the long side of each strip. Pin the folded side of each to the outside, along the top edges of bag, then pull the strips over to the inside of the bag, fold under the raw edge of each strip and pin to inside of bag. Stitch along folded edges from the inside to the outside of the bag, sewing through

all thicknesses. Pin and stitch remaining strip of trim to top front of bag, just below and adjacent to top front strip. Press well.

### Stitching strap to bag
Fold long edges of strap under to wrong side of fabric, overlapping edges slightly. Press; then sew overlapping edges together through all thicknesses of fabric. Overcast the two short edges closed. Insert strap into each side of bag 1 inch from top edge. Center between front and back, pin and stitch. Press entire handbag well; treat with fabric protector.

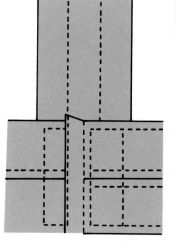

Seaming strap

Attaching strap to bag

# Etched aluminum tray

Etching designs on metal is a relatively simple process. This aluminum tray, for instance, is attractively etched with ducks on the wing. This design is easily copied or an original design may be etched by following the relatively simple directions.

Materials: The tray illustrated starts as a flat disk of 16-gauge aluminum, 16 inches in diameter. Other materials needed include: 1 pint of asphalt or tar paint; ½ pint of muriatic acid; and a small can of turpentine or naphtha. You also need: soft pencil; carbon paper; masking tape; No. 2 soft-hair pointed artist's brush; ⅛-inch soft-hair artist's brush; soft rags; clean porcelain or enamel pan; pliers; old newspaper; and rubber gloves. Obtain a picture or design for the tray from a magazine, or draw your own.

## Tracing the design

Wash the aluminum disk with hot, soapy water to remove any oily film from the surface. Rinse thoroughly in clear water and allow to dry.

Place the carbon paper (carbon side down) on the aluminum disk. Place the design to be copied over the carbon paper and fasten it

leaving uncovered those areas that are to be etched by the acid. In the illustrated design, the background is etched, and the border, the birds and the grass are left polished. Apply a heavy coat of asphalt or tar all around the 2-inch-wide border. Dry for at least four hours.

with masking tape over the edge of the disk. This allows you to move the carbon paper if necessary, without disturbing the position of the pattern. Trace the design onto the aluminum. Remove the pattern and the carbon paper. Draw a border around the disk, 2 inches in from the edge.

## Blocking off the shiny parts

Using the ⅛-inch brush for large areas and the No. 2 brush for details, apply a uniform, heavy coat of asphalt or tar paint to those parts of the design that are to remain polished.

## Fluting the rim

The next step is fluting the rim of the tray. Make a guide by cutting a paper pattern (newspaper will do the job) the same circular shape and size as the tray. Then, fold it in half, then in half again, then again to a pie shape, and then once more. Unfold the paper; there will be 16 folds. Tape the pattern to the top of the aluminum.

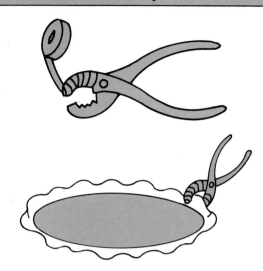

Wrap the jaws of the pliers with a heavy padding of masking tape to keep from marring the aluminum. At each fold in the paper pattern, use the padded pliers to bend up approximately 1 inch of the tray edge to an angle of 60 degrees. Always flute in pairs, one directly opposite another, until all pairs are completed, then remove the paper pattern. Be careful during this procedure not to mar the surface or disturb the asphalt paint. If the asphalt is chipped, touch up any exposed parts. Then paint the underside of the tray to protect it during the etching process. Let dry for four hours.

### Etching with acid

Working with muriatic acid can be as dangerous or as safe as you make it. If you use normal caution, you will have no trouble. Always wear rubber gloves when using the acid, and

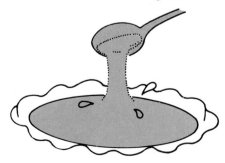

it is wise to wear protective goggles. If you accidentally splatter any of the acid on your skin or clothing, rinse it off immediately and thoroughly with plenty of water.

Spread a thick cushion of newspapers over the work surface. Set the porcelain or enamel pan on the papers. The etching mixture consists of one part muriatic acid to one part water. Pour the water into the pan first; then slowly add the muriatic acid. **Never pour water into the acid; always pour water first.** Set the tray on the newspaper-covered work surface.

Slowly and carefully pour on enough of the solution to cover the tray's surface to a depth of about 1/8 inch. **Do not let the solution overflow the edge of the tray.** Let the solution boil around the tray until it stops bubbling, indicating that the etching process is complete; this can take from 25 to 45 minutes. After the exposed metal has been etched, pour off the solution carefully and dispose of it down the drain, flushing it with lots of tap water. Rinse the tray thoroughly with water until all traces of the solution have been washed away.

### Finishing and painting the tray

Still wearing rubber gloves, saturate a soft cloth with turpentine or naphtha and wipe away the asphalt or tar paint. Use soap and hot water to wash the tray thoroughly. Rinse and wipe dry the completed tray. Buff with a soft cloth.

# Crocheted eyeglass case

Too frequently, crochet projects are time-consuming and too complicated in design to embark upon for a gift item. This eyeglass case, however, works up easily in a very short time and it makes a nifty gift. You can follow the color pattern illustrated, or use multicolored yarn and eliminate the second color band.

Materials: one ounce of blue knitting worsted and ¼ ounce of red knitting worsted (or one ounce of multicolored yarn); and a size H crochet hook.

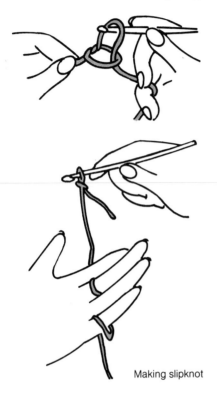

Making slipknot

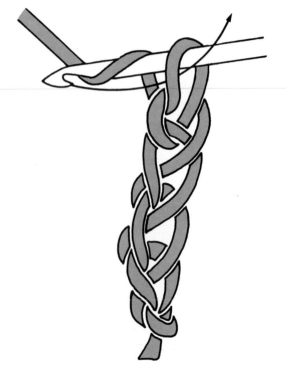

Making foundation chain

## Crocheting foundation chain

Start with the blue yarn, and attach yarn to the crochet hook by making a slipknot in the following manner. Grasp yarn near end between thumb and forefinger of left hand, make a loop by lapping long yarn over short yarn. Hold loop in place between thumb and forefinger, hold hook in right hand and put it horizontally through loop, catching long end of yarn and drawing it through. Leave hook in yarn. Pull short end and ball yarn in opposite direction to close loop around end of hook, firmly but not too tightly. Thread ball yarn between small and ring fingers of left hand, palm facing up, and thread yarn under ring finger, over middle finger and under forefinger firmly.

Hold knot of loop between thumb and forefinger, and begin to crochet a chain stitch. The chain stitch is the foundation of all crochet work. Pass hook under yarn and catch yarn with hook, called "yarn over," then draw thread through loop on hook to make one chain stitch. Continue this procedure until you have made 26 chain stitches. This chain is the length of the eyeglass case. One loop always remains on hook. Make sure the chains are all the same size, about ¼ inch in length.

# Crocheted eyeglass case

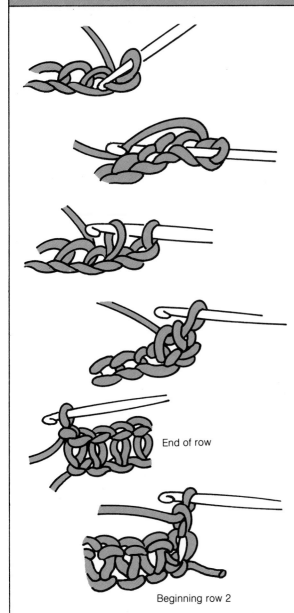

End of row

Beginning row 2

## Crocheting the first row

For first row, single crochet in second chain from hook. Insert hook from front under top strand of second chain. Yarn over and draw through stitch. There are now 2 loops on hook. Yarn over again and draw through 2 loops. One loop remains on hook, completing first single crochet. Insert hook under top strand of next stitch and work as for first stitch. Single crochet across row, ending with chain 1. Turn work and begin row 2.

## Crocheting rows two to twelve

Rows 2 to 12 are worked evenly, with single crochet in each stitch, ending with chain one; then turn work. Single crochet row 13, working in back loop only.

Band of red

## Working with the red yarn

Single crochet rows 14 through 16. Break off blue yarn, leaving a short tail, which will be worked into stitches to hide it. Start with red yarn, leaving a small lead piece before starting row 17. For row 17, single crochet in each of first 2 stitches, then single crochet in stitch below next single crochet. Repeat this pattern across; ending with 1 single crochet and chain 1, then turn work. Single crochet rows 18 through 20. Break off red yarn, leaving a small tail as before. Start row 21 with blue yarn.

## Finishing with blue yarn

Single crochet first stitch of row 21. Repeat a pattern of single crochet in stitch below next stitch, then 2 single crochets. Repeat these across. End row with 2 single crochets. Single crochet rows 22 through 24. Do not break off thread at end of row 24.

## Completing the case

Fold case in half. Then join the two edges together with single crochet through both layers along the long side and along the edge of one of the short sides. Finish with single crochet stitches along the open edge.

# Knitted hat with mittens

This colorful knitted hat with matching mittens requires only basic knitting skills. This project will be a helpful refresher if you have neglected knitting for some time, and beginners will find it quick and easy to complete.

Materials: a pair of No. 8 single-pointed needles; 8 ounces of varicolored knitting worsted; a tapestry needle; and scissors.

Sample of pattern

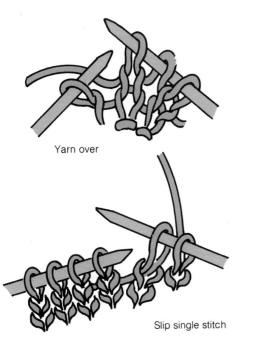

Yarn over

Slip single stitch

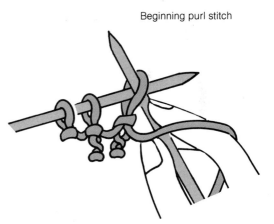

Beginning purl stitch

### Beginning the hat

To make the hat, cast on 58 stitches. (See Knitted shawl for casting-on instructions.) For first row, knitting from the front, knit 1 stitch. (See Knitted shawl for instructions on the knit stitch.) Wind yarn around needle once to create an additional stitch. This is called yarn over. Slip next stitch by passing right needle into back of next stitch on left needle, and slipping stitch off left needle onto right without working it. This is called a slipstitch. Then knit 1 stitch. Continue across row, working the following sequence of stitches: yarn over, slip 1 stitch and knit 1 stitch, ending row with knit 2.

### Knitting row 2

Knit first stitch of row 2; then yarn over, slip 1 stitch, and knit 2 together (knit the yarn over and slipstitch from previous row together). Continue working across the row in the same pattern: yarn over, slip 1 stitch, knit 2 together, ending the row with knit 1.

Repeat row 2 until your work measures 11 inches.

Work next row as follows: knit first stitch, purl 1 stitch. To purl (the reverse of knit stitch), hold left needle with yarn in front of

Purl stitch

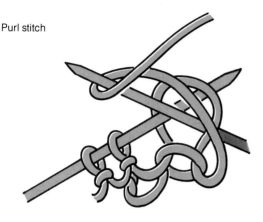

Knit two together

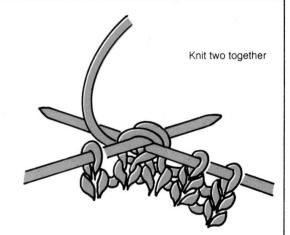

work. Insert tip of right needle from right to left through front loop of first stitch on left needle. Hold yarn in right hand as if to knit, but in front of needles; pass yarn over, then under, tip of right needle, forming a loop. Holding yarn firmly to prevent it from slipping off, draw loop through stitch on left needle. Slip this stitch off left needle, leaving new stitch on right-hand needle. Then, knit 2 together. Repeat pattern of purl 1, knit 2 together, until end of row, ending with knit 1.

### Knitting crown of hat

Work the next 5 rows in a pattern of knit 1, purl 1. This will form a ribbed pattern. Then, work a row decreasing to 30 stitches by

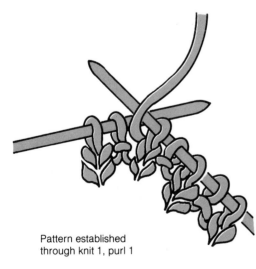

Pattern established through knit 1, purl 1

knitting first stitch, knitting next 2 stitches together, and continuing to knit 2 stitches together across, ending row with knit 1.

Next row: purl across.

Next row: decrease to 15 stitches by knitting 2 together across.

Cut yarn, pull through remaining stitches, and fasten. Thread yarn through a tapestry needle and, right sides together, sew the seam at the back of the hat, using either an overcast stitch or backstitch.

### Knitting mitten for right hand

To knit mitten for right hand, cast on 26 stitches. For the ribbing which will form the cuff, work in knit 1, purl 1, for 10 rows or until work measures 2 inches. Continue in the following pattern. Row 1: knit 1, yarn over, slip 1 stitch, knit 1; yarn over, slip 1 stitch, knit 1 across row, ending with knit 2. Row 2: knit 1, yarn over, slip 1 stitch, knit 2 together. Repeat yarn over, slip 1 stitch, knit 2 together across row. Repeat row 2 for as many rows as needed, so work measures 4½ inches from cast-on row.

418

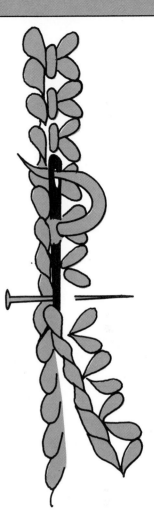

### Knitting thumb of mitten

For right thumb, work in pattern across for 13 stitches. Cast 6 stitches onto left needle. Knit the 6 cast-on stitches, then the next 6 stitches. Turn work and purl the 12 stitches you have just knit. Continue a stockinette stitch pattern of knit 1 row, purl 1 row of 12 stitches, until thumb measures 2¼ inches. Decrease 3 stitches in next knit row. (To decrease, work 2 stitches as 1.) Knit 2, knit 2 together, knit 2, knit 2 together, knit 2, knit 2 together, knit 1. Purl 1 row. Decrease 3 stitches in next knit row. Knit 1, knit 2 together, knit 1, knit 2 together, knit 1, knit 2 together. Six stitches remain. Break off yarn and thread through the 6 stitches. Pick up and knit 6 stitches where stitches were cast on for thumb. Finish row in the row 1 mitten pattern, establishing pattern on the 6 picked-up stitches as for row 1. Continue in pattern until mitten is desired length.

Work a decrease row as follows: knit first stitch, then knit next 3 stitches together. Repeat knit 3 stitches together across, ending with knit 1. Fourteen stitches remain. Purl 1 row. Next row, knit 1, then knit 2 stitches together across, ending row with knit 1. Break yarn and pull through remaining 8 stitches. Thread yarn through a tapestry needle, and with right sides together, sew seams, using overcast stitch or running backstitch.

### Knitting mitten for left hand

To make mitten for left hand, follow same instructions as given for right mitten, reversing the placement of the thumb to opposite side of work, by knitting pattern across for 19 stitches instead of 13.

# Baby bunting

A handmade baby gift is always very special, and this attractive bunting for an infant's first outing is sure to be appreciated. Warm and cozy in cold weather, the fake-fur fabric acts as a windbreaker. For warmer climate or summer-weight bunting, select a quilted cotton knit or lined seersucker fabric. The bunting is easy to make, and does not require advanced sewing skills. It works up quickly on a sewing machine, but it can be sewn by hand if necessary.

Materials: a 22-inch zipper; folded cotton bias braid 48 inches long and 1 inch wide; matching thread; a small hook and eye; and a piece of reversible fake fur measuring 30 inches by 32 inches. Select a colorful print fabric for the outside of the bunting if the fake-fur fabric is not reversible. The pile side forms a lining and fold-over collar.

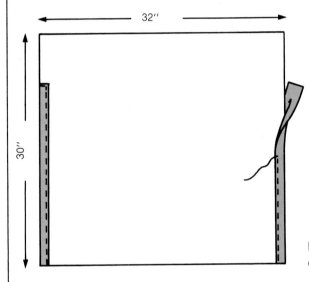

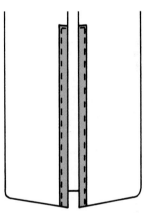

With the pile side out, fold over each of the braided sides 8 inches so that they meet in the center.

### Stitching braid to fabric
Cut the folded cotton braid into two 24-inch lengths. Fold one piece of braid over each of the 30-inch front edges of the fabric, starting at the bottom (this will leave a 6-inch exposed edge at the top of each side). Use a straight stitch to fasten the braid in place.

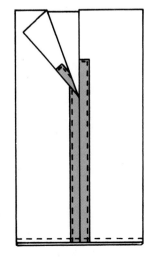

### Stitching the bottom seam
Stitch the bunting across the bottom, allowing a ½-inch seam.

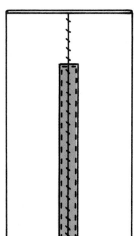

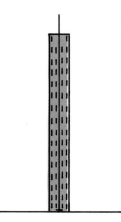

Again turn the bunting right side out. Hand-sew or use a zipper foot on the sewing machine, stitching from the top down one side, across the bottom, and up the other side. Remove the basting threads holding the closed front.

Turn the bunting right side out (with the print on the outside). Close the unbound opening temporarily by basting.

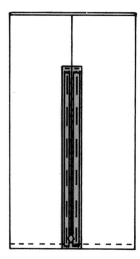

### Inserting the zipper
Turn the bunting inside out. Open the zipper and place it face down on the braid. Baste the zipper in place from top to bottom.

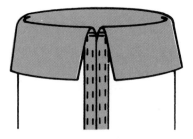

### Finishing the bunting
Fold over the top flap so that the fake fur shows.

With the zipper open, sew the hook and eye about 1 inch below the foldover to complete the baby bunting.

# Ceramic lamp

This sculptured ceramic lamp is an example of the coiled pottery method, differing in construction from some of our other ceramic projects. Here, the cylinders are formed by stacking long coils, each ½ inch thick, on top of each other. The cylinders are smoothed with fingers, modeling tools and slip (a binder paste of clay mixed with water) to form three columns of varying heights and widths, connected at their midsections by other coils. The central column of the lamp and the lighting fixture insert piece are bottomless, to permit installation of the electrical fixture when the lamp has been completed. Formulas for two colored glazes compatible with the malleable, high-fire clay used in this project are given below. Ceramists gauge the temperature at which a certain clay or glaze has completed firing by the melting point of cones placed inside the kiln with the object being fired. A cone's melting point is given a numerical plus or minus rating rather than measured by Fahrenheit or Centigrade degrees. Firing temperature for this clay and glaze is a high cone of five plus.

Materials: high-fire red clay; water and slip mixture; powdered ferric oxide to make the stain; ingredients to make the turquoise glaze (2% copper carbonate, 5% tin oxide, and 93% water) and lavender glaze (2.5% rutile, 2.5% tin oxide, 2.5% manganese dioxide, and 92.5% water); a modeling tool or butter knife; metal kidney-shaped tool, or the back of a cheap spoon for smoothing; and a shaving tool with a triangular-shaped wire on one end and an oval wire on the other, to remove excess clay from surfaces while drying. All are available at clay suppliers. Also needed are: wooden spoons and brushes for mixing and applying the stain and glaze; a rolling pin; a large, flat, non-metallic work surface area (preferably wood), well protected by several layers of newspaper; plastic sheeting or a plastic bag; and a sponge to remove excess water.

½'' thick

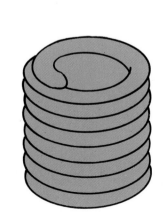

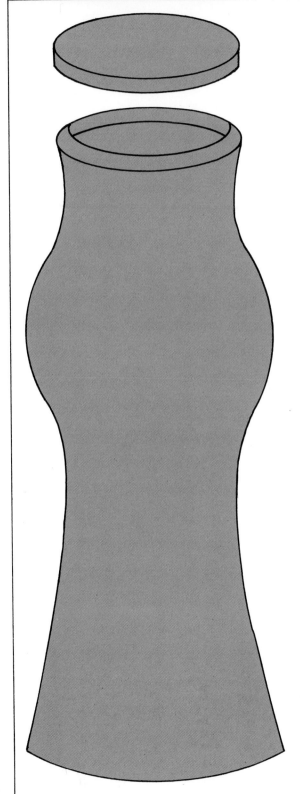

### Modeling the first two columns

The lamp's two shorter columns have unequal measurements. The shortest column, 7 inches high, has circumferences of 8½ inches at base, 12 inches at midsection, 5½ inches at neck, and 9½ inches at top. The second column, 9⅜ inches high, has circumferences of: 6¾ inches at base, 10¼ inches at the widest point of the midsection, 6 inches at neck, and 9½ inches at top.

Roll several snakelike coils, each ½ inch thick, using palms of hands and rolling on a flat surface. Shape each column of the lamp by placing several coils in a rising spiral to form a cylinder 2 to 3 inches high and ½ inch thick. Apply slip thinly in grooves. Use modeling tool and metal kidney to smooth grooves and even surface inside and outside. When smoothing outside, support cylinder from inside with the palm of your hand. Repeat this procedure of layering in spirals, applying slip and smoothing surfaces every 2 to 3 inches. For the two shorter columns, begin to widen the cylinder circumference when about a quarter of its total height. Continue widening the circumference of the spirals until half the height of the column has been formed, then decrease the circumference until the cylinder is three quarters of its estimated height. Next, increase the circumference of coiled spirals again until the column is at full height. Apply slip, smooth, and level top with shaving tool. Now turn the column over and insert a small, flat clay circle that has been rolled to ½ inch thickness. Apply slip and smooth, then turn right side up. If newspaper sticks to clay, just peel it off.

2″

Funnel

6″

### Forming the main column

Model the central and tallest column of the lamp in the same manner as the other two, but use different proportions. Increase the coil circumference at one third of the desired height, until half the total height is reached, then decrease circumference until the column stands a little less than two thirds of its full height. At this point, increase circumference once more until the column is full height. Finish modeling the top just as instructed for the other two columns, leaving the bottom open to permit threading of electrical fixture. Cut a small notch about ½ inch square at the base, so that when the lighting cord is threaded through, it will not prevent the lamp from standing evenly. This column is 12¼ inches high, with circumferences of 5 inches at the base, 9 inches at midpoint, 5½ inches at neck, and 13 inches at top.

### Making the fixture insert

The insert for the lighting fixture is another column of layered coils, worked similarly to the others, but in a different shape. The base circumference is 3 inches, worked gradually wider until you have a funnel 2 inches high, with a 7¼-inch circumference. Flatten the top of the funnel until only about ¾ inch remains open in the center. While applying slip and smoothing with tools and fingers, layer a cylinder on top of the funnel, spiraling until this section of the lamp is 6 inches high. Smooth top, leaving center opening, and set aside.

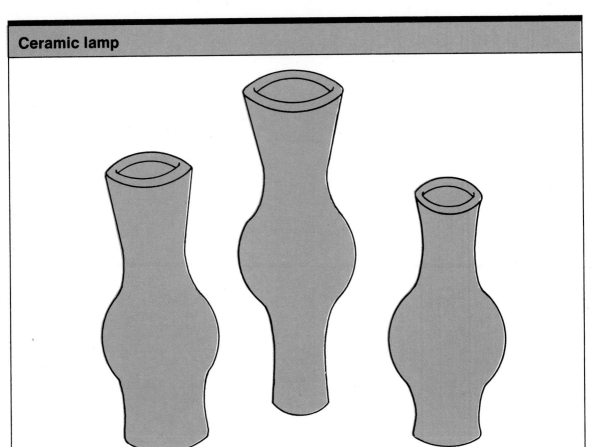

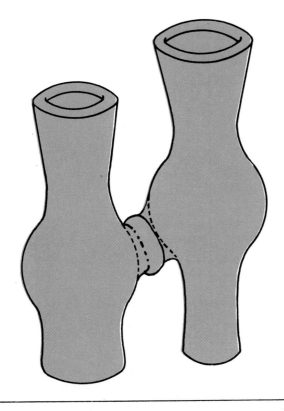

### Joining the columns

Stand the three columns close to one another, the tallest in the center, with the notched part of the bottom facing away from you, the shortest column on the right side, and the middle-sized column on the left. The two shorter columns should be slightly forward of the center column. Roll three long coils, each ½ inch thick. Use one of these to join the left column to the midsection of the central column, using a wrapping motion to make an oval joint 8 inches in circumference. At the widest part of the right column, wrap a connecting coil in a 7½-inch oval to join with central column, smoothing as you wrap. The final joint is a coiled oval 7 inches in circumference, connecting the widest portion of the middle column with the right column.

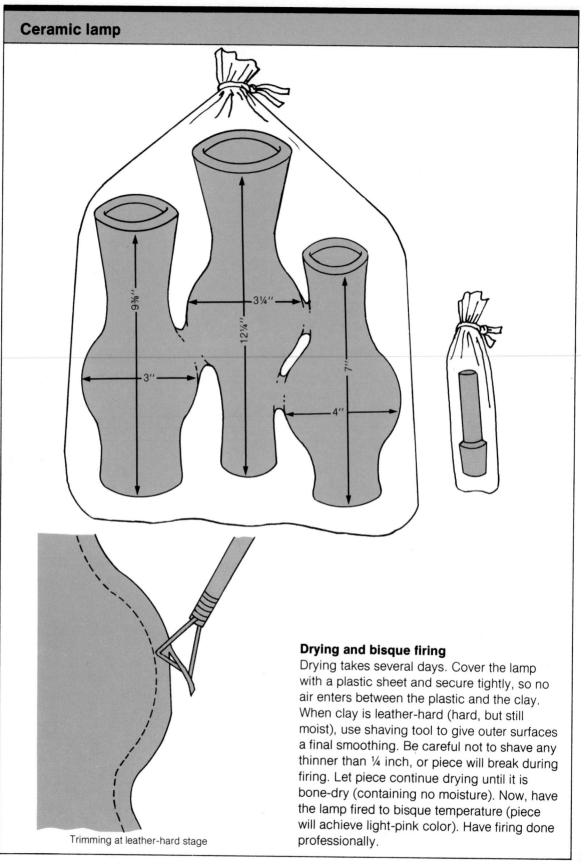

9⅜"

3¼"

12¼"

3"

7"

4"

Trimming at leather-hard stage

## Drying and bisque firing

Drying takes several days. Cover the lamp with a plastic sheet and secure tightly, so no air enters between the plastic and the clay. When clay is leather-hard (hard, but still moist), use shaving tool to give outer surfaces a final smoothing. Be careful not to shave any thinner than ¼ inch, or piece will break during firing. Let piece continue drying until it is bone-dry (containing no moisture). Now, have the lamp fired to bisque temperature (piece will achieve light-pink color). Have firing done professionally.

### Staining and second firing

Stain lamp with the red liquid mixture of powdered ferric oxide and water. To test glaze for adequate dryness, which takes about two days, place wet finger on surface and if it sticks slightly to the surface, the piece is ready to be fired again. Prepare the turquoise and lavender glazes following the formula instructions in the introduction and keep them tightly covered until you are ready to apply to the piece after second firing.

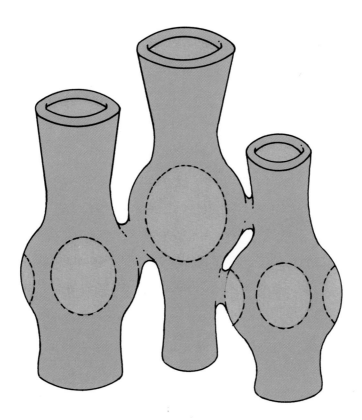

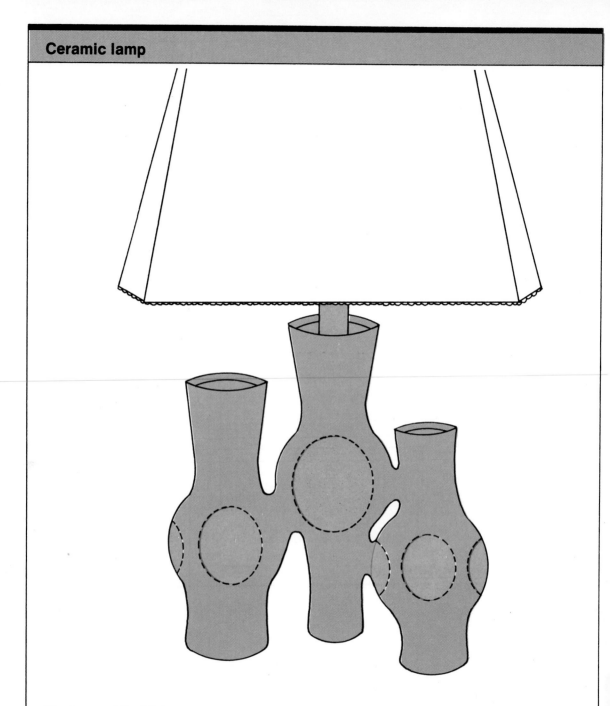

### Glazing and final firing

Brush lavender glaze liberally inside the three lamp columns, also painting large lavender circles on the outside to emphasize the bulbous contours. Apply turquoise glaze generously to entire lamp-fixture insert (except funnel bottom and base), and to outside of lamp, being careful to brush around the circles. When glaze sticks only slightly to wet finger, it is ready for the final firing. After firing, the glaze colors will thin just enough to allow some of the stain to show through in a subtle pattern of vertical streaks that complement the circle design and the varying widths and heights of the columns. The total effect is an attractive blend of soft semigloss tones counterpointing bold shapes. Select a lampshade in a size and shape proportional to the base, such as the rectangular one shown in the photograph, or a pleated shade.

# Handmade buttons

Decorative buttons give fashions a distinctive custom appearance, especially handmade buttons. There are countless ways to design buttons that are unique; the most frequently used method is to cover the button. You start with a button finding, a two-piece form that snaps together, available in a wide range of sizes and shapes. For coverings, embellish matching or contrasting fabric covers with embroidery, or crochet a plain or fancy pattern.

Materials: two-piece button forms; metallic 6-strand green and gold embroidery floss; embroidery needle; small swatches of fabric; red, green and yellow tapestry yarn (use single strand); a tapestry needle; and white glue.

### Embroidering the black fabric

For the embroidered black chained button, cut out two pieces of black fabric, slightly larger than the top and bottom pieces of the button form. Cover the back piece of the form with

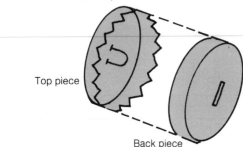

Top piece

Back piece

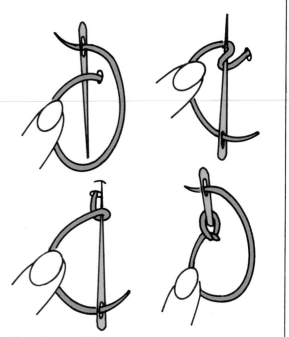

one fabric piece and with white glue, secure fabric to button form. With pencil, mark embroidery pattern on the other fabric piece. The green chain and two diagonal gold chains are formed with broad or threaded chain stitches.

Thread needle with green embroidery thread, and take a small stitch at one edge of the fabric, then bring the needle out approximately ⅛ inch away. Pass the needle behind the stitch from right to left, and insert needle where you brought it out. Pull through gently to avoid distorting stitches. Repeat, sliding the needle behind each preceding stitch, until the other edge is reached. Tie off thread. Thread needle with gold embroidery thread and stitch gold chains in same manner. Glue the embroidered piece to the top piece of button form and snap the two pieces together.

### Making the daisy button

The embroidered daisy button is similarly made. Cut out the two fabric pieces for the top and back of each button form. Glue the

first piece of fabric to the back piece of the button form, and mark the embroidery pattern on the second piece. Using the needle and single-strand tapestry yarn, stitch single daisy chains to outline the flower. Use green yarn for the stem and leaves, red for the petals, and yellow for the bud. To make a daisy-chain stitch, bring the needle out to edge of the fabric. Hold down the yarn with your thumb and form a loop with the needle to the right, inserting it back through the same hole. Bring it out at the bottom of the loop, over the loop, and back through the fabric to anchor the bottom of the loop. When flower is completed, glue the embroidered piece to the top piece of button form and snap the two pieces together.

# Silhouette with shears

A silhouette portrait of a child or other loved one is a classic keepsake that you will cherish for a lifetime, one that will be handed down through the generations as a proud family heirloom. Yet you will be surprised at how easy it is to make such a fine work of art, an art that has been practiced for many centuries.

Materials: a piece of plain white paper; and one of black construction paper, each at least 10 by 14 inches; and a somewhat larger piece of oaktag or other mounting board; the size and color will depend on how you decide to display your silhouette. Ours are mounted on pieces of white cardboard measuring 12 by 16 inches each. You will also need some masking tape; staples and a stapler; scissors; pencil; and rubber cement. And you will need an electric lamp with a bright bulb. A gooseneck desk lamp will do the job best, but any other table lamp can be used.

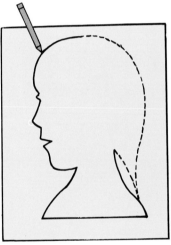

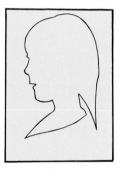

### Outlining the profile
Have the subject sit in a comfortable chair, in profile near a blank wall. Tape the white paper to the wall beside the subject's head. Place the lamp, with shade removed, on the opposite side of the subject, again at the head level. Turn lamp on so the light casts a shadow on the paper. Experiment by moving the subject and the lamp until you have a perfect profile outlined on the paper. It is important to keep the light source, the subject, and the paper in line so that there is no distortion.

With the pencil, copy the outline of the subject's head on the white paper. Pay particular attention to such details as eyebrows and eyelashes. If the subject moves while you are drawing, realign his head with the portion already drawn.

Finish off the bottom of the silhouette with a straight, horizontal line or draw a line from the nape of the neck angled or curving down toward the front.

### Cutting out and mounting the silhouette
Remove the paper from the wall and turn off light. Staple the white paper to the black paper around the edges. Holding paper firmly, cut out the silhouette in both pieces of paper simultaneously. Discard the white paper, or use it to make a white-on-black silhouette.

Coat the back of the black construction paper lightly with rubber cement. Press down firmly on the mounting board.

# Rushed chair seat

It takes practice more than skill to learn the craft of seat weaving, and you are sure to be pleased with the results of your handiwork: handsome, sturdy and durable chair seats. You can weave with either rush or fiber. Rush is made of twisted leaves of the cattail family, and must be soaked before use. For the beginner, fiber is recommended. It is a twisted cord that closely resembles rush but is much easier to work with and does not have to be soaked before use. The seat shown measures 12 inches deep by 15 inches wide in front and 12½ inches in back.

Materials: 2 pounds of fiber; a few small tacks; and 1 pint of shellac.

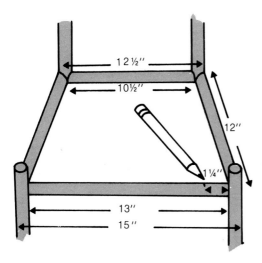

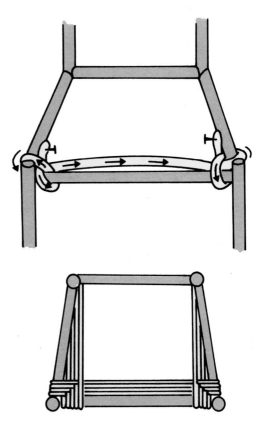

## Filling in the front and sides

Measure both front and back rails of the chair seat between the posts. On the chair shown, the front rail is 13 inches, the back 10½ inches. Figure half the difference between these two dimensions, which is 1¼ inches. Measure and mark with a pencil this distance from each post on the front rail.

Roll off 10 feet of fiber into a coil small enough to be handled conveniently. Tack the end to the inside of the left side rail behind the front corner post. Carry the fiber over and around the front rail; bring it up over itself and over the side rail. Pull the cord tightly across to the right side rail, over the top of the rail, then under and up over itself. Wrap around the front rail, then tack the end to the side rail and cut off excess. Repeat this procedure until the front rail has been filled from corner posts

to pencil marks. On the second and all following times around, consider the fiber already in place as part of the rails, and wrap around them accordingly. Keep strands tightly pushed together as they go around the rails.

Tack the end of the fiber for the next round to the left side rail, then wrap around front, left side, right side, and front rails as before. Pull the fiber across to the back rail, over, under, over itself and over the right side rail.

## Rushed chair seat

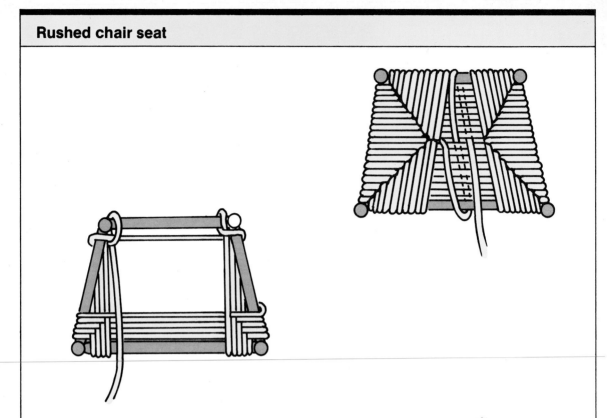

Then pull it across to the left side rail, over, under, over itself and over the back rail. Carry it back to the front rail to complete the round. Continue in this manner until the sides of the seat are filled. When fiber runs out, add more by tying a knot on the underside where it will be concealed by the weaving. Or you can overlap old and new strands about 2¾ inches and tie them together with heavy silk thread or very fine wire.

### Final weaving and finishing

When the side rails are filled, weave the remaining space by bringing the fiber over and around the front rail, up between the two center rows of strands, over and around the back rail, up between the center rows, and repeat in the form of a figure 8 until the space is filled. Flatten the strands of fiber where they cross in the center to fill in evenly.

When weaving is finished, carry the fiber down through the center and tie to any cord on the underside of the seat. Finish the seat by applying three coats of very thin shellac. This will enhance the appearance of the fiber as well as preserve it.

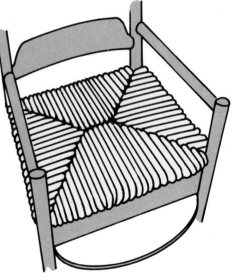

# Dried-apple heads

Country craftsmen have for generations carved doll heads from fresh, firm apples, resembling caricatures of wise old men and typical old grandmothers. The apple heads, wizened through drying, are invariably amusing to both children and adults; and surprisingly, they last for years. The principal material needed is a firm winter or late fall apple, the larger the better, generally uniform in shape. Neither a soft nor a bruised apple, nor a hard unripe one will carve satisfactorily.

Materials: an apple; an apple peeler and corer; sharp pocketknife; single-edge razor blade; nut pick; small quantity of lemon juice; small paintbrush; two small glass beads, cloves, or peppercorns for eyes; 4-inch length of wood dowel; small sheet of cardboard; toothpicks; small cuticle or fingernail scissors; fabric scraps for clothes; yarn scraps for hair; white glue; ruler; drafting compass; and a quantity of silica-gel, specially designed for drying flowers and available from a florist. In addition, to make the doll's torso you need: three slices of white bread; three tablespoons of white glue; three drops of lemon juice; and about 6 feet of pliable wire to make a full-length doll.

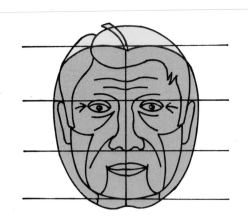

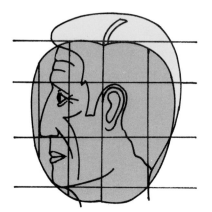

### Plotting face on grid

Begin by collecting some magazine pictures of interesting faces of old men and old women, the larger the better and full front face rather than profile. Select the best example of a strong-featured face of each sex. Superimpose on each of the chosen pictures the rough outline of an apple. Then square off the enclosed space, using a ruler and pencil, and draw a vertical line from top to bottom, so the head is divided in half. Draw three horizontal lines across the head so there are the following sections blocked off: chin to bottom of the nose; bottom of the nose to the top of the eyelids; and top of the eyelids to the top of the head. This face graph, which is divided into six (more or less) equal parts, serves as a guide in the analysis of the component parts you are about to carve.

### Preparing apple

With a pocketknife, peel a large, near perfect, hard winter or late fall apple of suitable shape. Make very thin peels so the shape of the apple is not distorted and also to keep the size of the apple as large as possible. Remove all ridges created by the peeler by gently scraping the ridges with the nut pick or pocketknife blade, so the surfaces are rounded all over. Using the small paintbrush, cover the entire surface of the apple with lemon juice to keep it from discoloring.

# Dried-apple heads

## Carving apple head

With the apple stem side up, use a pocketknife to block out a face on one side, using the proportions determined when you plotted the face. If you are starting with the female doll, remember that somewhat softer facial contours are appropriate than for the man. With nut-

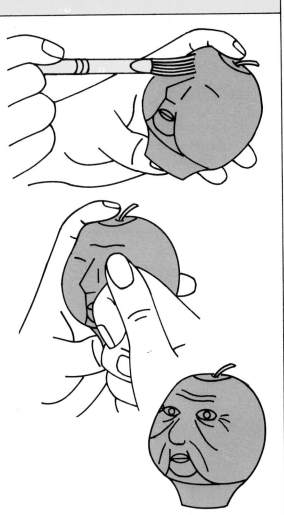

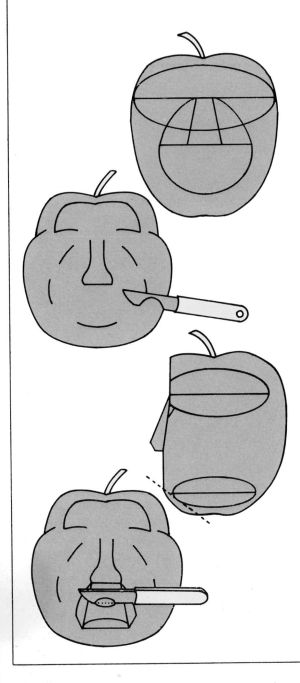

pick, score lines on either side of where the nose will be. Score lines where the eyes and mouth should be. Remember that only slight indenting is necessary when scoring these features, because as the apple dries, these lines become more pronounced. Carve deeply into the apple with the point of the knife, cut away the apple on either side of the nose, and then carve the other features, shaping the cheeks, forehead, and chin. With your fingernail, carefully score the forehead and outer edges of the eyes with shallow lines for wrinkles. Brush on more lemon juice, covering the newly-carved areas to protect them from discoloration. Insert beads, peppercorns, or cloves into the eye holes. (If you wish, you can also insert rice grains into the mouth for teeth.)

## Dried-apple heads

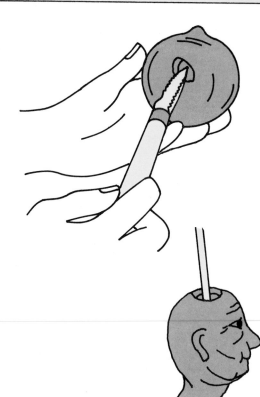

### Oven drying

Use the apple corer to remove carefully the core of the apple. Place the apple in a very low oven, not more than 200 degrees Fahrenheit, for about 12 hours. You can also dry the apple head more slowly near a warm radiator or near a furnace, in which case you should occasionally turn the apple to expose it evenly to the heat on all sides over a period of three weeks. During the drying process, check to see that the inserted eyes and teeth are not forced out. If they are, press them back gently as often as necessary. You will notice the head slowly shrinking to roughly half its original size as the water in the apple tissue evaporates. Also during the shrinkage, you will note that the cuts and incised lines remain the same size, so that they become very prominent and large in appearance.

### Silica-gel drying

When the apple is dry but still soft and pliable, rather like a plastic sponge, remove from heat and manipulate the features by gently pinching and pressing to give the face its particular character. When you are pleased with the results, give the head its final drying in the silica-gel. Use any convenient container to hold the drying agent. Do not force the head into the granular material, but instead make a small well in the granules and set the head top side up in the well. Sprinkle the silica-gel in the hollow core and all around the apple until it is completely covered with silica-gel. Cover the container tightly and leave it for 2 to 3 days. Remove the apple head, and check to see if all the moisture is removed from tissues. If not, replace in silica-gel and leave for another day or until apple head is completely dry. Trim any loose apple on head with the fingernail scissors before joining to the body.

# Dried-apple heads

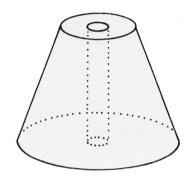

## Forming the body

To form body, mix up a bread-dough base using three torn-up slices of white bread, crusts removed; 3 tablespoons of white glue; and three drops of lemon juice. Knead until the material no longer sticks to your fingers and has a smooth consistency. To save leftover material for the second doll, store it in a plastic bag in the refrigerator. (It will keep up to three weeks.) Work the mixture down into the hollow core and mold a cone shape suggesting shoulders below the apple base. Use toothpicks poked through the mixture to help hold the shape together. With the razor blade, trim off any exposed ends of the toothpicks.

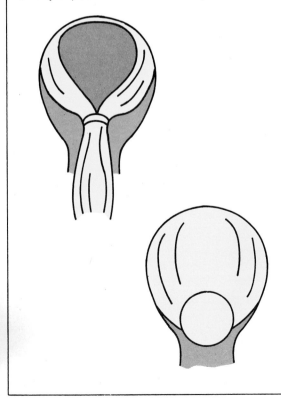

## Finishing the woman

To finish the apple-head woman, glue 6-inch-long strands of white yarn on the head for hair. Wrap the yarn around the head in an old-fashioned style and tie it in back in a bun. Trim the excess yarn away with scissors. Make the upper torso dress in whatever fashion your scrap materials and imagination suggest, gluing the parts to the shoulder form and tucking the edges underneath and out of sight with more glue.

## Finishing the man

To finish the apple-head man, glue small snippets of yarn on the face for a mustache. Glue a small swatch of knitted material to the top front of the torso, leaving a ¼-inch strip free on top to turn over as a collar. Roll over and stitch the collar edge down all around. At the back of the torso, fold the edges of the knit material where they come together and whip-stitch together for a tight fit. Finish off the torso by gluing edges of the material under the torso. The cap is fashioned with fabric-covered cardboard. Cut out a strip of cardboard 6 inches long and ¼ inch wide for the hat band. Cut out a circle 1¾ inches in diameter for the crown. Cut out a triangular piece for the visor that will fit comfortably under the circle. Cover all pieces with cotton fabric glued to the surfaces and tucked neatly underneath with more glue. Glue the cap to the head.

Depending on how you plan to use your dolls, you can either set them on display as they are or insert a wooden dowel through the soft bottom of the bread dough mixture before it hardens. If a full-length doll is desired, use the pliable wire to attach arms and legs to the body. Hands and feet are formed from apple pieces cut away from apple when carving the head, in which case they should be processed the same as the apple head, brushed with lemon juice and dried in the same manner before the doll is assembled.

444

# Pine-needle basket

The coiled method of basket making, one of the simplest, originated with the Indians of North and South America and is still prevalent today. The coiled basket shown here is assembled with bundles of pine needles wrapped with raffia and stitched together in rows around a hub to form a disc or oval for the base of the basket. The sides are formed with the same roping of pine needles wrapped with raffia, placed one on top of the other.

Materials: six 1-inch metal rings; long-eye embroidery needle; scissors; plastic beverage straw; can of clear acrylic spray; hank of raffia; and a quantity of pine needles, at least 20 or 30 branches. Needles of the slash pine, growing to a length of 10 to 12 inches are best, but shorter ones will serve the purpose. Use those pine needles that are newly browned in the sun and still attached to the branch.

## Preparing needles and raffia

Do not remove pine needles from branch until they have been washed in a solution of warm water and detergent. Rinse well. Remove from branches and soak overnight in fresh water. Drain, put needles in a plastic bag and place in refrigerator until ready to use. Soak raffia in water for about 15 minutes before using.

## Covering metal rings with raffia

For each of the six rings, select two medium-width strands of raffia about ½ to ⅝ inch. Stitch counter-clockwise in a double buttonhole stitch. Loop one strand over the ring from the outside, then under the ring and back up over itself. Loop the second strand over the ring from the inside, next to the first loop, then under the ring and back up over itself. Repeat with alternating loops of first and second strand until the ring is covered. Thread end of top strand through embroidery needle. Pass the needle through the stitch on the right and bring it back through the last loop. Cut the end of the raffia. Thread the end of the other strand through embroidery needle and stitch same as other strand, but do not cut the strand.

Bring the still-threaded needle across the middle of the ring to the opposite side and through a stitch, forming the first spoke. Bring the needle up two stitches to the right and again across the middle of the ring to opposite side of the ring and down through a stitch. Continue until there are four spokes in the ring. Then pass needle through the stitch on the right, looping to tie off stitch. Cut off excess raffia. Fill in center of the ring by weaving raffia between spokes in an over-and-under stitch.

## Pine-needle basket

### Forming the basket

Use one ring as hub of the inner disk which, when completed, measures approximately 3½ inches. Cut a 1-inch length from the beverage straw and slip seven pine needles into it. The straw piece will act as a holder for pine needles

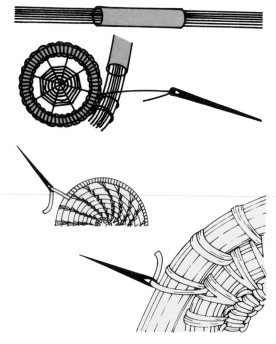

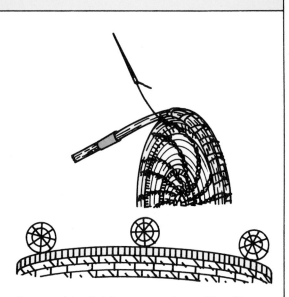

all around by tightly overcasting with raffia.

Start an outer disk around inner disk just as you did around the ring. Proceed as before, continuing until 12 rows have been added. Bind off by overcasting.

Begin still another disk and work four rows. Then begin forming side of basket by stitching a fifth row tightly atop the previous row. Continue upward for six more rows. Bind off by overcasting.

while working. Thread embroidery needle with a strand of raffia 1¼ inches wide and fasten it through one of the raffia loops covering the ring. Take the bundle of pine needles in plastic straw and, working counterclockwise, hold ends of pine needles against the ring. Then bring raffia-threaded needle over pine needles, back under, and through a loop on the ring. In this process the raffia is being wrapped around bundles of pine needles as they are secured to the ring. Continue stitching needles all around ring, spacing stitches ½ inch apart. When the first row is completed, continue to next row, feeding more pine needles into straw as needed. Add another strand of raffia, just before the strand being worked runs out, by overlapping previous strand and working new strand into the stitch. As you work, split each stitch in previous row about two-thirds up, making a chain stitch. Continue until disk measures 3½ inches in diameter. Bind off last row

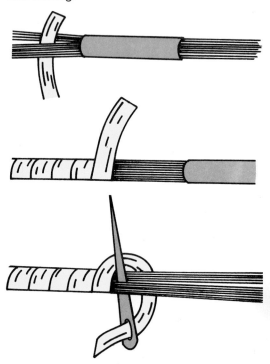

# Pine-needle basket

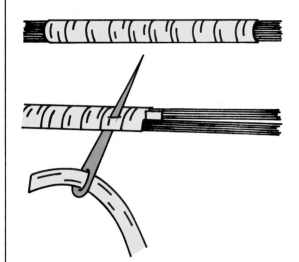

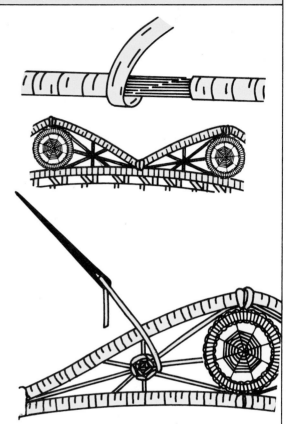

## Decorating the top of the basket

Stitch the five remaining covered rings in an upright position on top of last row, spaced evenly around basket perimeter.

Make a rope of raffia and pine needles approximately 36 inches long. First soak four or five strands of raffia and flatten them out. Cut off hard ends. Using the beverage straw holder, place four or five pine needles in it, and slip one end of a piece of flattened raffia between them, about 1 inch from the ends of the pine needles. Wrap the raffia tightly around needles, lapping each wrap halfway over previous one. Keep raffia flat by dipping fingers in water and smoothing. Continue wrapping, feeding needles into straw as needed. When nearing end of first strand, thread it into embroidery needle and pull through the pine needles. Cut off excess. Thread needle with a

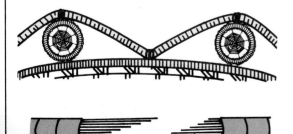

new piece of raffia, and pull about ⅞ inch through pine needles (¼ inch) behind the other, and through the stitch. Flatten raffia and continue to wrap. When rope is long enough, anchor raffia in same way, leaving 1 inch of needle ends exposed.

Starting midway between two upright rings, attach the rope around the basket top by stitching between rings and to the top of each ring. When this is completed, make a perfect splice of the two rope ends by cutting half of the needles from the top of one end and half from the bottom of the other. Lay left end on top of right end and wrap with a small piece of wet, flat raffia.

Stitch three more rows of pine needles onto rope; bind off last row by overcasting.

Use thin strands of raffia to fill in decorative stitching around the five rings. Where the stitches intersect, take several over-and-under stitches.

Spray the finished basket with a coating of clear acrylic.

# Braided rug

The American colonists braided rags and worn fragments of cloth into rugs out of necessity, but today these charming floor coverings are colorful room accents. Contemporary craftspeople need not collect old fabrics; they simply go to a craft-goods supplier or remnant outlet where quantities of mill-end fabrics are sold by the pound.

Materials: collect a large supply of woolen cloth, discarded old coats, suits, blankets or remnants from a mill-end supply house. Cottons are possible alternatives, but they will not endure years of usage. Choose fabrics that provide a balance of light and dark colors. You can continue to expand the size of your rug almost indefinitely. Therefore, have enough fabric on hand at the start to establish a basic color scheme. Also needed are carpet thread, a sack (curved) needle, basting thread and a heavy basting needle.

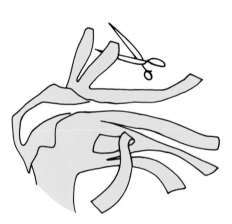

center line, so that the strip is four layers thick with the raw edges tucked deep inside the strip. Follow the same procedure for lightweight fabrics, but fold them lengthwise once more, making extra layers. It is important to make all the cables, of whatever fabrics, a uniform thickness.

### Cutting and cabling the fabric
Cut the wool fabric lengthwise in strips 2 inches wide. (If you are working with lightweight wool or cotton, cut the strips 3 to 4 inches wide.)

Before braiding, the strips must be cabled, that is, formed into flattened tubes of fabric. To cable, fold a strip lengthwise, so the outer edges meet in the center of the strip. Fold the strip lengthwise again, this time along the

With a stout needle and a noncontrasting thread, make long basting stitches along the seam to hold the strip together. This step, though time-consuming, will save valuable time later when you are braiding. To join strips, cut the end on the diagonal and sew to the next matching strip. Continue in this manner, cabling and splicing, until you have several yards of fabric rope. Roll it into a ball and make two more cabled ropes.

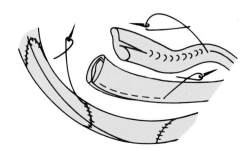

## Braided rug

### Braiding a three-strand rope of fabric

To begin braiding, first sew the ends of the three ropes together, tucking the loose, raw tips out of sight. Put a long nail into the end of a worktable or devise some other means to hold the joined end of the three ropes firmly in place while braiding. Loop the joined end of the ropes over the nail and begin to braid, pulling the ropes taut as you go. You may find that braiding is easier if you stand. Keep the sewn

seams of each rope turned in toward the inside of the braid, so that the seams are made invisible.

When you have braided enough of your first color to make a center of five to nine turns, switch to one of the other colors. For example, if you started braiding in light tones, splice on, cable, and then braid rug in dark tones. Continue in this color until you have braided enough to make a contrasting band of one or two turns. Then switch back to your first tone or introduce a third to make another band of color. Continue in this fashion until you have enough braided rope to make a whole rug.

### Cutting and sewing the rug

To assemble the rug, take the starting end of the braid and lay out the first 6 inches on a flat surface. This will be the center of your oval. Take the attached end of the braid and wrap it snugly around this center line in an oval coil, stitching the two together along the touching

edges. Use carpet thread and a sack needle. Sew firmly but not too tightly or the rug coils will begin to cup or curl. If this happens, try flattening the rug down overnight by covering it with a damp towel and something heavy placed on top. If the problem is severe, take out some of the stitches and resew them more loosely. Make the rug flat before continuing, for you cannot resolve the difficulty later.

When you have reached the dimensions desired, finish off the rug on a curve rather than along a flat side in order to hide the ends. Taper the three ends of the braid. Tuck them back into the braid and fasten securely.

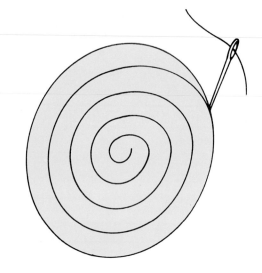

Should you wish to enlarge the rug later, simply withdraw the end and attach additional lengths of rag strips. Proceed with cabling, braiding and assembling, as above. Similarly, if the rug becomes damaged and you wish to replace a band of color, simply cut the old one free and splice in a new one.

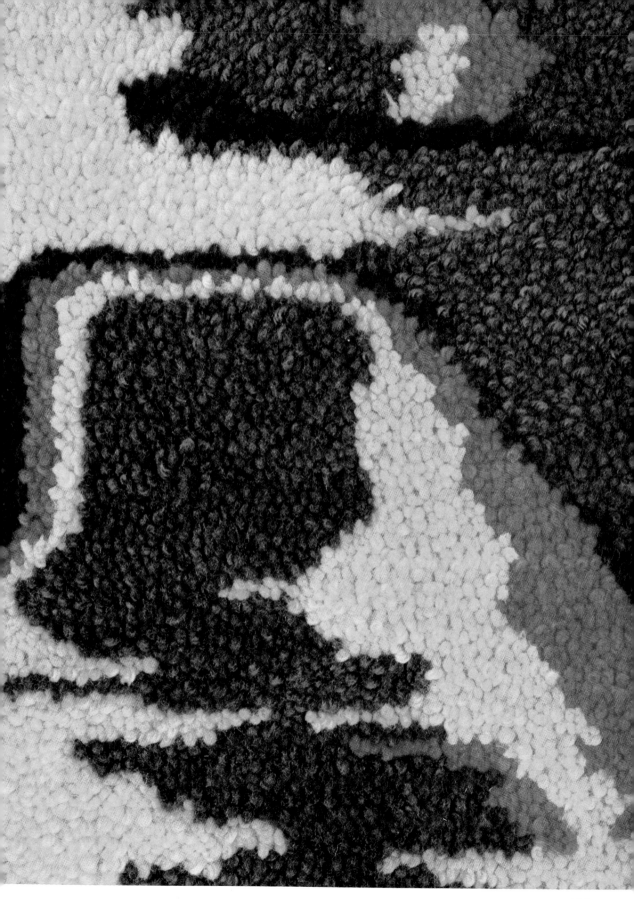

451

# Hooked rug

This striking, handmade rug, with its warm colors and supple pattern, has a rich pile texture that feels soft and luxurious underfoot. Unlike woven floor coverings, the yarn or pile is attached to a mesh fabric by hooking or looping. There are several ways to hook or loop a rug, two of which are described below. One uses a latch hook to secure precut strands of yarn, referred to as the pile, to a mesh canvas. The other uses a blunt-end tapestry needle to stitch a looped pile onto mesh canvas.

Materials: rug latch hook or No. 15 blunt-end tapestry needle; 4-foot-2-inch square of rug canvas, 5 meshes each 1 inch; one roll of masking tape; 3 yards of 1-inch-wide rug binding; heavy-duty carpet thread; No. 3 curved mattress needle; 20-inch-by-30-inch piece of jute or foam rug backing; rug glue (optional); 20-inch-by-30-inch sheet of brown wrapping paper; assorted waterproof felt markers, the same or similar to rug yarn colors; and any one of the following yarns: wool, orlon or acrylic rug worsted, rya or quickpoint yarn in the desired colors.

Since the suitable types of yarn vary in thickness, the amount of yarn required for this project depends on choice of yarn; therefore have the supply store estimate amount you need for each color. Buy skeins or precut packs of yarn according to method you choose. If you select a thin yarn, like rya, work with double or triple strands.

### Transferring the design
Plan your design on wrapping paper to fit the size of rug when finished. Sketch each shape actual size. When satisfied, place rug canvas over design and trace design onto rug canvas with waterproof felt-tip markers. (Felt markers must be waterproof; if not, the markings will bleed if rug gets wet. Test markers for color fastness by marking on a small corner of the canvas and then wetting.)

### Making a looped rug
To make the looped rug illustrated, cut each hank of yarn into 4-foot-strand lengths (or the length comfortable for you) before starting. Thread strands through tapestry needle by doubling yarn and pushing loop formed through eye needle. Work each row of looped stitches on 2 mesh rows of rug canvas, working from bottom to top, from right to left edges.

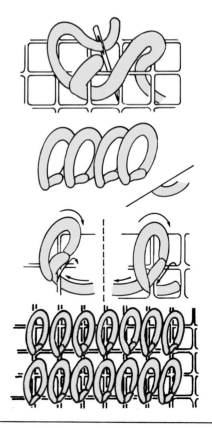

# Hooked rug

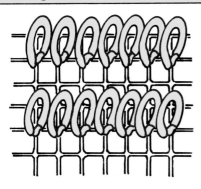

Start by bringing needle up through second mesh of second row, leaving a 2-inch tail on wrong side and pulling up a 2-inch loop (or to the exact height of pile desired). For second stitch, bring needle up through third mesh of second row and down again through second mesh of first row, making a taut stitch. Return needle through these same two meshes in the same direction, again pulling up a 2-inch loop (or height desired) and make a taut stitch as described above. Work rest of row in same manner.

Fold canvas under as you finish each row. When ending strand, make a half stitch by pulling a 2-inch loop diagonally through 2 meshes as shown, leaving a 2-inch tail of yarn at end of strand on wrong side. Complete stitch with new strand by bringing needle up through upper mesh of diagonal stitch and down through lower mesh of last loop made with previous strand to secure it. To resume working in stitch pattern, bring needle up through mesh row and down diagonally through lower mesh row of same stitch, then continue looped stitch, bring needle up, through lower row of mesh and down diagonally through upper mesh row, as shown. Stitch second row of loops on next 2 rows of canvas, for very closely spaced loops. Or, if you wish to conserve yarn, you can skip one row and stitch the following row of loops on the next two rows of canvas with no visible gaps, due to the thickness of each yarn loop.

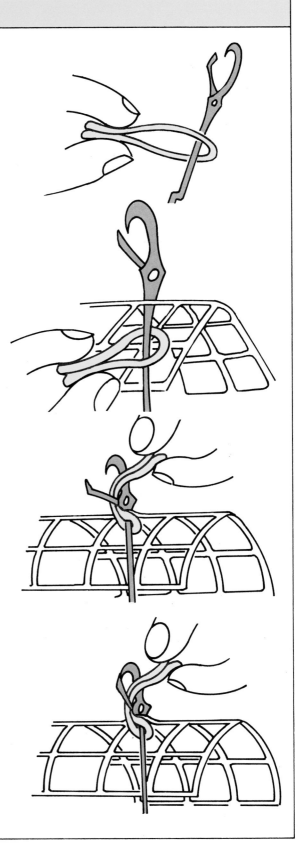

## Hooked rug

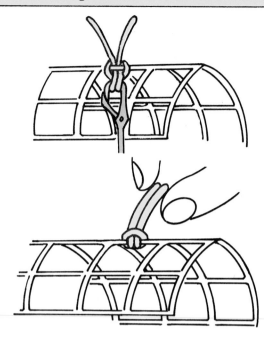

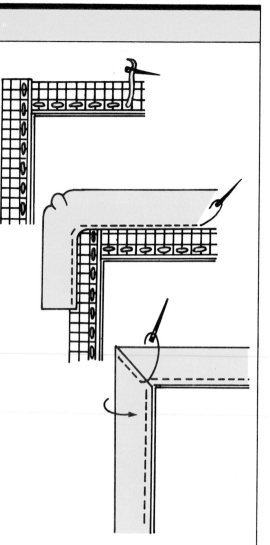

### Hooking rug

To hook a rug, begin by placing near you a small amount of precut strands of the colors to be used in the first few rows of the design. Fold a precut strand of yarn in half over the shank of latch hook just behind latch and hold ends between thumb and forefinger. Fold canvas back along first row of mesh. Push hook down through first mesh of canvas, under the horizontally held strand and up through the hole directly above. Pull hook back. With the latch vertical, bring the two loose ends you have been holding over the shank hook, between latch and hook. Pull hook toward you until latch closes, then release loose ends, continuing to pull back until ends pass all the way through looped yarn. Tug ends to tighten knot formed. Hook and knot each piece of yarn to form the pile of the rug in this manner, working from bottom to top horizontally, always in the same direction. As you complete rows, continue folding finished work underneath to prevent hook from snagging finished rows. Trim any uneven ends as you work, to keep pile even. When you have finished hooking, shake rug well and check for evenness of pile; clip to even, if necessary.

### Finishing rug

Trim all unworked edges of rug canvas to 1 inch. Fold opposite edges to wrong side and baste to back of rug with a No. 3 curved mattress needle and heavy nylon thread. Fold remaining two edges back and baste with back of rug facing up. Place one edge of rug binding 4 inches from corner and sew to edge, then continue sewing binding around rug. Fold other edge of rug binding toward back of rug and sew to inside edge, folding under corners to miter, as illustrated. Sew loosely, otherwise rug may curl. If finished rug is to be placed on a bare floor, you can glue a burlap, jute or foam backing to rug or have it done professionally at a craft or rug store. Keep rug looking fresh by washing periodically with rug shampoo or cold-water detergent.

# Patchwork quilt

Patchwork quilts are beautiful examples of needlecraft which often become collector's items. Colorful and exquisitely pieced (almost like a mosaic in fabric), the traditional quilt designs require time and patience to make. Since each square of the quilt is assembled separately, the work can be done almost anywhere, once all the pieces are cut out and pressed. Then the completed squares of appliqué are joined together in rows. To make a quilt 72 inches by 90 inches, you need the materials listed below.

Materials: a pad of tracing paper; several pieces of sandpaper or blotter paper; 7 yards of 45-inch-width fabric for the diamond-shaped pieces; a layer of dacron batting approximately 72 inches by 90 inches or a batt cut into 18-inch squares; 4 yards of 45-inch-width backing material; 1 yard of 45-inch-width material for a border (if desired); quilting needle and thread; and straight pins.

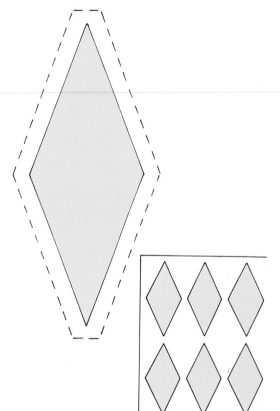

The center star is made with 8 diamond pieces and the border with 24 diamond pieces. Since the entire quilt is made up of 20 appliqué squares, the total number of diamond-shaped pieces needed is 640.

Once the patterns are cut, ready the fabric. First, even the fabric by tearing it or pulling a thread; next, use a damp cloth to cover the fabric and press it. Threads running lengthwise and crosswise are known as the lengthwise and crosswise grain. Place the sandpaper pattern on the lengthwise grain of the fabric and make a tracing line with a pencil. Trace 32 diamond patterns (the number needed for one block) on a sheet of fabric, leaving a ½-inch allowance on all sides between tracing lines.

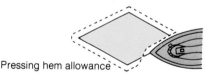

Pressing hem allowance

## Making the patterns

The Eccentric Star, an eight-point star surrounded by a border, is a classic quilt design. To duplicate the basic design, trace the diamond pattern and place this over a piece of sandpaper. Holding both papers firmly in your left hand, cut out the shape. Make a number of duplicates because they become frayed quickly. This one diamond shape is used throughout the design.

## Pressing and cutting the pieces

Cut out the pieces ¼ inch from the tracing lines on all sides of the pattern piece to allow for individual seams. Take the sandpaper pattern and place it directly over the tracing line on each pattern piece already cut out. With a moderately hot iron, press back the seam allowance, which will serve as a guide for sewing the seams. Be sure to press these to the wrong side of the material. Pressing is just as important in quiltmaking as it is in dressmaking. Press before cutting the material and after cutting the material. Press after sewing sections together and again after joining them in strips. All seams should be pressed in the same direction to one side so the finished piece is smooth and flat.

Assembled star pattern

## Sewing the blocks

To sew the 8 pieces together to form the star, join them from the center point outward. Join the 24 border pieces in the same manner following the illustrated diagram. Appliqué each unit on an 18-inch square of plain white material after each has been pieced. Joinings are

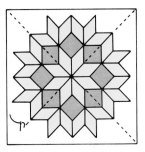

Quilted block

made by turning under the edges and stitching the pieces together with a fine running stitch on the wrong side. The units are appliquéd to the white background material with a running stitch. (See CRAFTNOTES.)

## Applying backing and batting

Lay backing flat on a table; top with a thin layer of dacron batting or a piece of batt cut to size. Place the appliquéd block on top; pin in place. Keeping the layers smooth, baste them together with large running stitches, first around the edges of each appliquéd piece,

and then in a large "X" across the center. Sew with small running stitches as directed in CRAFTNOTES. Remove basting threads.

## Sewing blocks together

To sew the quilt together, first assemble the blocks and the border of the quilt. Some quilts have borders and others a binding. The quilted blocks are joined in strips. For instance, if there are twenty blocks, four wide and five long, arrange them so that you have five strips of four blocks each. In this way, the blocks that make up the width of the quilt will be sewn together first. The rows should line up evenly, so that a quilted border will conform to the strips. (See CRAFTNOTES.)

## Adding the border

Cut 3-inch-wide strips of fabric into four lengths to fit the edges of the quilt, adding 6 inches to the two strips that border the top and bottom. With right sides together, place side borders on quilt along edges, pin and stitch borders in place, leaving ½-inch seams. Place the batting between the layers and baste the raw corners together. Repeat with bottom and top borders.

Stitching border

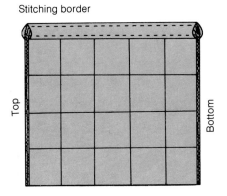

## Making the tulip design

To make a quilt using a floral motif, follow the same directions as for the Eccentric Star quilt, except use the Modern Tulip pattern to determine the size and shape of your pieces. For the center square, use one piece of pattern A and 4 pieces of pattern B. To make the corner squares, use pattern C for the base of each flower, and 4 pieces of pat-

# Patchwork quilt

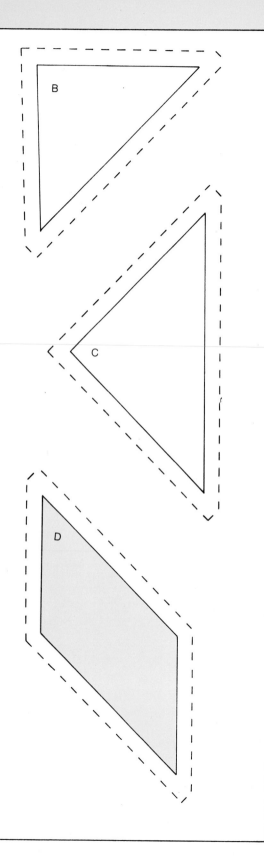

tern D and one piece of pattern E for the petals of the tulip. Use a solid color for the pieces cut from patterns E, D and A. For pieces cut from patterns B and C, use assorted prints. Go back to the instructions for the other quilt design and follow the directions from the making of the patterns to the final step of sewing all squares together.

To make matching quilted pillows, use one appliquéd square for each pillow. Miniature quilts are also attractive coverlets for baby gifts. For these, smaller appliquéd squares are more suitable.

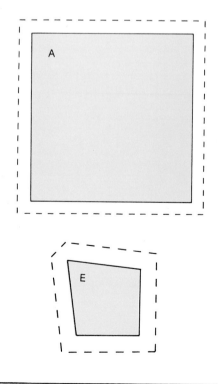

# Tinsel glass painting

The technique of tinsel glass painting, extremely popular during the Victorian Period, is a simplified form of the ancient Oriental and Egyptian art of painting a décor on gilded or enameled glass. Paint is applied in various thicknesses on the reverse side of clear glass, and foil is placed behind the painted décor simulating the effect of gilded glass. The foil reflects light on the different areas, producing a sparkling brilliance where the paint is almost transparent and an intensified appearance to the more opaque colors.

To start a tinsel glass painting project, select a picture, photograph, print, or drawing which will transfer well. A floral print, such as the one illustrated for this project, is a good choice, particularly for the novice painter.

Materials needed: a frame to fit the picture to be painted; glass and cardboard backing to fit the frame; 1-ounce bottle of India ink; a very fine penpoint with holder; low-gloss white enamel for the background of the picture (use black, if desired); a small amount of turpentine; liquid glass stain (suggested colors: purple, orange, light green, yellow, royal blue, red, brown, black, white); two small paintbrushes (No. 1 and No. 3); aluminum foil; some rags; two small screw eyes; and some picture wire. These materials are available at hobby shops or art supply stores.

### Drawing the picture with ink

First check the mirror image of the picture to be painted. Should the reverse image seem unsuitable or if there is lettering on the picture, trace it onto onion skin paper first, reverse and paint from the tracing. Otherwise, it will be backward in the final version.

Remove the glass from the picture frame. Place the picture to be copied under the glass

(make sure that you are working on a smooth, flat surface). With the pen and India ink, trace the picture onto the glass. Be careful not to dip too much ink on the penpoint at one time; surplus ink runs out and smears the glass. Wipe clean immediately any smears that do occur. When the entire picture is traced on the glass, let the ink dry thoroughly.

### Painting in the colors

Paint the background of the picture on the glass with low-gloss enamel. Use the smaller brush to get into tiny corners, such as between flower petals and leaves. When the painting is finished, clean the brushes in turpentine and allow the enamel to dry overnight.

## Tinsel glass painting

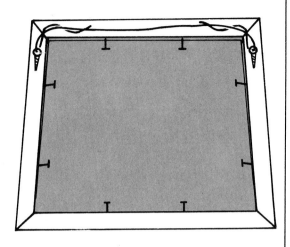

To paint the objects in the picture, in this case the flowers and foliage, apply the various color stains with the smaller brush, cleaning it in turpentine after painting each color. To shade colors, apply the lightest first, let it dry, then apply a darker shade over it. For example, for a deep yellow, first apply the yellow stain. Allow it to dry, then paint over it with a small amount of orange or red to darken it. Experiment with shading various colors on a piece of scrap glass before applying the stains to the project picture.

### Completing the picture with tinsel
When all the colors have been applied, allow the painting to dry thoroughly. Cut a piece of aluminum foil the same size as the cardboard backing. Crinkle the foil, then smooth it out on a flat surface. Set the glass in the frame with the unpainted side out, then set the aluminum foil in the frame against the painted side of the glass.

Place the cardboard backing in the frame and secure it with brads (small nails) or clips. The foil backing shows through the painted glass, giving the picture a tinseled appearance.

Fasten screw eyes to the back of the frame approximately 2 inches down from the top edge, and ⅜ inch in from the edges. Insert picture wire through the screw eyes and twist over the ends of the wire. Hang the picture where it will reflect light.

# Cornhusk doll

This miniature doll, created almost entirely from cornhusks, is a fine example of primitive folk art practiced by agrarian peoples. Like the delicate straw figures and images made by Mexican Indians and the detailed ornaments found in remote African villages, the cornhusk doll is a decorative piece exhibiting ingenuity and craftsmanship. The doll stands just under 5 inches tall when it is finished.

Materials: about 6 to 8 cornhusks; corn silk; a quart of glycerin; heavy-duty thread; a foamed plastic ball ¾ inch in diameter; 8 inches of thin, flexible wire; small wad of cotton; white glue; a few sprigs of babies' breath; and a black marking pencil.

## Making the arms

Separate the cornhusks. Soak them briefly in glycerin, then place them in a bowl of luke-

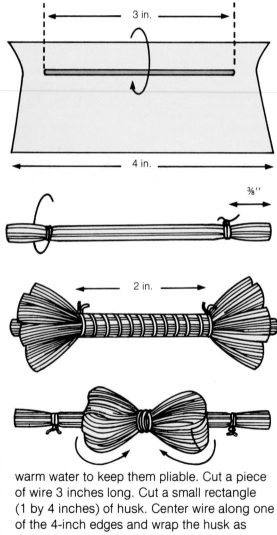

warm water to keep them pliable. Cut a piece of wire 3 inches long. Cut a small rectangle (1 by 4 inches) of husk. Center wire along one of the 4-inch edges and wrap the husk as tightly as possible around the wire. Wrap thread tightly around rolled husk ½ inch from each end. Cut another 1-by-4-inch rectangle

of husk and wrap it around the middle 2 inches of the covered wire. Wrap tightly with thread. Fold back the outer edges of husk and bring to middle of wire. Wrap thread to secure edges where they meet at center to form puffed sleeves. Set aside this part of the doll, which is the arms.

## Assembling head, body, and arms

Cut a 4-inch length of wire and insert halfway through the foamed plastic ball. This wire is for the body, and the ball is the head. Place the arms across the wire inserted in the foamed plastic ball, approximately ½ inch below the head. Tie securely by crisscrossing several times with thread, then wrapping thread around sides of head and tying. Cut a

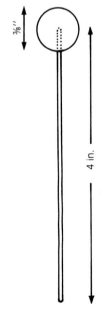

husk rectangle, 2 by 6 inches. Lay the head in the middle and wrap the husk tightly around

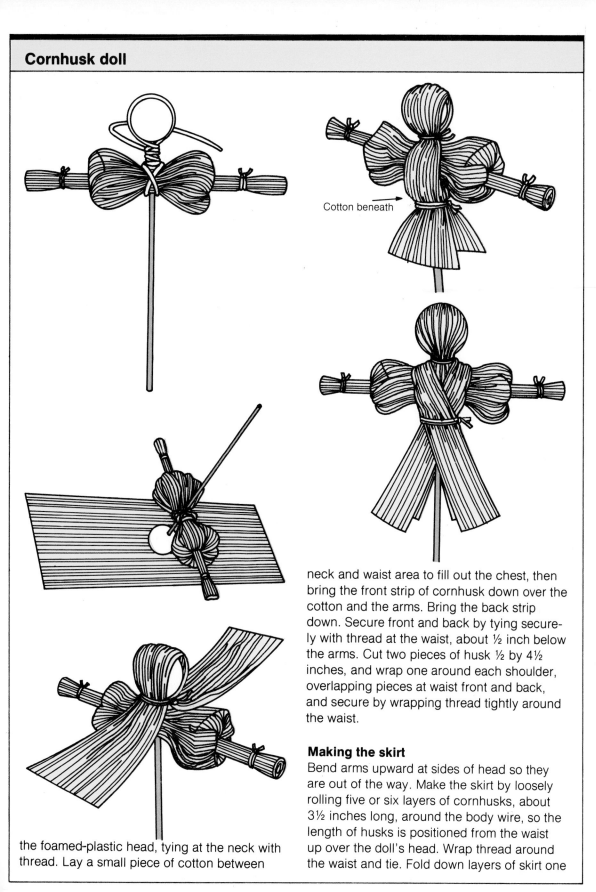

# Cornhusk doll

neck and waist area to fill out the chest, then bring the front strip of cornhusk down over the cotton and the arms. Bring the back strip down. Secure front and back by tying securely with thread at the waist, about ½ inch below the arms. Cut two pieces of husk ½ by 4½ inches, and wrap one around each shoulder, overlapping pieces at waist front and back, and secure by wrapping thread tightly around the waist.

**Making the skirt**
Bend arms upward at sides of head so they are out of the way. Make the skirt by loosely rolling five or six layers of cornhusks, about 3½ inches long, around the body wire, so the length of husks is positioned from the waist up over the doll's head. Wrap thread around the waist and tie. Fold down layers of skirt one

the foamed-plastic head, tying at the neck with thread. Lay a small piece of cotton between

Cotton beneath

at a time and smooth out. Trim husks at skirt bottom, so the doll is approximately 5 inches tall from the head to the bottom of the skirt. Pull arms down beside the body and fluff sleeves.

### Gluing hair and bonnet to head

Trim edges of husks around side of head. Glue corn silk in place on top and back of head. The corn silk should be long enough to trail down the doll's back. For a bonnet, cut a piece of husk to fit the head, approximately 1 by 2 inches. Cut points or scallops along one 2-inch side. Glue onto head (scalloped edge facing front), folding over the sides at back. Then fold down the scalloped edge to form the bonnet. Make eyes with black marking pencil. Glue a few sprigs of dried baby's breath on one of the doll's hands to simulate a bouquet.

# Embroidered place mats

The cross-stitch is one of the simplest and most widely used embroidery stitches. Children and adults alike can learn to do it skillfully in a few minutes. It consists of even rows of diagonal stitches that cross each other within a square area of fabric. The stitch is most frequently used for filling a solid area and is worked with transfers on fabric whose threads can be counted easily, or on fabric with equal-size small checks, such as the gingham background of these place mats. The sprightly shapes and spring-time colors of the flower patterns used on the place mats are also suitable for wall hangings, aprons and linens.

Materials: to duplicate the two flower patterns on two place mats, you need: one 9-yard skein of 6-strand embroidery floss in each of the following colors: orange, yellow, purple, bright green and dark green; an embroidery hoop to keep the stitches neat and even and the fabric flat; and a size 7 embroidery needle. Each place mat requires a 13-inch-by-19¼-inch piece of gray and white checked gingham with 8 squares per inch; a spool of sewing thread; and 2 rectangles of white flannel (13 inches by 19¼ inches) for backing. If you use fabric other than gingham, you also need: a pencil; sheet of graph paper; and dressmaker's carbon paper.

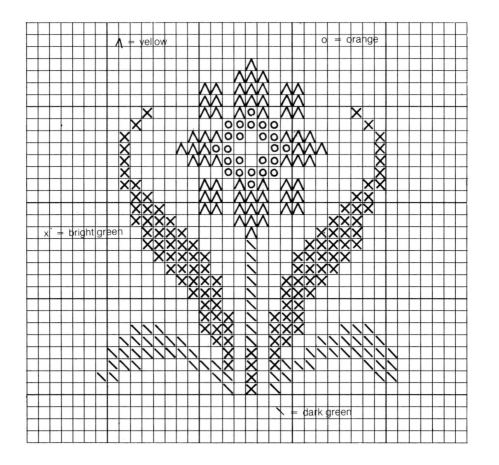

## Embroidered place mats

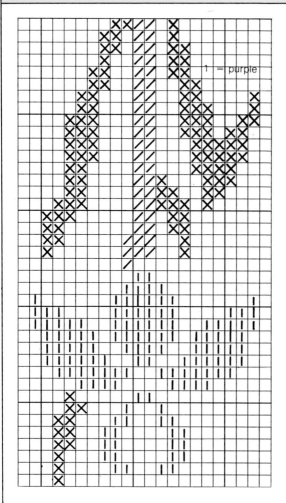

1 = purple

Transfer diagram to fabric, using a sharp pencil to trace over all the symbols on the diagram. Trace each area systematically to avoid any omissions. Each symbol represents a different color thread, so be sure to refer to the key on the paper diagram.

### Embroidering place mats

Once the design is marked on the place mat fabric, secure an area of design to be stitched inside an embroidery hoop. Thread needle with 2 strands of embroidery floss, about an arm's length. Knot end of strands by wrapping thread near ends around moistened forefinger 2 or 3 times, holding thread in place with thumb; then slip thread off forefinger and pull toward ends into a knot. Start stitching by bringing needle up from the wrong side in the right corner of the square to be stitched. To make a cross-stitch, simply make a diagonal stitch covering one ⅛-inch square of gingham (or an equal number of fabric threads), to form the first half of the cross. Then work a slanting stitch backward the same way to complete the cross. Work cross-stitches individually or in rows, making sure all crosses are made in the same direction. Backstitch or weave ends of strands through stitches on wrong side.

### Marking the design

If you are working on gingham fabric that is 8 squares per inch, stitch the design directly onto fabric, referring to the diagrams, which are also 8 squares per inch. However, if you are using other fabric, draw the diagram on graph paper, then position it on the fabric with a sheet of dressmaker's carbon paper (carbon side down) between. The flower designs are placed in the upper left area of the mats.

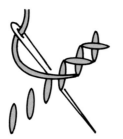

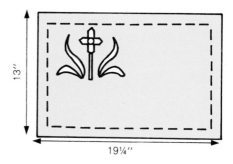

13″

19¼″

### Sewing place mats

To sew place mats, back-stitch fabric to flannel backing, right sides together, leaving a 3-inch opening at one edge. Allow a ¼-inch seam allowance. Turn fabric right side out and press. Close the 3-inch opening with slipstitches. Press well. For a finishing touch, top-stitch around place mat, ⅛ inch from edge. Press well again.

# Découpage wall plaque

Classic découpage, the decorative art of pasting cutouts to surfaces, was developed during the late seventeenth century by Venetian craftsmen as an inexpensive way to simulate rich inlaid designs on imported Oriental furnishings. It is achieved by mounting a cutout print on a surface and then applying as many as 25 coats of varnish or lacquer, creating an illusion that makes the print appear to recede into the background. From this basic method, the technique of découpage is varied and applied to different objects in more intricate designs.

A very simple wall plaque is suggested as the first project for the amateur.

Materials: one pint of water-base paint (light blue); one pint of sealer; one pint of découpage finish or lacquer; two 1-inch brushes; découpage paste or paper paste; finishing wax; thinner or brush cleaner; two sheets of medium sandpaper; two sheets of fine wet-or-dry sandpaper; a small package of very fine steel wool; sanding block; a 4-inch brayer or roller; wax paper. You will also need a small piece of wood (the oval shown measures 5½ inches long by 3½ inches wide); a decorative print; and a hanger for the back of the plaque.

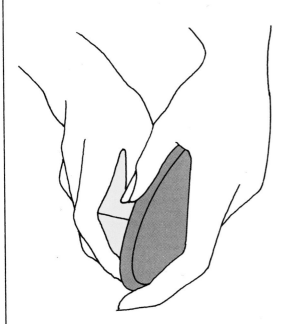

### Preparing the wooden plaque

Cut the wood piece to the desired size and shape. For the oval shape shown here, a jig saw or coping saw is used, followed by a router or shaper to contour the edges. It is not necessary to acquire the above-mentioned tools, or the skills to use them. Substitute a simple rectangular shape for the oval plaque. Or use the oval shape but eliminate the contoured edge by having the print cover the entire surface. To sand the surface smooth, wrap a piece of medium sandpaper around a sanding block (a small block of wood that fits comfortably in the hand) and sand the wood surface smooth, using broad strokes. Always sand in the direction of the wood grain. For contoured surfaces, hand-sanding with fingertips is best. Wipe thoroughly with a clean, dry cloth to remove all dust particles.

Apply sealer to both front and back surfaces of the plaque. When dry, sand again. Apply a coat of water-base paint to the plaque, again covering both front and back. Allow to dry for 24 hours, then apply a second coat to those surfaces that will be exposed when project is complete (such as the contoured edge in the sample shown). Allow to dry completely.

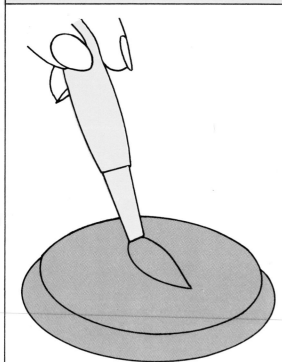

Cut a softly beveled edge, rounded toward the underside so the outer edge is thinner than the rest of the print. Keep the print flat until you are ready to use it by pressing it between the pages of a book.

### Aging the print

Select the print to be used. It can be from a book, from gift wrap, from wallpaper, or from a greeting card, such as the one shown. Cut the print carefully to the exact shape of the surface to be covered. In this project, it is easy because the entire surface of the oval is covered.

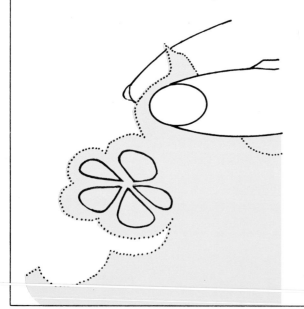

An aged parchment or "burnt-edge" effect is sometimes attractive and easy to achieve. Cut the print to the desired shape, but slightly oversized. Use thumb and forefinger to pinch and tear along the edges of the print. Hold each of the "scallops" thus formed over the flame of a candle and singe by simultaneously lighting the paper and blowing it out. Remove soot that is formed, leaving a brown burnt edge.

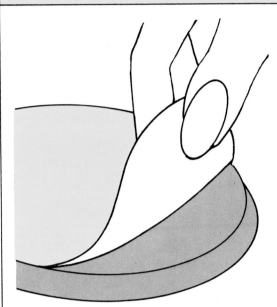

Cover with wax paper, then roll with the brayer, bonding the paper to the wood surface, and forcing out all the excess paste and air bubbles. Remove the wax paper and wipe the surface with a clean, damp cloth to remove the excess paste. Let dry for 24 hours.

### Attaching the print to the plaque

To affix the print to the plaque, spread a smooth, even coating of paste on the wood surface, then position the print on the surface. Découpage paste dries slowly, allowing repositioning of the print slightly until the edges align perfectly with the edges of the plaque.

### Applying a dulcet finish

The true art of découpage is in the finishing. It requires patience and careful workmanship. The liquid finish (in this project, a quick-drying varnish) is delicately floated on with a brush, rather than brushed into the surface. Apply the first coat and allow to dry for 45 minutes; place the brush in a lacquer thinner between coats so the brush will not be damaged. Continue in this manner, applying at least 25 coats of finish (allow each coat to dry thoroughly) until the print appears to recede into the painted surface and become part of the background. Allow the final coat of finish to dry for 24 hours.

Soak fine wet-or-dry sandpaper in a bowl of water for five minutes. Sand the flat surface with gentle, even pressure, keeping the sand-

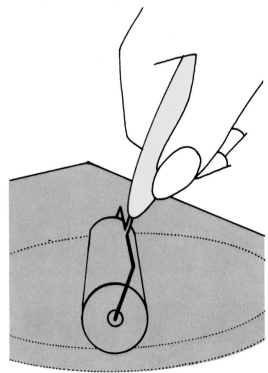

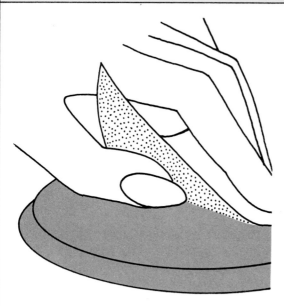

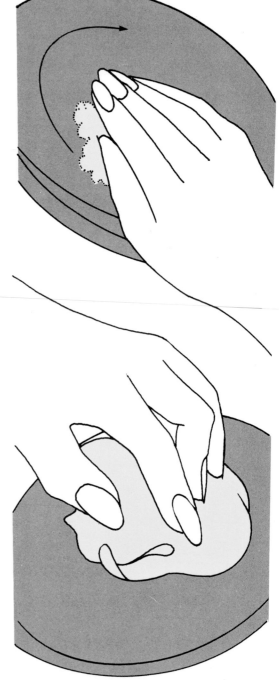

paper constantly wet. Use fingertip sanding for the contoured edge. Dry the surface at frequent intervals to check progress.

Inspect the surface by holding the plaque up to a light to see how effectively the shine is being removed. Be careful not to damage the finish during this operation. When the high gloss is completely removed, and the appearance of the surface is smooth and flawless, wipe with a damp cloth and dry thoroughly.

Buff gently with very fine steel wool to restore a shine to the surface. Again, be careful not to rub too hard and damage the finish. When the surface takes on a glossy appearance, remove  dust particles with a dry cloth.

Apply finishing wax with a damp cloth, then polish dry. Buff immediately to a bright finish. Fasten the hanger hook to the back of the plaque to complete the project. Be careful not to damage the front of the plaque.

### Other projects with découpage

The skills of découpage are not difficult to acquire, and once mastered, their application is almost limitless. The selection of prints and the development of intricate designs then become a challenging hobby. It is also possible to apply découpage to metal, plastic, glass or cork surfaces; but these materials require experienced hands. It is recommended that additional work on wood surfaces be accomplished first. Try ready-made boxes, trays, or wastepaper baskets, then attempt a small table, cabinet, or a chest of drawers.

# Stenciled furniture

Stenciling provides a quick, rewarding way to paint stylized flowers, vines, garlands and geometric patterns on almost any surface. This technique has been used over the years for room decoration as well as furniture embellishment.

    Materials: To prepare the stencil: waxy stencil paper, a single-edged razor or mat knife; a sharp pencil; and carbon paper. To paint the stencil design: one or more stencil brushes; japan paints (a quick-drying type of paint, sold in tubes or small jars); thinner; a ruler; and masking tape. Note: the surface to be stenciled must be clean of all wax and grease, even though freshly painted, for the ornamental paint to adhere properly. If the surface is very glossy, a fine sanding is also recommended. All materials can be purchased at art supply or hardware stores.

### Preparing the stencil
First measure the surface area to be decorated, so the design can be placed in the area with proper balance. For example, a design for the front surface of drawers should be created so it has more width than height.

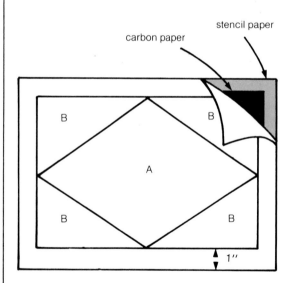

carbon paper

stencil paper

B  B

A

B  B

1″

When satisfied with the motif, lay the drawing, with a 1-inch border, over a sheet of stencil paper, with a sheet of carbon paper between them. Be careful to have all the layers straight. If the stencil ornament requires two colors (no more than two are recommended for the beginner), two stencils must be cut; one for each color.

    With a pencil, trace the lines around the parts of the drawing to be stenciled in color A, bearing down hard enough to leave an impression on the stencil below. For the second stencil (color B) follow the same procedure, placing the design on a second sheet of stencil paper with a sheet of carbon paper between. Then retrace all the parts of the motif which are to be painted in color B.

    Stack the two stencils together, then cut notches in the top right and bottom left corners as register marks. With a razor blade or sharp knife, cut out the holes marked on stencil A and stencil B.

### Experimenting with the painted design
Mix the japan paints, using small amounts of paint thinner, and following the directions of the manufacturer. Make a small amount at a time as this type of paint dries quickly. Lay stencil A on a sheet of newspaper and tape it down so that it will not move. Mark your registers, top and bottom. With the outer border of the stencil securely taped to the flat surface, daub a small amount of color A in the holes with a stencil brush. Work from the sides of the holes to their centers so that the bristles do not push paint under the stencil and blur the

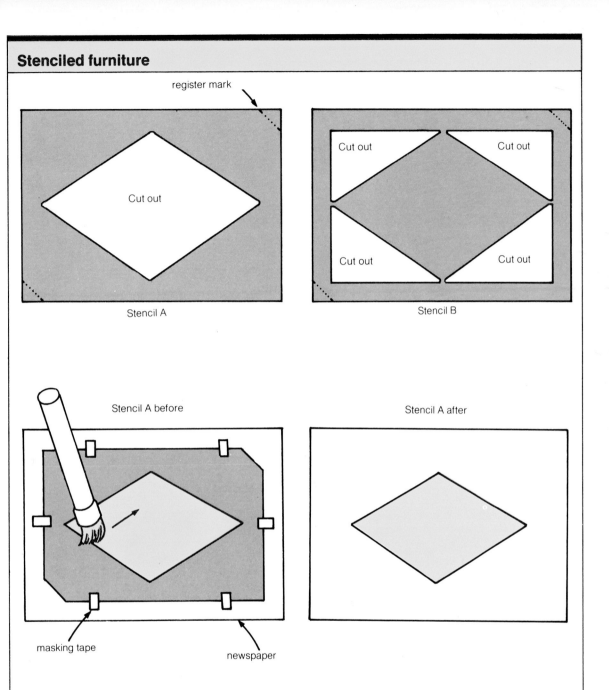

register mark

Cut out

Stencil A

Cut out

Cut out

Cut out

Cut out

Stencil B

Stencil A before

Stencil A after

masking tape

newspaper

design. This method of brushing should also prevent excess paint from seeping under. When all the openings have been painted, carefully lift the masking tape and remove the stencil from the newspaper. Wait a few minutes until the paint is completely dry on the newspaper. Meanwhile, use the thinner to clean paint from the brush and the stencil.

Lay stencil B on the newspaper, align the register marks, and tape it in place. Using color B, brush the paint into the holes. Remove and

clean the stencil and brush with thinner. Study the design painted on the newspaper. This is how the completed stencil ornament will look. Check to see if the stencils work well together. If they overlap, the registers were not followed carefully. If the images are not sharp, too much paint was used, or the paint may be too thin and runny. Thirdly, it is also possible that you have not pressed down on the edges of the hole as you filled it in. If necessary, repeat the above procedure several times, until perfected.

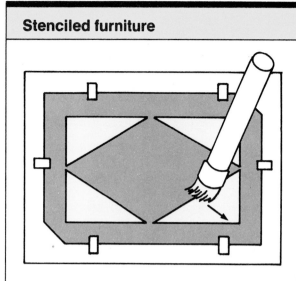

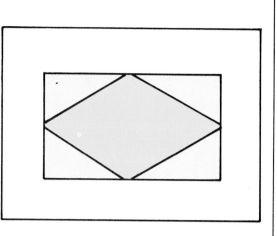

### Painting the design on the furniture

Position stencil A on the drawer front, measuring from the sides, top and bottom until it is centered. Tape the stencil in place; mark the registers and, using the appropriate brush, paint all the holes. Remove the stencil and allow the design to dry while cleaning the stencil. Repeat the process on the remaining drawer fronts, using the same stencil A, being careful to treat the stencil sheet with care.

Place stencil B in position on the first drawer front, check register marks, and tape securely. Using the other brush, fill the holes with paint, color B. Remove the stencil and allow the design to dry while you clean the stencil. Repeat the process on the remaining drawer fronts, using the same stencil B. If an impression becomes blurred during any of these steps, wipe it off as soon as discovered with a tiny tissue or cotton swab moistened lightly in thinner. When all the painting is finished, thoroughly clean the brushes and stencil. Allow the designs to dry for a day. If the furniture is likely to get much wear and tear, brush a coat of transparent polyurethane varnish over the stencil ornament. If varnish is not used, a coat of wax is suggested.

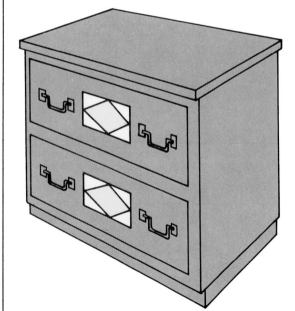

### Stenciling designs on walls and floors

Once you have mastered the technique of stenciling, consider decorating walls or floors with a stencil border that coordinates with a motif from a fabric in the room. Folk art motifs are also easily adapted to stenciling.

## Enlarging patterns

Many of the patterns for designs illustrated in *Joy of Crafts* are printed on a network of squares, called a grid, proportionally smaller than actual size. Patterns illustrated without a grid are placed on a grid before enlarging. Designs are easily enlarged to full size, following the method described below. If you are reproducing or enlarging a design not drawn on a grid, trace the original design and draw a rectangle around it. Place the tracing over graph paper (5 or 10 squares per inch) and tape in place. Or, if desired, draw your own grid on the traced design, as follows: Divide the rectangle into 4 equal rectangles by marking and connecting dots at midpoint of each side of the rectangle. Draw diagonals connecting the 4 corners of each rectangle. (These diagonal links are helpful when pattern is being drawn on the enlarged grid.) Mark midpoints of all sides of each of the 4 rectangles and connect, intersecting centers of diagonals, to form 4 more rectangles. Divide each smaller rectangle again into 4 still smaller rectangles by connecting the midpoints of the sides.

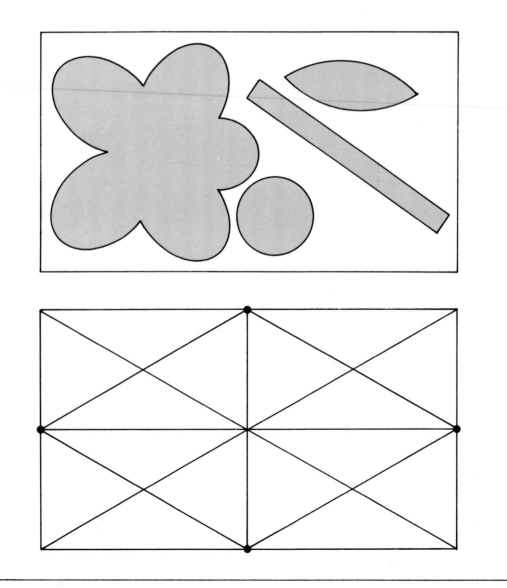

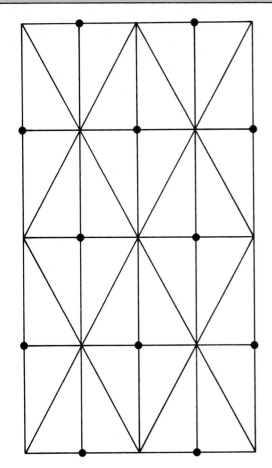

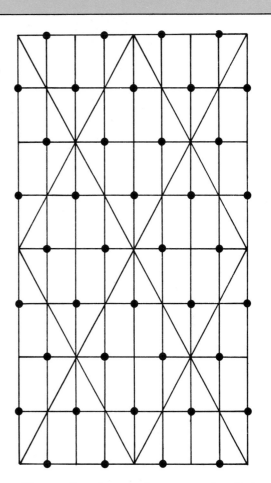

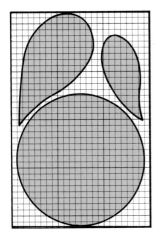

Observe the given scale or gauge to which the pattern is drawn, as well as the number of squares contained within the outlines of the grid. Count the number of squares on the grid occupied by the design along the horizontal plane and the vertical plane, and record these numbers. Determine the full-size dimensions of the design. For example, an illustrated design measures 2¼ inches by 1½ inches, and the actual size of the design should be about 6 or 7 inches by 4 or 5 inches. Then the design is to be enlarged three times. If the number of squares covering the design is 36 by 24 (on a grid of 16 squares per inch), then the grid for the enlargement will be gauged to 6 squares per inch. Buy grid or graph paper printed to the gauge you need to reproduce the pattern full size, or draw the enlargement grid yourself. If necessary, tape together two or more pieces of paper, cloth, or cardboard to produce sufficient area in which to draw the

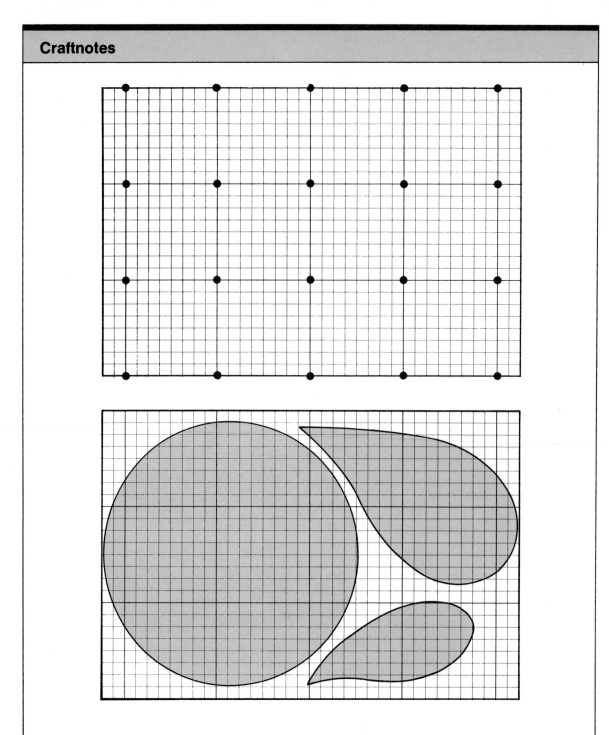

grid. Outline a rectangle large enough to contain the actual size of the enlarged dimensions of your pattern pieces. Mark off with dots to form squares. You have now drawn a grid to full scale. Although your enlargement grid contains the same number of squares as the grid you copied, the measurements of each square are proportionally larger.

Copy pattern lines within each square, one square at a time. Use a ruler or yardstick to reproduce straight lines; use a French curve and compass to reproduce curved lines. Label each piece, then cut. If a required seam allowance is not included within pattern dimensions, add to each piece as specified in the project.

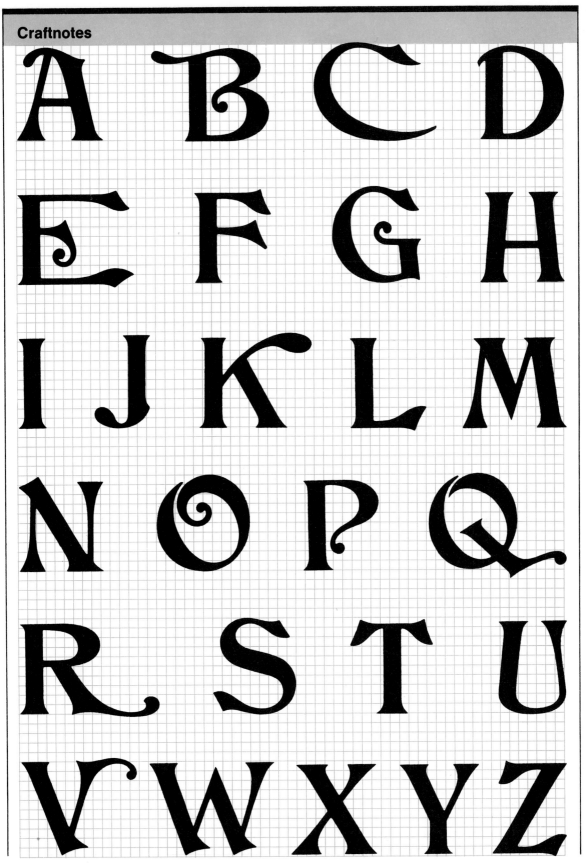

## Embroidery and needlepoint

To thread the needle, make a loop near the end of a 20-inch strand of yarn, pull it taut over the eye, and slide it off the needle; then push the loop through the eye. To begin the first strand, hold about one inch against the back of the row you are working on and cover it as you work the stitches on that row. End a thread and begin all other threads by weaving it through the wrong side of the stitches previously made.

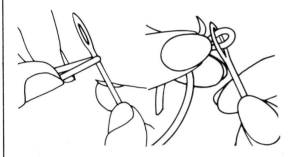

## Mounting and framing embroidery

If an embroidered piece is to be mounted and framed, you can have it done professionally or follow these instructions.

To mount the embroidered piece, you need a frame; a piece of heavy cardboard or hard composition board (⅛ to ¼ inch thick) cut ⅛ inch to ⅜ inch smaller than the opening at the back of the frame (to allow room for the embroidery fabric); heavy straight pins or push-pins; heavy rug-sewing thread; and needle. Center the piece on the board, right side up, then fold surplus fabric to the back. With pins secure embroidery along the top edge, pushing pins into the edge of the board. Pull embroidery taut over the lower edge in the same manner and secure with pushpins. Repeat the procedure for the two sides. With a needle and heavy sewing thread, lace the top and bottom margins together, drawing thread taut as you lace evenly from top to bottom. Lace the two side margins in the same manner. Remove the pins after all four sides have been laced. Fasten the embroidered piece into the frame with brads or glazier's points. Glass is generally not used in front of embroidery.

## Washing

If the fabric is washable, wash the piece in a solution of cool water and mild detergent, as used for nylons and woolens. Soak for a few minutes and rinse well in cold water. Do not squeeze or wring. Roll in a Turkish towel to absorb moisture, then leave folded over towel rack until dry. Place a double thickness of a Turkish towel on ironing board, then lay the dry embroidered piece rightside down on the towel. Press with a steam iron or a regular iron and a damp cloth. Press lightly, working from the center out. Work carefully so you do not flatten the stitches. It takes experience and patience to iron a piece of stitchery.

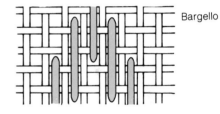

Bargello

## Working Bargello

Florentine or Bargello is a series of upright stitches passing over three or more meshes of the canvas to form a pattern. The stitch, which works best when making a zigzag design, is formed with the stitches worked over four horizontal threads. You may vary the length of the stitch by increasing or decreasing the number of threads over which you work. The fewer threads you pass, the shorter the stitches, and vice versa. On ten-mesh canvas, use needlepoint thread doubled to insure complete coverage of the canvas.

### Blocking needlepoint

Use a clean towel tacked taut over a board. Place needlepoint wrong side down on towel and wet wrong side with damp sponge. Tack one unworked edge to board with pushpins in a straight line. Gently pull one perpendicular side into shape and tack in a straight line to form a right angle. Repeat for other corners, gently pulling canvas into shape. Dampen wrong side again and allow work to dry for about four days. Do not remove canvas until work is completely dry. If piece is still out of shape, reblock and dry again. Remove tape.

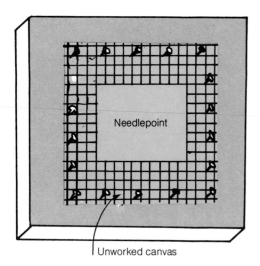

Needlepoint

Unworked canvas

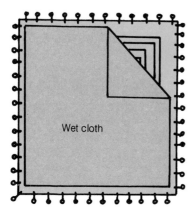

Wet cloth

### Patchwork quilting

Basically a quilt is a bed covering that consists of two layers of fabric with a layer of batt or batting in between. The three layers are held together with a series of evenly spaced running stitches, gauged nine stitches per inch. These quilting stitches also serve as decorative designs on the quilt.

The bottom layer or backing is generally one large piece or two seamed pieces of muslin or cotton fabric in solid colors or simple prints. Cotton or polyester batts or batting, available in varied widths and sold by the yard, are most frequently used for the middle layer or filler. There are many improved cotton batts that will not tear or mat; however, the newer polyester batts are easier to handle and they retain their shape after laundering far better than most cotton types do.

The top layer of the quilt is created with pieced, appliquéd, or patchwork fabric designs. The pieces may be joined together to form a square or block, as they are called, or the pieces may be joined to form a geometric pattern and then appliquéd to a square of fabric to create the block. The blocks, usually 8 to 10 inches square or larger, are joined together in rows to form the top layer. For example, if your blocks are 10 inches square and the desired size of the finished quilt is 70 inches by 90 inches, the blocks are assembled with 9 rows using 7 blocks for each row. To determine the desired size of the quilt, use a sheet or blanket to guide you in the measurements.

# Sewing

Many of the projects in *Joy of Crafts* require very simple sewing stitches, such as basting or topstitching, or basic embroidery stitches for finishing the borders of either patchwork or appliqué. There are some projects that call for some skill in adjusting patterns to fit either a doll or a person, while others might involve using dressmaker's carbon paper to trace a design or mark notches and slits. If you need further explanation regarding some of the tools, materials, and the know-how of sewing, we have highlighted these below.

# Needles

Both sewing-machine needles and those used for hand stitching are gauged by numbers. The machine numbers graduate from low for fine fabrics, to high for heavyweight fabrics. The reverse applies to needles for hand sewing: the higher the number, the finer the needle and the lighter weight the thread used.

When purchasing needles for hand sewing, look for the gauge number on the package (most include a range of four or five sizes) and the classification (sharps, betweens, milliners', or crewels) on the package. The sharps, all-purpose needles, have round eyes and are medium in length, while the betweens are similar but shorter in length and used for fine work. Milliners' are round-eyed, long, and slender, and are used for basting and hand-shirring. Crewels are of medium length but they have long eyes to make threading easy and to accommodate several strands of thread or yarn. For machine sewing, use No. 16 for heavy fabrics, No. 14 for general use, and No. 11 for fine fabrics.

# Beeswax

Beeswax comes in a holder with grooves, through which you pull sewing thread to straighten it before working on heavy fabrics or sewing on buttons.

# Sewing threads

For most sewing projects, mercerized cotton thread No. 50 is recommended for lightweight fabrics and No. 40 for heavier fabrics, including duck, corduroy, and upholstery fabrics. Nylon and polyester threads are both suitable for knits and most man-made fiber fabrics because of their elasticity. Buttonhole twist is a strong silk thread with a special twist which lends itself to decorative machine or hand stitching. Button-and-carpet thread is extra heavy for hand stitching only, such as the border stitching on the back of a hooked rug, or heavy upholstery fabric.

# Pins

The best pins to use are medium-sized steel which will neither rust nor leave holes in the fabric. Pins are usually used to hold seams and appliqué pieces in place before basting. In fact, with the modern sewing machine that sews over pins, pin basting is recommended.

# Tracing and marking tools

Pattern markings can be duplicated on the wrong side of the fabric by using dressmaker's carbon paper (not to be confused with typing carbon paper) and a tracing wheel, tailor's chalk, or chalk pencils. All three come in a range of pale to dark colors to match as closely as possible the fabric color. The pencils are best for very fine detail. Tailor's chalk, which rubs off easily, should be used for temporary markings only. Dressmaker's carbon is used extensively in transferring designs to canvas or fabric for needlepoint, embroidery, and for appliqué cutouts.

# Pressing and iron-on interfacing

Pressing is very important to give the sewing project a finished appearance when complete. Press after each step, even if it seems unimportant as you work. This applies in projects throughout the book wherever there are seams, or where fabric is to be turned under. Pressing cloths are helpful to protect fabric from coming in contact with a hot iron. The pressing cloth should be used dry over delicate fabrics, and damp over linen or cotton. See the special Craftnotes on pressing embroidered and stenciled fabrics.

## Adjusting patterns to body size

First, take your own measurements for your bust, hips, waist, and back waist length (the distance on your back from the nape of the neck to the waist). For pants, also measure the crotch depth, front and back (from waist to crotch) and the side length (from waist to desired length on outside of leg). Hold tape around your body snugly but not tightly.

Measure corresponding areas on patterns (taking seam allowances and darts into consideration). Compare with your body measurements. If pattern is too small, cut across the pattern in its center and tape in an insert to enlarge it to your measurements. If pattern is too large, fold it in a tucking fashion in the center of the piece to make it the right size.

## Basting

Basting is a preliminary joining of pieces with long, loose running stitches, removed after the final stitching is finished. It is used in difficult areas such as armholes and necklines. Use white thread for dark fabrics and a pale or contrasting color on fabrics in lighter shades. Use a long needle and take long running stitches, several at one time, before drawing the thread through fabric.

## Threading the needle

Threading the needle is simple if you use thread of the proper weight to accommodate the needle eye. Moisten and flatten the end of the thread and pass through the eye. Generally a small knot is made on the end of threads when basting, gathering, or shirring. To make a knot, wind thread end in a loop around your forefinger. With the thumb, roll the end away from you, around and under the loop. Continue rolling with thumb until thread rolls off tip of finger. Then hold the resulting knot with the thumb, pulling thread from needle end to tighten. No other hand-sewing stitches require knots, but begin and end with tiny backstitches in the line of sewing.

## Basic sewing stitches

*Running stitch.* A tiny straight-line stitch used for seams, gathers, tucking, quilting, and delicate work. The needle is passed through the material and back again, taking up a very small amount of material for each stitch. Use a long, slim needle, size 7 or 8, and weave the point in and out of the fabric several times before pulling thread through. Keep the stitches uniform.

*Basting stitch.* A large straight-line stitch, similar to a running stitch, used to hold material in place temporarily, until a finer and more permanent stitch is made.

*Overcasting stitch.* This stitch is made with the needle held in a slanted position to finish raw edges of seams, especially fabrics that fray easily. Bring the needle from the back to front, carry thread over edge of fabric, and insert needle in the back again. Continue in the same manner, making all stitches the same length. On heavy fabrics, take one stitch at a time over the edge; on lightweight ones, take several stitches on the needle before pulling it through. Keep the thread easy and never draw it tight enough to pucker the edge.

*Whip or whipping stitch.* A shallow version of the overcasting stitch. The stitches are smaller and placed closer together. Bring the needle out at edge of fold in position for the first stitch. Insert the needle diagonally, catch one or two threads in fabric, and then bring needle through folded edge of hem. Pull thread through and make another stitch below in the same manner. Continue working toward yourself. The stitches on the right side are almost invisible while the slanting stitches of even length are on the wrong side.

*Backstitch.* A straight-line stitch that can take strain. Stitches should be even and made in a line. Use a short needle and bring it up through the fabric, then insert the needle a few threads to the right and, coming up, bring the needle out a few threads to the left. You are taking a stitch through fabric; then putting the needle in halfway back through first stitch and taking another stitch underneath. This makes the forward stitch on the underside and the short backward stitch on the surface.

## Crocheting

Crochet is worked by pulling one loop through another loop with a crochet hook. All the stitches are based on this method. The work begins by making a slipknot on the hook and then crocheting a foundation chain made with the chain stitch. If the pattern is worked flat, the crocheting is worked up from the chain. However, if the work is to be crocheted in a spiral or circle, as in crocheting hats, then the foundation chain is joined to form a ring. The work is crocheted in rounds instead of rows.

If you have never crocheted, it will be much easier for you to understand the method of creating each stitch by crocheting a practice piece. Use a large crochet hook and heavy cord to make the slipknot and crochet the foundation chain. Work slowly, following the diagrams for each step.

## Foundation chain

Make a slipknot on hook about 6 inches from the end of yarn. Pull one end of yarn to tighten knot. Place hook between right index finger and thumb, holding hook as you would a pencil. Thread yarn over index finger, holding short end between thumb and middle finger. If more tension is desired, wrap yarn around little finger. Insert hook under and over strand. Catch strand with hook and draw through loop. Make the chain the desired length, depending on the pattern. In *Joy of Crafts*, the crochet projects utilize two basic stitches, the single crochet and the double crochet.

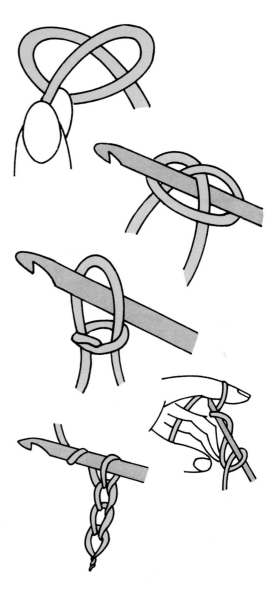

## Slipstitch

The slipstitch is used to give the foundation chain a firm edge when the pattern is worked flat rather than in a ring. It is also used for joining, fastening, or repositioning the yarn without adding to the dimensions of the work. To make a slipstitch on a foundation chain, insert hook under top strand of second chain from hook, yarn over. With single motion, draw through stitch and loop on hook. Insert hook under top strand of next chain, then yarn over and draw through stitch and loop on hook. Repeat to end of chain.

## Turning work

When crochet is worked straight (rather than in rounds), it is not as simple as in knitting. This is because in crocheting you are working from the top down and the stitches have more depth. Generally, you work a certain number of extra chains to form an upright stitch at the end of a row before turning the work. The exact number depends on the stitch you are using, and this information will be specified in the pattern instructions.

### Tension

Tension, as in knitting, refers to the number of stitches and rows worked to each square inch. Check your tension for a particular project by working about four inches of chain, using yarn and hook size recommended in the pattern, and crochet about a three-inch sample of the stitch pattern. Press, then with ruler and pins mark off one inch of the sample, and count the stitches between the pins.

Double crochet

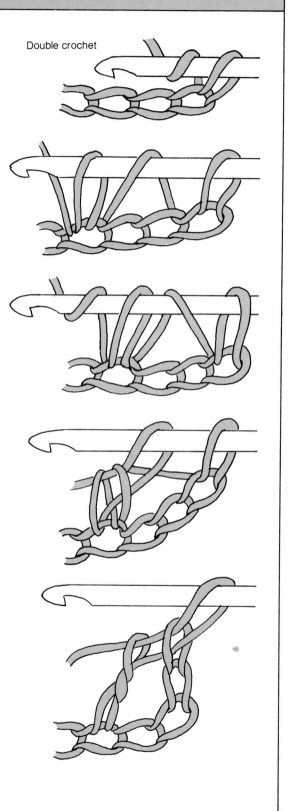

Single crochet

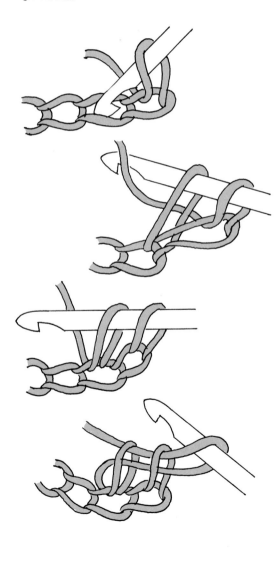

## Knitting

When learning to knit, start with a ball of yarn and a pair of knitting needles. There are only two basic knitting stitches, knitting and purling. The most common combination of the two is the stocking stitch which is achieved by working one row of knitting stitches and the second row in purling, and repeating throughout. The stocking stitch has a smooth surface created by a series of interlaced loops running horizontally up the fabric. The back of the stocking stitch consists of a series of close ridges. The garter stitch is produced by working the knit stitch on every row, and this is also called plain knitting.

The foundation at the beginning of a piece of knitting consists of loops made from a continuous length of wool or yarn. This is called casting on and can be done by several methods. In *Joy of Crafts*, the knitting projects call for the same casting-on method.

Casting off refers to the last row of knitting when the stitches are worked off the needle to make a finished edge. Knit the first 2 stitches from the left-hand needle onto the right-hand needle. With the point of the left-hand needle draw the first stitch knitted over the second and let it drop. Knit the next stitch. There are now 2 stitches again on the right-hand needle. Draw the first over the second as before, and let it drop. Continue this way all along the row until only 1 stitch is left. Cut the yarn, slip the needle out of the stitch and pull yarn gently to enlarge loop; pass the free end through loop and pull securely.

## Tension

In knitting as in crocheting, the number of stitches worked per square inch determines the tension. The number of stitches per inch depends on the weight of yarn and size of needles and the looseness or tightness of the stitches. It is important to test your tension before starting a pattern, for this will influence the dimensions of the piece. To check tension, knit a sample 3 to 4 inches square, using the recommended yarn and needles for the pattern to be knitted. Press square and lay it on a flat surface and with pencil mark off a

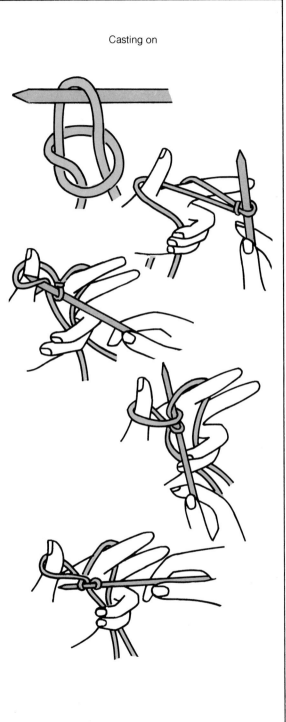

Casting on

2-inch square in the center. Count stitches across and then count the number of rows down within the pinned square. This will give you an accurate count of stitches across per inch, and the number of rows down per inch.

491

## Macramé

Before you begin to do macramé, you must have an anchor for your work: a nail (or nails) hammered into a board, table or other flat working surface, or for small items, a clipboard covered by several layers of corrugated cardboard and used with T-pins (available in stationery and art supply stores).

The first step is to select one cord as the mounting cord (sometimes also called the holding cord) and to secure this cord to the anchor. The rest of the cords, with which you do the knotting, are called the working cords. (Note: some macramé projects are worked without a holding or mounting cord. Instead, working cords can be knotted onto a ring, as described in Knotted plant hanger, or onto a wooden dowel, as in Macramé wall hanging.) Cords that remain stationary and have knots tied around them are called foundation cords. They add extra body and fullness to the knots.

## Basic knots

Here are some common macramé knots you will need to know for the projects in this book:

*Mounting loop* (also called Lark's head knot). The easiest knot, usually employed to begin a macramé piece.

To work the mounting loop, fold your working cord in half to double it and form a loop. With your right hand, hold looped cord in front of mounting cord (or ring or dowel) and with your left hand, bend it over the mounting cord away from you. Hold in this position with your left hand. Reach through this loop with thumb and forefinger of right hand and bring both the free ends backward out through the loop. Tighten the knot. (See diagram above right.) If you prefer not to have the loop showing on the front of your work, you can reverse the mounting loop to make the loop face the back of the work, without affecting the outcome of the rest of the piece: hold the loop initially behind the mounting cords and pull the free ends through the loop toward you.

*Square knot.* Described in Macramé vest, Macramé wall hanging, and in Knotted plant hanger. Also used in Macramé necklace.

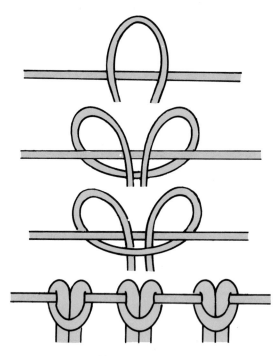

Mounting loops

Often worked in a vertical chain braid called sennit or in an alternating pattern.

## Making the square knot

Cross right outer cord over both center foundation cords and under the left outer cord. With cords in this position, pick up outer left cord, place it under the 2 center cords and

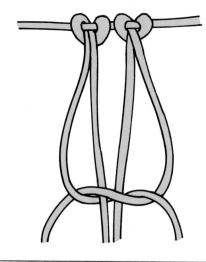

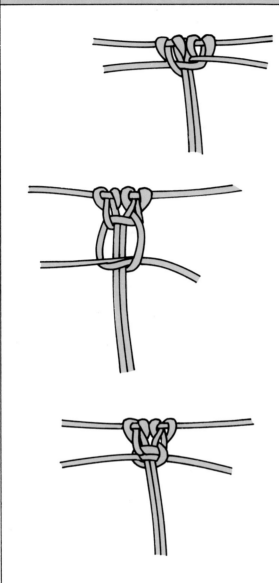

*Double half hitches.* Each working cord is looped twice around a holding cord, which determines the direction of the chain of knots. It can be done horizontally or diagonally or vertically.

## Working the double half hitch

Starting on the right side, take the last cord (holding cord) and place it horizontally across the other cords, pinning it taut. Then, starting with adjacent cord, lay each free length under the horizontal cord, bring end up and loop it

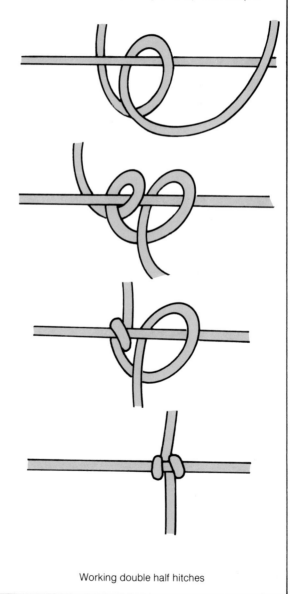

up through the loop. Draw outer cords up and tighten. Step 2 of the square knot follows the same procedure, but from opposite sides. Cross left outer cord over 2 center cords and leave it in this position. Pick up right outer cord, place over left outer cord, under 2 center cords and up through left loop formed. Pull tightly.

*Half knot.* The same as the first half of a square knot (the second half is known as a reverse half knot, since it is done in the same manner but in the opposite direction). When you knot cords vertically in succession, they form a spiral chain of half knots.

Working double half hitches

over horizontal cord. Drop free end behind horizontal cord and pull loop tight. Again, pass same free length behind anchor or holding cord and through the loop formed. Pull knot tight. Continue from edge across row to left edge of working cords, making 2 loops with each knotting or working cord. Take the holding cord on the left edge and in the same manner, work back to right edge, to complete two rows.

To work the double half hitch in a vertical position, pin the working cord and place it under the first holding cord, holding it taut with your right hand. Then loop the working cord behind the holding cord and through the loop at your left, pulling upward. Make a second loop and then pull tight to complete the knot. Continue across the row of free-hanging cords.

*Overhand knot.* Often used to finish off dangling cords neatly. May be combined with a bead (see Macramé vest).

*Tassels.* To learn two ways to tie tassels, see Macramé vest. For a third type of tassel, see Knotted plant hanger.

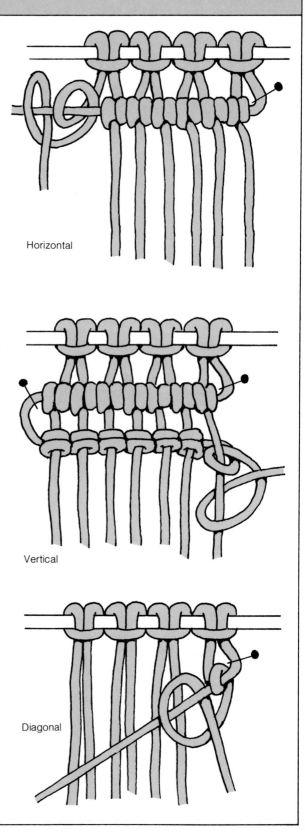

Horizontal

Vertical

Diagonal

## Candles

### Molds for casting candles
Empty cardboard or plastic containers are suitable for molding large, bulky candles, while cardboard tubes from plastic wrap, paper towels, or aluminum foil will do nicely for molding candles that are smaller in diameter. If the inside surface of the container is not waxed or plastic coated, apply a thin coat of vegetable oil to the inside surface so the molded candle will slip out easily when the wax has hardened. The same procedure should be followed if metal molds are used. Should the metal mold be fluted, coat the inside surface of each groove thoroughly. To make a cardboard tube into a functional mold, tape a piece of aluminum foil over one of the open ends to form a base for the mold.

### Anchoring candle wicks
Wicks should be cut at least 2 to 3 inches longer than the height of the mold. The wick is anchored by one of two methods. If the bottom of the mold can be pierced, make a small hole in the center of the base, then thread the wick through the hole from the inside of the mold and knot the end of the wick to anchor it. Draw the wick up taut and tie the end of the wick to a pencil or dowel that is longer than the width of the mold. The pencil is placed across the center of the mold. Instead of using the pencil, you can tie string to the wick and tape the ends of the string to the outside rim of the mold. The object is to keep the wick centered while pouring the wax.

A second method is adaptable to empty juice cans, glass containers, or molds made of hard materials that cannot be pierced at the bottom. One end of the wick is tied to the center of a pencil and the other end of the wick tied to a weight such as a metal bolt or nut which will serve as an anchor. Place the pencil or dowel across the top of the mold so the wick hangs down at the center of the mold.

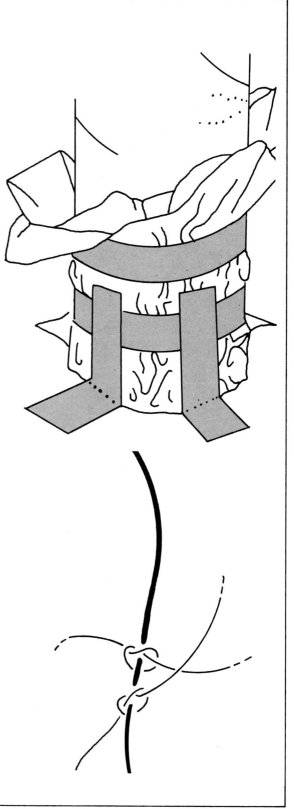

## Unmolding candles

Cardboard molds will tear off easily once a cut is made in the rim. Tear the mold off in pieces to release the candle when wax is sufficiently hardened. To unmold candles cast in glass, metal or plastic, dip the mold in warm (not hot) water for about one minute and the candle should release. Allow candles to cure or completely harden after unmolding. Cure for about a week before burning candles.

## Block printing

Block printing is the process of stamping a surface with an inked design which has been cut out of a block of wood, linoleum, or other material. In *Joy of Crafts*, we are confining our printing techniques to the linocut, a linoleum block on which a design has been carved. The raised surface of the pattern is inked and then carefully pressed against the surface to which the design is to be transferred.

## Cutting tools

A set of basic cutting tools includes both U-shaped and V-shaped gouges of different sizes, a flat chisel, and a cutting knife. The blades for these tools are easily replaced in permanent handles, as you replace a razor blade when it becomes dull or breaks. The U-shaped gouges are generally most effective to carve out large areas of background, while the V-shaped gouges perform the detail work and the cutting of fine lines. To cut clear, sharp lines in the design, and to trim edges, use the knife. The chisel is useful in working over large flat cutout areas to be sure they are smooth.

## Cutting techniques

Once the design is drawn and traced onto the block, cut the outline of the design with one of the smaller V-shaped tools, sometimes called a liner. Then take a large V-shaped gouge and make a deeper cut directly over the cut made with the liner. Select the proper gouge to carve out the areas around the design, and the details. It is suggested that you practice by cutting simple shapes such as leaves or circles on a piece of foamed plastic or scrap linoleum. By experimenting with the cutting tools, you will determine the usefulness of each, and at the same time acquire skill in working with them. To be sure the cutting is done safely, secure the block with a bench hook or, lacking this, with clamps, and never permit your free hand to be in the path of a cutting tool that may slip. Remember to keep your left hand behind the tool being worked with your right hand and vice versa. A bench hook, obtainable in a hardware store or hobby shop, is a device to hold your work at the front of your working space. Its dropped forward edge, in front of the bench, prevents it from moving away, and its raised rear edge prevents the linoleum block from moving away while cutting.

## Rubbings

In making reproductions of incised designs through the technique of rubbing, the best results are achieved with smooth-textured, lightweight papers. Art supply stores usually stock special paper for this purpose, available in white, black, and a few pastel shades. You may also use a lightweight bond or rice paper that is strong enough to withstand the friction of the marker and at the same time thin enough for the marker to transfer the incised markings.

Almost any wax-base marker will produce clean and detailed prints if properly applied, such as ordinary wax crayons, crayon pencils, or shoe-finishing wax, sometimes called a shoemaker's heel. Any marker that has a tendency to build up on the paper (charcoal or ordinary soft graphite pencils) is not recommended. Experiment with various markers on bond paper, using objects found at home, to determine the best color and paper combination and also to get the feeling of working the marker across the incised area.

We recommend storing the paper in a cardboard tube to carry it to the site if you are going to make a rubbing of a historical marker. After successfully transferring the incised marker, store the rubbing in the tube as a safety measure in transporting it back home.

### Leather

For beginners, calfskin and cowhide are recommended in making simple tooled and carved leather articles. The skins vary in size and most craft suppliers will sell less than a full skin. If you are making a belt, decide on the width and know the proper length needed before you purchase the leather.

### Cutting tools

There are a number of tools used in cutting leather but a sharp knife will serve nicely. Leather cutting can be accomplished easily and accurately if a large flat surface is used for the working area. Place the leather on a board or heavy cardboard and use the edge of a steel ruler or T-square to guide the knife. If a belt length is to be cut, mark off the measurement and cut to within one inch of the mark, then reverse the knife and cut from the opposite direction to where you stopped cutting. This avoids overcutting.

### Tooling and carving leather

Designs may be tooled on leather very simply by outlining the pattern with the ball end of a modeler, tracing the design on the moistened leather. Keep going over the outlines until the grooves are the desired depth. To embellish the background of a pattern, use the stippler or a stylus. The effect achieved by stippling is a patch of many small impressions that resemble dots. If you wish to depress the

background of a design, the deerfoot is used to bevel the leather away from the design outline. The deerfoot is also used to make a tooling pattern in the background. The only way you can judge your ability with leather modelers is to practice on scraps of leather. After working with one or two of these basic tools, you might try carving with a swivel knife.

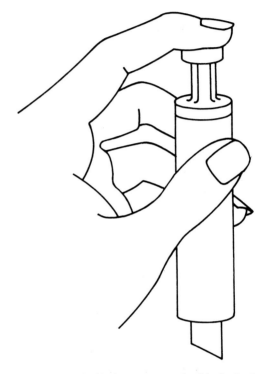

The swivel knife has an angular blade that incises the leather as pressure is applied by the index finger on its yoke. The tool should be held upright while incising the leather. With a steady hand, you can carve flower petals or a sunburst, making curved lines and detailed designs. To complete a cut design, the background should be beveled to make the pattern more pronounced. Use the stippler or deerfoot to work the background away from the design.

### Apply dyes after tooling

To dye leather evenly, work with caution and use broad, systematic strokes, applying the dye with cotton swabs or a small camel's hair brush. Do not dye leather that has already been treated with wax or a protective finish.

Deerfoot modeler

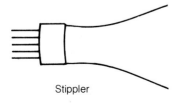

Stippler

## Plants and flowers

For success in horticulture, you must select plants suitable to the growing conditions your environment provides. The charts on the opposite page provide guidance in matching plants to the environment and assistance in keeping them thriving.

## Lighting

The charts explain which different lighting conditions provide the best growing conditions for each plant. Check how much light your windows provide; then select plants suited accordingly. Or provide artificial lighting for your plants (see Indoor light garden project).

## Watering

The charts also indicate how much water various plants need. To insure best results in watering, make sure your pots have proper drainage. For continuous moisture, place pot in a larger container and surround with sphagnum moss. Moisture from watered moss will seep into potting soil.

## Humidity

For plants which require a higher relative humidity than that which is found in the average household, the best solution is to set them in a humidity tray. Select a shallow dish large enough to accommodate your humidity loving plants and fill it with pebbles, gravel, sand, or perlite, and some water, being sure to keep the water level below the bottom of the pots. Plant roots may rot if they stand in water. Some other solutions to the humidity problem are to keep plants near one another, since each plant emits some moisture; to place plants in the bathroom near the shower; or to hang them in the kitchen over the sink.

## Soil

Almost all foliage house plants need special soil mixtures for optimum growth. Many flowering house plants grow well in the ordinary packaged potting soil found at variety stores, nurseries, and garden centers. Those that need special treatment are indicated by # after the name. Some common potting mediums are: loam, humus, mulch, peat moss, leaf mold, sharp sand, finely ground fir bark, crushed charcoal, vermiculite, ground limestone, bone meal, perlite, and well-rotted or dried cow manure. These ingredients are combined in various proportions. Consult the store where you obtain the plants for the exact combinations.

## Fertilizing and feeding

Not all plants respond well to fertilizing and feeding; some suffer from it. To learn exactly what your plants need, ask at the store where you buy them.

## Propagation

While many plants can be started only from seeds or bulbs, many can be multiplied by a simple process of rooting a new plant from a stem cutting. Basically, this technique involves cutting a healthy stem during its growing period, placing it in a rooting medium (a hormone that stimulates root growth is optional), and nursing it inside a clear plastic bag until growth begins again, indicating that new roots have formed.

## Beware these symptoms

Roots emerging from the bottom of the pot, excessive wilting, stunted growth or no growth, and browning, yellowing or dropping leaves all tell you your plant needs special attention fast. Often, the problem lies in improper environmental conditions. Or you may need to repot the plant to give its roots more room.

## Repotting

Moisten soil, invert pot, and tap bottom until soil ball falls out. Prepare a new pot 2 inches wider and deeper than the old one. To insure proper drainage, place a 2- to 3-inch layer of clay shards on the bottom of the pot, covered by a 1-inch layer of sphagnum moss and enough potting medium to bring the final soil level to 1 inch below the top of the pot once the plant is placed in it. Add more potting mixture around the sides of the soil ball. Smooth the top surface and soak the plant until water seeps out the bottom.

# Craftnotes

## Foliage house plants

With 4 hours of direct sunlight and keeping the soil moist at all times:

Chamaerops
Cordyline
Cyperus

With bright indirect or curtain-filtered sunlight and keeping the soil moist at all times:

Acorus (t)
Calathea (t)
Chlorophytum (hp)
Chrysalidocarpus
Cyathea
Dracaena (t)
Livistona
Maranta (t)
Platycerium
Rhapis
Tolmiea

With light reflected off walls or in poor light from northern windows and keeping the soil moist at all times:

Adiantum (t)
Asplenium (t)
Chamaedorea (t)
Fittonia (t)

With 4 hours of direct sunlight and keeping the soil barely moist at all times:

Acalypha *
Buxus *
Caryota
Codiaeum
Fatshedera *
Fatsia
Gynura (hp)
Hedera (t)
Laurus *
Ligustrum (mg) *
Nicodemia *
Osmanthus *
Podocarpus *
Polyscias *
Tetrapanax (hp)

With bright indirect or curtain-filtered sunlight and keeping the soil barely moist at all times:

Asparagus (hp)
Aucuba
Callisia (hp) (t)
Cibotium
Coleus (Rehnelt coleus: hp)
Costus
Dizygotheca *
Euonymus
Ficus
Geogenanthus *
Howeia
Hypoestes *
Monstera*
Nephrolepis (hp)
Pedilanthus *
Philodendron * (t)
Pilea *
Piper * (saffron pepper: hp)
Plectranthus * (hp)
Pleomele
Polypodium (hp)
Rhoeo
Senecio (hp)
Scindapsus (hp)
Syngonium * (hp)
Zebrina * (hp)

With light reflected off walls or in poor light from northern windows and keeping the soil barely moist at all times:

Aglaonema * (t)
Araucaria
Aspidistra
Aucuba
Cyrotomium
Davallia (hp)
Polystichum (t)
Pteris (t)

With 4 hours of direct sunlight and allowing the soil to become moderately dry between thorough waterings:

Adromischus
Agave
Aloe (mg)
Aporocactus (hp)

Beaucarnea
Begonia (basket begonia: hp)
Brassaia
Cephalocereus (mg)
Crassula (mg)
Echeveria (mg)
Echinopsis
Euphorbia (mg)
Grevillea (mg)
Gymnocalycium
Kalanchoe *
Lobivia (mg)
Mammillaria (mg)
Myrtus (mg)
Notocactus (mg)
Opuntia
Pachyphytum
Pittosporum *
Sedum (hp)
Setcreasea * (hp)

With bright indirect or curtain-filtered sunlight and allowing the soil to become moderately dry between thorough waterings:

Begonia
Ceropegia (hp)
Cissus
Crassula (mg)
Cycas
Dieffenbachia (t)
Echeveria
Gasteria (mg)
Haworthia
Pandanus
Peperomia
Phoenix
Scindapsus * (hp) (t)
Tradescantia * (hp)

KEY

* = may be propagated from stem cuttings
(t) = suitable for a terrarium
(hp) = suitable for a hanging planter
(mg) = suitable for miniature gardens

## Flowering house plants

With 4 hours of direct sunlight and keeping the soil moist at all times:

Abutilon *
Acalypha *
Agapanthus
Ananas #
Azalea # *
Billbergia #
Brassia #
Browallia *
Brunfelsia
Capsicum
Carissa *
Cestrum *
Chirita *
Chrysanthemum *
Crinum
Crocus
Crossandra * #
Cuphea *
Cymbidium #
Eranthemum *
Evratamia *
Felicia *
Fuchsia *
Gardenia # *
Gelsemium *
Gloriosa
Haemanthus
Heliotropium
Hibiscus *
Hippeastrum
Hoya
Ixora #
Jacobinia *
Jasminum *
Lachenalia
Malvaviscus *
Muscari
Nicotiana
Osmanthus *
Oxalis
Passiflora
Pentas *
Punica *
Rosa
Scilla
Senecio
Sprekelia
Stephanotis *
Streptosolen *
Thunbergia
Tropaeolum
Tulbaghia
Vallota
Veltheimia
Zantedeschia
Zephyranthes

With bright indirect or curtain-filtered sunlight and keeping the soil moist at all times:

Acalypha *
Achimenes #
Aeschynanthus # *
Anthurium (hh)
Browallia * #
Camellia *
Campanula *
Clerodendrum or Clerodendron *
Coffea
Columnea # *
Cyclamen #

Dendrobium # (hh)
Epidendrum #
Epiphyllum #
Episcia # *
Eucharis # *
Exacum #
Gloxinera (hh)
Guzmania #
Hydrangea
Hypocyrta # *
Impatiens # *
Kohleria # *
Lilium
Maxillaria (hh) #
Narcissus
Neofinetia # (hh)
Neomarica
Nidularium #
Phalaenopsis (hh) #
Quesnelia #
Rodriguezia # (hh)
Ruella #
Schizocentron
Schlumbergera #
Sinningia #
Smithiantha #
Streptocarpus # *
Tetranema
Tillandsia #
Trichocentrum # (hh)
Tulipa
Vriesia #

With light reflected off walls or in poor light from northern windows and keeping the soil moist at all times:

Manettia *
Spathiphyllum #

With 4 hours direct sunlight and keeping the soil barely moist at all times:

Aeschynanthus or Trichosporum (hp) *
Calliandra *
Campanula *
Citrus *
Fuchsia *
Ipomoea or Pharbitis
Lobularia *
Veltheimia

With bright indirect or curtain-filtered sunlight and keeping the soil barely moist at all times:

Aechmea
Angraecum # (hh)
Aphelandra (hh) *
Begonia
Calceolaria *
Daphne *
Epiphyllum *
Primula
Rechsteineria (hh) #
Saintpaulia (hh) #

With 4 hours direct sunlight and allowing the soil to become moderately dry between thorough waterings:

Begonia
Beloperone
Bougainvillea *
Cattleya # (hh)
Crinum
Dyckia #
Euphorbia
Fortunella *
Gazania
Gloriosa
Hoya
Kalanchoe *
Lealia #
Lnatana *
Malpighia
Odontoglossum (hh) #
Oncidium #
Ornithogalum
Passiflora
Pelargonium *
Petunia
Rosmarinus
Russelia *
Solanum
Sprekelia
Stephanotis *
Strelitzia
Trachelospermum or Rhychospermum *
Vallota
Veltheimia

With bright indirect or curtain-filtered sunlight and allowing the soil to become moderately dry between thorough waterings:

Brassavola (hh) #
Clivia
Cryptanthus #
Dipladenia *
Laeliocattleya (hh) #
Saxifraga
Sophrolaeliocattleya (hh) #
Trachelospermum or Rhychospermum *

KEY

* = may be propagated from stem cuttings
# = special potting mixture required
(hh) = high humidity required

499

# Resources

## General Art and Craft Supply Stores

Arthur Brown & Bro., Inc.
2 West 46th St.
New York, NY 10036

Lee Wards
Creative Crafts Center
1200 St. Charles St.
Elgin, IL 60120

American Handicrafts
8113 Highway 80 West
Fort Worth, TX 76116

Sears, Roebuck and Co., Inc.
Customer Service Dept. (or check Yellow
Pages for your local stores)
1633 Broadway
New York, NY 10019

Earth Guild/Grateful Union
15 P. Tudor St.
Cambridge, MA 02139

## Specialized Stores for Hard-to-Find Items

BASKETRY SUPPLIES:

Ace Rattan Products
60-19 54th Pl.
Maspeth, NY 11378

H. H. Perkins
10 S. Bradley Rd.
Woodbridge, CT 06525

Dick Blick Co.
P.O. Box 1267
Galesburg, IL 61401

BATIK MATERIALS:

Utrecht Linens
33 35th St.
Brooklyn, NY 11232

Polyproducts Corp.
13810 Nelson Ave.
Detroit, MI 48227

BEADS:

Grey Owl Indian Mfg. Co., Inc.
150-02 Beaver Rd.
Jamaica, NY 11433

Del Trading Post
P.O. Box 248
Mission, SD 57555

The Bead Game
8071 Beverly Blvd.
Los Angeles, CA 90048

BEESWAX FOR CANDLES:

A. I. Root
1106 East Grand St.
Elizabeth, NJ 07201

BOTTLE-CUTTING TOOLS:

Avalon Industries, Inc.
200 Fifth Ave.
New York, NY 10010

BRAIDED RUG SUPPLIES:

Tinkler & Co., Inc.
P.O. Box 17
Norristown, PA 19404

CERAMICS SUPPLIES:

Long Island Ceramic Center
1190 Route 109
Lindenhurst, NY 11757

American Art Clay & Co., Inc.
4717 W. 16th St.
Indianapolis, IN 46222

ENAMELING MATERIALS:

Allcraft Tool & Supply Co.
100 Frank Rd.
Hicksville, NY 11801

Thomas C. Thompson Co.
Highland Park, IL 60035

Seaire
17909 So. Hobart Blvd.
Gardena, CA 90248

FIBERS FOR KNOTTING AND WEAVING:

P. C. Herwig Co., Inc.
264 Clinton St.
Brooklyn, NY 11201

Boin Arts & Crafts
91 Morris St.
Morristown, NJ 07960

JEWELRY SUPPLIES:

Magic Novelty Co., Inc.
95 Morton St.
New York, NY 10014

Allcraft Tool & Supply Co., Inc.
22 W. 48th St.
New York, NY 10020

Jewelart, Inc.
7753 Densmore Ave.
Van Nuys, CA 91406

KNITTING NEEDS:

Home Yarn Co.
1849 Coney Island Ave.
Brooklyn, NY 11230

Oregon Worsted Co.
8300 S.E. McLaughlin Blvd.
Portland, OR 97202

Colonial Woolen Mills, Inc.
6501 Barberton Ave.
Cleveland, OH 44102

Cottage Crafts
Pomfret Center, CT 06259

Walter McCook & Son, Inc.
31 No. 10th St.
Philadelphia, PA 19107

## Resources

**LEATHERWORKING SUPPLIES:**

P. C. Herwig Co., Inc.
264 Clinton St.
Brooklyn, NY 11201

California Crafts Supply
1096 N. Main St.
Orange, CA 92667

Tandy Leather Co. of Canada
1224 Rue Drummond
Montreal, H3GIV7
P.Q., Canada

Berman Leather
147 S. St.
Boston, MA 02111

Leathercrafters Supply Co.
25 Great Jones St.
New York, NY 10012

**MAKE-UP:**

Van Walters & Rogers
P.O. Box 3200
San Francisco, CA 94119

Irving's Theatrical Make-Up Supply
305 E. Ridgewood Ave.
Ridgewood, NJ 07415

Paramount Theatrical Supplies
32 W. 20th St.
New York, NY 10011

**METAL SUPPLIES:**

Apollo Metals, Inc.
6650 S. Oak Park Ave.
Chicago, IL 60638

**NEEDLECRAFT NEEDS:**

Mazaltov's Custom Needlepoint
758 Madison Ave.
New York, NY 10021

Goldman's Yarn Stores, Inc.
4417 13th Ave.
Brooklyn, NY 11219

Lee Wards
1200 St. Charles St.
Elgin, IL 60120

Alice Maynard
724 Fifth Ave.
New York, NY 10019

Naturalcraft
2199 Bancroft Way
Berkeley, CA 94704

Meribee
2904 W. Lancaster
Fort Worth, TX 76101

**OILS, FRAGRANCES, ESSENCES AND POTPOURRIS:**

Aphrodisia Products, Inc.
28 Carmine St.
New York, NY 10014

Caswell-Massey Co., Ltd.
518 Lexington Ave.
New York, NY 10017

**PLASTICS, MOLDING AND CASTING SUPPLIES:**

Industrial Plastic
309 & 324 Canal St.
New York, NY 10013

The Plastics Factory
119 Ave. D
New York, NY 10009

Polyproducts Corp.
13810 Nelson Ave.
Detroit, MI 48227

Smooth-On Corp.
1000 Valley Rd.
Gillette, NJ 07933

**RUSHING AND CANING MATERIALS:**

Alnap Co., Inc.
66 Reade St.
New York, NY 10007

Dick Blick Co.
P.O. Box 1267
Galesburg, IL 61401

Naturalcraft
2199 Bancroft Way
Berkeley, CA 94704

H. H. Perkins
10 S. Bradley Rd.
Woodbridge, CT 06525

The Caning Shop
1279 Gilman St.
Berkeley, CA 94704

**SILKSCREEN SUPPLIES:**

Arthur Brown & Bro., Inc.
2 W. 46th St.
New York, NY 10036

**TJANTING TOOLS FOR BATIK:**

Aljo Manufacturing Co.
116 Prince St.
New York, NY 10012

Naturalcraft
2199 Bancroft Way
Berkeley, CA 94704

Dick Blick Co.
P.O. Box 1267
Galesburg, IL 61401

**WOODFINDINGS:**

Duplex Novelty Co.
315 W. 35th St.
New York, NY 10001

# Acknowledgments

The Blue Mountain Crafts Council gratefully acknowledges
the creative and editorial contributions to this book by:

Designer: Ron Gross; Photographers: Enrico
Ferorelli, Benno Friedman, Paul Levin; Art
Director: Jacques Chazaud; Editors: Nancy
Jackson, Ellyn Polshek, Ruth Viscount;
Craftspeople: William Accorsi; Suzanne Austin;
Ellen Applebaum; Sal Baron; Albert J.
Bradicich; Susan Becker; Janet Booth; Debi
Bracken; Carl Caronia; Terry Cooper; Rose
Crofford; Arlene Demske; George A. Elbert;
Vivian Gedman; Anita M. Golia; Kenny
Goodman; Dorothy Grader; Ellen Green;
Robert Charles Heitman; Florence Horn;
Richard A. Hodge; Harrieta Isles; Charles
Jackson; Nancy Jackson; June Johnson;
Frederick J. Koelbel; Dick Laughton; Doris
Laughton; Janet Leeds; Diane Lennox; Nancy
Bruning Levine; June McDermott; Betsy
Meyer; Marilyn Nierenberg; Inge Nissen; Carol
M. O'Brien; Lucille O'Brien; Liz Pannell; Mary
Pannell; Catherine Philbin; Alfred Pruitt;
Marilyn Ratner; Suzan Rose, Bright E. Sage;
Bonnie Schiffer; Mary Grace Skurka; Harry
Steinberg; Hope Stevens; Ruth Viscount; Joan
Walter; Rod Young; and the following writers,
researchers and artists: Ayako Abe; Debi
Bracken; Judy Bray; Jerry Curcio; Jesarielle
Damora; Richard Demske; Candice Eaton;
Leonard Everett Fisher; Rodney Friedman;
Marina Givotovsky; Becky Johnston;
Christopher Jones; Rochelle Lapidus; Patricia
Lee; Lynn Matus; Wendy Murphy; Marilyn
Nierenberg; Ruth Nowakowski; Lucille
O'Brien; Catherine Philbin; Thomas Philbin;
Sally Shimizu; Mary Grace Skurka; Harry
Steinberg.

# Index

Boldface numbers refer to full-color illustrations

# Index

# Index

# Index

# Index

# Index

# Index

# Index